London presbyterians and the British revolutions, 1638–64

Manchester University Press

Politics, culture and society in early modern Britain

General Editors

Professor Alastair Bellany
Dr Alexandra Gajda
Professor Peter Lake
Professor Anthony Milton
Professor Jason Peacey

This important series publishes monographs that take a fresh and challenging look at the interactions between politics, culture and society in Britain between 1500 and the mid-eighteenth century. It counteracts the fragmentation of current historiography through encouraging a variety of approaches which attempt to redefine the political, social and cultural worlds, and to explore their interconnection in a flexible and creative fashion. All the volumes in the series question and transcend traditional interdisciplinary boundaries, such as those between political history and literary studies, social history and divinity, urban history and anthropology. They thus contribute to a broader understanding of crucial developments in early modern Britain.

Recently published in the series

Chaplains in early modern England: Patronage, literature and religion   Hugh Adlington, Tom Lockwood *and* Gillian Wright (*eds*)

The Cooke sisters: Education, piety and patronage in early modern England   Gemma Allen

Black Bartholomew's Day: Preaching, polemic and Restoration nonconformity   David J. Appleby

Insular Christianity: Alternative models of the Church in Britain and Ireland, c.1570–c.1700   Robert Armstrong *and* Tadhg Ó Hannrachain (*eds*)

Reading and politics in early modern England: The mental world of a seventeenth-century Catholic gentleman   Geoff Baker

'No historie so meete'   Jan Broadway

Writing the history of parliament in Tudor and early Stuart England   Paul Cavill *and* Alexandra Gajda (*eds*)

Republican learning: John Toland and the crisis of Christian culture, 1696–1722   Justin Champion

News and rumour in Jacobean England: Information, court politics and diplomacy, 1618–25   David Coast

This England: Essays on the English nation and Commonwealth in the sixteenth century   Patrick Collinson

Gentry culture and the politics of religion: Cheshire on the eve of civil war   Richard Cust *and* Peter Lake

Sir Robert Filmer (1588–1653) and the patriotic monarch   Cesare Cuttica

Civil war London: Mobilising for parliament, 1641–5   Jordan S. Downs

Doubtful and dangerous: The question of succession in late Elizabethan England   Susan Doran *and* Paulina Kewes (*eds*)

Brave community   John Gurney

Revolutionizing politics: Culture and conflict in England, 1620–60   Paul D. Halliday, Eleanor Hubbard and Scott Sowerby (*eds*)

'Black Tom'   Andrew Hopper

Reformation without end: Religion, politics and the past in post-revolutionary England   Robert G. Ingram

Freedom of speech, 1500–1850   Robert G. Ingram, Jason Peacey *and* Alex W. Barber (*eds*)

Connecting centre and locality: Political communication in early modern England   Chris R. Kyle *and* Jason Peacey (*eds*)

Revolution remembered: Seditious memories after the British Civil Wars   Edward James Legon

Royalists and Royalism during the Interregnum   jason mcelligott *and* David L. Smith

Laudian and Royalist polemic in Stuart England   Anthony Milton

The crisis of British Protestantism: Church power in the Puritan Revolution, 1638–44   Hunter Powell

Lollards in the English Reformation: History, radicalism, and John Foxe   Susan Royal

The gentlewoman's remembrance: Patriarchy, piety, and singlehood in early Stuart England   Isaac Stephens

Exploring Russia in the Elizabethan Commonwealth: The Muscovy Company and Giles Fletcher, the elder (1546–1611)   Felicity Jane Stout

Loyalty, memory and public opinion in England, 1658–1727   Edward Vallance

Church polity and politics in the British Atlantic world, c.1635–66   Elliot Vernon *and* Hunter Powell (*eds*)

Full details of the series are available at www.manchesteruniversitypress.co.uk.

London presbyterians and the British revolutions, 1638–64

Elliot Vernon

MANCHESTER UNIVERSITY PRESS

Copyright © Elliot Vernon 2021

The right of Elliot Vernon to be identified as the author of this work has been asserted by them in accordance with the Copyright, Designs and Patents Act 1988.

Published by Manchester University Press
Oxford Road, Manchester M13 9PL
www.manchesteruniversitypress.co.uk

British Library Cataloguing-in-Publication Data is available

ISBN 978 1 5261 5780 5 hardback
ISBN 978 1 5261 7461 1 paperback

First published by Manchester University Press in hardback 2021

This edition published 2023

The publisher has no responsibility for the persistence or accuracy of URLs for any external or third-party internet websites referred to in this book, and does not guarantee that any content on such websites is, or will remain, accurate or appropriate.

Typeset by Servis Filmsetting Ltd, Stockport, Cheshire

Contents

Acknowledgements	page vi
List of abbreviations	viii
Note on conventions	xiv
Introduction	1
1 The radicalisation of conformist puritanism, c. 1638–40	15
2 Smectymnuus and the attack on episcopacy in 1641	35
3 The emergence of the London presbyterian movement, 1642–3	67
4 London presbyterians and the fracture of parliamentarianism, 1644–5	94
5 The campaign for presbyterian church government, 1645–6	118
6 The political presbyterian moment, 1646–7	138
7 Presbyterian church government in the Province of London, 1646–60	168
8 The London presbyterians and the projected settlements of the British civil wars, 1647–9	195
9 'Mr Love's case' and the London presbyterian struggle against the English republic, 1649–51	220
10 Cromwellian Britain, c. 1653–9	242
11 The Restoration, 1659–60	267
12 Epilogue: the Cavalier Parliament, the Great Ejection of 1662 and the first years of dissent	294
Conclusion	311
Index	319

Acknowledgements

This book began life as a series of essays written as part of a master's degree I took with Nicholas Tyacke at University College London in 1994. I was fortunate enough to receive a British Academy scholarship to go to Robinson College, University of Cambridge, where in 1999 I completed my Ph.D under the ever-friendly supervision of John Morrill. The academic job market at that point in time was particularly dire and so I chose to leave academia for a career in law. My legal practice left me content to abandon scholarship for the next ten years, until a conversation with John Adamson convinced me to return to the archives. The product of that conversation was my collaboration with Philip Baker and others on the *Agreements of the People*, but my thoughts returned to a history of the London presbyterian movement, a work that has been (all too slowly) completed when my day job has permitted me the time to research and write.

The publication of this work has been made possible by a generous grant from the Marc Fitch Fund. I would like to express my gratitude to the trustees of the Marc Fitch Fund for their kind assistance in bringing this work to print.

I have also incurred a substantial number of personal debts over the years. My first round of gratitude goes to those who have taught or supervised me: Jimmy Green, Christopher Husbands, David Dean, Philip Broadhead, Janet Clare, Nicholas Tyacke, Charles Stewart and John Morrill. My Ph.D examiners Peter Lake and Ann Hughes have both given me much guidance and encouragement over the years. D'Maris Coffman and Duncan Needham gave me employment at Newnham College, Cambridge, affording me invaluable access to the University of Cambridge's databases at a critical time. Chris Thompson let me use his superb transcripts of Yonge's diary and Sylvia Brown provided me with invaluable information on the manuscripts of Mary Love and Elizabeth Jekyll. Whitney Gamble graciously shared her knowledge of the Westminster assembly antinomian committee via email and Mark Jones answered multiple questions on obscure aspects of puritan theology. John Adamson, Sean Kelsey, David Como, Michael Winship,

Scott Spurlock, Crawford Gribben, James Mawdesley, Lloyd Bowen, Anthony Milton, Clive Holmes, Chris Kyle, Michael Mendle, Stephen Roberts, Andrew Barclay, Patrick Little, David L. Smith, Tom Charlton, Alison Searle, Isaac Stephens, Sarah Mortimer, John Miller, Judith Maltby, Chad Van Dixhoorn, John Coffey, Andy Hopper, Noah Millstone, Tom Cogswell, Paul Griffiths, David Magliocco, Alan Orr, Jonathan Moore, Rachel Foxley, Adam Richardson, Paul Lim, Frank Bremer, Ted Vallance and Blair Worden have all provided me with much intellectual stimulus for this work over the years.

I would also like to thank those whose friendship has made worthwhile the years this book has been coming together. In particular Jeremie Fant, Jenny Macleod, John Philips, Helen McCartney and Natasha Conway made my time at Cambridge bearable and prevented me from throwing myself into the Cam on many occasions.

Gratitude must also go to those who have made this book and its research possible. The team at Manchester University Press have, as always, provided exemplary assistance. Jane Giscombe, Alan Argent and David Wykes made my trips to Dr Williams' Library highly enjoyable and the staff of Cambridge University Library often went out of their way to assist in the early days of my research.

My greatest thanks go to those who have suffered the writing of this book for many years: David Scott and John Morrill both read the complete draft and gave me invaluable and constructive criticism. Michael Winship, Jason Peacey and Jordan Downs gave me valuable feedback on the early chapters of the book when those chapters were in a decidedly incomplete state. Tim Cooper and Edward Legon helped me immensely by reading early drafts of the final chapters. Philip Baker and Joel Halcomb were always available for advice when called upon (frequently) by telephone. Ann Hughes, Peter Lake and Mike Braddick gave me many helpful pointers over the years and Hunter Powell provided important discussions concerning the book. The late, great and much missed Justin Champion shared information, sources and ideas over coffee in the Institute of Historical Research. All errors and omissions in this work remain my own.

I would also like to thank my family who have long supported me through this project and especially Ane, Edmund and Sonja, who have often lost a husband or a father for many hours and days to the world of London presbyterians and the British revolutions.

Abbreviations

Abernathy, 'The English presbyterians' G. R. Abernathy, 'The English presbyterians and the Stuart Restoration, 1648–1663', *Transactions of the American Philosophical Society*, n.s., 55:2 (1965), 1–101.

A&O *Acts and ordinances of the Interregnum, 1642–1660*, eds C. H. Firth and R. S. Rait, 3 vols (1911).

Acts of the general assembly *Acts of the general assembly of the Church of Scotland, 1638–1842*, ed. T. Pitcairn (Edinburgh, 1843).

Adamson, 'Peerage in politics' J. S. A. Adamson, 'The peerage in politics 1645–49' (Ph.D thesis, University of Cambridge, 1986).

Ashton, *Counter-revolution* R. Ashton, *Counter-revolution, the second civil-war and its origins, 1646–1648* (New Haven, CT, 1994).

Baillie, *L&J* *The letters and journals of Robert Baillie, 1637–1662*, ed. D. Laing, 3 vols (1841–2).

Baxter, *RB* Richard Baxter, *Reliquiae Baxterianae: or, Mr Richard Baxter's narrative of the memorable passages of his life and time*, ed. M. Sylvester (1696).

BL British Library, London.

Bosher, *Restoration* R. S. Bosher, *The making of the Restoration settlement: the influence of the Laudians, 1649–1662* (Oxford, 1957).

Brenner, *Merchants* R. Brenner, *Merchants and revolution: commercial change, political conflict, and London's overseas traders, 1550–1653* (Princeton, NJ, 1993).

Cal. Clarendon SP	*Calendar of the Clarendon State Papers*, ed. F. J. Routledge, 5 vols (Oxford, 1872).
CCRB	*Calendar of the correspondence of Richard Baxter*, eds N. H. Keeble and G. F. Nuttall, 2 vols (Oxford, 1991).
Cary, *Memorials*	*Memorials of the great civil war in England*, ed. H. F. Cary, 2 vols (1842).
CCEd	Clergy of the Church of England database.
CH	*Church History*.
CJ	*The journals of the House of Commons* (1802).
Clarendon, *History of the rebellion*	Edward Hyde, Earl of Clarendon, *The history of the rebellion and civil wars in England*, ed. W. Dunn Macray, 6 vols (Oxford, 1888).
Clarke papers	*The Clarke papers: selections from the papers of William Clarke*, ed, C. H. Firth, 2 vols in one volume (1992 reprint; originally 1901).
Coffey, *John Goodwin*	J. Coffey, *John Goodwin and the puritan revolution: religion and intellectual change in 17th century England* (Woodbridge, 2006).
Cromwell Letters and speeches	*The letters and speeches of Oliver Cromwell*, eds T. Carlyle and S. C. Lomas, 3 vols (1904).
CSPD	*Calendar of State Papers Domestic Series* (1875–86).
CSPV	*Calendar of State Papers [...] relating to [...] Venice* (1864).
Davies, Dunan-Page and Halcomb, *Church life*	*Church Life: Pastors, Congregations, and the Experience of Dissent in Seventeenth-Century England*, eds M. Davies, A. Dunan-Page and J. Halcomb (Oxford, 2019).
De Krey, *London*	G. S. de Krey, *London and the Restoration, 1659–1683* (Cambridge, 2009).
De Witt, *Jus Divinum*	J. R. de Witt, *Jus divinum: the Westminster assembly and the divine right of church government* (Kampen, 1969).
DWL	Doctor Williams' Library, London.
DWL transcript	Dr Williams' Library MS 201.12–13, Charles Surman's transcript of the Records of the London Provincial assembly, with the editor's notes.

Edwards, *Gangraena*	Thomas Edwards, *Gangreana*, 3 vols (Ilkley, 1977; originally 1646).
EHR	*English Historical Review*.
Fairfax Memorials	*Memorials of the civil war, comprising the correspondence of the Fairfax Family*, ed. R. Bell, 2 vols (1849).
Farnell, 'Politics of the City of London'	J. Farnell, 'The politics of the City of London (1649–1657)' (Ph.D thesis, University of Chicago, 1963).
Gardiner, *CD*	*The constitutional documents of the puritan revolution 1625–1660* ed. S. R. Gardiner (3rd edn, Oxford, 1906).
Gillespie, *Notes*	George Gillespie, 'The notes of debates and proceedings of the Assembly of divines', in *The works of Mr George Gillespie*, ed. W. Hetherington, 2 vols (Edinburgh, 1846), II.
Ha, *Presbyterianism*	P. Ha, *English Presbyterianism, 1590–1640* (Stanford, CA, 2011).
Haykin and Jones, *Controversie*	*Drawn into controversie: Reformed theological diversity and debates within seventeenth-century British puritanism*, eds M. A. G. Haykin and M. Jones (Göttingen, 2011).
HJ	*The Historical Journal*.
HMC	Historical Manuscripts Commission.
Hughes, *Gangraena*	Ann Hughes, *Gangraena and the struggle for the English Revolution* (Oxford, 2004).
JBS	*Journal of British Studies*.
JEH	*Journal of Ecclesiastical History*.
Jus divinum regiminis ecclesiastici	*Jus divinum regiminis ecclesiastici, or the divine right of church government asserted*, ed. C. Coldwell (Dallas, TX, 1995; originally 1646).
Juxon, *Journal*	*The journal of Thomas Juxon, 1644–1647*, eds K. Lindley and D. Scott (Cambridge, 2011).
Kishlansky, *New Model Army*	M. Kishlansky, *The Rise of the New Model Army* (Cambridge, 1979).
Lightfoot, *Journal*	John Lightfoot, 'The journal of the proceedings of the assembly of divines' in *The whole works of John Lightfoot D. D. master of Catherine Hall, Cambridge*, ed. J. R. Pittman, 13 vols (1824), XIII.

Lindley, *Popular politics*	K. Lindley, *Popular politics and religion in civil war London* (Aldershot, 1997).
LJ	*The journals of the House of Lords* (1767–1830).
LMA	London Metropolitan Archives.
LMA, JCC40	London Metropolitan Archives, MS COL/CC/01/01/041 (Journal of Common Council, vol. 40 (1640–9)).
LMA, JCC41	London Metropolitan Archive MS COL/CC/01/01/042 (Journal of Common Council, vol. 41 (1649–60)).
Matthews, *CR*	A. G. Matthews, *Calamy revised: being a revision of Edmund Calamy's account of the ministers and others ejected and silenced, 1660–2* (Oxford, 1934).
Mahony, 'The presbyterian party'	M. Mahony, 'The presbyterian party in the London Parliament, 2 July 1644–3 June 1647 (D.Phil thesis, University of Oxford, 1973) (https://ora.ox.ac.uk/objects/uuid:2c94758f-f66e-4a9c-9122-275b2254d4e9).
Montereul	*The Diplomatic Correspondence of Jean de Montereul*, ed. J. G. Fotheringham, 2 vols (Edinburgh, 1899).
Mordaunt, *Letter book*	*The letter book of John Viscount Mordaunt, 1659–1660*, ed. M. Coate (1945).
MPWA	*The Minutes and Papers of the Westminster Assembly, 1643–1652*, ed. C. Van Dixhoorn, 5 vols (Oxford, 2012).
MS	Manuscript.
NA SP	State papers held at the National Archives, Kew, London.
Nagel, 'The militia of London'	L. C. Nagel, 'The militia of London, 1641–1649' (Ph.D thesis, King's College, University of London, 1982).
Nicholas papers	*The Nicholas papers*, ed. G. F. Warner, 4 vols (1886–1920).
ODNB	*The Oxford Dictionary of National Biography*, eds H. C. G. Matthew and B. Harrison (Oxford, 2004).
P&P	*Past & Present*.
PA	Parliamentary Archives, Victoria Tower, Houses of Parliament, London.

Paul, *The assembly*	R. S. Paul, *The assembly of the Lord: politics and religion in the Westminster assembly and the 'grand debate'* (Edinburgh, 1985).
Pepys, *Diary, 1660*	Samuel Pepys, *The Diary of Samuel Pepys*, vol. 1 1660, eds R. Latham and W. Matthews (1970).
Pearl, *London*	V. Pearl, *London and the outbreak of the puritan revolution: city government and national politics, 1625–43* (Oxford, 1961).
Powell, *Crisis*	H. Powell, *The crisis of British protestantism: church power in the puritan revolution, 1638–1644* (Manchester, 2015).
RLPA	Records of the London Provincial assembly, Lambeth Palace Library, London MS ARC. L40.2/E17.
Rushworth, *Collections*	John Rushworth, *Historical Collections*, 8 vols (London, 1721).
Scott, *Politics and war*	D. Scott, *Politics and war in the three Stuart kingdoms, 1637–49* (Basingstoke, 2003).
Schneider, 'Godly order'	C. G. Schneider, '*Godly order* in a church half-reformed: the disciplinarian legacy, 1570–1641' (Ph.D thesis, Harvard University, 1986).
Sharpe, *London*	R. R. Sharpe, *London and the kingdom*, 3 vols (1895).
Shaw, *HEC*	W. A. Shaw, *The history of the English Church during the civil wars and under the Protectorate*, 2 vols (1900).
State papers, Clarendon	*State papers collected by Edward Earl of Clarendon* ed. T. Monkhouse, 3 vols (Oxford, 1786).
State Trials	*Cobbett's complete collection of state trials*, ed. T. B. Howell, 13 vols (1808–26).
Tapsell and Southcombe, *Revolution England*	G. Tapsell and G. Southcombe, *Revolutionary England, c.1630–c.1660: essays for Clive Holmes* (London, 2017).
Thurloe SP	*A collection of the state papers of John Thurloe*, ed. Thomas Birch, 7 vols (1742).
TRHS	*Transactions of the Royal Historical Society*.

Vallance, *Revolutionary England*	T. Vallance, *Revolutionary England and the national covenant: state oaths, Protestantism and the political nation, 1553–1682* (Woodbridge, 2005).
Wallington, *Notebooks*	*The notebooks of Nehemiah Wallington 1618–1654: a selection*, ed. D. Booy (Farnham, 2007).
Walwyn, *Writings*	*The writings of William Walwyn*, eds J. R. McMichael and B. Taft (Athens, GA, 1989).
Webster, *Godly clergy*	T. Webster, *Godly clergy in early Stuart England: the Caroline puritan movement, c.1620–1643* (Cambridge, 1997).
Wodrow, *Sufferings*	Robert Wodrow, *The history of the sufferings of the Church of Scotland from the restauration to the revolution*, 2 vols (Edinburgh, 1721–2).
Worden, *God's Instruments*	B. Worden, *God's instruments: political conduct in the England of Oliver Cromwell* (Oxford, 2012).
Worden, *Rump*	B. Worden, *The Rump Parliament, 1648–1653* (Cambridge, 1974).

Note on conventions

The dating used in this study is old style, but the year is taken to begin on 1 January. Quotations from primary sources are reproduced with the original spelling and punctuation, except that capitalisation has been modernised, as have i/j, v/u and vv/w (save in the name 'Smectymnuus'). The place of publication for all works cited is London unless otherwise stated.

Introduction

This book is a study of what might loosely be termed the 'London presbyterian movement' and its relationship to the politics of religion during the period *c.*1638–64.[1] It is a study of a historical failure, of a political and religious movement that, with the restoration of the Stuart monarchy and the rise of 'Anglicanism' in the 1660s, failed to achieve its hopes or aspirations. History, the saying goes, is written by the winners and thus it may seem odd to study a movement that failed. Yet, as Gerald Aylmer once wrote, 'nothing fails in history like failure, but when it can be recovered and reconstructed, the story of some failures is of greater interest to posterity – and more rewarding in its own right – than many superficial success stories'.[2] The London presbyterian movement fits Aylmer's criterion perfectly, presenting an important case study in the mid-seventeenth-century politics of religion. The London presbyterians, while little explored by historians on their own terms, are a ubiquitous voice in histories of the period, having given impetus to many of the debates that made up the fractured parliamentarian cause.[3] Further, as part of the 'political presbyterian' alliance in the late 1640s, the presbyterians came close to controlling the terms of political settlement. This led more radical and opposing voices to find common cause with the New Model Army, thus triggering the political revolution of December 1648. Although presbyterians were eclipsed during the first years of the Commonwealth, their distinctly early modern rhetoric of reformation, magistracy and ministry remained a centrifugal force for many old parliamentarians, pulling the Cromwellian Protectorate away from the radical moment. In the end, in 1659, with the bankrupt wreckage of the radical parliamentarian experiment collapsing about them into incoherent military rule, London presbyterians made a significant contribution to bringing about the political settlement that ended the civil wars and interregnum. Ironically, but perhaps true to form, the presbyterians rapidly lost control of both the terms and the narrative of that final settlement.

The first question that arises in this study is dealt with in the first chapters of this book; it concerns the genesis of mid-seventeenth-century English presbyterianism. As the word 'presbyterian' suggests, the focus of this study is on church polity. This is not to deny that theology proper or liturgical reform were important. The recent history of the Westminster assembly pioneered by Chad Van Dixhoorn has shown that theological questions were at the front of the minds of many of the presbyterian ministers and laity studied in this book.[4] Recent work, especially that originating from Reformed seminaries in North America, has revealed the wealth of theological reflection of many of the London presbyterian ministers who did not attend the assembly.[5] Likewise, the issue of liturgical reform has been the focus of work by the late Christopher Durston and Judith Maltby.[6] Nevertheless, the presbyterians studied in this book were theologically within the gatefold of 'Reformed orthodoxy', along with Calvinist episcopalians and congregationalists, even if that enclosure has turned out to be wider than perhaps was once thought. The emphasis on church polity in this book, therefore, is justified as it was the distinctive area of thought and identity that gave the movement discussed here its name.

The term 'presbyterian' itself presents some difficulty as it can be used in at least three distinct ways.[7] The most direct usage applies to those who held to a system of ecclesiastical polity that was structured around the authority of elders in the congregation and whose governance of the church was through a hierarchy of church councils, from the congregational presbytery to the classis (the church assembly, overseeing about a dozen parishes) and beyond to provincial, national (and theoretically ecumenical) synods. As John De Witt noted, many of the London presbyterians held to this position with 'unmistakable clarity'.[8] The term 'presbyterian', however, had a wider meaning in the seventeenth century. The famous seventeenth-century dissenter Richard Baxter alludes to this meaning when he states that the 'name of presbyterians' was applied by 'the vulgar' as a blanket term to those formerly called 'the godly', or 'puritans', most of whom were of 'no sect or party at all' but were 'mere Catholics'. For Baxter, the presbyterianism developed by the Westminster assembly was 'but a stranger' to these English puritans, imported by the Scottish covenanters as the price to be paid by Parliament for military assistance.[9] Like Baxter, a number of influential London 'presbyterians' (such as Thomas Gataker or Richard Vines) would reject some of the touchstones of the stronger presbyterian position, such as the divine warrant for ruling elders, or would advocate the retention of a bishop who, though not distinct in order, held presidency over local presbyters. Other ministers, although called 'presbyterians', would hold that scripture did not set out a model of church polity that was binding on the church for all time and that the civil magistrate had a discretion to structure the church following general patterns laid out in the bible and church history according to what was convenient in the state.[10] It must also be recognised that there was considerable variation and flexibility as to the exact particulars of church polity, even for those who professed to hold to the divine warrant for presbyterianism. Although early modern views of presbyterian polity were structured around the basic ideas of reforming the church to have only the offices named in scripture, a system of consistorial government and the equality of presbyters, there was, in practice, considerable variation in these ideas. This variation was due to presbyterian polity developing in the various sixteenth-century Reformed churches in parallel, with many of these churches being dispersed and subject to persecution.[11] In addition, most London presbyterians had been raised and ordained in the episcopal Church of England and, while they held that scripture held forth a presbyterian polity, they conceded that this 'externall government and discipline of Christ' was 'not necessary to the being' of a church but was required for its 'well-being'.[12] This potentially equivocal formula, the distinction between *esse* ('being') and *bene esse* ('well-being') dated back to the pre-civil war English presbyterian tradition.[13] It allowed space for even those who maintained the divine right of presbyterianism to accept that a church where true doctrine was preached and the sacraments were properly delivered could be submitted to, even if it was defective in terms of discipline and polity.

One consequence of this terminological confusion has been that historians have sometimes sought to deny that English presbyterians were, in actuality, presbyterians. Ethyn Williams Kirby, exploring differences of opinion over a range of issues at the Westminster assembly and drawing on the hard choices that many presbyterians faced in 1660–2, concluded that English presbyterians did not 'wholeheartedly' support the polity because presbyterianism was 'not deeply rooted in their thought'.[14] Following the Baxterian analysis, it has sometimes been claimed that English presbyterians were really 'primitive episcopalians' and not true presbyterians, at least not on the Scottish model.[15] While the distinction between the two positions is valid, the terms 'presbyterian' and 'primitive episcopacy' were remarkably plastic concepts. The exact structure of presbyterian church government was subject to debate within the Reformed churches and definitions of 'primitive episcopacy' could range in definition from full-blown 'Scottish' presbyterianism to the Elizabethan ideal of a pastorally focused diocesan episcopate. Mid-seventeenth-century presbyterians, therefore, could legitimately claim that at the extremes there was no difference between presbyterian polity and the 'primitive episcopacy' of the very early church.[16]

In a similar vein, historians have generally had difficulty accepting that presbyterianism had much in the way of lay support. Keith Lindley could even assert that the London turner and presbyterian ruling elder Nehemiah Wallington was no 'high presbyterian', apparently because Wallington could find spiritual comfort in the writings and sermons of godly episcopalians like Bishop Joseph Hall or congregationalists like Jeremiah Burroughes and did not shun those with opinions differing from his own.[17] Yet Wallington, whose writings often bemoaned England's breach of the Solemn League and Covenant and the disrespect for the presbyterian ministry, attended regularly as a delegate of the fourth London presbyterian classis. He was chosen an uncharacteristic fifteen times to attend the sessions of the London Provincial assembly (the highest council of the London presbyterian system) between 1647 and his death in 1658.[18] Professor Lindley's test for a 'high presbyterian' appears, therefore, unduly sectarian and quite off-target in Wallington's case. Nevertheless, it provides a warning not to treat definitions such as 'presbyterian', 'congregationalist' or 'episcopalian' as hermetically sealed sects or through the lens of present-day denominational conflicts. The godly of the mid-seventeenth century, many of whom had come out of the early Stuart 'Calvinist consensus' and had experienced the common threat of Laudianism together, were capable of appreciating each other's spiritual talents, even if they differed on matters of church polity or varied on points of doctrine. While incidents of religious violence can be found in civil war and interregnum London (for example the antinomian Giles Randall or the general baptist Edward Barbour both suffered physical attacks for their beliefs) godly opponents remained neighbours and were largely on civil, even cordial, terms despite their differences. Irenicism and 'getting along' were just as common factors as conflict in the mid-seventeenth-century politics of religion.[19]

As has been alluded to above, a third meaning of 'presbyterian' grew out of the politics of religion around late 1644 and early 1645. This was the political alliance centred around the person of the Earl of Essex, the parliamentary 'peace party' of the early 1640s, the Scottish covenanters, London's religious presbyterians and former 'war party' parliamentarians who had become disillusioned or disappointed with the controlling faction within Parliament.[20] Many of those within this composite alliance were not presbyterians in the first sense of the word given above; some were not even presbyterians in the second, Baxterian, sense, but were christened 'presbyterians' through their political association.

This last definition brings us to one of the major aims of this book: to provide a case study in the interconnected nature of civil war and interregnum politics and religion. Jason Peacey has drawn attention to how political practices in the civil war led to what he terms an 'integrated' or shared 'common politics' that calls into question the traditional division between 'high' and 'popular' politics.[21] The London presbyterian movement demonstrates how such common politics worked, integrating the machinations of aristocratic cabals with the politics of the parish, the street and the crowd. In addition, through their alliance with their Scottish covenanter co-religionists, the London presbyterians were often referred to as the 'Scotified interest' in English politics, demonstrating that the British dimension remained a constant feature of the political culture of the period.

Such a political culture required institutions and media through which the various 'levels' of the politics could integrate. Of key importance were the networks of patronage and mercantile endeavour that connected godly ministers, city merchants and tradesmen to country gentlemen and, particularly in the case of London's presbyterians, dissident aristocrats. The relationships of patronage and commerce spanned out to wider connections through the parish, guild or civic community, or through the private groups of godly that met for religious conference as well as attending the parish church. Of particular importance to these networks were spaces in the city where individuals could meet, confer and plan courses of action. These 'hubs' of communication could range from public spaces such as London's Royal Exchange or the area around Westminster Hall, where rumour, gossip and news could be swapped, to taverns and bookshops, which in the 1640s served a similar function to that of coffee houses later in the century (which has been more fully explored). Beyond these public spaces, institutional assemblies such as the parish vestry, or the city's common council meeting at Guildhall and Sion College, London's clerical 'club', provided the means for the dissemination of news and the planning of political strategy. The importance of such networks to political organisation in 1640s and 1650s London found in this study confirms the importance of the focus on mobilisations advocated in the work of Michael Braddick and others.[22] It was through such mobilisations that extended networks of individuals became politicised, especially in the distrustful atmosphere of the 1640s and 1650s.

Recent historical writing about the civil war period has stressed the importance of print and print culture in creating and extending the reach of politics during the civil wars. These clandestine measures can be contrasted with the London presbyterians, whose representation in the upper echelons of the Stationers' Company and near-hegemony of the licensing process meant that presbyterians had little difficulty in getting their voice heard in public. Nevertheless, in the various crises of the late 1640s and 1650s presbyterian stationers and ministers also reverted to anonymous printed material to make their case against their adversaries. The effect of the wide use of print was to create a 'market place' of ideas and, as the work of Ann Hughes has shown, presbyterians engaged and competed in this market place at all levels of political and religious discourse.[23] The focus on print culture, however, should not detract from the importance of gossip and rumour in city politics. In an urban environment such as London, at a time when even putative allies were embroiled in mutual suspicion of each other's motives, the oral spread of 'informal news' formed part of the culture of political communication and manipulation. Indeed, print and orality were still intertwined to a degree to which they can often be classed as extensions of each other. In mid-seventeenth-century London politics, print and gossip, news and rumour, fed into each other to create an adversarial dynamic that permeated politics, especially in the religious sphere.[24]

This work also presents a case study of the connections between theology and politics. A major dispute of the period was a questioning of the notion of the supremacy of the civil magistrate in matters of religion, which had been intrinsic to the Tudor Reformation settlement. In part spurred by the desire to protect the church from future royal interference and in part inspired by Scottish 'Melvilianism', the London presbyterians became advocates of a high Calvinist two-kingdoms theory. This political theology fleshed out previous godly concerns for the co-ordination of ministry and magistracy, while keeping the spheres of church and state as separate 'kingdoms' under Christ. By the mid-1640s, the dispute over the two-kingdoms position had given rise in presbyterian polemic to the term 'Erastian', after Thomas Erastus, a sixteenth-century opponent of the independence of the church in matters of ecclesiastical discipline. Originally meant as a slur aimed at common lawyers and Hebraists such as John Selden, William Prynne and Thomas Coleman, the term encapsulated the way in which theological positions impacted on the political and highlights the importance of presbyterians in London (both Scottish and English) in directing political debate.

The London presbyterians of the mid-seventeenth century are most known, and infamously so, for Thomas Edward's *Gangraena* and their rejection of religious toleration. Richard L. Greaves saw the 1640s debate over toleration in stark terms as the battle between 'the basic rights of the people' and the 'authoritarianism' of presbyterianism.[25] A more recent stream of historiography, however, has suggested that the issue needs to be understood in early modern terms.[26] A major feature of early modern Reformation thought was what Bob Scribner called the 'sacral corporatism' of social life. Religious heterodoxy therefore was seen to challenge the cosmology that underwrote civil peace, communal coherence and individual salvation.[27] Intolerance of confessional variation was understood as being necessary for the peace and unity of the commonwealth and the salvation of individual souls.[28] Thomas Edwards expressed this view, arguing that the law of nature requires 'that the severall parts and particular members' of any society be united 'for the good of the whole', with the consequence that 'the whole being greater than a part, the severall parts should be subject to, and ordered by the whole'.[29] As will be seen in this study, other voices among the London presbyterians show that the presbyterian theory of 'intolerance' was not always as extreme as has sometimes been averred by historians. However, as the London presbyterian ministers argued in 1647, the toleration of outright heresies opposed the advancing of God's kingdom and threatened the withdrawal of the 'presence of Grace' from God's people.[30] The need for the preaching of right doctrine meant that presbyterians could not accept that religious heterodoxy was anything other than a threat, both to the community of the saints and to civil society in general.

Finally, the London presbyterian movement can be seen as part of the *longue durée* of the history of puritanism. The now well-established work of scholars such as Patrick Collinson and Peter Lake has cast puritanism as an evangelical movement within the early modern Church of England, seeking to preserve the Reformed character of the national church. The vast majority of London presbyterians, clerical or lay, emerged out of either the moderate puritan or nonconformist traditions within the Church of England. The presbyterianism of the 1640s and 1650s, therefore, can be seen as a puritan reform movement within the national church, rather than as a sect or a break with the Church of England. The mid-century presbyterian insistence on the continuation of the national church and their polemic against sectarian religion would lead to the dilemma of dissent in the aftermath of the Great Ejection of 1662, a discussion of which concludes this book.

The scope of this study

This book covers the period between c.1638 and 1664. The call for presbyterian reformation emerged first as a clerical movement and the first three chapters focus on the development of presbyterianism among the clergy. However, by 1644, as the parliamentarian cause began to fracture over the terms of a future settlement with the king, it became critically important that lay supporters with access to institutional power in the city enter the political fray to push for the aims of the presbyterian movement. As the narrative from chapter 4 shows, the London ministers could call on a committed group of lay activists, identifying themselves as 'covenant-engaged citizens', for support and mobilisation in city politics. The majority of the ministers and laity examined in this study had been born between 1595 and 1615 and thus grown up in the Jacobean Church of England. The work of modern scholars of the pre-Laudian Church of England has shown that, despite its rifts and disagreements, it more or less co-existed around a Calvinistic doctrinal consensus and (a not necessarily strictly enforced) ceremonial conformity. Prior to the civil wars many of the ministers studied in this book had been conforming ministers and had accepted conformity, looking to godly bishops for the leadership of the church. These ministers had grown increasingly discontent under the 'new' conformity imposed by Archbishop Laud and his fellow travellers. While Elizabethan presbyterianism and Jacobean nonconformist thinking on church polity must have been known to these godly conforming clergy, there appears little evidence beyond the few small pockets of presbyterianism (such as that uncovered by Polly Ha) that there was any widespread discussion of, let alone plotting for, a presbyterian reformation of the Church of England.[31] The general view of most historians is that those puritans who crossed the boundary from the 'old' Jacobean conformity to nonconformity during the Laudian period looked to the congregationalism of New England as the model of ecclesiastical reform. The hopes and dreams of those who continued to conform often envisaged models of episcopacy that essentially looked to the ideal of, to use Ken Fincham's phrase, 'prelate as pastor'.[32]

The question of the adoption of presbyterianism by many English godly clergy between the calling of the Short Parliament and the outbreak of the first civil war is a pertinent one that is addressed in the first two chapters of this study. The common argument that presbyterianism was only adopted as a result of the need to court and obtain Scottish military aid in the struggle against Charles I is modified. These chapters look at the literary and oral debate from the first months of the Long Parliament to the opening debates on church government in the Westminster assembly to argue that a variety of genuinely presbyterian platforms and arguments were produced by influential English clergy. While the importance of Scottish propaganda and argument for presbyterianism cannot be overestimated, the presence of these English advocates for a presbyterian reformation complicates the common historiographical picture of presbyterianism as an alien offshoot grafted on to the English political scene by Scottish covenanter religious imperialism.

Another focus of this study is the emergence of a coherent presbyterian movement with both clerical and lay participants in London in the 1640s and 1650s. It is clear that the origins of this movement can be detected in the opposition mounted by networks of godly clergy to the Laudian canons of 1640, networks that also served to promulgate Scottish covenanter propaganda into England. But the existence of such organisation begs the question what existing structures were in place to allow the godly to mobilise against the Laudian canons? Peter Lake and David Como have argued that one aspect of puritanism prior to the late 1630s was 'underground' edifices that allowed the godly to manage internal conflict outside the gaze of the political state or episcopal disciplinary machinery.[33] Indeed, the management of rivalries and disputes to prevent potentially embarrassing public divisions can be identified in many of the same informal networks that Tom Webster found acting to inculcate sociability and stability among the Caroline godly. These networks also provided the means by which talented young clergy could obtain access to patronage and protection from those gentlemen and aristocrats who held both the advowsons and the influence necessary to float a career in the church.[34] Under the pressures of the Laudian disciplinary machinery of the late 1630s the godly clergy transformed these 'unrevolutionary' meetings and conferences of the early Stuart church into networks of mobilisation and resistance. It was from these radicalised clerical networks that calls for presbyterian reformation emerged.

Yet presbyterianism was but one form of church polity under consideration in the early 1640s and one that conflicted with the godly episcopacy advocated by influential and well-respected prelates such as Joseph Hall, James Ussher and John Williams. What would come to be called the 'Erastian' notion of a church 'by law established' under the royal supremacy was ingrained in the thought of the common lawyers and many other lay people who made up the bulk of the membership of the Long Parliament. In addition, advocates of reformation based on self-governing congregations were surfacing and becoming increasingly vocal. It is also clear that even among those who were self-consciously presbyterian there was no complete consensus on the exact particulars of presbyterian polity. Some presbyterians stressed the primal authority of the congregational unit, while others argued that congregations were not fully churches unless associated with other local ecclesiastical assemblies. Chapter 3 examines how these early debates over church polity would prove divisive in the polemically fuelled public environment of civil war print culture. Chapter 4 explores the theoretical development of presbyterianism among the London ministers. It also analyses attempts between presbyterians and Independents to find an accommodation over the terms of the projected national reformation of the church.

During the period 1645–8 the London presbyterian movement became a potent extra-parliamentary political force in the post-civil war politics of settlement. Although ultimately stopped by the rise of the New Model Army, the political strategies of the London presbyterian movement are an important case study of the politics of religion after the end of the first civil war. Chapters 5, 6 and 8 explore the mobilisation of networks of citizens, politicians and clergy to attempt to force a confessionally directed settlement of the English church and the exclusion of political and religious rivals within parliamentarianism.

Despite the importance of London presbyterian involvement in the politics of settlement after the end of the civil wars, London presbyterianism was first and foremost a religious movement aimed at reforming parish churches while retaining the national Church of England. Chapter 7 explores how, despite facing a succession of problems, ranging from the chronic economic condition of London's parish churches, through an absence of political will, to unpopularity and local resistance, the London presbyterians clung to the hope that they could make presbyterian polity work in practice.

The political revolution following Pride's purge and the execution of Charles I effectively sounded the death knell to hopes for a national presbyterian reformation. As John Morrill has noted 'without central backing [...] and *de jure* toleration from 1650, the whole rationale [behind Presbyterianism] failed'.[35] Chapter 9 will investigate how the revolution substantially weakened the institutional and political bases that the London presbyterians had built to mobilise the 'covenant-engaged interest' in the 1640s. After purging Parliament, one of the first steps of the new republic was to exclude the vast majority of lay presbyterians from their power base in the common council of the City of London. The Commonwealth's attempt at something akin to an oath of loyalty, the Engagement, was seen by presbyterians as being directly contradictory to the Solemn League and Covenant, leading to a wave of resistance to the new regime. The presbyterian ministry and citizenry in London, unable to submit to what they saw as the illegality of the Rump Parliament, took the dangerous path of supporting their presbyterian brethren in Scotland and Charles II, the newly covenanted King of the Scots, as a means to satisfy their consciences. Although London's presbyterians had been among the most vigorous supporters of the parliamentarian cause in the first civil war, the events of Pride's purge, the regicide and the Engagement controversy begged questions of allegiance and what proper action to take in the face of a political and military coup. Such questions would lead to a round of presbyterian plotting extending into continental Europe, with ultimately fatal consequences for the presbyterian minister Christopher Love, and thus provide a case study of the issues of legitimation and resistance in the English republic.

The fall of the Commonwealth and the removal of the Engagement in 1653, discussed in chapter 10, brought some cheer to London's presbyterians. Although presbyterianism was a spent force as a movement for the reformation of the Church of England, London's presbyterians began to regain ground under the Cromwellian Protectorate. While London's presbyterian government barely functioned, the presbyterians undertook numerous initiatives seeking to rescue and refocus presbyterian discipline.[36] That this task ultimately proved unsuccessful should not detract from the continuing vivacity and presence of London presbyterians in Cromwellian politics. Outside the failing operation of the presbyterian discipline, London's presbyterian ministers acted, often in concert with the more magisterially minded congregationalists, to seek a religious settlement that stressed the pre-civil war puritan ideal of the union of magistracy and ministry. The Cromwellian period saw presbyterian ministers contesting the *de facto* triumph of toleration and sectarian models of ecclesiastical polity. The Protectorate's concerns to rebuild the old parliamentarian centre also saw a cautious return of leading London presbyterians to positions of power and counsel in the Cromwellian administration.

However, the Army officers' intervention against what promised to be a political and religious, presbyterian-leaning settlement under Richard Cromwell's Protectorate, shattered the Cromwellian equilibrium. As the Army followed its erratic course in 1659 of *Putsch* and purge, London's presbyterians were stirred towards finding a solution that best protected the godly parochial ministry from chaos.

The shape of the Restoration, which is the subject of chapter 11, was never an inevitability and was subject to a mixture of political calculation, miscalculation and contingency equivalent to that at the outbreak of the civil war. As calls grew for a free parliament and ultimately the return of the Stuart monarchy, London presbyterian ministers acted to further the re-establishment of the house of Stuart, hoping that a political restoration led by presbyterians would establish a favourable settlement on terms similar to those agreed with Charles I at the treaty of Newport in 1648. It became increasingly clear to the London ministers, however, that the Stuart monarchy would not adopt a presbyterian polity in any new Church of England settlement. This reality led to divisions among presbyterians as to how to proceed. For the majority of London presbyterians, comprehension within a national church that retained something of the polity 'according to the word of God and the best Reformed churches' was seen as a better option than acquiescing to a toleration that afforded liberty to papists and quakers. Yet, if comprehension within a restored episcopal Church of England retaining aspects of Reformed polity looked to be within reach, the hope collapsed soon after as the Cavalier Parliament and the restored episcopate set about constructing the 'Anglican' Church of England.

The final chapter explores the period when London's presbyterians had to make a choice between accepting a Church of England that went against their consciences or refusing to conform to a national church that they had defended and hoped to reform for some twenty years. The majority of presbyterian ministers accepted nonconformity on 24 August 1662, providing important leadership to early dissent. While 'Black Bartholomew's day' was not the end of English presbyterianism, it marked the conclusion of the story that had begun with the English puritan clergy's resistance to Laudianism and the hope for a second reformation of the Church of England. Although presbyterians would continue in dissent, and presbyterian churches of various guises would revive in England, the end of this study marks the end of the presbyterian moment in the history of the Church of England.

Notes

1 I have intentionally used the phrase 'the politics of religion' to signal that I have adopted the approach to the subject explored in the influential set of essays of Restoration history edited by Tim Harris, Paul Seaward and Mark Goldie: *The politics of religion in Restoration England* (Oxford, 1990).
2 G. E. Aylmer (ed.), *The Levellers in the English revolution* (Ithaca, NY, 1975), p. 55.
3 The notable exception being the work of Ann Hughes, especially Hughes, *Gangraena*.
4 See C. Van Dixhoorn, 'The strange silence of Prolocutor Twisse: predestination and politics in the Westminster assembly's debate over justification', *The Sixteenth Century Journal*, 40 (2009), 395–418; C. Van Dixhoorn, 'The Westminster assembly and the Reformation of the 1640s' in *The Oxford History of Anglicanism*, vol.1: *Reformation and identity 1520–1662*, ed. A. Milton (Oxford, 2017), pp. 430–1; L. Gatiss, '"Shades of opinion within a generic Calvinism". The particular redemption debate at the Westminster assembly', *Reformed Theological Review*, 69:2 (2010), 101–18 and J. D. Moore, 'The extent of the atonement: English hypothetical universalism versus particular redemption' in Haykin and Jones, *Controversie*, pp. 124–61.
5 Recent examples of such work include Won Taek Lim, 'The covenant theology of Francis Roberts' (Ph.D thesis, Calvin Theological Seminary, 2000) and Chin How Wong, 'The overlapping realms: William Jenkyn's exposition on Jude' (Ph.D thesis, Westminster Theological Seminary, 2014).
6 C. Durston, 'By the book or with the spirit: the debate over liturgical prayer during the English revolution', *Historical Research*, 79:203 (2006), 50–73; J. Maltby, '"Extravagencies and impertinencies": set forms, conceived prayer and extemporary prayer in revolutionary England' in *Worship and the parish church in early modern Britain*, eds N. Mears and A. Ryrie (Farnham, 2013), pp. 221–43. See also my 'Godly pastors and their congregations in mid-seventeenth century London' in Davies, Dunan-Page and Halcomb, *Church life*, pp. 45–62.
7 Ann Hughes gives a similar typology of the term 'presbyterian' in A. Hughes, 'Print and pastoral identity: presbyterian pastors negotiate the Restoration' in Davies, Dunan-Page and Halcomb, *Church life*, p. 153.
8 De Witt, *Jus Divinum*, pp. 233–4, 245.
9 Baxter, *RB*, I, p. 146; G. Yule, 'Some problems in the history of the English presbyterians in the seventeenth century', *Journal of the Presbyterian History Society of England*, 13:2 (1965), 9; Paul, *The assembly*, pp. 531–4.

10 Yule, 'Some problems in the history of the English Presbyterians', pp. 9–11.
11 A summary of the history of Reformed church polity can be found at J. Ballor and W. B. Littlejohn, 'European Calvinism: church discipline' in *European History Online* (EGO). URL: www.ieg-ego.eu/ballorj-littlejohnw-2013-en URN: urn:nbn:de:0159-2013032507 [last retrieved: 17 January 2020].
12 London Provincial assembly, *A vindication of the presbyterial-government and ministry* (1650), p. 1.
13 See e.g. John Paget, *A defence of church-government* (1641), p. 33.
14 E. W. Kirby, 'The English presbyterians in the Westminster assembly', *CH*, 33:4 (1964), 426.
15 For example, the collection edited by C. G. Bolam, J. Goring, H. L. Short and R. Thomas, *The English presbyterians: from Elizabethan puritanism to modern Unitarianism* (1968), pp. 34–46.
16 See John Geree, *Siniorragia: the sifters sieve broken* (1648), pp. 48, 59–60 for a contemporary argument for this point.
17 Lindley, *Popular politics*, pp. 279, 409.
18 Wallington was in the top rank of those serving the London Provincial assembly. Only 5 out of a total of about 199 elders were delegated more times than Wallington.
19 For a discussion of the dynamic of neighbourliness and toleration in civil war London see K. Lynch, '"Letting a Room in London-House": a place for dissent in civil war London' in Davies, Dunan-Page and Halcomb, *Church life*, pp. 63–81. More generally, see the collection of essays in *Getting along? religious identities and confessional relations in early modern England: essays in honour of Professor W. J. Sheils*, eds N. Lewycky and A. Morton (Farnham, 2012).
20 For a succinct typology and chronology of party politics see D. Scott, 'Party politics in the Long Parliament, 1640–8' in Tapsell and Southcombe, *Revolutionary England*, pp. 163–75.
21 J. Peacey, *Print and public politics in the English revolution* (Cambridge, 2013), pp. 397, 400–2.
22 M. Braddick, 'Mobilisation, anxiety and creativity in England during the 1640s' in *Liberty, authority, formality: political ideas and culture, 1600–1900*, eds J. Morrow and J. Scott (Exeter, 2008), pp. 175–93.
23 See A. Hughes, '"Popular" presbyterianism in the 1640s and 1650s: the cases of Thomas Edwards and Thomas Hall' in *England's long reformation, 1500–1800*, ed. N. Tyacke (1998), pp. 235–60; A. Hughes, 'Religious diversity in revolutionary London' in *The English revolution, c.1590–1720: politics, religion and communities*, ed. N. Tyacke (Manchester, 2013), pp. 111–28. This topic is also a major theme explored in Hughes, *Gangraena*.
24 For an essay exploring the power of rumour and gossip in early modern England see D. Coast and J. Fox, 'Rumour and politics', *History Compass* 13:5 (2015), 222–34. For a survey of alternative theories drawn from the anthropology of politics and social psychology see P. J. Stewart and A. Strathern, *Witchcraft, sorcery, rumors and gossip* (Cambridge, 2004), pp. 29–58.

25 R. L. Greaves, 'The ordination controversy and the spirit of reform in puritan England', *JEH*, 21:3 (1970), p. 233.
26 See, for example, A. Zakai, 'Religious toleration and its enemies: the Independent divines and the issue of toleration during the English civil war', *Albion*, 21:1 (1989), 1–2, 33; J. C. Davis, 'Religion and the struggle for freedom in the English revolution', *HJ*, 35:3 (1992), 510–11, 515, 521, 523; B. Worden, 'Toleration and the Cromwellian Protectorate' in Worden, *God's instruments*.
27 B. Scribner, 'Preconditions of tolerance and intolerance in sixteenth-century Germany' in *Tolerance and intolerance in the European Reformation*, eds O. P. Grell and B. Scribner (Cambridge, 1996), p. 43; H. Oberman, 'The travail of tolerance: containing chaos in early modern Europe' in Grell and Scribner, *Tolerance and intolerance*, p. 17.
28 M. Goldie, 'The theory of religious intolerance in Restoration England' in *From persecution to toleration: the Glorious Revolution and religion in England*, eds O. P. Grell, J. Israel and N. Tyacke (Oxford, 1991), pp. 331–59.
29 Thomas Edwards, *Reasons against the independent government of particular congregations* (1641), p. 10.
30 *A testimony to the truth of Jesus Christ* (1647), pp. 1–2.
31 See generally Ha, *Presbyterianism*.
32 P. Collinson, *The religion of protestants: the Church in English society 1559–1625* (Oxford, 1982), ch. 2; K. Fincham, *Prelate as pastor: the episcopate of James I* (Oxford, 1990), ch. 8.
33 P. Lake and D. Como, '"Orthodoxy" and its discontents: dispute settlement and the production of "consensus" in the London (puritan) "underground"', *JBS*, 39:1 (2000), 34–70.
34 Webster, *Godly clergy*, pp. 9–92.
35 J. Morrill, 'The church in England, 1642–1649' in *The Nature of the English Revolution: essays by John Morrill* (Basingstoke, 1993), p. 156. See also L. H. Carlson, 'A history of the presbyterian party from Pride's purge to the dissolution of the Long Parliament', *CH*, 11 (1942), 83–122.
36 I deal with this to some degree in my 'A ministry of the gospel: the presbyterians during the English revolution' in *Religion in revolutionary England*, eds C. Durston and J. Maltby (Manchester, 2006), pp. 115–36.

1

The radicalisation of conformist puritanism, c. 1638–40

In May 1639 the godly minister Edmund Calamy arrived in London having resigned his living of the Essex parish of Rochford, a parish he had served at the personal invitation of the Earl of Warwick, a patron and friend. Calamy's move to London had been brought about by the election of the parishioners of St Mary, Aldermanbury, a wealthy parish located in the centre of the city of London.[1] The Aldermanbury living was owned by the parish itself and had been rendered vacant by the death of its puritan minister Dr John Stoughton. Calamy's election was fortuitous. With Charles I's personal rule about to collapse, this London location and Calamy's friendship with the dissident Earl of Warwick placed him at the centre of the opposition to the Caroline administration of church and state. In 1643 a royalist propagandist would complain of a 'junto' meeting at Calamy's Aldermanbury house. From here, the propagandist alleged, parliamentarian 'emissaries' among the godly ministry would 'receive directions' as to 'what concerns the present opportunity, and what is necessary to be preached unto the people'.[2]

There is very little evidence from the 1620s and 1630s to mark Calamy out as a future parliamentarian activist. In matters of doctrine, he held to the pastorally driven 'hypothetical universalism' advanced by the English delegates at the Synod of Dort.[3] He had attended Pembroke Hall in Cambridge in 1616, before becoming the household chaplain to Nicholas Felton, the Calvinist Bishop of Ely. His ministry at Bury St Edmunds in the late 1620s and early 1630s, a town ministry he shared with the future congregationalist Jeremiah Burroughes, suggests a picture of a godly preacher who nevertheless accepted the conformity required by the Church of England.[4] Yet, by 1641 Calamy would be at the centre of parliamentarian opposition to Laudian prelacy, advocating fundamental reform of the polity of the Church of England in a presbyterian direction.

This chapter will explore the radicalisation of many of London's moderate puritans during the period 1637–40 in the wake of the crisis that erupted in the Churches of England and Scotland under the Laudian administration of the 1630s. The discussion will then turn to the godly ministers' mobilisation of opposition to Convocations' new canons of 1640. It will be argued that the opposition to the canons revitalised the godly clergy as a political force and ushered in a somewhat cautious movement seeking further reformation of the polity of the Church of England.

The London godly scene in the 1630s

The origins of the London presbyterian movement that emerged in the 1640s can be found in the reaction of godly ministers and laity who were marginalised and harassed under the Laudian administration of the late 1630s. Throughout the 1620s and 1630s the number of beneficed ministers in London who can be happily described as 'puritan' or 'godly' was relatively small, making up 15 to 20 per percent of the beneficed clergy in the City of London's 109 parishes.[5] While the term 'puritan' and its cognate 'the godly' have proven contentious among historians, by the 1640s presbyterian ministers could adopt 'puritan' to describe 'the best Protestants' who did not separate from the Church of England but who 'bewailed' its lack of full reformation.[6] The ministers stressed the 'experimental' application of Reformed theological doctrine both to the individual and collective lives of the faithful. However, at least until the late 1630s, moderate puritans did not aim at fundamentally reforming the polity of the Church of England.[7] Many of these ministers accepted the Jacobean episcopate's compromise of affording a tacit forbearance on issues of strict conformity in return for subscription to its doctrine and discipline.[8] This semi-official position of latitude, often effected by the Jacobean bishops of London turning a blind eye towards partial, ceremonial conformity would come to be described in the 1640s as the 'old conformity'. This was in contrast to the rigorous 'new conformity' imposed on the Church of England in the late 1620s and 1630s under Archbishop William Laud.[9] The Laudian campaign of pressure put substantial strain on the viability of this puritan 'old conformity' within the national Church of England.[10]

The rise of William Laud, first as Bishop of London and then Archbishop of Canterbury, and the style of religious piety that historians have termed 'Laudianism', progressively disrupted this tacit Jacobean equilibrium. The Laudian focus on 'the beauty of holiness' in the parish church, with lay devotion centred on corporate participation in the church's liturgy, was undoubtedly popular among a substantial section of London's population.[11] In addition the Laudian drive for the 'beauty of holiness' fed into Londoners' existing concerns to improve the fabric and aesthetic of their church buildings.[12] Nevertheless, these changes of focus in the religion of the established Church were at odds with the godly style of 'experimental' application of Calvinist predestinarian doctrine. This was not helped by the Laudian administration re-envisioning the godly as 'dangerous enemies' of the church and monarchy.[13]

The Laudian marginalisation of puritan ministers was brought into effect by a campaign of intimidation and pressure against the godly. One of Laud's early campaigns as archbishop of Canterbury was to promote the prosecution of the 'feoffees for impropriations', a group of merchants, clergy and lawyers whose aim was to purchase advowsons in order to present godly ministers to livings. Among the leading trustees of the feoffee group were the London ministers William Gouge of St Anne, Blackfriars and Charles Offspring of St Antholin, Budge Row, as well as John White, the lawyer and later Long Parliament MP.[14] Laud characterised the feoffees as 'main instruments for the puritan faction' and 'dangerous to both Church and state'.[15] The feoffees' operation did not survive the Laudian challenge in the court of Exchequer in 1633 and the operation was closed down with the forfeiture of the advowsons in the feoffees' control.[16]

A major aspect of the Laudian reforms was designed to bring about a stricter observance of the 'new conformity' required by the Laudian conceptualisation of corporate worship. In the mid-1630s Edmund Calamy, then town preacher at Bury St Edmunds, had felt compelled to conform to the requirements to wear clerical dress, but had drawn the line at reading set prayers towards the altar.[17] Kenneth Fincham has noted 'the firm and sustained pressure for conformity' under the Laudian administration, which used extensively the tools of suspension and excommunication against godly ministers.[18] In London, David Como's research has found that in the 1630s Laud used 'behind the scenes methods quietly to bully London's Calvinist ministers into compliance'.[19] Laudian enforcement of the 'new conformity' entailed a thorough policy of requiring conformity to the ceremonies of the Church of England. Ministers who failed to wear the prescribed clerical dress or strictly use the Book of Common Prayer, whose preaching ventured into issues such as the doctrine of predestination or questioned the Church of England's hierarchy, might find themselves under surveillance, censured and even prosecuted.[20]

The Laudian imposition of stricter conformity in the 1630s acted to unseat the latitude and forbearance that had characterised the practice of the Jacobean episcopate in the city. The ritualism of the Laudian reforms also served to raise fears among London's godly that the protestant religion itself was under attack. Tom Webster's research has shown how Laudian changes to the nature of conformity caused a growing number of godly ministers throughout England to begin to rethink the old arguments for conformity.[21] The Laudian marginalisation of moderate puritan ministers in London and elsewhere therefore began to reawaken old puritan criticism of the established church that had been subsumed by the 'old conformity' during the Jacobean period.

The Laudian campaign for more rigorous conformity did not aim just at harassing ministers. The 1637 trial and bloody punishment of Henry Burton, John Bastwick and William Prynne for publishing books against the Laudian prelacy sent a shock wave through the godly community in London and the nation at large.[22] Burton, Bastwick and Prynne took every opportunity to turn their prosecution into a public spectacle of resistance to the Laudian regime. Bastwick, who would serve the later London presbyterian movement both as a polemicist and as a ruling elder, played up his imprisonment in London's notorious Gatehouse prison by holding readings of his controversial works with his visitors.[23] The persistence and rigour of Laud's investigation into those connected with Bastwick, Burton and Prynne only served to radicalise local networks of godly Londoners. An example of this can be seen in the February 1639 Star Chamber investigation of Nehemiah Wallington, a relatively obscure Eastcheap wood turner.[24] Wallington, together with his brother John and friends such as the future presbyterian elder Daniel Sowton, had owned a number of the controversial works of Burton and Prynne.[25] The investigations into, and harassment of, relatively lowly puritans such as the Wallingtons and their friends served to increase the local sense of resentment among the godly against the Laudian prelacy. The wide-ranging harassment of local puritans sublimated the fear of punishment into narratives of godly suffering and martyrdom, and in some cases created eschatological expectations that the end time was approaching.[26] Laud's efforts to harass and cow local puritan networks therefore served to radicalise and strengthen the godly in the opposition to the Laudian church.

Alongside the perceived Laudian persecution of the godly in England, the Scottish 'Prayer Book' rebellion in July 1637 also provided a further catalyst for English opponents to organise against Laudian and Caroline policies.[27] Between November 1637 and November 1638 the Scottish national assembly dismantled the edifice of the Stuart kings' policy of imposing episcopacy on Scotland. In so doing the covenanters challenged the foundations of Charles I's prerogatives and authority in plain sight of the godly in England.[28]

The Scottish rebellion fed a growing sense among some of the English godly that the English prelacy, even episcopacy itself, was defective as a form of church government. This question had already been explored by William Prynne in his anonymous 1636 work *The unbishoping of Timothy and Titus*, which advanced a presbyterial interpretation of the primitive church against the claims that diocesan episcopacy was established by divine right.[29] The emerging question of episcopacy can be seen in the case of the Essex minister Constant Jessop, who recorded that the Laudian imposition of the Prayer Book on Scotland, the cruel treatment of John Bastwick and the imposition of the new canons of 1640 caused him to begin to question the scriptural warrant for episcopacy. Jessop began to focus on the themes discussed in Prynne's 1636 tract, as well the emerging scholarship on the early church, such as the 1633 publication of the first-century letter attributed to Clement of Rome, a work that could be interpreted as showing a presbyterial structure to the immediately post-apostolic church.[30] This period of reflection caused Jessop to abandon his former conformity and become a convinced presbyterian by the early 1640s.[31] The radicalisation of moderate puritans such as Jessop caused by Laudian policy in the 1630s was a process that would lead to a reform-minded constituency in the early years of the Long Parliament.

The perceived threat to the godly caused by the Laudian campaign for the 'new conformity' also caused godly merchants in the city to begin to seek out one another for deliverance. Anne Venn, the daughter of the future Long Parliament MP John Venn, remembered that in 1638–9 'the people of God' in the city, including her father, 'met often and spake one to another, and kept days of humiliation, and seeking the Lord in the behalf of the nation and his poor people'.[32] Godly London merchants such as John Venn were also connected to opposition peers such as the Earl of Warwick and Viscount Saye and Sele through business interests in colonial ventures. These connections would link London's puritans to the 'junto' that made up the principal opposition to Charles I's regime.[33] This network was made plain in September 1640, when Venn and other godly merchants would organise a city petition to the king supporting the junto peers' own petition for the calling of a new Parliament.[34]

The Laudian campaign to enforce the 'new conformity' in 1630s London, coupled with the investigation into godly criticism of Laudian policy, served to radicalise and connect what had been largely politically inert networks of local piety among those called puritans. The politicisation of these connections would gather momentum in 1640 with the calling of Parliament and Convocation.

The Canons of 1640 and the mobilisation of godly discontent

The covenanter rebellion in Scotland, beginning in 1637, saw the resurgence of militant Scottish presbyterianism and the first Bishops' War in the summer of 1639.[35] Although a temporary peace was agreed at Berwick on 18 June 1639, this truce existed to give both sides room to manoeuvre and necessitated Charles I calling an English parliament to quell the Scots. The gathering of the 'Short Parliament' of 1640 stimulated the lines of communication that existed between London and the localities. As we have seen from the example of Constant Jessop, the Convocation's making of new canons contributed to the erosion of the already dwindling puritan commitment to the 'old conformity'. In drafting the canons, Convocation had attempted to project the appearance of consensus by including Calvinist ministers on the drafting committee. However, the canons were offensive to many godly clergy both within and outside Convocation.[36] One aspect of this criticism was of a legal-constitutional nature, as Convocation claimed to be entitled to make canons without parliamentary consent, and to grant a £20,000 subsidy to the king.[37]

Alongside legal-constitutional criticism, the godly's protests were aimed specifically at the content of the canons.[38] This included criticism of the first canon (that monarchy and the monarch's right to taxation were divinely ordained), the seventh canon (which set a position for the communion table *vis-à-vis* the altar and genuflexions associated with it, that, to the godly, were reminiscent of Roman Catholic practice) and the '*et cetera* oath' contained in the sixth canon.[39] This oath required that a minister refuse to give 'consent to alter the government of this Church, by archbishops, bishops, deanes and archdeacons, *&c*, as it stands now established, and as by right it ought to stand'. The inclusion of the ominous '*et cetera*' at the end of the list of episcopal offices was perceived as a future trap that gave the ecclesiastical hierarchy a blank page to force innovations on the clergy. Arthur Jackson, the godly minister of St Michael, Wood Street, who would become a leading London presbyterian in the 1640s, commented on 10 July 1640 that the oath was such that 'if God be with me, I hope I shall never take. The Lord be merciful to us!'[40] It also seemed to its critics to contradict the oath of allegiance and, as its opponents among the clergy of Devon protested, to 'clip the wings' of the crown's supremacy to determine the polity of the church.[41]

A further sub-clause of canon six, 'I doe approve the Doctrine and Discipline or Government, establish in the Church of England, as containing all things necessary to salvation' was criticised on the basis that neither the doctrine nor the discipline of the Church of England were defined by the canons.[42] The reference to discipline as being 'necessary to salvation' presumed, it was argued, a divine right for episcopacy, implying that the Scottish and continental Reformed churches were not true churches.[43] To their godly opponents, the canons of 1640 therefore confirmed the worst of the Laudian reforms and made them binding on the church.

The new canons triggered the godly into mobilising a national campaign to protest against their contents. The first wave of petitions voicing concerns against the canons broke in late July and early August 1640 and originated from ministers from London, Northamptonshire, Kent and Devon.[44] The London ministers' petition, although circulated for signatures in July, was completed at a meeting convened at the house of John Downame, the godly minister of Allhallows the Great, on 6 August 1640. According to the intelligence of Sir John Lambe, the meeting was attended by a number of London godly ministers including Cornelius Burges, Edmund Calamy, Arthur Jackson, Charles Offspring, John Downame and John Goodwin.[45] This group appears to have been in correspondence with networks of provincial godly clergy. Nicholas Tyacke and Jacqueline Eales have charted a 'puritan continuum' that connected pockets of godly clergy and laity who could look back to the Elizabethan period.[46] This continuum often found expression in voluntary conferences of local ministers. For example, Samuel Clarke, the mid-century presbyterian minister of St Benet Fink, London, had preached alongside the Elizabethan presbyterian Humphrey Fenn in 1620s Coventry.[47] Of particular importance was the conference in the midland and north-western counties formed around Arthur Hildersham, John Dod and John Ball. This conference included ministers known for presbyterian views such as Simeon Ashe, William Rathband and Julines Herring.[48] Panels of godly clergy often acted as private advisers to local godly gentry and peers, such as the Northamptonshire ministers around the minister Thomas Ball, who advised godly patrons such as Viscount Saye and Sele and John Crewe about which clergy to present to the livings in their gift.[49] The 'radicalism' of such groups, however, was more latent than overt, at least until the call for reformation was reactivated by the national petitioning campaign against the canons of 1640.

The similarity of the county petitions against the canons all indicate that this campaign was organised by ministers who had connections to the London clergy meeting at Downame's house.[50] At the start of the campaign, the London ministers sent out a series of 'queries' to the localities, which circulated throughout England at remarkable speed.[51] An example of the influence of the London ministers can be seen in a meeting of around thirty local clergy on 25 August 1640 at the Swan Tavern in Kettering in Northamptonshire.[52] The participants in this meeting included Thomas Ball, who was corresponding with Edmund Calamy in 1639 on matters of church government, and the future London presbyterians Jeremiah Whitaker, James Cranford, Daniel Cawdrey and Andrew Perne.[53] Ball and his circle of Northamptonshire ministers had become notorious to the Laudian authorities for their growing opposition to the 'new conformity' in the 1630s and for working in concert with godly dissidents such as Richard Knightly and Viscount Saye and Sele.[54] During the Kettering meeting Jeremiah Whitaker produced the queries 'which came from the London ministers' and a Scottish covenanter tract justifying the Scots' invasion of northern England.[55] The Northamptonshire meeting resolved to oppose the canons and to join the petitioning campaign against them.

Similar meetings to raise opposition to the canons also took place in other counties, including Shropshire, Worcestershire and Cheshire.[56] These connected prominent country ministers such as Samuel Clarke and John Ley to the London campaign. The importance of the London ministers to the campaign against the canons in the localities can be seen in the fact that John Ley, disgruntled by the northern Convocation's support for the canons, had travelled to London to seek the advice of the city ministers as to how to direct regional opposition.[57]

The radicalising effect of the meetings can also be seen in the anecdotes of individual ministers. We have already noted the effect of the canons in causing the Essex minister Constant Jessop to question the validity of episcopacy. The thoughts of a 'Mr S. M. of Essex', possibly Stephen Marshall, were circulating in response to the 1640 canons, attacking the episcopate's claims to sole jurisdiction in the church and the requirement that the clergy subscribe to episcopacy by divine right. The note advised that 'in the primitive church the Bish. was onely the præses of the assembly, and did nothing without the rest of the clergy' and that the local clergy, not the king, elected this president.[58] Richard Baxter remembered that his troubles with the canons led him to begin to seek out and study anti-episcopal works such as Paul Baynes's *The Diocesans Tryall* or Gerson Bucerus's *Dissertatio de Gubernatione Ecclesiae*.[59] The effect of this course of reading was to alienate Baxter and many other 'quiet conformists' from the corrupt 'English diocesan frame' of church government.[60]

The godly campaign against the canons of 1640 saw the nationwide networks of godly ministers politicised against Laudian episcopacy. These local conferences and meetings had been put under strain by the more thorough imposition of Laudian reforms in the Church of England. The enforcement, expansion and vigorous prosecution of the Laudian style of 'new conformity' in the later 1630s acted to transform local conferences of godly clergy into vehicles of resistance and caused previously conforming clergy to rethink the issue of further reformation in the Church of England. At the centre of this mobilisation were the London clergy, who organised the national opposition to the canons. The calling of the Long Parliament would only serve to further London as the centre of godly activism in the winter of 1640–41.

The opening of the Long Parliament and the call for further reformation

With the opening of the Long Parliament in November 1640, godly ministers close to the opposition junto expressed the expectation that Parliament should not just address their complaints against Laudian 'innovations', but also seek further reformation of the church. From the beginning of the Long Parliament there were fierce private discussions on ecclesiastical polity among ministers and laity alike. With a number of potentially incompatible positions held by the ministers in the circle of the opposition junto and the pragmatic realities of politics there was no consensus for a programme of reform. Nevertheless, the London 'Root and Branch' petition demonstrated that anti-episcopal positions were being advanced by the city's godly citizens. Similar debates were taking place among the London ministers, whose meetings in the city were augmented by the arrival of representatives sent from the provincial clerical networks that had opposed the Laudian canons earlier in 1640. These provincial agents came to London to join the city ministers in drafting a national Petition and Remonstrance of the godly clergy. While this document, perhaps intentionally, lacked the strident anti-episcopalianism of the London Root and Branch petition, or any mention of a change of ecclesiastical polity, the submissions made before the Parliamentary committee hearing the Petition and Remonstrance showed that the London ministers were cautiously setting out the foundations for a reformation of the polity of the Church of England.

The opening of the Long Parliament on 3 November 1640 created considerable expectation among the ministers that a new wave of reformation in the Church of England was about to commence. This expectation can be seen in the sermons preached for the opening parliamentary fast on 17 November 1640 by Cornelius Burges and Stephen Marshall. The sermons went beyond a call to merely roll back the Laudian innovations and enjoined Parliament to effect a more comprehensive reformation of the church.[61] While renewing the traditional puritan call for local ministers to be empowered to exercise parochial discipline, the sermons at the opening fast left open the question of the precise shape of further reformation of the ecclesiastical polity.

This guarded position was prudent, as the clerical caucus that had emerged from the campaign against the canons of 1640 did not agree among itself as to how far the anticipated second wave of reformation should go. Between 1640 and 1641 the godly ministers' desire to maintain consensus often sat in tension with the aspirations of some of their number to reform the polity of the Church of England. In addition, the clergy linked to the parliamentary opposition to Charles I were aware that political issues had higher priority in the early Long Parliament and that the reformation of the Church of England would prove divisive.[62] An example of such circumspection can be seen in the words of Calybute Downing, the minister of Hackney, who in 1641 publicly advocated 'a prudent and peaceable spirit' on issues of church government, counselling against declaring matters of polity to be prescribed by divine right.[63] At the same time, however, he published an anonymous tract advocating the adoption of a thorough-going presbyterian polity in the church.[64] The sermons and polemical works in these early months of the Long Parliament often display a studied ambiguity, or even silence, on the exact particulars of the ecclesiastical settlement being aimed at. This ambiguity was essential to maintaining consensus among the opposition to the administration of the church by leaving room for the pragmatism and compromise needed to effect further reformation.

If the need to maintain consensus and trim to the winds of what was politically possible muted public expression of further reformation among godly ministers, it is clear that there was, nevertheless, a resurgence of debate on the various alternative positions concerning church polity. The result of the clerical conferences begun in mid-1640 was that ministers began to consider issues of church polity afresh. This process would be exacerbated by the arrival of the Scottish commissioners and their chaplains in London on 13 November. During and after the Bishops' Wars, covenanter propaganda, which advanced the newly restored presbyterianism of the Church of Scotland and poured scorn on the Prayer Book and Laudian episcopacy, had been posted or delivered to the godly throughout England.[65] This propaganda campaign heralded a greater discussion of alternative positions on church order when the Scots arrived in London. The Scottish chaplains were accommodated in the parish of St Antholin, Budge Row, the location of regular puritan lectureships and were afforded the use of the parish's pulpit.[66] The Scottish sermons, particularly those of Alexander Henderson, became popular events.[67] Royalist propaganda would later describe St Antholin as the 'pratique seminary' of puritanism and 'a *classis* or clero-laicall consistory' from which opposition to Laudianism was planned.[68] Upon their arrival, the Scottish ministers set about advancing their aim of establishing the rightness of the covenanter's presbyterian cause through the agency, as Robert Baillie put it, of 'praying, preaching, and printing'.[69]

At the same time as the arrival of the Scots, the London Root and Branch petition, with its demand that episcopal government 'with all its dependencies, roots and branches, may be abolished' was in circulation in the city.[70] The Scots first saw a copy the London petition in mid-November and the Glasgow minister Robert Baillie reported that by 2 December it had been signed by 'some thousands of hands'.[71] Nevertheless, the extreme anti-episcopal stance of the London Root and Branch petition frightened the parliamentarian junto as its demands were potentially counterproductive to their immediate political programme of dismantling the mechanisms of Charles I's personal rule.[72] Baillie noted that the Root and Branch petition 'had not friends in both the Houses' and that it was beginning to polarise opinion in Parliament. The petition's organisers were warned by the junto's Parliamentary managers against presenting the petition until after the conclusion of the business of the Earl of Strafford and the removal of the bishops from the House of Lords.[73] Despite these warnings, the petition was presented on 11 December by the godly city merchant and London MP Isaac Pennington, accompanied by a large crowd of citizens.

There is some debate as to who was behind the London Root and Branch petition. Conrad Russell and Austin Woolrych argue that the London ministers, acting with the Scots, were the 'undoubted' originators and organisers of the petition.[74] On the other hand, Anthony Fletcher, Nicholas Tyacke and Keith Lindley see the petition as the work of 'radical citizens' in the parishes, with Pennington being its 'organizing genius'.[75] On balance, the latter view seems more convincing. Baillie described the petition as coming from 'the Toun of London and a great world of men' when the Scots arrived in London.[76] Isaac Pennington would later be the petition's greatest advocate, defending the social standing of those citizens who signed it. This may suggest that he was also one of its principal authors and organisers.[77]

Whatever the connection between the godly clergy in London and the Root and Branch petition, London's puritan ministers were at work at Edmund Calamy's house in Aldermanbury on a national Petition and Remonstrance against the abuses of the Laudian period.[78] The ministers meeting at Calamy's house were building on the national network that had developed during the campaign against the Laudian canons in 1640. Conferences of puritan ministers from all over England sent clerical delegates to London to act as deputies in preparing the Petition and Remonstrance. For example, the Warwickshire minister Samuel Clarke was sent to London at the behest of the ministers of the diocese of Worcester. Clarke recalled that at 'London we met with many ministers from most parts of the kingdom; and upon some meetings and debates, it was resolved that a committee should be chosen to draw up a remonstrance of our grievances, and to petition Parliament for reformation'.[79] On 12 December 1640 Baillie noted that the Petition and Remonstrance had been begun by 'sundrie countrie ministers [...] which, in the name of the Church, shall shortlie be presented against the bishops'.[80] It is also apparent that the text of the Petition and Remonstrance was communicated by the regional delegates to their home areas via the chaplains of godly peers who were present in London for the Long Parliament. On 28 December, Baillie told his colleagues that the Petition and Remonstrance 'is now posting through the land for hands to make it stark'.[81] These chaplains, whose position invariably involved travelling on secretarial engagements for their patrons, acted as go-betweens between godly ministers in the country and the metropolis. One such emissary was Lord Brooke's presbyterian-leaning chaplain Simeon Ashe, who took the Petition and Remonstrance from London to receive subscription from ministers in Warwickshire.[82]

The Petition and Remonstrance, which had amassed between 700 and 800 signatures by January 1641, represented a comprehensive catalogue of complaints against the Laudian innovations in the Church of England, attacking, as Baillie put it, the 'corruptions of the Church, in doctrine, discipline, lyfe, and all'.[83] It was presented to the Commons on 23 January 1641 by Sir Robert Harley accompanied by a number 'of the eldest and gravest' of the godly clergy, including Cornelius Burges, Calybute Downing, Edmund Calamy and Stephen Marshall. William Shaw argued that the Petition and Remonstrance was 'a standard of moderate reform' issued by 'the moderate majority' of the clergy in reaction to the radicalism of the London Root and Branch petition.[84] The Petition and Remonstrance did not call for the abolition of episcopacy, nor the establishment of presbyterian church polity, but there is good reason to believe that there were more radical voices behind it than Shaw allowed. Richard Overton, the future Leveller, reported that objections were raised by the clerical delegates during the discussions at Calamy's house that a call for outright abolition of episcopacy would encourage 'heresies [to] further spread'. This led Calamy to meet with the leaders of separatist churches to convince them to worship less openly.[85] Likewise, Cornelius Burges claimed in 1659 that the abolition of episcopacy did not form part of the policy discussions taking place at the Earl of Warwick's Holborn house between the leading puritan ministers and the junto grandees in 1640–41.[86] It seems likely, therefore, that the Petition and Remonstrance was purposefully designed to build consensus among the anti-Laudian clergy rather than suggest the more radical approach of the Root and Branch petition. Baillie dated the commencement of the Petition and Remonstrance to 12 December 1640, the day after the presentation of the London Root and Branch petition. This may suggest that the Petition and Remonstrance was strategically planned to attenuate any damage caused by the overt anti-episcopal demands of the Root and Branch petition.[87]

It therefore seems possible that the timing of the presentation of the ministers' Petition and Remonstrance was calculated to reduce the damage that the naked anti-episcopalianism of the London Root and Branch petition might cause. In this regard, it was successful. The ensuing debate on 8–9 February showed that the Commons were more interested in regulating the abuses of episcopacy than venturing into the uncharted territory of establishing a non-episcopal form of church polity. In particular, the long-running early modern theme of the incompatibility of presbyterianism with the royal supremacy was aired in the debates. On 9 February, the Commons passed the ministers' Petition and Remonstrance together with the Root and Branch petition to the important Parliamentary committee of twenty-four.[88]

If the ministers' Remonstrance presented a wholesale catalogue of grievances against Laudianism, the London ministers' arguments before the committee revealed a somewhat sharper attack on prelacy.[89] In the sessions of 12 and 15 February 1641 the ministers' spokesman, almost certainly Edmund Calamy, defined episcopacy as the doctrine that the bishop had 'a sole power in ordination, and jurisdiction by vertue of a distinct order superior to a presbiter'. Calamy offered a rebuttal to this proposition, citing scripture, Jerome and Cyprian of Carthage to show that 'sole ordination and sole jurisdiction is not in bishopps, but the presbiters were equal to them in all things'.[90] He stressed that in scripture the terms 'presbyter' and 'bishop' were synonyms used interchangeably for the pastoral office and thus opened one of the foundational arguments for presbyterianism.[91] He argued '[t]hose that have the same name and same offices in scripture are all on[e]. But bishopps and presbiters have the same name and office, *ergo*, they are all on[e].'[92] In advancing this case, Calamy and his fellow ministers were seeking to redefine the concept of 'episcopacy' so that it would be more consonant with the continental Reformed churches and the Scottish Kirk. The direction of this readjustment can be seen in Cornelius Burges's arguments on ecclesiastical jurisdiction made on 17 February 1641. After stating that all ministers held ecclesiastical power equally in the ancient church, he stated '[t]he ordinary place [for the exercise of discipline] was the presbiterie or consistory' where one minister was 'chosen to preside, but he was not *jure devino*, nor *ex ordinis potestate, sed ex humano*'.[93]

It is significant that when Burges referred to the president of the consistory, he did not use the title 'bishop'. Burges would emerge as a steadfast advocate of reduced episcopacy, yet he left open whether the president of the presbytery would hold the title 'bishop' or be called by another title, such as 'president' or 'moderator'. The ambiguity can be seen as an attempt by the ministers before the committee of twenty-four to maintain consensus among differing positions on church polity. In any event, Burgess need not have been so circumspect, as the committee of twenty-four understood the ministers' submissions to be calling for a reformation of episcopacy based on a reduction of the bishop's role and power. When the Northamptonshire MP John Crewe presented the committee's report to the Commons on 1 March, the proposals outlined a brief scheme for the reduction of episcopacy in England.[94]

It is probable that the large majority of English godly clergy at this point in time were uncommitted to the idea of adopting a presbyterian structure on the Scottish model. Certainly, Richard Overton reported that some ministers saw the retention of episcopacy as a bulwark against separatism and Baillie stated that that the London ministers were 'for the erecting of a kind of presbyteries, and for bringing doun the Bishops in all things, spirituall and temporall, so low as can be with any subsistence'.[95] However, he reported that for the majority of English ministers 'the knott of the question' was the total abolition of episcopacy.[96] This does not mean that all English ministers were opposed to a presbyterian reformation in the Church of England. For example, the Lancashire minister William Bourne advised Sir Robert Harley on 8 January 1641 to establish a 'perpetuall accord betwixt the kingdomes [of England and Scotland]' by reforming the Church of England in conformity with the rule of 'the apostles times; whereof wee haue presidents in France, Geneva, Scotland, & other reformed churches'.[97]

In late December 1640 Baillie had detected three positions among the London clergy. With probable wishful thinking, he was confident that 'the farr greatest part' of the ministers in London were 'for our discipline' or at least 'for all the considerable parts of it'. A few ministers advocated the congregationalism of New England. These included Henry Burton, whose pamphlet *Christ on his throne*, published soon after his release from imprisonment in November 1640, set out the outlines of congregationalist polity.[98] More ominously for the Scots, a 'great faction' of the clergy called only for a reduction of episcopacy, a threat made worse by rumours that Archbishop James Ussher was preparing such a model of church government for publication.[99] The fact that two of the Scottish clergy in London prepared tracts refuting notions of reduced episcopacy illustrates how great a threat the Scots considered this model to be to the covenanter's presbyterian revolution in Scotland.[100] Reduced episcopacy was, and would remain, an idea popular in England with many ministers, including John Ley, Thomas Gataker and Richard Baxter, favouring a system of presbyterial government supervised by a permanent presidential bishop.[101] Although not recorded as a distinct idea by Baillie, a fourth position was that scripture was ambiguous as to the exact form of church government. This position avoided a rigid commitment to episcopal, presbyterian or congregationalist forms of church government and looked to the magistrate to choose a form of ecclesiastical polity that, while according with scripture, was most prudent for the age. As will be seen in chapter 2, by the spring of 1641, with the *de facto* collapse of censorship in the London press, these private discussions would become a matter of public debate.

Conclusion

By the first months of 1641 the coalition of godly ministers who had campaigned against the canons of 1640 had begun to reject the 'old conformity' that had sustained the godly within the Church of England during the early decades of the seventeenth century. The Laudian reforms and the more thorough policing of conformity had effected a structural change in the church that appeared to the godly as a rolling-back of the Reformation, or more ominously, a return to popery. This growing sense of menace was followed by the crisis of conscience that the canons of 1640 triggered in many moderate puritan ministers. Yet these perils to godly religion created the environment for formerly conforming puritan clergy to combine to challenge the Laudian reforms. Organised largely from London and relying on regional conferences of ministers, many moderate puritan clergy were radicalised by this process. By the first few months of the Long Parliament, a growing number of godly ministers had begun to perceive that further reformation of the Church of England's polity was necessary to prevent prelatical and royal power from further threatening the gospel. It is these 'new motions' and the emergence of a London presbyterian movement that chapter 2 explores.

Notes

1 LMA MS P69/MRY2/B/002 (Vestry minutes of St Mary, Aldermanbury), fos 43–4; J. Fielding (ed.), *The diary of Robert Woodford, 1637–1642* (Cambridge, 2012), pp. 313, 315.
2 *A Letter from Mercurius Civicus to Mercurius Rusticus* (1643), p. 27.
3 Examples of Calamy's 'hypothetical universalism' in his parish preaching can be found in Bodleian MS Eng c 2693, pp. 157, 187–8 (I am very grateful to Professor Ann Hughes for this reference).
4 S. Achenstein, 'Edmund Calamy (1600–1666)', *ODNB*.
5 Alan Argent has calculated that 18 per cent of the London clergy in the late 1630s were 'puritans': see A. Argent, 'Aspects of the ecclesiastical history of the parishes of the City of London, 1640–1660 (with special reference to the parish clergy)', (Ph.D thesis, University of London, 1984), pp. 76–80.
6 John Ley, *The fury of warre, and folly of sinne* (1643), pp. 21–2; John Geree, *The Character of an Old English Puritan* (1646). For historiographical discussions of attempts to define the terms 'puritan' and 'godly', adopted throughout this work, see P. Lake, 'Defining puritanism – again?' in *Puritanism: transatlantic perspectives on a seventeenth-century Anglo-American faith*, ed. F. J. Bremer (Boston, MA, 1994), pp. 3–29 and J. Coffey and P. C. H. Lim, 'Introduction' in *The Cambridge companion to puritanism*, eds Coffey and Lim (Cambridge, 2008), pp. 1–15.

7 P. Lake, *Moderate puritans and the Elizabethan Church* (Cambridge, 1982), pp. 1–5.
8 K. Fincham, 'Episcopal government, 1603–1640' in *The early Stuart Church*, ed. Fincham (Basingstoke, 1993), pp. 74–6; K. Fincham, *Prelate as pastor: the episcopate of James I* (Oxford, 1990), ch. 7.
9 My use of the terms 'old conformity' and 'new conformity' derives from Jeremiah Burroughes, *A vindication of Mr Burroughes* (1646), p. 17. See more generally, K. Fincham, 'Clerical conformity from Whitgift to Laud' in *Orthodoxy and conformity in the English Church 1560–1642*, eds P. Lake and M. Questier (Woodbridge, 2000) pp. 125–58.
10 For a study of the pressure put on moderate puritans in London see D. R. Como, 'Predestination and political conflict in Laud's London', *HJ*, 46:2 (2003), 263–94.
11 P. Lake, 'The Laudian style: order, uniformity and the pursuit of the beauty of holiness in the 1630s' in Fincham, *The early Stuart Church*, pp. 166, 169–75; P. Lake, *The boxmaker's revenge: 'orthodoxy', 'heterodoxy' and the politics of the parish in early Stuart London* (Manchester, 2001), ch. 11.
12 J. Merritt, 'Puritans, Laudians, and the phenomenon of church-building in Jacobean London', *HJ*, 41:4 (1998), 935–60.
13 Lake, 'The Laudian style', pp. 178–9, 182; J. Peacey, 'The paranoid prelate: Archbishop Laud and the puritan plot' in *Conspiracies and conspiracy theory in early modern Europe: from the Waldensians to the French revolution*, eds B. Coward and J. Swann (2004), p. 113; M. Reynolds, 'Predestination and parochial dispute in the 1630s: the case of the Norwich lectureships', *JEH*, 59:3 (2008), 407–25, p. 422.
14 N. Tyacke, 'The fortunes of English puritanism, 1603–1640' in *Aspects of English Protestantism, c.1530–1700*, ed. Tyacke (Manchester, 2001), pp. 121–3.
15 William Laud, *The Works of Archbishop Laud*, ed. J. Bliss, 7 vols (Oxford, 1853), III, pp. 216–17, 253.
16 E. W. Kirby, 'The lay feoffees: a study in militant puritanism', *Journal of Modern History*, 14:1 (1942), 16–21.
17 [Lawrence Womock], *Sober sadness: or historical observation* (Oxford, 1643), p. 32; Henry Burton, *Truth still truth though shut out of doors* (1645), pp. 5, 7; E. Calamy, *A just and necessary apology* (1646), p. 8; K. W. Shipps, 'Lay patronage of East Anglian puritan clerics in pre-revolutionary England' (Ph.D thesis, Yale University, 1971), pp. 198–9.
18 Fincham, 'Episcopal government, 1603–1640', p. 84.
19 Como, 'Predestination and political conflict', 283. For a differing view see, e.g., Ian Green, 'Career prospects and clerical conformity in the early Stuart church', *P&P*, 90 (1991), 108.
20 Examples of future London presbyterian ministers who fell foul of Laudian measures include James Nalton (R. N. McDermot, 'James Nalton', *ODNB*; P. S. Seaver, *The puritan lectureships: the politics of religious dissent 1560–1662* (Stanford, CA, 1970), p. 249; NA SP 16/147 fo. 95; SP 16/154

fos 149–51; SP 16/400 fos 149–51); Obadiah Sedgwick (B. Donagan, 'Obadiah Sedgwick', *ODNB*); George Walker (D. Como, 'George Walker', *ODNB*; Philip Nye, *Beames of Former Light* (1660), p. 177; Cambridge University Library, MS Dd. ii. 21, fo. 85r; NA SP 16/401 fos 170–71; SP 16/412 fo. 103; SP 16/414 fo. 38; SP 16/472 fo. 63; SP 16/474 fo. 129) and Henry Roborough (P. S. Seaver, 'Henry Roborough', *ODNB*; Como, 'Predestination and political conflict', 288–9; NA SP 16/474 fo. 115).

21 T. Webster, *Godly clergy*, pp. 149–252; D. R. Como, *Blown by the spirit: puritanism and the emergence of an antinomian underground in pre-civil war England* (Stanford, CA, 2004), pp. 406–14.

22 S. Foster, *Notes from the Caroline underground: Alexander Leighton, the puritan triumvirate and the Laudian reaction to nonconformity* (Hamden, CT, 1978), p. 18; J. Fielding, 'Opposition to the personal rule of Charles I: the diary of Robert Woodford, 1637–1641', *HJ*, 31:4 (1988), 784; F. M. Condick, 'The life and works of Dr John Bastwick (1595–1654)' (Ph.D thesis, University of London, 1983), pp. 137–8.

23 Condick, 'The life and works of Dr John Bastwick', p. 106.

24 P. S. Seaver, *Wallington's world: a puritan artisan in seventeenth century London* (Stanford, CA, 1985), pp. 158–60.

25 Wallington, *Notebooks*, pp. 79–84. For the smuggling of puritan books by young separatists such as John Lilburne see Foster, *Caroline underground*, pp. 60–62; M. Tolmie, *The triumph of the saints: the separate churches of London, 1616–1649* (Cambridge, 1977), pp. 46–7.

26 Nehemiah Wallington, for example, recorded that he was 'glad and joy was in my heart that I should be put among them and to be made partaker of saints sufferings': Wallington, *Notebooks*, p. 81.

27 D. Stevenson, *The Scottish revolution 1637–1644: the triumph of the covenanters* (Newton Abbot, 1973), pp. 60–4.

28 C. Russell, *The fall of the British monarchies 1637–1642* (Oxford, 1991), pp. 53–5.

29 [William Prynne], *The unbishoping of Timothy and Titus* (1636).

30 The first-century Christian text known as '1 Clement', or 'The first epistle of Clement to the Corinthians', was published in Greek and Latin by the royal librarian Patrick Young in 1633.

31 Constant Jessop, *The angel of the Church of Ephesus no bishop of Ephesus* (1644), sigs A2v–A3r.

32 Anne Venn, *A wise virgins lamp burning* (1658), pp. 4–5; John Goodwin, *Certain brief observations and antiqueries* (1644), p. 7.

33 For the 'junto' see Scott, 'Party politics in the Long Parliament, 1640–1648', pp. 34–5.

34 Pearl, *London*, pp. 187–9, 325–7; J. Adamson, *The noble revolt: the overthrow of Charles I* (2007), p. 79; K. Lindley, 'Venn, John', *ODNB*; Lindley, *Popular Politics*, p. 46.

35 M. C. Fissel, *The Bishops' Wars: Charles I's campaigns against Scotland, 1638–40* (Cambridge, 1994), pp. 2–39.

36 J. Davies, *The Caroline captivity of the church: Charles I and the remoulding of Anglicanism 1625–1641* (Oxford, 1992), pp. 259–63; N. R. N. Tyacke, *Anti-Calvinists: the rise of English Arminianism, c. 1590–1640* (Oxford, 1987), pp. 240–2.
37 E. S. Cope, 'The Short Parliament of 1640 and Convocation', *JEH*, 25:2 (1974) 172–7; Russell, *Fall*, pp. 106–7, 109–10, 114–16; Davies, *Caroline captivity*, pp. 251–3.
38 Davies, *Caroline captivity*, pp. 280–2.
39 *The Stuart constitution: documents and commentary*, 2nd edn, ed. J. P. Kenyon (Cambridge, 1986), pp. 149–53.
40 *The court and times of Charles I*, ed. T. Birch, 2 vols (1849), II, p. 287.
41 Rushworth, *Collections*, III, pp. 1205–7.
42 *Ibid.*, p. 1206.
43 *Ibid.*, p. 1206.
44 BL Harley MS 4931, fos 52v–53v, 56r–59r.
45 NA SP 16/463, fos 199–200.
46 Tyacke, 'The fortunes of English puritanism', p. 126; J. Eales 'A road to revolution: the continuity of puritanism, 1559–1642' in *The culture of English puritanism, 1560–1700*, eds C. Durston and J. Eales (Basingstoke, 1996), pp. 184–209.
47 Eales, 'A road to revolution', p. 194.
48 Tyacke, 'The fortunes of English puritanism', pp. 125–6; Ha, *Presbyterianism*, p. 130–33.
49 J. Fielding, 'Conformists, puritans and the Church courts, the diocese of Peterborough, 1603–1642' (Ph.D thesis, University of Birmingham, 1989), pp. 20–1, 42; on the importance of lay patronage generally, see Eales, 'A road to revolution', pp. 185, 192.
50 J. Rushworth, *Collections*, III, pp. 1205–8.
51 Davies, *Caroline captivity*, pp. 279–80; Russell, *Fall*, pp. 139, 166.
52 NA SP 16/465 fo. 16; NA SP 16 465 fo. 65.
53 Sheffield University, Hartlib Papers 30/4/27B.
54 Fielding, 'Conformists, puritans and the Church courts', especially pp. 20, 46, 101, 124, 144 n. 52, 149–50, 171, 205 and 220; and Webster, *Godly clergy*, ch. 11.
55 John Fielding points out that the covenanter tract was probably *The intentions of the army of the kingdom of Scotland declared to their bretheren of England* (1640): see Fielding, 'Conformists, puritans and the Church courts', p. 250, n. 10.
56 Baxter, *RB*, I, p. 16; Samuel Clarke, *The lives of sundry eminent persons in this later age* (1683), pp. 7–8; A. Hughes, *Politics, society and civil war in Warwickshire 1620–1660* (Cambridge, 1987), p. 134.
57 John Ley, *Defensive doubts, hopes and reasons for refusall of the oath* (1641), sigs a3v, c1v.
58 BL Harley MS 4931, fos 61r–62r.
59 For a summary of Bucerus's arguments see A. Milton, *Catholic and Reformed:*

the Roman and protestant churches in English protestant thought, 1600–1640 (Cambridge, 1995), p. 457, n. 26.
60 Baxter, *RB*, I, p. 16.
61 C. Burges, *The first sermon preached to the honourable House of Commons* (1641), pp. 6, 14–15; S. Marshall, *A sermon preached [...] November 17, 1640* (1641), p. 35; J. F. Wilson, *Pulpit in parliament: puritanism during the English civil war, 1640–1648* (Princeton, NJ, 1969), pp. 36–41, 255.
62 Eales, 'A road to revolution', pp. 186–7.
63 Calybute Downing, *Considerations towards a peaceable reformation* (1641), p. 4.
64 [Calybute Downing], *An Appeale to Everye Impartiall, Judicious and Godly Reader* (1641); B. Donagan, 'Downing, Calybute (1606–1644)', *ODNB*.
65 BL Harley MS 4931, fos 70r–71v; BL Add. MS 35331, fos 70r–v; S. Waurechen, 'Covenanting propaganda and the conceptualizations of the public during the Bishops' Wars', *HJ*, 52:1 (2009), 70–1.
66 For the St Antholin's lectures, see Seaver, *The puritan lectureships*; Baillie, *L&J*, I, p. 273.
67 Baillie, *L&J*, I, p. 295; Clarendon, *History of the rebellion*, III, p. 251.
68 *A letter from Mercurius Rusticus to Mercurius Civicus*, p. 6.
69 Baillie, *L&J*, I, pp. 273, 295, 299.
70 Gardiner, *CD*, pp. 137–44.
71 Baillie, *L&J*, I, p. 275.
72 Lindley, *Popular politics*, p. 16.
73 Baillie, *L&J*, I, pp. 274–5.
74 Russell, *Fall*, pp. 180–1; A. Woolrych, *Britain in revolution 1625–1660* (Oxford, 2002), pp. 169–70.
75 A. Fletcher, *The outbreak of the English civil war* (1981), pp. 91–2; Tyacke, 'The fortunes of English puritanism', p. 127; Lindley, *Popular politics*, pp. 14–16.
76 Baillie, *L&J*, I, pp. 273–4.
77 Lindley, *Popular politics*, p. 15 n. 43.
78 BL Harley MS 5108, fos 45v–110v; Calamy, *A just and necessary apology*, p. 9.
79 Clarke, *The lives of sundry eminent persons*, p. 8; Hughes, *Politics, society and civil war in Warwickshire*, p. 134.
80 Baillie, *L&J*, I, p. 282.
81 Baillie, *L&J*, I, p. 286.
82 Hughes, *Politics, society and civil war in Warwickshire*, p. 134.
83 Baillie, *L&J*, I, p. 292; see also BL Harley MS 5108, fos 45v–110v; *CJ*, II, p. 72; J. Eales, *Puritans and roundheads: the Harleys of Brampton Bryan and the English civil war* (Cambridge, 2001), pp. 111–13.
84 Shaw, *HEC*, I, pp. 23, 26.
85 Richard Overton, *A sacred decretal* (1645), p. 12.
86 *CCRB*, I, p. 409. Given the date and context of this letter (i.e. Baxter was seeking support for his plan for Ussher-style reduced episcopacy) and that

Burges was a life-long advocate of reduced episcopacy, how far this letter reveals what other ministers close to the junto believed in 1641 should be treated with a degree of caution. Nevertheless, Burges's letter is probably an accurate reflection of the extent of the discussions between the ministers and the parliamentary junto leaders in 1640–41.

87 Baillie, *L&J*, I, p. 282. For controversy over the Petition and Remonstrance in Parliament see *CJ*, II, p. 17; Shaw, *HEC*, I, pp. 23–4 and J. S. McGee, *An industrious mind: the worlds of Sir Simonds D'Ewes* (Stanford, CA, 2015), p. 196.
88 For the speeches of 8–9 February, see Shaw, *HEC*, I, pp. 29–42. The committee had been appointed to prepare a declaration of the state of the nation. Despite its name, the committee of twenty-four had thirty members by the time the Remonstrance was discussed. For the debate on episcopacy, presbyterianism and the royal supremacy prevalent among the Long Parliament's common lawyers see J. Rose, *Godly kingship in Restoration England: the politics of the royal supremacy, 1660–1688* (Cambridge, 2011), pp. 45–73.
89 Calamy, *A just and necessary apology*, p. 9.
90 *Verney papers: notes of proceedings in the Long Parliament*, ed. J. Bruce (1845), p. 5. Verney did not record which minister spoke on these days but Calamy later intimated that he had been the speaker: see Calamy, *A just and necessary apology*, p. 9.
91 This had been the subject of John Rainolds' 1588 letter to Sir Francis Knolles, first printed in 1608 in the presbyterian tract *Informations, or a protestation and a treatise from Scotland* (Amsterdam?, 1608), pp. 73–87.
92 *Verney papers*, pp. 8–9.
93 *Ibid.*, p. 11.
94 The final report, presented by John Crew on 9 March, put forward three heads, two of which encapsulated the ministers' remonstrance. See Shaw, *HEC*, I, pp. 45–8.
95 Baillie, *L&J*, I, p. 303.
96 *Ibid.*, p. 303.
97 BL Add MS 70105 (William Bourne to Sir Robert Harley).
98 Henry Burton, *Christ on his throne* (1640), especially pp. 57–71.
99 Baillie, *L&J*, I, pp. 275, 287.
100 [Alexander Henderson], *The unlawfulnes and danger of limited prelacie* (1641); Robert Baillie, *The unlawfulnesse and danger of limited episcopacie* (1641); a third, anonymous, tract, *Certaine reasons tending to prove the unlawfulness of [...] all diocesian episcopacy* (1641) appears to be written from the perspective of an English author. See M. Mendle, *Dangerous positions: mixed government, the estates of the realm and the answer to the XIX propositions* (Tuscaloosa, AL, 1985), pp. 144–5.
101 Mendle, *Dangerous positions*, p. 141.

2

Smectymnuus and the attack on episcopacy in 1641

The London godly ministers' submissions before the committee of twenty-four, seen in chapter 1, had left the question of church polity open. From early 1641 the English parliamentarian clergy began to develop their ideas for the reformation of the Church of England more fully. This chapter begins by surveying the range of ideas concerning church polity discussed by the English godly prior to the Long Parliament. These ideas often had a subterranean existence, repressed by a culture of self-censorship, or shared by small conferences of ministers who kept alive the flame of earlier reformers. As a result, these ideas would only fully resurface as Charles I's administration began to collapse. This chapter will argue that, contrary to the impression sometimes given by historians that there was little in the way of English presbyterian thought until the Scots forced the issue at the Westminster assembly, there is ample evidence of a re-emergent English presbyterianism by 1641.

The chapter provides a presbyterian reading of the 'Smectymnuus' tracts, a collective writing group made up of the leading junto clergy Stephen Marshall, Edmund Calamy, Thomas Young, Matthew Newcomen and William Spurstowe, and will situate these works in the alliance of godly clergy who were meeting at Calamy's house in Aldermanbury. The Aldermanbury group were key allies of the parliamentary junto and joined in the mobilisation against Charles I's administration in the spring and summer of 1641. Nevertheless, as we have noted, the junto at Westminster and their godly allies outside Parliament's doors lacked consensus on issues of religion and church polity. They were also circumscribed by what was politically possible in 1641. By the early summer of 1641 attempts to reach a consensual settlement of religion had failed. The summer debates over the so-called 'Root and Branch' bill saw various models for the national church aired in the House of Commons. These debates ultimately revealed deep tensions among those seeking to reform the polity of the church. The chapter concludes by exploring the emerging divisions among the godly on the issue of the proper location of power in church government and how, in light of those divisions, the parliamentarian clergy closest to the junto struggled to maintain unity, if not consensus, in the fight against prelacy.

Pre-civil war puritan thinking on church polity

Ideas for further reform of the Church of England in the middle decades of the seventeenth century did not come out of a vacuum. During the Elizabethan period, presbyterians such as Thomas Cartwright, Walter Travers and William Fulke had set out a system for the presbyterian reform of the polity of the national church. These proposals envisaged that each parish church would be governed by a consistory made up of pastors, teachers, elders and deacons.[1] In this scheme, local churches would combine into classes for the 'mutuall help' of each church. In turn, these local conferences would elect members to attend biannual provincial synods and ultimately national and ecumenical assemblies.[2] It has sometimes been argued that such higher assemblies would have only persuasive authority over individual congregations and that Elizabethan presbyterian theory focused on individual congregations as the prime ecclesiastical unity. However, Elizabeth presbyterians were clear, drawing on the precedent of Acts 15, that conferences and synods existed 'according to the Word of God' and would have the power to admonish, censure and, ultimately, depose wayward pastors in order to maintain discipline.[3] In relation to the civil state, Elizabethan presbyterians looked to civil magistrates as 'nurses and foster-fathers to the Church', charged with protecting the church by punishing heretics or calling synods when it was disordered.[4] Nevertheless, Elizabethan presbyterians deployed a Calvinist two-kingdoms perspective that saw ecclesiastical and civil society as 'distinct and diverse one from another', with ecclesiastical government being left by Christ to the officers of the church.[5]

While presbyterianism survived the failure of the Elizabethan presbyterian movement, many of the godly in England reimagined ideas for the reformation of church polity. These ranged from arguments for the necessity of conformity to the reduction of episcopacy, or a focus on parish congregations as the manifestation of the visible church.[6] This section surveys ideas about church government in the early Stuart period in order to set the scene for the intellectual sources of the debate on church government in 1641.

The majority of godly ministers in the early Stuart period conformed to the Jacobean Church of England without, at least publicly, demanding further reformation of its polity. This stance, defined by Peter Lake as 'moderate puritanism', was justified on the basis that the Church of England needed a godly preaching ministry to teach true gospel religion more than it needed governmental reform.[7] Historians have long stressed that polemic against the dangers of popery acted as a structuring rhetoric that gave meaning, unity and identity to English protestantism.[8] Working in a similar manner at the other end of the spectrum to anti-popery were warnings against separatism. Anti-separatist polemic often argued that the Church of England was in the same position as the Church of Laodicea in the Book of Revelation. Like Laodicea, the Church of England was a church that, despite its manifold faults, retained true doctrine in its teaching and sacraments.[9] Anti-separatists therefore maintained that even if the government of the Church of England deviated from New Testament patterns, it was still an efficacious vehicle for the gospel and thus to separate from it was an unacceptable schism.

Godly conformity was also maintained by a culture of self-imposed censorship whereby conforming ministers actively avoided reading or circulating works discussing different visions of ecclesiastical polity. The Worcestershire minister Richard Baxter found that prior to 1640 the works of nonconformist authors such as Paul Baynes or Robert Parker on church polity were unavailable to him. Baxter had to content himself with material written by godly conformists such as John Burges or John Sprint, or divine-right episcopalians such as George Downame.[10] An extreme example of this self-censorship can be found in the Essex minister Constant Jessop, who had been forbidden by his godly father to engage in either private or public discussion about the scriptural warrant for episcopacy.[11] As we have seen, this culture of self-censorship would not change until the challenge to the Laudian church began to gather speed.[12]

Despite the hurdles that godly conformists set themselves on the issue of church polity, attempts to envisage the further reform of the Church of England remained.[13] The notion of emulating the 'primitive' episcopacy of the early church provided an impetus to imagining a reformation of ecclesiastical polity. Ideas about the nature of 'primitive', 'reduced' or 'limited' episcopacy, however, were imprecise and ambiguous concepts that could signify a wide range of positions. By the early 1640s these ideas could range from a hankering after an idealised, 'Grindalian', Elizabethan preaching prelacy to government by classes and synods moderated by president-bishops having no additional jurisdiction over their fellow clergy.[14] The ambiguity of the idea betrays the fact that reduced episcopacy was often a way for conforming puritans to think through alternatives to diocesan episcopacy without venturing into the perils of nonconformist or separatist patterns of thought. Because 'reduced' or 'primitive' episcopacy was an ambiguous, even heuristic, position to take, its more extreme expressions were not starkly distinct from ideas of presbyterianism. Many leading theologians in the sixteenth century, including Calvin and Beza, saw presidential bishops (whom they associated with the episcopate of the patristic era) as an acceptable, if not optimal, historical development in the church.[15] Late Elizabethan and early Stuart presbyterians and nonconformists conceptualised the diocesan bishop as a minister of state, an interface between royal power and the church. At the same time, they asserted the presbyterian position of ministerial parity, arguing that in scripture the term 'bishop' (from the Greek *episkopos*, an 'overseer' or 'guardian') applied to the pastor of a local congregation.[16]

Advocacy for measures that would reduce the power of the episcopate in the early seventeenth century can be found in John Rainolds's proposal at the Hampton Court conference in 1604 that the parish minister should have the power to bar unworthy communicants from the Lord's supper. He suggested, to the horror of James VI and I, that this could be done by relocating the power of confirmation in the local minister, rather than the bishop. Rainolds's scheme sought further reform by converting the Church of England's deaneries into classes of local clergy 'to heare and censure the offences committed within their circuite'. This system of 'presbytery within episcopacy' would give the local clergy the leading role in ecclesiastical discipline, with the bishops presiding over yearly diocesan synods 'for [the] determination of matters of greater importance'. King James would have none of Rainolds's proposals, however, declaring 'when I mean to live under a presbytery, I will go into Scotland again. But while I am in England, I will have bishops.'[17]

Further evidence of 'primitive episcopalianism' can be found in a 1639 Latin treatise published by the Smectymnuan presbyterian divine Thomas Young, later a member of the Westminster assembly. Young argued that 'the name of *bishop* is a general appellation, signifying all those that labour in the Word of God, and attend upon the cure of souls', which comprehended both 'bishops and presbyters'.[18] The title of 'bishop' as a separate order in the church was not an institution of Christ or the apostles, but one that derived from 'the custom of the church or [...] the words of honour' deployed in the early patristic period.[19] Young's view of primitive episcopacy was that of a single, preaching bishop, acting as the president of a consistory of presbyters. His arguments provided a model to reform the Church of England on lines more consonant with the continental Reformed church polities, but without directly advocating the abolition of the episcopate.

Despite the self-censorship apparent among many godly clergy on the question of episcopacy, alternative models of ecclesiastical polity were available from either the continental Reformed churches or the English nonconformist tradition. As Polly Ha's research has shown, properly presbyterian ideas and arguments survived the collapse of the Elizabethan presbyterian movement. In particular, when Walter Travers and his circle were confronted with the Independency of Henry Jacob in around 1620, they restated the scriptural warrant for presbyterianism and the authority of synods as essential to preserving the unity and purity of the visible church.[20] While the arguments of presbyterians in Travers's circle would continue to be made throughout the early seventeenth century, many nonconformist theorists of church polity increasingly began to see the congregation as the primary location of the 'church', rejecting the binding authority of the higher assemblies found in presbyterianism.[21] William Bradshaw, writing anonymously in 1605, held that the title 'church' properly applied only to each particular congregation. For Bradshaw, the use of the term 'church' for 'consociations, synods, societies, combinations or assemblies' was an unsuitable attribution. Likewise, William Ames, in the 1620s, argued that the visible church was to be been seen in individual professing Christians and the particular congregations to which they belonged. Should an individual church fall into error, Bradshaw thought, neighbouring churches or consociations had no direct ecclesiastical power to impose a formal judgement, but were to first advise, then admonish and finally withdraw communion from the erring congregation.[22]

These developments did not mean that ideas of the universal visible church and synodical authority were jettisoned by the Jacobean nonconformist successors to Elizabethan presbyterian thought.[23] In addition to the subterranean continuation of presbyterian ideas through Travers and his successors, relatively strong notions of synodical authority can be found in the writings of those nonconformists often classed as 'non-separating congregationalists'. Many of these thinkers were engaged in countering Bishop George Downame's 1608 sermons on the divine right of episcopacy.[24] Paul Baynes, for example, while locating the origin of ecclesiastical power in the particular congregation, held, using the example of the twenty-four churches of Geneva, that such congregations could make an authoritative 'consociation' in order to act together as a single 'political' church. This was particularly the case for 'weak' congregations, which lacked the resources to have a full complement of elders and deacons.[25]

For Robert Parker the starting point for arguments as to the authority of any particular ecclesiastical assembly derived from Jesus's donation of the 'keys of the kingdom of heaven' to Peter in Matthew 16:19. There was disagreement among protestants as to Peter's status as the recipient of the keys. Parker's view was that the keys were given to Peter as the first person to profess faith in Christ and therefore Peter was representative of the faithful Christian believer. The consequence of this was that the keys of the kingdom of heaven resided in the body of believers. Nevertheless, Parker introduced the distinction that, although ecclesiastical power resided 'virtually' in the body of the faithful, it was 'actually' to be exercised by each congregation's eldership.[26] Parker's interpretation of Matthew 16:19, however, was not universally held. An alternative, and probably dominant view, held for example by the influential 1630s nonconformist leader John Ball, was that the keys were given to Peter as the representative of the apostles and their clerical successors.[27] This position was also implied in the marginal notes to the 1599 edition of the Geneva Bible, which glossed Matthew 16:19 with Isaiah 22:22, explaining that the reference to 'the keys' was a 'metaphor taken from stewards who carry the keys' and that this 'power is common to all ministers'. It followed that 'the ministry of the gospel may rightly be called the key of the kingdom of heaven'.[28]

The issue of the location of power in the church would be the subject of disputes among English exiles in the Netherlands during the mid-1630s. The protagonists of the dispute were William Best, a lay member of the English Church in Amsterdam, the minister John Davenport, later a leading New England congregationalist, and John Paget, the presbyterian minister of the English Church in Amsterdam.[29] In 1634, Best had published a private dispute between Paget, Davenport and the Amsterdam classis relating to Davenport's refusal to baptise the infants of parents who had not made a profession of faith.[30] The debate moved on to the authority of classes and higher synods over congregations. Paget argued that presbyterianism, which afforded an aggrieved individual a right of appeal to the classis, was 'a sanctuary against tyranny'. He considered that Independency brought 'manifold disorders, confusion and dissipation' to churches. Further, Paget pointed out that each individual church had an equal voice in classes and synods and so presbyterianism in no way diminished the authority of an individual congregation.[31] Davenport, while accepting that individual churches should consociate into classes and synods for advice and fellowship, argued that a classis could only advise and not give judicially binding decisions. The final implementation of any decisions remained with the particular congregation. The purpose of classes and synods, therefore, was to preserve the consent of local congregations, to provide a remedy to problems that all congregations within the consociation shared and to provide a forum for those aggrieved by the decisions of their particular church to have grievances heard.[32] Because a classis or synod worked on the basis of consent, it lacked the authority to excommunicate, impose or remove ministers or to specify doctrines or practices to be observed by individual congregations.[33] Davenport is alleged to have said that an authoritative classis, such as those advocated by Paget and the Dutch Reformed church, 'sets up many bishops instead of one'.[34]

The principal difference between Paget and Davenport in the 1630s was thus an understanding of where power and authority lay in the church. Paget argued that 'the execution and judiciall exercising' of power in a particular church, and by extension in classes and synods, resided in the eldership 'chosen with the publick knowledge and free consent of the Church'.[35] Paget argued against the position that authoritative decisions were to be made by the minister and congregation joined together. For Paget, 'the church' in Matthew 18:15–20 referred to the rulers of the synagogue and thus to the eldership and not the people.[36] Paget's debates with Davenport and the separatists were in part influenced by the practice of the Dutch Reformed church, but they also highlight the survival of an English presbyterian tradition which developed over the early seventeenth century.[37]

The issue of the location of ecclesiastical authority was again taken up in the 1630s in a debate between a number of conferences of English nonconformist ministers and the Massachusetts churches over the increasing role of the laity in New England congregations.[38] The principal thrust of the English nonconformists' argument with the Massachusetts Bay churches was that the exercise of church authority had been given by Christ directly to the eldership rather than to, or through, the community of the faithful.[39] For these English nonconformists, the Massachusetts churches' growing readiness to encompass the laity in church governance went perilously close to the doctrines of the separatists.[40] American congregationalist practice, therefore, provided a timely warning for English nonconformists of the continuing dangers of separatism.

The leading group among these English critics was the godly conference centred on the ministers John Ball and John Dod. Ball's responses to the New Englanders, as well as against the separatist leader John Canne, saw a number of key developments in the nonconformist tradition on church polity that would impact substantially on the debates of the 1640s. Alongside the critique of the laity wielding the power of the keys, Ball attacked the position that the New Testament churches were always single congregational churches. Ball argued that some of these apostolic churches were single churches that were of such a size that they worshipped in multiple congregations.[41] His analysis, which had previously been avoided by nonconformists as it was thought to give credence to arguments for diocesan episcopacy, was aimed at countering the atomising effect of New England congregationalism. Ball opened up the argument that the New Testament pattern for churches was based on presbyteries rather than singular particular churches. This development would have an important effect on the 1640s debate on church polity.

These 1630s nonconformist debates over the structure of the church or the power of the keys would provide the fertile ground from which the debates on ecclesiastical polity in the 1640s would spring. However, until the early 1640s the content of these debates appears to have been available to only a limited number of English nonconformist ministers who could learn about them from face-to-face discussions or read them in privately shared manuscripts and books. Despite the growing unease with episcopacy under Laudianism, many moderate puritan ministers continued to apply the traditional arguments for conformity to their pastoral careers, seeing the ministry of the gospel as more important than issues of ecclesiastical polity or discipline. The subterranean debates on church polity during the early Stuart period, however, would burst out into public discussion in 1641 as effective censorship of godly speculation on the nature of the government of the church collapsed.[42]

Early 1641 ideas of church reformation

The early months of 1641 would see a kaleidoscope of differing viewpoints on church government made available to the public through the printing presses.[43] This section surveys some of the earliest works in favour of Reformed church government after the opening of the Long Parliament and links these early discussions to the circle of English and Scottish ministers meeting at Edmund Calamy's house in Aldermanbury.

In January 1641 the bookseller George Thomason obtained two tracts advocating the replacement of the diocesan framework of the Church of England with a presbyterian system of church polity. The first, a tract ascribed to either Richard or John Bernard, presented a model of presbyterianism that could be grafted onto the parishes and deaneries of the Church of England.[44] The traditional parish offices were left undisturbed, with churchwardens taking on the role of ruling elders and overseers for the poor standing in the place of deacons. His presbyterian scheme privileged the clergy by denying a role for the laity in higher church assemblies.[45] According to Bernard, his plan would bring England into conformity with the Church of Scotland and the continental Reformed churches and reverse the self-imposed exile of many of the godly abroad.[46] The second work advocating presbyterian reformation in January 1641, *The beauty of godly government in a church reformed*, used a style and language very similar to Bernard's scheme, but allowed one lay elder from each parish in classical and synodical meetings to counterbalance the clergy.[47] As well as arguing for the superiority of presbyterian over 'prelatian' government, *The beauty of godly government* saw the extra-parochial assemblies as a mechanism for keeping the dangers of separatism in check. A system of parish presbyteries under the jurisdiction of classes and regional synods would ensure that 'the parochiall government is upheld, *and yet kept within bounds*, Christ's doctrine and worship kept pure, good ministers honoured, and the rest either reformed, or cast out'.[48]

Although these proposals reveal that a presbyterian settlement of the Church of England was being contemplated from very early in the tenure of the Long Parliament, they do not appear to have emanated directly from ministers at the heart of the Aldermanbury junto. For this we have to look to February 1641's *The petition of the prelates briefly examined* and Smectymnuus's *An answer to an humble remonstrance*, published in late February and March 1641. The primary author of *The petition of the prelates* was the congregationalist Jeremiah Burroughes, who had returned from the Netherlands in late 1640.[49] *The petition of the prelates* was published to refute a petition circulating in London in favour of episcopacy, although the latter part of the tract set out a broad statement of principles of Reformed church government.[50] It is clear that Burroughes's tract was written alongside and intended to complement Smectymnuus's *An answer*.[51] The Smectymnuans and many of the returning congregationalists from the Netherlands had been godly comrades in the late 1630s. Burroughes and Calamy had worked together in Bury St Edmunds in the mid-1630s and were both close confidantes of the Earl of Warwick.[52] Other ministers among the later 'dissenting brethren' were also connected to the Smectymnuans in the late 1630s and early 1640s. On 30 September 1638, Thomas Goodwin, just prior to his flight to the Netherlands, had preached alongside William Spurstowe at Calybute Downing's parish of Hackney. In August 1640 William Greenhill, newly returned from the Netherlands, was invited by Edmund Calamy to preach at Aldermanbury. Greenhill's text, Jeremiah 31:31: 'Behold, the days come, saith the Lord, that I will make a new covenant with the house of Israel, and with the house of Judah', was a potentially controversial theme given the typological comparison between Judah and Israel and England and Scotland.[53]

In addition to collaborating with the Smectymnuans, Burroughes was also in conversation with the Scottish ministers residing in the city, with Alexander Henderson writing the preface to *The petition of the prelates*.[54] In December 1640 Burroughes had met with Henderson and the other Scots Commissioners to discuss whether they agreed with the power afforded to the parochial eldership set out in George Gillespie's 1637 *A dispute against the English popish ceremonies*. Henderson, Burroughes claimed, answered positively to his queries and allowed Burroughes to believe that congregationalists could work with the Scots on the matter of reformation in England.[55]

The petition of the prelates therefore provides a window on the internal workings of the Aldermanbury junto, which included Calamy's group, the Scottish ministers and the congregationalists recently returned from the Netherlands. Burroughes states that the 'prelatical party' had mocked the godly ministers for not being able to reach an agreement on the 'common forme' of church government to replace episcopacy. In a candid acknowledgement of this criticism, Burroughes admitted that there was division among the godly on the issue of polity, but stated that if 'episcopacy were gone, the agreement would be easie' as many 'are afraid to discover themselves freely, for feare if episcopacy hold, it will be hereafter revenged upon them'. Further, Burroughes declared, in what was probably a reference to agreement between the Aldermanbury ministers, that the godly 'professe one to another that they can walke as brethren together'. To this end, Burroughes warned episcopalians, '[y]ou seeme to rejoyce in the supposall of dissensions between others, thinking therby to gaine time, but [...] there is not so vast a difference amongst us'. In order to show this Burroughes set out principles upon which 'wee are all agreed': that the church should only be governed by 'pastors, teachers, elders and deacons'; that each particular parish congregation 'hath her owne power and authoritie' in the use of ordinances; that 'higher assemblies' such as synods were expedient to the good ordering of the church and that any reform of the church was to be guided solely by scripture and the light of reason.[56]

Smectymnuus and the emergence of London presbyterianism

Smectymnuus's *An answer to a booke entitled an humble remonstrance* would set the tone of the debate on the reform of the Church of England for the next twenty years. In May 1662 Sir Robert Turner, the Restoration speaker of the House of Commons, would describe the attempted mid-seventeenth-century reformation as a '*Smectymnian plot*', which 'sought to erect a popular authority of elders, and to root out episcopal jurisdiction' such that 'the means whereby distinction or inequality might be upheld among ecclesiastical governors' were removed.[57] Ostensibly written as a reply to Bishop Joseph Hall's anonymous *An humble remonstrance*, in June 1641 Smectymnuus would publish a second work, *A vindication*, in answer to Hall's also anonymous reply to *An answer*.[58]

What the Smectymnuus tracts advocate in terms of church polity has presented something of a conundrum for historians. Traditionally historians have seen them as presbyterian tracts, while others have claimed Smectymnuus only offered a 'vague' call for 'the riddance of prelatical episcopacy' and supported 'any scheme of church government that would secure essentials'.[59] Tom Webster has argued that the Smectymnuus tracts are wrongly classed as presbyterian and primarily contend for a 'primitive' or 'reduced' episcopacy.[60] By contrast, Carol Schneider reads the Smectymnuus tracts as a statement of a 'latitudinarian presbyterianism'. She argues that, in order to maintain consensus within the anti-Laudian alliance, Smectymnuus self-consciously left the ultimate model of church polity unresolved. This need to maintain consensus meant that the Smectymnuans made 'symbolic gestures to *each* of [... the] competing interpretations of the apostolic churches, and the consequent structure of church presbyteries'.[61] One problem with this modern discussion is that too sharp a distinction is often drawn between what would have been understood as presbyterian (or 'presbyterial') polity and 'primitive episcopacy'. As the example of post-Reformation Geneva shows, 'presbyterians' accepted that consistorial government should have a moderator or president and, as with the examples of Calvin and Beza, a single person could hold the presidential post for many years in succession.[62] John Williams, the Bishop of Lincoln, is said to have seen the debate on reduced episcopacy in 1641 as part of the policy for those seeking to institute 'Beza's moderator [... and] Cartwright's president' in the Church of England.[63] The distinction between presbyterianism and 'primitive episcopacy', therefore, was not always entirely clear to contemporaries of the debate and this ambiguity has often pervaded modern discussion of the subject. This section, while acknowledging that ambiguities exist in Smectymnuus on the question of church polity, which kept open the possibility of compromise through the reduction of the office of the bishop, provides a reading that understands these works as advocating a presbyterian view of polity.

The Smectymnuus tracts analyse the titles of ecclesiastical offices in scripture and early church history to suggest an essentially presbyterian structure as the scripturally prescribed model for the church. One of the keys to understanding Smectymnuus's argument is their projection of the history of episcopacy based on Beza's figure of *de triplici episcopatu*.[64] Beza saw episcopacy as gradually developing greater corruption throughout church history from the *episcopus divinus*, established by the apostles, to the *episcopus diabolicus* of popish polity. The *episcopus divinus* for Beza was the presbyter-bishop of the New Testament period, the pastor of a single flock of believers. Succeeding the divine office of bishop was *episcopus humanus*, the presidential or superintending bishops of city churches during the patristic period. Ultimately, the *episcopus diabolicus* emerged: the prelatical, 'monarchical' episcopacy of the churches of Rome and England, who usurped to themselves a sole power of ordination and jurisdiction.[65] Using Beza's figure to structure their work, Smectymnuus argued that in true 'primitive episcopacy' the terms 'presbyter' and 'bishop' were applied synonymously to the pastor of a particular church.[66] Smectymnuus therefore saw the original 'primitive episcopacy' as one where the overseers of a particular church or association of churches held parity with each other. Criticising those, like Joseph Hall, who argued that there was always a bishop ruling over a diocese composed of many parishes, Smectymnuus argued that as the parochial structure did not develop until the second or third centuries, neither did the diocesan bishop.[67]

In their June 1641 *Vindication*, the Smectymnuans expanded this argument in a significant presbyterian direction. They argued that by the time narrated in the Acts of the Apostles, the church in Jerusalem had become so large that believers met in 'divers meeting places'. This did not mean, however, that the church of Jerusalem could be equated with a diocese, as scripture referred to the church of Jerusalem as 'but one Church'. These meeting places, Smectymnuus argued, 'were frequented promiscuously, and indistinctly, and were taught and governed by all the presbyters promiscuously'.[68] The scriptural synonymity of the words 'bishop' and 'presbyter' for the same office in the apostolic church provided Smectymnuus with the argument that the title of 'bishop' should be applied to all pastors equally. 'The best way to confute' the arguments of episcopalians, Smectymnuus asserted, 'is by bringing in a community of the name bishop to a presbyter as well as to a bishop'.[69]

The early modern churches that most closely resembled the New Testament order were, for Smectymnuus, the presbyterian churches represented by the Gallic and Belgic confessions, with the offices of pastors, elders and deacons, rather than the episcopal order of bishops, priests and deacons.[70] One of the main objectives of *An answer* was to press for reform of the Church of England to nearer conformity with the biblical model, which in their discussion of the confessions, Smectymnuus took to be represented by the continental Reformed churches.[71] Arguing another significant presbyterian position, Smectymnuus demonstrated that the office of ruling elder was mandated by scripture and found in the practice of the apostolic and early church.[72]

If the continental Reformed churches provided the model that Smectymnuus considered closest to New Testament 'primitive episcopacy', Smectymnuus went on to analyse why the church had lost its purity and descended into popery.[73] Smectymnuus cited Jerome to argue that presbyters acted together as a common council in ecclesiastical government until 'the devil's instinct' created schism in the church.[74] In order to prevent divisions caused by schism, a presbyter was elected to preside over the consistory, initially according to seniority of age, and later of ability. This presidential bishop acquired the title of 'bishop' 'upon Ecclesiastical custome, and not upon divine institution'.[75] Smectymnuus cited 'the commentaries that goe under the name of St Ambrose' (i.e. by Ambrosiaster, a fourth-century commentator on the epistles of St Paul) to show that another reason for the creation of the separate orders of bishop and presbyter was 'the increase and dilatation' of the church. Following the Bezan theme of *episcopus humanus*, Smectymnuus argued that these early president-bishops differed from prelates in deriving their origin from human contingency, not apostolic institution, were locally elected by the clergy and claimed no separate power of ordination and jurisdiction.[76]

Relying on Beza's description of the decline of episcopacy into a diabolical form of polity, and probably echoing the Elizabethan presbyterian Walter Travers, Smectymnuus argued that these president-bishops were ultimately a negative step in the history of the church. The emergence of the bishop as a separate office resulted from a 'diabolicall occasion' which 'would not onely be ineffectual to the cutting off of evil, but become a stirrup for Antichrist to get into his saddle'.[77] The description of Satan's role in bringing about a separate episcopal order shows how far Smectymnuus had moved from Young's previously positive account of the early church bishops in his 1639 *Dies Dominica*.

Smectymnuus therefore argued that the episcopate of the patristic church was not the pristine creation of Christ or the apostles. Episcopacy in a single person had emerged as a human response to schism and heresy and was ultimately part of Satan's long-term ploy to set the church on its trajectory towards popery.[78] Nevertheless, the adoption of Beza's three-fold order does allow Smectymnuus to imply that the early model of *jure humano* episcopacy was a model of ecclesiastical polity not entirely tainted by Antichrist in the same way as the English prelatical model and thus might be considered a model for ecclesiastical reformation.[79] Nevertheless, it was a model of church polity that lacked the scriptural purity of the presbyterianism of the French and Dutch Reformed churches.[80]

Smectymnuus stressed that the time for compromise with prelacy had passed. The blame for the religious crisis of 1641 fell squarely on the *jure divino* pretensions of the Laudian episcopate. The Laudian drive for conformity, particularly the canons of 1640, had shattered the arguments for the 'old conformity' that had formerly accommodated moderate puritans. Prior to the canons, Smectymnuus asserted, 'many conscientious men [...] hitherto conformed to ceremonies and episcopacie [...] as supposing that authoritie did not make them matters of worship but of order and decencie'.[81] As has been noted above, these godly conformists could satisfy their qualms about episcopacy by seeing it as a political order issuing from the king rather than as the divine government of the church. Smectymnuus argued that 'the best charter pleaded for episcopacy in former times was ecclesiasticall constitution, and the favour of princes'.[82] However, the Laudian tactic of forcing the clergy to accept divine right episcopacy by the *et cetera* oath meant that the old arguments for conformity could no longer satisfy the consciences of godly professors. Episcopacy had now become 'an idoll, and like the Brazen Serpent to be ground to powder'.[83]

Further evidence of Smectymnuus's presbyterian position on church government can be seen in their interpretation of the status of Timothy and Titus found in the pastoral epistles and the nature of the 'angels' of Revelations 2–3. The ecclesiastical status of Timothy and Titus and the angels was important as it supplied advocates of divine right episcopacy with proof texts for the apostolic status of prelacy.[84] Relying on church tradition, it was argued that Timothy and Titus had been the Bishops of Ephesus and Crete respectively and the 'angels' of the seven churches were the bishops of those churches. In the late 1630s and early 1640s the debate over the apostolic origins of episcopacy had centred on these New Testament figures. In 1636 William Prynne had published a tract denying that Timothy and Titus were apostolic models of later diocesan bishops and arguing that ordination rested by divine right in presbyters collectively.[85] Smectymnuus contended that the true office of Timothy and Titus was that of evangelist, an extraordinary office of the apostolic era no longer extant and thus of a different 'sphere above bishops and presbyters' altogether.[86]

The angels of the seven churches of Revelation, however, presented a more problematic argument for Smectymnuus. Eminent Reformed theologians such as Beza and John Rainolds had advanced the view that the angels were individuals presiding over each of the seven churches. Defenders of episcopacy argued that these 'angels' were early proof of the existence of monarchical bishops and, by extension, their churches were ancient dioceses. Smectymnuus set out two alternative cases to meet this argument. Their primary case was to argue that the exegesis of the angels by Beza and Rainolds was incorrect. Smectymnuus cited the English tradition of interpretation exemplified by Thomas Brightman, which argued that the word 'angel' in the singular had to be taken synecdochically to mean the collective presbytery of each of the seven churches.[87] At the same time Smectymnuus put an alternative, secondary case that, even if the word 'angel' did signify a singular individual, there was no indication from scripture that the angel was equivalent to a diocesan bishop.[88] Smectymnuus deployed Acts 20:28 to show that the church of Ephesus, one of the seven churches of Revelation 2–3, was a church ruled collectively by many ministers, all of whom were called 'bishop' by the apostles.[89] Despite the multiplicity of bishops at Ephesus there was 'no colour of any superintendency or superiority of one bishop over another'.[90] Indeed, in their *Vindication* of June 1641, Smectymnuus argued that Rainolds and Beza would have characterised the angels of Revelation as '*Angelus praeses*, not *angelus princeps*. And he was *praeses mutabilis*, and *ambulatorius*, just as a moderator in an assembly, or as the speaker in the House of Commons, which is onely during the Parliament'.[91] For Smectymnuus, 'this *individual angell* may be nothing else than a moderator of a company of Presbyters [...] and this is also mutable and changeable, according as *Pareus* and *Beza* hold'.[92]

Tom Webster has argued that Smectymnuus's alternative understanding of the meaning of the angel in Revelations 2–3 demonstrates that they were not advocating presbyterianism but were arguing 'for the most extreme form of primitive episcopacy'.[93] Webster is correct to highlight the ambiguous play between definitions of 'primitive episcopacy' and presbyterianism in the 1641 debates. However, given Smectymnuus's characterisation of the 'angel' in each church as a rotating, ambulatory presidency, Webster's argument presents a distinction between presbyterianism and 'extreme' primitive episcopacy that is without a difference. In both practice and theory, almost all early modern presbyterian churches accepted that a moderator or president of the presbytery was mandated by both scripture and the practice of the early church. As Ethan Shagan has shown, the early modern concept of a 'moderator' envisaged a potentially more regulatory and coercive function than our present-day signification of the term, although this meaning was tempered in presbyterian thought by the insistence on the essential parity of presbyters.[94] An example of this can be found in the Genevan Company of Pastors, where the moderatorship of the Company remained Calvin's during his lifetime. After Calvin's death, the Company adopted annual elections for the position of moderator, but even then Beza was re-elected for sixteen continuous years, a point made in the seventeenth century by the pro-episcopalian John Bridges in his critique of presbyterianism.[95] The Smectymnuus tracts, by arguing for a mutable and ambulatory, rather than fixed, presidency, betray a position closer to continental presbyterianism than the 'primitive episcopacy' of contemporaries such as Archbishop Ussher.

One impetus in early 1641 for arguing against a fixed president of an ecclesiastical assembly came from the Scottish covenanters. In January, Alexander Henderson had published a tract against the institution of a 'perpetual presidency'. He pointed to the inconvenience that the Scottish church had experienced from their bishops under King James.[96] Another anti-episcopal author considered the 'least and most moderate' or 'petite' episcopacy to be one where an individual acted as a constant moderator of a presbytery. What made such a polity unlawful in scriptural terms was not the length of the presidential bishop's term of office, but that they held a 'negative or double, or at least a casting voyce' in the decisions of the presbytery. This 'petite' episcopacy could not be viewed as a lawful 'circumstantial' that the church was free to adopt, for it affronted the scripturally mandated 'substantials' by offending against the rule of parity between ministers.[97]

This point is essential to understanding Smectymnuus's position on the presiding 'angel' of the presbytery. If the 'angel' was indeed a single individual rather than a collective presbytery, such a person held only a situational presidency over a particular session of a church consistory, with no additional power deriving from their presidential position. This was a pertinent question in the debate with Joseph Hall, as Hall had argued that continental Reformed churches effectively had a separate 'episcopal' order in the form of their moderators or superintendents. For Hall the difference between the continental churches and England was that English bishops held their office for life.[98] Countering Hall's argument that presbyterian moderators were in substance the same as English bishops, Smectymnuus pointed out that such moderators had no power of veto, no separate power of ordination and jurisdiction and no additional financial maintenance.[99] In their *Vindication*, the issue of the length of the moderator's office was revisited by citing Wilhelm Zepper, an influential late-sixteenth-century German Reformed theologian, to show that the superintendents of the German Reformed churches 'are only presidents while the synod lasteth; when it is dissolved, their prerogative ceaseth', and that when the meeting of the synod ceased 'they returne to the care of their particular churches'.[100] Smectymnuus, while allowing for one minister to preside over church assemblies, argued for the more properly presbyterian position that such a president or moderator should hold the office only for the duration of the synod and should have no additional jurisdiction over fellow presbyters by virtue of that office.

Nevertheless, Smectymnuus's primary argument is that the 'angel' in Revelations 2–3 signifies by synecdoche the collective presbytery of one church. They affirmed this point by drawing on William Tyndale's translation of the New Testament, in which the seven churches are described as 'congregations'.[101] Such congregational churches were to govern themselves but act in combination with their neighbours. Smectymnuus argued '[w]ee reade in scripture, of the churches of *Judea*, and the churches of *Galatia*; and why not the churches of *England*? Not that we deny the *consociation*, or *combination* of churches into a provinciall or nationall synod for the right ordering of them.'[102] The reference to the language of 'consociation' and 'combination' derives from English nonconformist writers such as Robert Parker and Paul Baynes. This suggests that in *An answer* Smectymnuus was drawing on the English nonconformist tradition that saw the power of assemblies and synods deriving from an 'ascending' theory of presbyterian polity, with synodic authority originating from the delegated consent of individual congregations.[103] This was followed up in their *Vindication*, where Smectymnuus argued that discipline should be exercised by 'the minister or ministers of each congregation with the advice, and consent of the presbyters adjoining'.[104] The Smectymnuus tracts were, therefore, describing a form of ecclesiastical polity that followed the contours of presbyterian positions on church government.

The final thrust of Smectymnuus's attack on Hall's *Humble remonstrance* was to call on Parliament to legislate the 'abrogation of episcopacie'.[105] Citing Sir Edward Coke, Smectymnuus argued that episcopacy in England was historically the creation of statute. As such, Smectymnuus averred that episcopacy may 'by the same authoritie be abrogated; by which it was first established'.[106] To assist in showing how episcopacy had been anathema to English history, Smectymnuus added a postscript, generally ascribed to John Milton, cataloguing the maladministration of the bishops throughout English history.[107] In the work of further reformation, Parliament is asked to consider 'whether it be best to walk after the president [precedent] of man, or the prescript of God'.[108]

Between *An answer* and their *Vindication*, the Smectymnuans present two variations of presbyterian polity for the church. The first model, the mainstay of *An answer*, was that of a single congregation ruled by its pastors and ruling elders 'consociated' with other congregations through provincial and national assemblies. The *Vindication*, on the other hand, advanced an alternative position where the local church consisted of a consistory of ministers and elders ruling a group of congregations. In both of these paradigms, churches were to consociate into a synodic structure presided over by a moderator or superintendent whose presidency would be temporary, lasting only for the duration of the meeting of the synod.[109] Joseph Hall considered that the Smectymnuans were arguing for presbyterianism, an accusation that the Smectymnuans did not deny, stating 'we heartily desire that Christ may rule, and wee shall most willingly subject ourselves to his government'.[110] While the possibility of a *jure humano* 'reduced episcopacy' was not entirely closed off, the Smectymnuans' explicit call to Parliament to 'abrogate' episcopacy and their advocacy of church government by congregations governed by presbyter-bishops and ruling elders, 'consociated' into assemblies under the temporary presidency of a moderator, show that the Smectymnuus tracts move beyond the reduced or primitive episcopacy advocated by the likes of Archbishop Ussher, or indeed Thomas Young in 1639. The Smectymnuan tracts advocate (to use Carol Schneider's apposite term) a 'latitudinarian presbyterianism' and one that was left purposefully vague in order to afford room to manoeuvre in the situation current in the first half of 1641.[111]

The radicalisation of Parliament: spring and summer 1641

Despite the presbyterianism of the Smectymnuus tracts, the authors were close enough to the pulse of the parliamentary junto to realise that the best hope for reformation in early 1641 would be to find a compromise with

Calvinist episcopalians. As noted in chapter 1, the leaders of the parliamentary junto and many godly clergy at this time appear to have been more committed to the reform of episcopacy than its abolition. In addition, most of the ministers meeting in Aldermanbury followed the long-standing moderate puritan imperative to preserve the integrity of the Church of England, while seeking its reformation. As has been noted earlier, this tradition held that the form of polity in the church was a matter of its 'well-being' and not an essential mark of the true church.[112] The need for the godly clergy to retain unity while the attack on Laudianism was under way meant that the issue of church government and of the ultimate fate of episcopacy was often studiously avoided in the collective petitions and public statements of the ministers.

One potential opportunity to bring about a compromise over grievances in the Church of England was the meeting of the Lords' sub-committee on innovations in religion, chaired by Bishop John Williams of Lincoln, which met between March and late May 1641 and included many of the leading Calvinist episcopalians, including the bishops Joseph Hall, James Ussher and Thomas Morton, as well as other leading conformists such as Daniel Featley and Ralph Brownrigg.[113] According to Thomas Fuller the conformist group were dubbed 'doctrinal puritans' by the Laudians. A smaller number of 'disciplinary puritans' were invited by Williams to attend the committee, including the Smectymnuans Marshall, Calamy and Young as well as Cornelius Burges, John White of Dorchester, William Twisse and Thomas Hill.[114]

The work of the committee, on Williams's guidance, focused on the consensual areas of addressing complaints about issues of doctrine and ceremony, including many of the 'innovations' of the Laudian period.[115] The conformist members made substantial concessions to the puritan ministers' grievances, with Hall later claiming that he had declared 'my open dislike of all innovations, both in doctrine and rites'.[116] Nevertheless, the conformists sought to keep the issue of church government out of the discussions.[117] Hacket remembered that Williams had made clear his distaste for presbyterianism, declaring that the church 'must not be built like a barn, all on one floor, but must be framed with gradual subordinations'.[118] A further indication that Williams kept back discussion of ecclesiastical polity was his presentation on 1 July 1641, two months after the committee had ceased to meet, of a bill for the regulating of episcopacy that addressed some of the complaints of the 'disciplinary puritans', such as requiring bishops to exercise jurisdiction and ordination with a committee of local presbyters.[119] One purpose of inviting members of the Aldermanbury junto to join the sub-committee may have been to win back influential members of that group from their drift towards the more Reformed positions on polity. Thomas Fuller believed that the committee 'might [...] not only have checked, but choked our civil war in the infancy thereof' by agreeing on a reformation of the ceremonies and establishing a more pastorally sensitive episcopacy. In a similar vein, Hacket stated that the guiding motif of the committee was 'for the settlement of a general peace' and that Williams had conceded that 'sometimes a little loss is a great gain'.[120] The conformists' concessions on matters of doctrinal and ceremonial reform appear to have been partially effective. Edmund Calamy's grandson recorded that 'by mutual concessions, things were bro[ugh]t into a very hopeful posture'.[121] However, by the time of the final meetings of Williams' sub-committee, in the last days of May 1641, the chances of consensus were beginning to fade. Stephen Hampton has shown how (to the dismay of the aged puritan John White of Dorchester) the 'disciplinary puritan' members like Calamy and Marshall demanded more concessions than the conformists were prepared to give.[122] Both Hacket and the younger Calamy considered that the introduction in the Commons of May's Root and Branch bill, as well as the disputes within the two houses over the removal of the bishops from the House of Lords, were the key factors that wrecked the progress of the Williams committee.[123]

This turn against both compromise and episcopacy was partly the consequence of the hardening of positions induced by the threat to Parliament of April and May's royalist plots to seize the Tower of London.[124] On 21 April, a large crowd of the city's godly citizens, led by the godly merchant John Venn, submitted a petition, allegedly subscribed by 20,000 citizens, blaming the Earl of Strafford for the 'incendiaries' threatening Parliament.[125] The reformist mood would continue into the summer as Parliament debated, pursuant to the Root and Branch bill, alternative models of church government to episcopacy. These discussions, however, would also reveal fundamental divisions among the godly on the issue of ecclesiastical polity, and would witness concerted attempts by the Aldermanbury circle to restore a public face of unity.

On 2 May a bungled attempt was made by the loyalist Sir John Suckling to seize the Tower of London in defence of the Earl of Strafford and the king's administration. This attempted coup led Parliament to introduce its 'Protestation', the swearing of which was designed to flush out its enemies.[126] Many of the puritan clergy, including John Geree, the Tewkesbury and later London presbyterian minister, saw the Protestation as a much-hoped-for covenant for further reformation.[127] Given the close political connections between the parliamentary junto and the Aldermanbury ministers, it is unsurprising to find that the latter were instrumental in distributing and promoting the Protestation in the city. In particular, sources singled out the ministers Calamy and Burges, as well as godly merchants including

John Venn, as those behind the campaign to get Londoners to take the Protestation.[128]

As Judith Maltby has noted, the real difficulty that the Protestation presented to conformist supporters of the Church of England was the 'Explanation' issued by Parliament on 12 May to elucidate its terms. The Explanation made it clear that the Protestation did not discount the possibility that Parliament might legislate a reformation of the 'worship, discipline, or government', or the liturgy and ceremonies of the church. This left the clause committing subscribers of the Protestation to the defence of the 'true Reformed religion' looking less certain and potentially more radical than the wording had initially suggested. The Explanation was probably issued to provide comfort to the more advanced English puritans, as well as the Scottish commissioners, who in May had published their plea for 'unitie in religion, and uniformitie of Church government'.[129] However, the Explanation also fed the fears of proponents of episcopacy that the Protestation was a Trojan horse that threated the established ecclesiastical order.[130]

These fears were exacerbated in the public arena by Henry Burton's publication of his barely anonymous tract *The Protestation protested*. This pamphlet urged the godly to separate from the established church into gathered congregations.[131] Such arguments aggravated many of the ministers of the Aldermanbury junto, who were committed to a national reformation of the Church of England.[132] Burton's *The Protestation protested* helps bring into focus the fact that many of the positions on ecclesiastical polity being arrived at in the printed public debate were too radical for almost all in Parliament. This would become evident between May and July as the Commons finally debated its Root and Branch bill.

The debate, initiated by Sir Edward Dering's presentation of the bill on 27 May and ending on 3 August, was an expression of the Commons' anger at the Lords' refusal to pass legislation removing the bishops from that House on 24 May.[133] The Root and Branch debates have been seen by historians as a manifestation of an increasingly 'Erastian' stance that would characterise parliamentary thinking about the proper relationship between church and state during in the mid-seventeenth-century crisis.[134]

The historiographical stress on parliamentary 'Erastianism', while undoubtedly the dominant voice in the debates, has often failed to recognise much of the fluidity of opinion in the Commons. Rather than exposing the threat of the civil state's dominance of the church, the ambiguities of the Root and Branch debate inspired the godly clergy to believe that Parliament would bring about the type of reformation of polity that they desired. During the debate on the Bishops' Exclusion bill, John White the member of parliament for Southwark made a speech, much of it similar in nature to the arguments of Smectymnuus, stating that in the New Testament 'there is no mention of other bishops than the presbyters' and that 'episcopacy in whatsoever exceeds the presbyters office [...] is a branch of the hierarchy of Rome, and of the antichrist'.[135]

It is apparent that the 'behind the scenes' management of the Root and Branch debates included clergy close to the Aldermanbury circle. On 11 June Stephen Marshall was sent from a meeting of the junto leaders to find Sir Simonds D'Ewes with instructions to return to the Commons and make a snap speech in favour of the Root and Branch bill.[136] At the bill's commitment, D'Ewes had made noises that some form of presbyterianism might be a suitable replacement for episcopacy, telling Parliament that if episcopacy was abolished 'nor shall we need to study long for a new church government having so evident a platform in so many Reformed churches'.[137] The upshot of the debate was that the question of the church would ultimately be settled on the advice of an assembly of divines.[138] In the meantime an interim administration established by Parliament would govern ecclesiastical matters. As it turned out, the final position of Parliament's scheme for interim administration, before the king's departure for Scotland stopped the debate dead, was the establishment of local committees of godly gentry, who would govern church affairs with a minimal role for the clergy. The 'Erastian' nature of this scheme has been rightly stressed by historians, who see it as the model for similar arrangements under the Protectorate. However, the proposed lay commissioners' scheme should not detract from the fact that other models for church governance were advanced that did involve significant clerical input. Sir Edward Dering suggested that the county administration should operate under a 'constant presbytery' of clergy overseen by a president. Even the original plan for local committees, as proposed by the trenchant anti-clericalist Sir Henry Vane junior, consisted of an equal number of clergy and laymen.[139]

The debates over the Root and Branch bill revealed a will in the Commons for parliamentary supremacy over the church. However, as Dering's and Vane's initial schemes show, many in Parliament were not entirely sure about dispensing with an element of clerical governance in the church altogether. For the Aldermanbury ministers, the Root and Branch debates could lead pro-parliamentarian clergy to envisage that Parliament was setting England on the path to finally completing the reformation of the church.

Godly divisions in the summer of 1641

While the Commons debated the Root and Branch bill, the core ministers of the Aldermanbury circle increasingly began to consider the question of reforming the polity of the church. Divisions arose between those who sought a more presbyterial (including 'primitive episcopalian') approach to the Church of England's government and those who advocated a congregational way, more in tune with New England or the separatist congregations in the Netherlands. The source of tension among these ministers in mid-to-late-1641, as later, was what specific division of authority would be held by congregations and higher assemblies when taken together. Thomas Edwards, in a pro-presbyterian tract published in August 1641, claimed that at their 'first coming over' from the Netherlands those in favour of congregationalism had declared they 'could take the charge of parochiall churches [...] upon the reformation hoped for, and they could yield to presbyteriall government, by classes and synods, so [long as they were] not enjoyned to submit to it, as *jure divino*'. By the summer of 1641 Edwards reported that this possible compromise had faded.[140] Since late 1640, Henry Burton had led the way in publicly advancing a congregationalist position on church government.[141] He would be joined in the spring of 1641 by others who openly advocated the congregational way.[142] On 30 May, Nathaniel Holmes used a fast sermon before Parliament to declare that 'every congregation is as a particular corporation' and thus should be self-governing.[143] In April 1641 a separatist, probably John Canne, launched a systematic attack in print on presbyterianism.[144] The issue of the authority of classes and synods, or perhaps more foundationally, the dispute between the principals advocating 'aristocratic' rule in the church by the ordained ministry and those propounding 'democratic' rule of the members of each congregation, represented a fault-line within the anti-episcopal alliance that threatened division before the battle against episcopacy had fully begun.[145]

As well as doubts about the scriptural warrant and desirability of authoritative classes and synods being raised, it is also apparent that questions were being expressed about the extent to which parish elders held authority independent from the members of the congregation. Evidence of the disputes on the issue of congregational governance and the power of extra-congregational presbyteries can be seen in a letter sent on 12 July 1641 by some of the London ministers to the general assembly of the Kirk at Edinburgh. The London ministers behind the letter sought the advice of the Kirk, complaining that a contingent of the ministers in London 'hold the whole power of Church-government [... is] to be decreed by the most voyces in [...] every particular congregation, which (say they) is the utmost bound of a particular Church [...] and only some formalities of solemne execution to be reserved to the officers'.[146] The July letter to the Kirk went on to state that a further point of disagreement was whether particular congregations 'ought to transact, determine, and execute all matters pertaining to the government of themselves [...] within themselves, without any authoritative [...] concurrence or interposition of any other persons or churches whatsoever'. Those of the London anti-episcopal alliance who held this position believed that the 'decisive power of classes, or compound presbyteries and synods' were 'a meere usurpation' of a congregation's independent authority. The Kirk's reply, written by Alexander Henderson and dated 9 August 1641, attempted to strike an irenic note. It advised that, while ecclesiastical power resided in the presbytery of ministers and elders, the presbytery should only exercise its powers of censure with 'the tacite consent of the congregation'. Further, the Scots tried to provide comfort to those fearing an oppressive authority in classes and synods. Henderson argued that synods were 'a help and strength, and not a hinderance or prejudice, to particular congregations and elderships' and that such classes and synods did not hold any 'extrinsecall power set over particular Kirks' in the manner of episcopacy. Yet, despite such words of comfort, the main thrust of Henderson's letter was the hope that the Churches of Scotland and England might become 'as one people' through the imposition of 'one confession, one directory for publike worship, one catechisme, and one forme of kirk-government'. The Scots therefore made it clear that they sought religious uniformity with England on a presbyterian model.[147]

In order to close the rift created by these discussions and the potentially devastating use that conformist episcopalians could make of a public pamphlet dispute between the godly, the Aldermanbury ministers set out to maintain the appearance of consensus by containing public discussion among themselves on issues of ecclesiastical polity. According to Thomas Edwards, all sides within the godly camp were 'sensible how much our differences and divisions might distract the Parliament, and hinder the taking away of episcopall government, and the reformation intended'.[148] To contain these divisions, the London brethren met at Calamy's house to agree a plan of action for the future. Although the exact date of the meeting is unclear, the London schoolmaster and presbyterian polemicist John Vicars placed it around November 1641. It is therefore likely that the effect of the disputes between the godly on parliamentarian unity was brought into sharp focus by the threat caused by the outbreak of the Irish rebellion.[149] Edwards alleged that a written agreement was drawn up, aptly described by Frank Bremer as the 'Aldermanbury Accord', which set out terms for how the puritan brotherhood would proceed against episcopacy without publicly revealing their internal differences.[150] It was also agreed that the less offensive parts of the Book of Common Prayer would continue to be used in church services in the interim. This denied the episcopal party a propaganda victory by playing on popular affection for the Prayer Book. In any event, many godly conformists did not object to the use of a 'stinted' liturgy in principle, so long as there was a latitude for the individual minister's conscience and talents.[151] The Accord further decided that the preaching of 'lay-men, tradesmen, and mechanicks' and 'the anabaptists and rigid Brownists' would be discouraged. The parties agreed that 'a mutuall silence' would be imposed 'both in preaching, printing, and conferring with the people (and especially parliament men) of any of the points in difference betweene us'. Finally, the congregationalists would be permitted to present a statement 'of all their opinions that they held in difference' with the main bulk of the reformist ministers.[152]

Although the evidence of this meeting is heavily coloured by the obviously biased testimony of Vicars and Edwards, it is apparent that the Aldermanbury junto reached its agreement with near-consensus.[153] Edwards later bemoaned the fact that, although he wished to continue his print battle against the Independents, he had been specifically leashed by the undertakings of his 'brethren' at the Aldermanbury meeting. The years 1642–3 remained relatively quiet in regard to the publication of tracts on topics prohibited by the Aldermanbury Accord, indicating that the terms of the agreement were largely observed.[154] It is also likely that the Scottish Kirk's irenic position in its reply to the London ministers in 1641 and the anticipation of the 'synod of the most grave, pious, learned and judicious divines of this island' promised in Parliament's Grand Remonstrance helped to maintain the public silence agreed at Aldermanbury.[155]

Conclusion

The November Accord represented the culmination of the efforts of the anti-prelatical network meeting at Calamy's house between 1640 and 1641. The coming months would see twelve bishops imprisoned in the Tower and from February 1642 excluded from their seats in the House of Lords. The regular monthly parliamentary fasts, which began in December 1641 with sermons by Calamy and Marshall, would confirm the parliamentary pulpit as the mouthpiece of the dissident junto. The connected clerical 'junto that meet at Calamy's house' would play a key role in using the pulpit and press to define and expound Parliament's ideological position as Charles I's monarchy collapsed.

Between the calling of the Short Parliament and the first months of 1642, London's godly ministers transformed themselves from a group of harassed parish clergy into a component of Parliament's political machinery. In this regard, they were aided by an influx of provincial godly ministers being sent to London from regional conferences as agents to observe events in the capital. 'Calamy's junto' therefore emerged as an important component of the nascent parliamentarian challenge to the

Caroline regime. However, a fundamentally clericalist strain of argumentation can be detected in the early discourse of many of the Aldermanbury ministers. The submissions before the committee of twenty-four and the Smectymnuus tracts envisaged a church in which the power of ecclesiastical discipline was transferred from the traditional episcopal hierarchy and church courts to largely independent presbyteries governed by clerics and laity raised to the status of ecclesiastical officers. While much of this new thinking on church government remained fluid, it is clear that an English presbyterianism emerged in the course of 1641. English presbyterian thought in 1641, however, was not yet fully worked out in all its particulars. The emerging clericalism would, in later years, come into conflict with the concurrently emerging 'Erastian' sensibility among leading parliamentarians of the need to preserve, and even extend, the civil supremacy of the state over the church.

Notes

1 [William Fulke], *A briefe and plain declaration* (1584), pp. 3–110; [Walter Travers], *A directory of church-government* (1645), sigs A2r–3r, Br–B3v. For the *directory* (not published until 1645), see P. Collinson, *The Elizabethan puritan movement* (1967), pp. 291–302 and M. Winship, *Godly republicanism: puritans, pilgrims and a city on a hill* (Cambridge, MA, 2012), pp. 54–5, 267 n. 39.
2 [Travers], *A directory*, sigs A3r, C1r–C4v; [Fulke], *A briefe and plain declaration*, pp. 111–25.
3 [Travers], *A directory*, sigs A2r, A3v; [Walter Travers], *A defence of the ecclesiastical discipline ordayned of God* ([Middelburg], 1588), p. 93.
4 Thomas Cartwright, *The rest of the second replie of Thomas Cartvurihgt* (n.p., 1577), pp. 151–70.
5 [Travers], *A defence*, pp. 166–8; [Fulke], *A briefe and plain declaration*, pp. 137–45. For the roots of the two-kingdoms doctrine in Calvin's political theology, see M. Tuininga, *Calvin's political theology and the public engagement of the Church: Christ's two kingdoms* (Cambridge, 2017).
6 Ha, *Presbyterianism*, especially ch. 6; Collinson, *Elizabethan puritan movement*, pp. 385–467. For case studies which chart the divergence of the puritan stance after the defeat of the Elizabethan presbyterian movement, see P. Lake, *Moderate puritans and the Elizabethan Church* (Cambridge, 1982), chs 10 and 11.
7 Lake, *Moderate puritans*, pp. 3, 245–9, 280–3; M. Winship, 'Straining the bonds of puritanism: English presbyterians and Massachusetts congregationalists debate ecclesiology, 1636–1640' in *Puritans and Catholics in the trans-Atlantic world 1600–1800*, eds C. Gribben and S. Spurlock (2015), p. 107.

8 P. Lake, 'Anti-popery: the structure of a prejudice' in *Conflict in early Stuart England: studies in religion and politics 1603–1642*, eds R. Cust and A. Hughes (Basingstoke, 1989), pp. 72–106.
9 Lake, *Moderate puritans*, p. 77; V. J. Gregory, 'Congregational puritanism and the radical puritan community in England c.1585–1625' (Ph.D thesis, University of Cambridge, 2003), pp. 206–48; Schneider, 'Godly order', pp. 202–46; F. D. Carr, 'The thought of Robert Parker (1564?–1614) and his influence on puritanism before 1650' (Ph.D thesis, University of London, 1964), pp. 133–7.
10 Baxter, *RB*, I, pp. 13, 16.
11 Constant Jessop, *The angel of the church of Ephesus no bishop of Ephesus* (1644), sig. A2v–A3r.
12 Baxter, *RB*, I, p. 16.
13 C. Prior, *Defining the Jacobean church: the politics of religious controversy, 1603–1625* (Cambridge, 2005), pp. 113–57.
14 W. Hudson, 'The Scottish effort to presbyterianize the Church of England during the early months of the Long Parliament', *CH*, 8:3 (1939), p. 266 n. 42; W. M. Abbott, 'Anticlericalism and episcopacy in parliamentary debates, 1640–1641: secular versus spiritual functions' in *Law and authority in early modern England: essays presented to Thomas Garden Barnes*, eds B. Sharp and M. C. Fissel (Newark, NJ, 2007), pp. 156–85, especially pp. 159–61 for a survey of contemporary sources showing the problem of the definition of 'primitive episcopacy'.
15 John Calvin, *Institutes of the Christian Religion*, trans. H. Beveridge (Peabody, MA, 2008), pp. 709–18; J. L. Ainslie, *The doctrine of ministerial order in the Reformed churches of the sixteenth and seventeenth centuries* (Edinburgh, 1940), pp. 93–119; T. Maruyama, *The ecclesiology of Theodore Beza: the reform of the true church* (Geneva, 1978) pp. 185–7, 193–4; G. S. Sunshine, 'Reformed theology and the origins of synodical polity: Calvin, Beza and the Gallican confession' in *Later Calvinism: international perspectives*, ed. W. F. Graham (Kirksville, MO, 1994), pp. 142–58; G. S. Sunshine, *Reforming French protestantism: the development of Huguenot ecclesiastical institutions, 1557–1572* (Kirksville, MO, 2003), pp. 28–9; A. Milton, 'Puritanism and the continental Reformed churches' in *The Cambridge companion to puritanism*, eds J. Coffey and P. C. H. Lim (Cambridge, 2008) pp. 109–26.
16 Ha, *Presbyterianism*, pp. 16–18; Winship, *Godly republicanism*, p. 272 n. 24.
17 R. G. Usher, *The reconstruction of the Church of England*, 2 vols (1910), II, pp. 345–52; Schneider, 'Godly order', pp. 141–5.
18 Thomas Young, *Dies dominica* (1639), pp. 89–92. Citations are from the 1672 English translation *The Lord's day*, pp. 277–9.
19 *Ibid.*, pp. 277–80.
20 Ha, *Presbyterianism*, pp. 50–5; *The puritans on independence: the first examination, defence and second examination*, ed. P. Ha (Oxford, 2017), pp. 48–9, 89–98.
21 Winship, *Godly republicanism*, ch. 4, pp. 277–8 n. 6.

22 William Bradshaw, *English puritanisme* (1605), pp. 5–8; William Ames, *The marrow of theology*, trans. J. D. Eusden (Grand Rapids, MI, 1997), p. 178–80; P. Lake, *Moderate puritans*, pp. 269–76.
23 Ha, *Presbyterianism*, especially chs 2–5.
24 George Downame, *Two sermons* (1608); Winship, *Godly republicanism*, pp. 96–7.
25 Paul Baynes, *The diocesans tryall* (1621), p. 21.
26 Carr, 'Robert Parker', pp. 165–7.
27 John Ball, *A friendly triall of the grounds tending to separation* (1640), pp. 238–9.
28 References are to the 1599 edition of the Geneva Bible printed by the deputies of Christopher Barker.
29 For Paget, see K. L. Sprunger, 'Paget, John', *ODNB*; Schneider, 'Godly order', pp. 339–50; Ha, *Presbyterianism*, pp. 69–70, 91–4, 104–5, 110–12, 127–36.
30 F. J. Bremer, *Building a new Jerusalem: John Davenport, a puritan in three worlds* (New Haven, CT, 2012), pp. 116–29.
31 John Paget, *An answer to the unjust complaints* (Amsterdam, 1635), sig. *4, p. 65; John Paget, *A defence of church-government* (1641), pp. 29–32.
32 John Davenport, *An apologeticall reply* (Rotterdam, 1636), p. 228.
33 *Ibid.*, pp. 224–32.
34 F. J. Bremer, *Lay empowerment and the development of puritanism* (Basingstoke, 2015), pp. 63–5.
35 Paget, *Defence of church-government*, pp. 2–4; Ha, *Presbyterianism*, pp. 56–9.
36 Paget, *Defence of church-government*, pp. 42–51.
37 Ha, *Presbyterianism*, pp. 56–9, 128–33.
38 The discussions of these disputes are detailed in B. R. Burg, 'A letter of Richard Mather to a cleric in old England', *William and Mary Quarterly*, 3rd series, 29 (1972), pp. 82–98; C. G. Schneider, 'Roots and branches: from principled non-conformity to the emergence of religious parties' in *Puritanism: transatlantic perspectives on a seventeenth-century Anglo-American faith*, ed. F. J. Bremer (Boston, MA, 1994), pp. 166–200; Webster, *Godly clergy*, pp. 301–5; Ha, *Presbyterianism*, pp. 59–67; Winship, *Godly republicanism*, pp. 291–2 n. 11; Winship, 'Straining the bonds of puritanism', pp. 89–111; J. Mawdesley, 'Peers, pastors and the particular church: the failure of congregational ideas in the Mersey Basin region, 1636–41' in *Church polity and politics in the British Atlantic world, c.1635–66*, eds E. Vernon and H. Powell (Manchester, 2020), pp. 48–51.
39 John Ball, *A tryall of the new-church way* (1644), pp. 72–4; [Richard Mather?], *Church government and church covenant* (1643), p. 4; [Richard Mather?], *An apologie of the churches in New England* (1643), p. 24.
40 Winship, 'Straining the bonds of puritanism', pp. 93, 95, 106.
41 Ball, *A friendly triall*, pp. 300–2; Ball, *A tryall of the new-church way*, pp. 25–7.
42 Ha, *Presbyterianism*, pp. 180–1.
43 For the sectary dimension to the attack on episcopacy see D. R. Como, *Radical parliamentarians and the English civil war* (Oxford, 2018), ch. 3.

44 [Richard or John Bernard?], *A short view of the praelaticall Church of England* (1641).
45 *Ibid.*, pp. 40–1.
46 *Ibid.*, p. 43.
47 [Anon.], *The beauty of godly government in a church reformed* (1641), pp. 7–8.
48 *Ibid.*, p. 8 (my emphasis).
49 [Jeremiah Burroughes], *The petition of the prelates briefly examined* (1641). For the publication of this tract, see Baillie, *L&J*, I, p. 303.
50 J. Maltby, 'Petitions for episcopacy 1641–1642' in *From Cranmer to Davidson: a Church of England miscellany*, Church of England Record Society, 7, ed. S. Taylor (Woodbridge 1999), 103–67.
51 [Burroughes], *Petition of the prelates*, p. 24.
52 Powell, *Crisis*, pp. 22–9.
53 Congregational Library, London, MS II.d.46 (Anonymous sermon notes, 1638–41 and 1672–77), no foliation, notes dated August 1640.
54 Baillie, *L&J*, I, p. 303.
55 Jeremiah Burroughes, *Irenicum* (1645), pp. 155–6. Burroughes was referring to George Gillespie's *A dispute against the English popish ceremonies* (1637), pp. 181–5.
56 [Burroughes], *Petition of the prelates*, pp. 30–2.
57 *LJ* XI, p. 470.
58 The sequence of pamphlets went [Joseph Hall], *An humble remonstrance* (1641); Smectymnnus, *An answer to a booke entitled an humble remonstrance* (1641); [Joseph Hall], *A defence of the humble remonstrance* (1641); Smectymnuus, *A vindication of the answer to the humble remonstrance* (1641); [Joseph Hall], *A short answer to the tedious vindication of Smectymnuus* (1641).
59 Paul, *The assembly*, p. 119; Hudson, 'The Scottish effort', p. 267 n. 46; C. G. Bolam, J. Goring, H. L. Short and R. Thomas, *The English presbyterians: from Elizabethan puritanism to modern unitarianism* (1968), p. 41.
60 Webster, *Godly clergy*, pp. 315, 319–21, 323, 327.
61 Schneider, 'Godly order', pp. 462, 465.
62 S. M. Manetsch, *Calvin's company of pastors: pastoral care and the emerging Reformed church, 1536–1609* (Oxford, 2012), pp. 61–7.
63 John Hacket, *Scrinia Reserata* (1693), II, pp. 143–4.
64 For the use of Beza's *de triplici episcopatu*, see Smectymnuus, *An answer*, pp. 86–7.
65 *Ibid.*, pp. 86–7.
66 *Ibid.*, pp. 16, 19, 23–9; Smectymnuus, *A vindication*, pp. 18, 152.
67 Smectymnuus, *An answer*, p. 16.
68 Smectymnuus, *A vindication*, p. 152. The probable source for the adoption of this position was Ball, *A friendly triall*, pp. 261–4, 298–302. George Gillespie also made similar arguments in *An assertion of the government of the Church of Scotland* (1641), pp. 138–41.
69 Smectymnuus, *An answer*, p. 91; *A vindication*, p. 73.
70 Smectymnuus, *An answer*, pp. 69–71.

71 *Ibid.*, pp. 13, 16–17, 67, 69–71, 91.
72 For Smectymnuus's favourable argument for ruling elders see *ibid.*, pp. 71–5; *A vindication*, pp. 183–95.
73 Smectymnuus, *An answer*, p. 16.
74 *Ibid.*, pp. 27, 33. These arguments explicitly looked back to Beza's dispute with Hadrian Saravia; see p. 29.
75 *Ibid.*, pp. 27–9, 33.
76 *Ibid.*, pp. 30–1, 33–5.
77 *Ibid.*, pp. 29–30. This argument is similar to that made by Henderson in *The unlawfulness and danger of limited prelacie*, p. 9. It may ultimately derive from [Travers?], *A defence*, p. 19, 76–81, 98–101.
78 Smectymnuus, *An answer*, pp. 29–30.
79 *Ibid.* pp. 35–8. In an influential passage, Webster (*Godly clergy*, p. 321) argues that Smectymnuus's discussion in these pages (section VIII of *An answer*) shows that the Smectymnuans' 'assumption is that a properly constituted church will include bishops but that they will be of the same order as their presbyters'. However, Smectymnuus in this section discussed the Bezan epoch of *episcopus humanus*, a time when, the Smectymnuan tracts argue, the pristine, apostolic constitution of the church had already been corrupted. The point of Smectymnuus's argument in section VIII is to show that the prelacy of the Church of England had fallen even further towards the diabolical frame than the already corrupted order of the *jure humano* bishops of the patristic era.
80 Smectymnuus, *An answer*, pp. 86–7.
81 *Ibid.*, pp. 85–6.
82 Smectymnuus, *A vindication*, p. 113.
83 Smectymnuus, *An answer*, p. 86.
84 For Downame, see Ha, *Presbyterianism*, p. 75; Hall, *Episcopacy by divine right stated*, pp. 42, 65–86, 112, 119, 159–60.
85 [Prynne], *The unbishoping of Timothy and Titus*; Ha, *Presbyterianism*, p. 76.
86 Smectymnuus, *An answer*, p. 48; *A vindication*, pp. 114–37.
87 Smectymnuus, *An answer*, pp. 53–6; *A vindication*, pp. 132–59. For Smectymnuus's use of Brightman, see Thomas Brightman, *A revelation of the apocalypse* (1611), p. 32, which identifies the angel of each church as the 'whole colledge of pastours'. Smectymnuus also appears to rely on a document entitled 'A question resolved by a learned doctor', printed with *Dr Reignolds his letter to [...] Sir Francis Knolles* (1641).
88 Smectymnuus, *An answer*, pp. 58–60.
89 'Take heed therefore unto yourselves, and to all the flock, over the which the Holy Ghost hath made you overseers [i.e. 'bishops' in Greek], to feed the church of God, which he hath purchased with his own blood.'
90 Smectymnuus, *An answer*, p. 58.
91 Smectymnuus, *A vindication*, pp. 150–1.
92 *Ibid.*, p. 159.
93 Webster, *Godly clergy*, pp. 321–2.

94 E. H. Shagan, *The rule of moderation violence, religion and the politics of restraint in early modern England* (Cambridge, 2011), pp. 15–16.
95 Manetsch, *Calvin's company of pastors*, pp. 60–7. For Bridges' critique, see Ethan Shagan's discussion in *The rule of moderation*, pp. 124–5.
96 Henderson, *The unlawfulness and danger of limited prelacie*, pp. 8–14.
97 [Anon.], *Certaine reasons tending to prove the unlawfulness [...] of all diocesan episcopacie* (1641), pp. 1, 10–12.
98 [Hall], *An humble remonstrance*, p. 32.
99 Smectymnuus, *An answer*, p. 71.
100 Smectymnuus, *A vindication*, p. 182. Zepper (1550–1607) was the author of *Politia ecclesiastica* (Herborn, 1607).
101 Smectymnuus, *An answer*, p. 58; *A vindication*, pp. 151–2.
102 Smectymnuus, *An answer*, pp. 80–1.
103 See for example, Davenport, *Apologeticall reply*, pp. 228–30; Baynes, *Diocesans tryall*, p. 21.
104 Smectymnuus, *A vindication*, p. 157.
105 Smectymnuus, *An answer*, p. 71; *A vindication*, pp. 59–60, 174–5.
106 Smectymnuus, *An answer*, pp. 20–1, 85.
107 *Ibid.*, pp. 85–104. For the basis of the ascription of the postscript to Milton see B. K. Lewalski, *The life of John Milton: a critical biography* (Oxford, 2003), p. 585 n. 43. Hall accused the Smectymnuans of drawing from Alexander Leighton's *An appeal to Parliament, or Sion's plea against the prelacy* (1620, reprinted in 1640) in the postscript, a fact which they conceded in *A vindication*, pp. 216–17.
108 Smectymnuus, *An answer*, p. 78.
109 *Ibid.*, pp. 58, 71; *A vindication*, pp. 151–2, 181–2.
110 [Hall], *A defence of the humble remonstrance* (1641), p. 160; Smectymnuus, *A vindication*, pp. 213–14.
111 For conclusions about the Smectymnuus tracts contrary to my own, see e.g. Webster, *Godly clergy*, p. 321–33; Como, *Radical Parliamentarians*, p. 92.
112 Preserving the integrity and unity of the Church of England against separatists had, for example, been a touchstone of the godly circle around the influential minister Arthur Hildersham, including the later London presbyterians Simeon Ashe and William Rathband. See L. A. Rowe, *The life and times of Arthur Hildersham, prince among puritans* (Grand Rapids, MI, 2013), ch. 7.
113 The leading analysis of the Williams committee, which discusses the committee and its historiography in full, is S. Hampton, 'A "theological junto": the 1641 Lords' subcommittee on religious innovation', *The Seventeenth Century*, 30:4 (2015), 433–54.
114 Thomas Fuller, *The church history of Britain*, ed. J. S. Brewer, 6 vols (Oxford, 1845), VI, p. 191; Hacket, *Scrinia reserata*, II, p. 146–7.
115 The probable heads of discussion of the sub-committee can be found in *A copie of the proceedings of some worthy and learned divines* (n.p., 1641). See also Fuller, *Church history*, VI, pp. 189–90; Hacket, *Scrinia reserata*, II, p. 147.

116 Hampton, 'A "theological junto"', pp. 438–46; Joseph Hall, *A letter lately sent by a reverend Bishop* (1642), pp. 5–7.
117 For a different view of the Smectymnuan position, see Hampton, 'A "theological junto"', pp. 436, 448.
118 Hacket, *Scrinia reserata*, II, pp. 143–4.
119 Shaw, *HEC*, I, p. 71.
120 Fuller, *Church history*, VI, p. 191; Hacket, *Scrinia reserata*, II, p. 147. Peter Heylin had a different view, seeing the committee as a foil for the machinations of the presbyterian faction: Peter Heylin, *Aerius redivivus, or, the history of the presbyterians* (Oxford, 1670), pp. 438–9.
121 Edmund Calamy the younger, *An abridgement of Mr Baxter's history* (1702), p. 186. The younger Calamy probably received his information about the committee by hearsay from Richard Baxter and possibly from reading Hacket, rather than his grandfather, who had died five years before his birth.
122 Hampton, 'A "theological junto"', pp. 447–8.
123 Hacket, *Scrinia reserata*, II, pp. 148; Calamy, *An abridgement of Mr Baxter's history*, p. 186.
124 C. Russell, 'The first army plot of 1641', *TRHS*, 5th ser., 38 (1988), 85–106; Shaw, *HEC*, I, pp. 60–63.
125 *CJ*, II, p. 125; J. Walter, *Covenanting citizens: the protestation oath and popular political culture in the English revolution* (Oxford, 2017), p. 51.
126 For the Protestation see D. Cressy, 'The Protestation protested, 1641 and 1642', *HJ*, 45:2 (2002), pp. 251–79; Vallance, *Revolutionary England*, pp. 51–3. The fullest study is Walter, *Covenanting citizens*.
127 Cressy, 'The Protestation protested', pp. 255–6; John Geree, *Judah's joy at the oath* (1641).
128 [Robert Chestlin?], *Persecutio undecima* (1648), pp. 57–8; Pearl, *London*, p. 218; Adamson, *The noble revolt*, pp. 284–5; Walter, *Covenanting citizens*, pp. 45–6, 53–61, 113–20.
129 *Arguments given by the Scots commissioners [...] perswading conformitie of church government* (1641).
130 J. Maltby, *Prayer book and people in Elizabethan and early Stuart England* (Cambridge, 1998), p. 90; Kenyon, *The Stuart constitution*, pp. 200–1, 235.
131 [Henry Burton], *The Protestation protested* (1641).
132 Hughes, *Gangraena*, pp. 122–3.
133 For the Root and Branch debate see Fletcher, *Outbreak*, pp. 99–108; Russell, *Fall*, pp. 344–6.
134 Fletcher, *Outbreak*, p. 104; D. A. Orr, 'Sovereignty, supremacy and the origins of the English civil war', *History* 87:288 (2002) 474–90; J. R. Collins, *The allegiance of Thomas Hobbes* (Oxford, 2005), pp. 76–9.
135 John White, *A speech of Mr Iohn White [...] concerning episcopacy* (1641), sigs Hhh2–Hhh3, Iii3v.
136 Shaw, *HEC*, I, p. 82.
137 *Ibid.*, I, p. 81; Russell, *Fall*, p. 244.
138 Adamson, 'Peerage in politics', p. 82.

139 Shaw, *HEC*, I, pp. 92–3; Fletcher, *Outbreak*, p. 104.
140 Thomas Edwards, *Reasons against the independent government* (1641), p. 31.
141 Henry Burton, *Christ on his throne* (1640), pp. 57–71.
142 J. Wilson, *Pulpit in Parliament*, pp. 46–51; P. Christianson, 'From expectation to militance: reformers and Babylon in the first two years of the Long Parliament', *JEH*, 24 (1973), 232–3.
143 A fast sermon was a sermon given on a day of religious fasting. In the 1640s and 1650s, the parliamentary fast sermons were a regular series of sermons preached (usually monthly) before the Houses of Parliament and published by authority of Parliament. Nathaniel Holmes, *The new world or the new reformed Church* (1641), pp. 52–3. Holmes's congregationalism did have room for 'lawfull synods orderly and lawfully gathered according to the scriptures' if individual churches should fall into error.
144 [John Canne?], *Syons prerogatyve royal* (n.p., 1641); [John Canne?], *The presbyterial government examined* (n.p., 1641). The latter tract, although undated, appears to have been published around April 1641.
145 Edwards, *Reasons against the independent government*, p. 16. For a useful discussion, albeit one that somewhat underplays what I see as the evident presbyterianism of these exchanges, see Como, *Radical Parliamentarians*, pp. 98–101.
146 *Acts of the general assembly*, p. 49; Baillie, *L&J*, I, p. 364.
147 *Acts of the general assembly*, pp. 49, 50–1.
148 Thomas Edwards, *Antapologia: or, a full answer to the apologeticall narration* (1644), pp. 240, 242.
149 For the dating of the meeting see John Vicars, *The schismatick sifted* (1646), pp. 16.
150 F. J. Bremer, *Congregational communion: clerical friendship in the Anglo-American puritan community, 1610–1692* (Boston, MA, 1994), pp. 132–3.
151 C. Durston, 'By the book or with the spirit: the debate over liturgical prayer during the English revolution', *Historical Research*, 79:203 (2006), 56–8.
152 Edwards, *Antapologia*, pp. 240–1.
153 *Ibid.*, p. 242. Edwards and Vicars alleged that the agreement began to turn sour when the congregationalist Philip Nye came to Calamy's house to 'borrow' the written agreement to show it to his gathered church in Hull: see *ibid.*, p. 243; Vicars, *Schismatick sifted*, p. 17. In response, John Goodwin claimed that Nye had returned the agreement: see John Goodwin, *Anapologesiates antapologias* (1646), p. 252.
154 Edwards, *Antapologia*, p. 243.
155 Kenyon, *The Stuart constitution*, p. 215.

3

The emergence of the London presbyterian movement, 1642–3

The two years following the Aldermanbury Accord of 1641 saw the emergence of a London presbyterian movement that would endure throughout the 1640s and 1650s. Intellectually, the London presbyterians would develop and expound ideas of limited monarchy and a 'co-ordinate' mixed constitution, Old Testament notions of national covenanting and sixteenth-century presbyterian two-kingdoms theory. As well as developing their ideological position, 1643 saw the London presbyterian clergy begin to build their key institutional power bases in the city. Calamy's house in Aldermanbury was replaced by London's Sion College, the Westminster assembly became increasingly dominated by English and Scottish presbyterians and an alliance was forged with godly elements of the parliamentarian citizenry in the city. At the same time the London presbyterian clergy began to develop the polemical tools to mobilise for the establishment of presbyterian government in the Church of England against rival claims to the polity of the church. This in turn would create tensions within the parliamentarian camp, particularly among some of the leading godly peers, who saw in presbyterianism a clericalism at least as virulent as Laudian episcopacy.

The consolidation of the London presbyterian clergy

It is apparent from an analysis of the printed output between the end of 1641 and the early summer of 1643 that the moratorium agreed at Aldermanbury on pamphlets discussing church polity largely held sway, at least among those who were subject to it.[1] Whether this was due to the descent into civil war or the agreement at Calamy's house is unclear. One of the concerns of the ministers in the Aldermanbury circle from late 1641 was that the populace was generally too wedded to the traditional forms and rituals of worship to be receptive to a new wave of reformation. In a fast sermon before Parliament on 22 December, Calamy noted that many 'fear that this is not the time appointed wherein God will have mercy upon

Sion'. He lamented that the people 'would not bear a thorow Reformation' because 'the bulk of our people are wicked, and their hearts are not as yet prepared to the yoke of the Lord'. The solution, Calamy believed, was to ensure that Parliament legislate to fill the nation with a godly preaching ministry.[2]

Despite the self-imposed censorship of public pronouncements on church polity, there is evidence that at least some of the ministers in London expressed a desire for a presbyterian settlement of the Church of England. In a letter sent to the Scottish Kirk's general assembly on 22 July 1642 the same London ministers behind the 12 July 1641 letter discussed in chapter 2 assured their Scottish brethren that 'the desire of the most godly and considerable part amongst us is, that the presbyterian government [...] may be established amongst us'. The authors of the letter hoped that England and Scotland 'may agree in one confession of faith, one directorie of worship, one publike catechisme, and form of [church] government'. The ministers recognised that their presbyterian 'designe' 'hath enemies on the left hand, and dissenting brethren on the right', but they assured the Kirk that they would 'adde what power the Lord hath given us with you to the same purpose'.[3]

The 22 July letter was sent at a time when Parliament recognised that it needed to court the Kirk over a possible military alliance with the covenanters.[4] On 9 May a bill had been laid calling for an assembly of divines to settle matters of religion, a demand repeated a month later in Parliament's nineteen propositions to the king.[5] It is tempting to view the exuberance of the London ministers' design for presbyterian uniformity with the Scots as part of the careful strategy being played at Westminster to woo a Scottish alliance. However, Parliament's own statements to the Scots in the summer of 1642 had avoided any promise of presbyterian uniformity. Even in September 1642, after hostilities with the king had finally broken out, Parliament would only go so far as to promise the abolition of the diocesan hierarchy and the calling of an assembly of divines.[6] It is likely, therefore, that even if the London ministers had been encouraged by their Westminster patrons to make overtures to the Kirk, their promises exceeded those which Parliament would have considered acceptable or prudent.

The London ministers' letter of July upset the careful balance agreed on at Aldermanbury in November 1641. Thomas Welde, the pastor of the church at Roxbury, Massachusetts, visiting London to renew the colony's charter, would complain in 1644 that the July 1642 letter, written by 'our brethren, of the Presbyterian way', was 'underhand' and had 'fore-determine[d] the matter' of church polity in favour of presbyterianism, thus prejudicing the freedom of discussion in the assembly.[7]

If the London ministers' 21 July letter pointed to the dispute waging internally within the anti-prelatical alliance, the period of silence on issues of church polity maintained the external appearance of unity and moderation during Parliament's principal assault on episcopal power. The courts of High Commission and Star Chamber had been abolished in July 1641, twelve of the bishops had been imprisoned in the Tower on 30 December 1641 and the episcopate was excluded from the House of Lords in February 1642.[8] In addition to the measures against the bishops, Parliament had established a committee for scandalous ministers chaired by the godly Southwark MP John White, which had been taking evidence since December 1640 against the Laudian and royalist parish clergy in the city. This, often formulaic, evidence would form the justification for the purge of these ministers, with between 81 and 86 per cent of London's parish clergy losing their livings between summer 1642 and 1644.[9] The singling out of 'malignant and scandalous' clergy was assisted from December 1642 when a committee of the London common council, comprising a number of future presbyterian ruling elders, co-ordinated the gathering of evidence against such malignant clergy in London.[10]

The removal of Parliament's clerical opponents in the city was a critical step in the emergence of a London presbyterian movement. The purges created vacancies in London parishes that were often filled by provincial ministers who either were doctrinaire presbyterians, or were willing to accept a presbyterian settlement in the church. Between 1641 and 1645 around thirty parishes in London were filled by such ministers, many coming from the godly networks of Warwickshire, Northamptonshire and the Welsh Marches. In particular many of the ministers drawn to London were clerical clients of the godly Earl of Warwick, or of other godly patrons connected to Warwick such as Lord Brooke or the Harley family.[11]

Presbyterian political thought: limited monarchy, co-ordinate powers and Parliament's 'defensive armes'

The outbreak of civil war in August 1642 required the London ministers to publish and preach in defence of Parliament against the polemics of the king's propagandists. By December, London experienced public protests as large numbers of its citizens became disillusioned with the descent into civil war. This dissatisfaction was seized upon by royalist propagandists, particularly Henry Ferne, the Archdeacon of Leicester and one of the king's royal chaplains.[12] Ferne sought to disabuse 'all misse-led people in this Land' of the idea that Parliament's claim to resist the king was anything other than 'unwarrantable' and 'damnable'.[13] In the face of such danger, the parliamentarian ministers associated with the Aldermanbury alliance continued to work together to provide justification for Parliament's 'defensive armes' against the king's party.

This section looks at the Aldermanbury ministers' development and deployment of a parliamentarian political thought based on ideas of mixed government, limited monarchy and lawful resistance. The idea of a mixed constitution in England had its roots in the medieval notion of 'the estates of the realm' found in authors such as Sir John Fortescue.[14] This stream of thought had converged with classical learning on the nature of the ideal commonwealth during the Tudor period and been developed by English and Scottish presbyterian thinkers during the late sixteenth century.[15] The idea of mixed monarchy, and of limiting Charles I's monarchy in particular, had been central to the political thinking and aims of the dissident junto in the run-up to the Long Parliament. In July 1640 Viscount Saye and Sele had told John Winthrop, the governor of the Massachusetts Bay colony, that a balanced constitution of monarchy, aristocracy and democracy was necessary for 'the settling and preserving of common right and liberty'.[16] This view had been developed further in parliamentary declarations issued from late 1641 throughout 1642 and in the works of Saye's nephew Henry Parker.[17] From December 1642 the idea of England being a limited monarchy would be developed by the clergy in London in their responses to Ferne's charge that resistance to the king was a damnable sin. The idea of limited monarchy would become increasingly important to London's religious presbyterians, particularly after 1645, when the more radical parliamentarian theory, which stressed popular sovereignty and classified magistrates as replaceable agents or trustees, would gain traction and challenge the ancient constitution.

The pattern of the London clergy's engagement with Parliament from late 1641 was exemplified by their preaching in the early fast sermons. These sermons cast Parliament as the divinely ordained vehicle to 'reform the Reformation itself' and to restore England to the truths of the gospel.[18] To resist or even remain neutral to Parliament's providential task to aid the church, as Stephen Marshall's famous sermon *Meroz cursed* claimed, was an act that would summon God's wrathful displeasure on the nation.[19] The city's presbyterian ministers were also actively involved in preaching to London's citizens the righteousness of supporting Parliament's war against the king. As well as being distributed in print, these sermons were often preached numerous times. It was alleged that Marshall had preached *Meroz cursed* some sixty times to stir the people out of their neutrality.[20] This preaching was often carried out in private meetings. For example, Edmund Ludlow reported that Daniel Axtell, the future regicide, had been convinced 'of the justness of the warr' by hearing the sermons of the presbyterians Francis Woodcock, Simeon Ashe and Christopher Love at a private prayer meeting in Lawrence Lane.[21]

Parliament's clerical propagandists were largely drawn from ministers close to the Aldermanbury circle of 1641. This included both presbyterians, notably Stephen Marshall and Samuel Clarke, and their congregationalist brethren Jeremiah Burroughes and William Bridge. However, the rising star among this group in late 1642 was Charles Herle, the pre-civil war rector of the Lancashire parish of Winwick.[22] Herle been among those active in opposing the canons of 1640 in Cheshire and Lancashire.[23] In 1642 he had fled to London, obtaining the sequestered living of St Olave, Southwark.[24]

The catalyst for the London ministers' defences of parliamentary constitutional thought and resistance theory was Henry Ferne's December 1642 tract *The resolving of conscience*. This work was published at a time when the legitimacy of Parliament's actions was being questioned on the streets of London by peace protestors. Ferne argued that Romans 13 obliged Christians to submit to their rulers or suffer eternal damnation. The correct response to the civil war was to obey the king and, if aggrieved, follow the model of primitive Christians, suffering with tears and prayers.[25] Ferne's theory of obedience had deep foundations in English protestant thought and must have provided an attractive option to many London citizens, who feared the collapse of the social and economic order from the continuation of civil war.[26] While Ferne accepted, as had the king in June's *Answer to the xix propositions*, that the English constitution was a mixed one, the powers of Parliament were of counsel and consent only. A mixed monarchy, Ferne argued, did not mean that the estates were equal to one another. The king was sovereign and the two houses of Parliament could not seize the power that reposed in the monarch.[27] The consequence of Parliament's unwarrantable declaration of its right to legislate in the king's absence was that the whole fabric of lawful authority was in the process of unravelling. Ferne warned his readers that the consequence of Parliament's claim to legitimate resistance was that the people, 'with rapine and confusion', could equally claim the right of resistance against Parliament, splintering the nation into an unstable cantonal system of government.[28]

Lining up against Ferne, the parliamentarian ministers, including Herle, Marshall and Burroughes, argued that Romans 13 did not prevent Christians from acting in self-defence against a ruler operating out of his own 'illegal will and ways'.[29] In making these arguments the ministers relied on the medieval idea that the monarch's office and person could be separated. When the king acted beyond the law, allegiance was owed to the king's political capacity and not to the king's physical person.[30] Samuel Clarke argued that the king's behaviour demonstrated that he was acting as a man 'whose passions may mislead him'. Consequently, he could be defensively resisted until Parliament could win his personal capacity back to his rightful body 'politic' in Parliament.[31]

The issue of Romans 13 also dovetailed into the ministers' deployment of the argument that England was a mixed constitution comprised of co-ordinate powers. The 'higher powers' of the Apostle Paul's commandment in the English state was king-in-Parliament, not the king alone.[32] In advancing this justification of defensive war, the ministers, particularly Herle, deployed and developed the political theory that the monarchy in England was made up of three equal, co-ordinate estates: king, Lords and Commons.[33] Herle argued that if the king were to 'faile and refuse, either to follow the rule [of] law, or its end safety', the houses of Parliament, as the 'co-ordinates in this mixture of the supreme power', were enabled to supply the deficit left by the erring king.[34] It followed that it was no disobedience to fight defensively for Parliament.[35]

In tackling Ferne's argument that parliamentary resistance created a slippery slope towards popular sovereignty, the ministers' responses were varied. Given the possibility in 1643 that a pro-peace faction in Parliament might gain the majority and impose an agreement with the king's party, some of the ministers were prepared to countenance the shadowy possibility of the people's resistance to Parliament itself. The right of popular resistance was largely found in works by congregationalist authors, such as Jeremiah Burroughes and William Bridge.[36] Charles Herle and most presbyterians took a different stance. Herle accepted, from 1 Peter 2:13's definition of government 'as an ordinance of man', that the people of any particular tribe or region had originally held the power to agree the nature and form of the government that should rule over them.[37] Nevertheless, Herle closed off Ferne's charge that parliamentary resistance theory was dangerously revolutionary by arguing that once a people fixed their form of government, they were bound to it. The people of England had designated that they should be ruled by a mixed monarchy and had failed to make any reservations for themselves that would allow them to take back their original power.[38] In any event, Herle argued, 'Parliament is the peoples own consent'.[39] As members of the Commons were themselves subjects drawn from, and elected by, the people, they were 'the people' in a representative capacity. In this regard, Herle and other presbyterians argued that the location of the final, 'arbitrary', element of power resided solely in both houses of Parliament.[40] As Rachel Foxley has noted, Herle's argument had the effect of implying that sovereignty ultimately resided in the two houses of Parliament.[41] In contrast to Jeremiah Burroughes's countenancing of the possibility of popular resistance against Parliament, Herle argued that the people had no right of resistance, even if, for example, a future Parliament attempted to settle paganism on the nation.[42]

When it came to fighting the civil war, the ministers argued that the co-ordinate nature of the English constitution legitimised Parliament in fielding armies against the king and his partisans. As the highest court in the kingdom, Parliament possessed the power 'to apprehend and bring delinquents' to justice and to raise the national equivalent of a *posse comitatus* to supress a rising.[43] As Glenn Burgess has noted, the presbyterian ministers' justification of civil war stressed that resistance against the king's forces was based on a legal defence of the constitution rather than a holy war.[44] Parliament's war was thus cast by the minsters as a war defending not only Parliament but also the king, who, using the commonplace justifications of medieval and early modern rebellions, had been 'seduced by wicked councell' into unlawful violence.[45]

The defensive character of Parliament's military efforts did not, however, detract from the fact that the war had to be conducted aggressively. At the most blood-thirsty end of the spectrum, the youthful presbyterians George Lawrence and Christopher Love declared that 'cursed be hee' that 'keepeth back [...] his sword from blood' and that parliamentarians should 'make ready for the battell'.[46] In a distinction that would become significant in 1649, the ministers explained that while Charles I, like king Saul in 1 Samuel 24:6, was 'the Lord's anointed', and must not be killed in cold blood, the parliamentarian armies should not hold back if the king was foolhardy enough to appear in arms on the battlefield. The London presbyterian ministers behind the tract *Scripture and reason pleaded for defensive armes* used a counterfactual argument from 1 Samuel 23 to justify the possibility of the king being killed in battle. They argued that had David defended himself against Saul, divine providence, in the form of 'an arrow or a stone' launched by David's army, might have killed Saul. In such a circumstance, Saul's 'bloud would have bin upon his own head' and not on David's.[47] Samuel Clarke stated that the king had received pleas from Parliament to leave his 'evill counsellors' but had remained in open arms with his malignant confederates. The blame for the potentially fatal consequences to the king in war therefore fell on his evil counsellors and not on parliamentarians who were defending themselves and the king's politic capacity against cavalier aggression.[48] Should Charles I die in battle, the ministers behind *Scripture and reason* argued, the fault would be 'wholly his owne and those wicked Councellors that have thrust him upon the fury of battell'.[49]

The political theory advanced by ministers such as Herle in the parliamentary crisis of 1642–3 was improvised to meet the unprecedented conditions of the early 1640s. It presupposed that once Parliament had restored the kingdom to order, the operation of traditional monarchical government would again be largely entrusted to the king, albeit with the monarch now advised by 'honest' rather than evil counsellors. Throughout the mid-century crisis, the presbyterians would not resile from this position. Presbyterian ministers agreed that it was the 'imminence of danger' to the public safety that permitted the extraordinary measures of the Lords and Commons and justified the civil war.[50] As Julian Franklin observed, the argument that Parliament could deploy its co-ordinate powers to preserve the constitution in times of emergency contained lingering theoretical contradictions that questioned whether the king was truly sovereign. This was especially true given Herle's argument that, in the final analysis, ultimate sovereignty rested in both houses of Parliament.[51]

If Herle struggled with his theory of co-ordinate powers to maintain the supremacy of king-in-Parliament against Ferne's attack, an alternative current of thought that stressed popular sovereignty through the House of Commons was also gathering momentum. This alternative stream of argument brought into sharper focus the idea that the king's powers were merely of executive significance.[52] It also developed Jeremiah Burroughes's notion that, if necessary, even Parliament itself could be resisted. These arguments were by no means exclusive to 'Independent' or sectarian thinkers, as some of its leading proponents included presbyterians such as Edward Bowles and William Prynne.[53] Nevertheless, as the 1640s progressed this more radical line of argumentation would increasingly become associated with Independent and sectary thought.[54] This clash of parliamentarian theory would become most apparent in the days that followed the military-backed revolution of 1648.

The Covenant and the London godly alliance

The ministers' sermons and pamphlets stressed that the civil war was a legal defence of constitutional rights and the protestant religion. Nevertheless, there can be little doubt that they were motivated by the promise of further reformation of the Church of England in the near future. In the first year of the civil war, Parliament had been reticent to commit on issues of church reform. The debates of 1641 had already shown that this would lead to divisions within the parliamentarian camp at a time when the cause needed unity among those committed to the war. The Aldermanbury ministers, along with many zealous London citizens and allies among religious Independents, had held together around war party themes. Co-operation among the London godly can be seen in a petition of 8 February 1643 in which the presbyterian ministers Thomas Case and Francis Woodcock joined Jeremiah Burroughes, Colonel Randall Mainwaring and four city militia captains to protest against proposals for a cessation of arms.[55]

Robert Brenner has stressed that in 1643 the city militants supporting Parliament's war efforts in this period showed congregationalist or sectary leanings.[56] There is traction in this argument, as is evidenced by the composition of the most militant of the city committees, such as the ill-starred Salters' Hall sub-committee.[57] Nevertheless, Brenner's argument that future religious presbyterian citizens were 'moderates' or 'conservatives' in 1643 is not entirely convincing.[58] Many future religious presbyterians were active in city militancy or supported war party positions in 1642–3. For example, Sir David Watkins, the future ruling elder of St Andrew Undershaft and, from 1647, a member of the London Provincial assembly's ruling grand committee, was a leading activist among the city militants in 1642–3.[59] Jeremiah Baines, who would serve as a ruling elder of St Olave, Southwark and would also be chosen as a delegate to the London Provincial assembly, gained notoriety in 1642 for tearing down copies of the king's commission of array in Southwark. Baines volunteered as a captain of dragoons in the Earl of Essex's army in 1642, before enlisting with Sir William Waller's Southern Association, rising to the rank of lieutenant colonel and being appointed Waller's quartermaster general of foot in 1644.[60] City militants (and later 'political Independents') who were religious presbyterians included William Underwood and John Warner. These two, both from the parish of St Stephen Walbrook, would serve as ruling elders alongside the presbyterian minister Thomas Watson.[61] The future presbyterian ruling elders John Vicars and Thomas Underhill were involved with Lord Mayor Isaac Pennington in the city mobilisation against the peace proposals of August 1643 led by Northumberland and Holles.[62] Although Pennington is sometimes classed as an 'Independent' in religion, he appears to have held moderate presbyterian leanings. For example, during his tenure as Lord Mayor in 1642 he chose the presbyterian minister Thomas Case to be his chaplain. Case had been a contemporary of Edmund Calamy and the Manchester presbyterian minister Richard Heyrick at Merchant Taylor's School in the 1610s and had had fallen under Laud's surveillance in 1639 for preaching in favour of 'the Scotch rebels' and 'against the discipline of the Church of England'.[63] In 1645–6 Pennington would promote the presbyterian William Taylor to replace the ousted John Goodwin as the minister of St Stephen, Coleman Street. Along with eleven other prominent citizens, Pennington would serve as one of the ruling elders at St Stephen's under Taylor's ministry.[64] The vast majority of the London ministers and citizenry who would subscribe to presbyterianism seem to have held to the 'war party' position at the outbreak of the first civil war.

While godly reform of the church was one of the key ideas encouraging support for Parliament's war in 1642–3, the impetus towards a specific second reformation would come as a result of the military setbacks of 1643.[65] The parliamentary junto began to see the Scottish alliance as the only means of breaking the military stalemate with the king's party. The first step in the parliamentary junto's wooing of the Scots was the imposition, from 9 June, of the Vow and Covenant on English parishes within Parliament's area of control.[66] This oath was more militant than the Protestation and caused controversy because it failed to repeat the requirement for the defence of the king's person.[67] Samuel Clarke, the minister of St Benet Fink, noted that the Vow and Covenant was designed to stop the practice of people supplying money and arms to both king and Parliament 'so by complying with both they might escape the displeasure of either'.[68] The Vow and Covenant was supported by sermons and encouragement from the London ministry, who treated it as a revival of the ancient biblical practice of national covenanting with God.[69] Nevertheless, the ministers placed the Vow and Covenant within the context of Parliament's previous declarations. Edmund Calamy stressed that the Vow and Covenant was a further aspect of Parliament's 'defensive armes' and was not designed to unleash 'an anabaptistical fury' against the ancient constitution.[70] Samuel Clarke argued that the Vow and Covenant was compatible with the oaths of allegiance and supremacy on the basis that the king had been corrupted by his evil counsellors.[71] Thomas Case, the presbyterian minister of St Mary Magdalen, Milk Street, and his wife Ann, led the whole parish in taking the Vow and Covenant unequivocally.[72]

One intent behind the imposition of the Vow and Covenant and the calling of the Westminster assembly in July was to signal to the Edinburgh regime that the English Parliament was seeking a military alliance with Scotland.[73] The key document of this alliance, the Solemn League and Covenant, drafted largely by Alexander Henderson, was negotiated in Edinburgh from 7 August 1643. The Covenant was approved by the English Parliament on 25 September after amendments were added to satisfy English 'tender consciences' and to tone down the requirement that the three kingdoms adopt Scottish presbyterian polity.[74] Even English presbyterians such as Thomas Case made it clear that the Covenant did not bind the Church of England to follow the exact form of presbyterianism found in Scotland.[75] These caveats were necessary, both to convince those who scrupled at taking the Covenant and to preserve the possibility of agreement on religious fundamentals within the parliamentarian alliance. In addition, there was a concern not to prejudice the Westminster assembly's deliberations on church polity, 'according to the Word of God and the example of the best Reformed Churches'.

For the Scots, the alliance would deploy a mutual commitment to Reformed protestantism as a means of keeping royal power in check by replacing regal union with a covenanted confederacy of England and

Scotland.[76] As Allan MacInnes notes, this was not the view of the majority of English parliamentarians, who were wedded to ancient constitutionalism and the doctrine of Parliament wielding the royal supremacy in matters of religion.[77] However, the London ministers saw in the Solemn League and Covenant a statement of principles that encapsulated their idea of a limited monarchy kept in check by a godly alliance of the three nations. At the centre of this vision was a reformation of the churches of England, Ireland and Scotland that would significantly diminish the king's power to interfere with the Reformed faith.[78] It was given eloquent expression in 1643 by Thomas Coleman, a Westminster assembly divine, who told Parliament that the hope of the Solemn League and Covenant was that 'England and Scotland after this religious union in one covenant, may ever be one people in this island of Great Britaine'.[79]

This is not to say, however, that all ministers within the parliamentarian camp wholeheartedly supported the Solemn League and Covenant. On 30 August, Cornelius Burges and William Price petitioned Parliament objecting to what they saw as the wholesale rejection of all episcopalian forms of the church polity envisaged by the Covenant.[80] When it was clear that the petition was not looked on favourably, Price quickly disavowed it. Burges, however, was suspended from the Westminster assembly until he recanted.[81] Despite these protests, the Covenant generally provided a welcome symbol of unity to the parliamentarian clergy. The congregationalist Philip Nye proclaimed at the taking of the Covenant by Parliament on 25 September that the three kingdoms were 'swearing fealty and allegiance unto Christ the king of kings; and a giving up of all these kingdomes [...] to be subdued more to his throne'.[82] In the winter of 1643, there was a general hope, expressed by Edmund Calamy, that the military alliance enshrined in the Covenant would lead to a royalist surrender without further bloodshed.[83] That these hopes would prove to be false would begin to become apparent in the events surrounding the calling of the Westminster assembly.

Tensions within the London godly alliance and the emergence of presbyterian polemic

The parliamentary ordinance creating the Westminster assembly, issued on 12 June 1643, declared that 'many things remain in the liturgy, discipline and government of the Church, which do necessarily require a further, and more perfect reformation then as yet hath been attained'. The ordinance roundly condemned the episcopal order as 'evil' and proposed establishing a form of church polity 'agreeable to God's Holy Word', in 'nearer Agreement with the Church of Scotland, and other Reformed Churches abroad'.[84] Parliament's ordinance made it clear that the assembly, which was to meet from 1 July 1643, was not to be a free-standing church council. The divines' role was 'to give their advice and counsel' on such matters as were 'proposed unto them' by the houses of Parliament.[85]

The initial task of the assembly was to review the Church of England's thirty-nine Articles of religion. Given that the Articles had not been substantially questioned by the godly in the 1630s and early 1640s, this task essentially put the assembly on a leash while the military alliance with the Scots was being negotiated. Nevertheless, the assembly still found time to debate controversial topics, such as the problem of antinomianism, a package of doctrines that challenged the orthodox Reformed view of the process by which a believer's salvation was worked out in earthly life. A commonly held antinomian position was that God's 'free grace' rescued the believer from the process of sanctifying their life through conformity to God's law. Orthodox Reformed theologians accused antinomians of teaching that justification, the imputation of Christ's alien righteousness that made the faithful right before God, cloaked the justified sinner so entirely that God did not see his or her sins.[86] The antinomians' teachings not only short-circuited the system of practical divinity worked out by Elizabethan and Jacobean Calvinists but also presented a menace to the social order by invoking the spectre of libertinism. One difficulty with the antinomians' errors was that, taken individually, they were often indistinguishable, or different only in degree, from those held by orthodox Reformed divines; yet, as a package, antinomian doctrines acted to dismantle the careful system of Calvinist practical divinity preached by the godly.[87]

On 10 August the assembly petitioned the Commons to take action against the publication of antinomian books, particularly those of John Eaton, Tobias Crisp and Henry Denne. In response, the Commons ordered that a committee, membership of which included noted puritans such Sir Robert Harley and Francis Rous, sit with a committee of the assembly to investigate antinomianism.[88] The committee, which was largely made up of London ministers, called in and examined those accused of antinomianism such as John Simpson and Giles Randall.[89] Rather than empower a new Inquisition, the Commons proceeded with caution, calling on the assembly to produce a report on the differences between antinomian doctrine and the Church of England's thirty-nine Articles.[90] The Commons' concerns were expressed by John Selden, who told the assembly to demonstrate how antinomians could be prosecuted according to English law. For Selden this meant identifying which doctrines were either contrary to the thirty-nine Articles, so that any beneficed ministers teaching such doctrines could be deprived of their living, or were contrary to law, so that antinomians could be proceeded against by criminal prosecution. The problem, as many of the assembly members on the committee recognised, was that it was difficult to pinpoint what in antinomianism went beyond the theologically disputable into heresies that could be prosecuted and punished. Edmund Calamy succinctly summarised the problem when he declared to the assembly that 'a man may hold an error and yet not be an heretique'. The pugilistic George Walker, on the other hand, thought proving that antinomians were heretics was 'as easy as to sit up and down'.[91] The problem of antinomianism presented the assembly with a taste of the difficulties in combating theological errors in the absence of the church courts. Nevertheless, despite Selden's legalism, Parliament was not entirely unhelpful to the assembly, convening a committee on 10 October to take measures to 'hinder those of the antinomian opinion from preaching'.[92]

One reason for the Commons' caution in supporting the assembly's attack on antinomianism was that it raised the spectre of vilifying those on the margins of godly orthodoxy who were committed to Parliament's cause and thus risked dividing the parliamentarian camp. The ministers' agitation against 'error' also threatened the fragile peace agreed at Aldermanbury in 1641. Although the Accord had prevented works from being published by presbyterians and congregationalists against each other, it was challenged indirectly when works issuing from either New England or Scotland appeared in London's bookshops. The works were brought to public consumption by London printers and publishers, many of whom were emerging as partisans in the religious debate. The publication of material from New England or Scotland was therefore an intentional attempt to circumvent the Accord. In 1644 Thomas Edwards identified the New England congregationalists Hugh Peters and Thomas Welde as the main culprits for this breach. Edwards charged these ministers with using their colonial status to circumvent the agreement by publicly preaching for congregational government. Edwards also implied that Welde and Peters had published two works by the respected New England minister John Cotton advocating the congregational way in the summer of 1642 to side-step the Aldermanbury Accord.[93]

Congregationalists, on the other hand, claimed that the first blows could be traced back to a series of works published by presbyterians between 1641 and 1643.[94] The most significant and prejudicial work was Samuel Rutherford's 1642 *A peaceable and temperate plea for Pauls presbyterie in Scotland*. Rutherford's *Peaceable and temperate plea* set out to undermine Robert Parker's arguments that ecclesiastical power was primarily held by the body of faithful believers and delegated to the elders as their representatives.[95] Although Rutherford allowed the people a role in the election of church officers, he argued, contrary to Parker and many English congregationalists, that presbyters received ecclesiastical power directly from Christ.[96] It is clear that this tract, with its stress on the location of ecclesiastical authority in the presbytery, went to the heart of the debates on church power that had been circulating in England since 1641. Rutherford's work forced English ministers to make what were often implicit and undefined positions around which consensus could be obtained into explicit and divisive stances. The consequence of this was that irenic ambiguities and omissions in the debate on church government became less possible and positions hardened. By December 1646 the London presbyterian ministers would cite *A peaceable and temperate plea* to make the argument that scripture located the power of keys in the 'ruling church' of elders alone. Rutherford's *Peaceable and temperate plea*, therefore, was a publication that significantly influenced the process of the crystallisation of previously fluid principles and positions.[97]

The perception that the Aldermanbury Accord began to fracture as a result of the printing of various opposing treatises needs to be set in the context of the beginnings of partisan religious conflict. A key event that struck a heavy blow to the *détente* reached at Aldermanbury was the decision in April 1643 by Henry Burton and Nathaniel Holmes to gather congregational churches.[98] Burton and Holmes set a precedent and a number of additional gathered churches either were founded or came to London in 1643. John Goodwin's private conventicle made the transition to gathered church in around September and Nicholas Lockyer had established his gathered church in Soper Lane by early November.[99] In the same month the London turner Nehemiah Wallington sought the advice of his minister Henry Roborough on what to think of some of his godly neighbours 'settling a church by themselves'.[100] In the assembly, Edmund Calamy reported that a broadsheet 'ticket' was circulating in London arguing 'it is not fit to wait or attend upon [the assembly's] determination for settlement' and that the saints should begin gathering churches.[101] The semi-public gathering of churches in the midst of the city triggered a wave of publishing activity from London presbyterians to counter Independency. One of the leading works against the gathering of churches was Charles Herle's *The independency on scriptures of the independency of churches*, a defence of presbyterianism published in May 1643, a month after Burton and Holmes' churches were set up. A further indication of the reaction to the gathering of churches was the publication of two pamphlets in June and July that deployed vintage anti-separatist arguments to satisfy the godly of the lawfulness of participating in mixed-parish communions.[102]

A further blow to the Aldermanbury Accord came in June when Hugh Peters published the manuscript response on behalf of the New England churches to a series of questions critical of the congregational way sent by Lancashire ministers in the late 1630s.[103] The timing of Peters' publication suggests that the publication of Herle's defence of presbyterianism had been the catalyst that led to its publication. Herle's work had largely cited the works of outright separatists such as John Robinson, John Canne and Katherine Chidley as examples of 'Independency'. However, in the marginalia he had linked the views of these separatists to the respected New England divine John Davenport.[104] In 1644 Peters's compatriot Thomas Welde recognised that the term 'Independency' was being used ambiguously in London polemic. The term was being 'abusively taken', signifying 'such a [church] society as are neither subject to magistracy, nor regard the counsel of other churches, but are conciepted and selfe sufficient people, that stand only on their owne leggs'.[105] This definition was fraught with danger for supporters of the congregational way as it conveyed an association with the continental anabaptists' denial of the magistrate's authority, a position that was anathema to the New England form of church order.

This pattern of publication and counterpublication in mid-1643 marked the beginning of a series of events that would render the agreement settled at Aldermanbury void by mid-1644. Peters's publication of what had previously been treated as semi-private correspondence provoked the presbyterians Simeon Ashe and William Rathband to publish further communications between the New England churches and their English conference from the 1630s. Alluding to Peters's recent publication, Ashe and Rathband bemoaned that the late 1630s debates between New and old England would not have been 'made thus notorious if some who cry up the church way in New England as the only way of God, had not been forward to blow them abroad in the world'.[106] Ashe and Rathband's publication of the 1630s debate is significant as it marks one of James Cranford's first acts as a partisan presbyterian licenser. Cranford had already shown his understanding of the use of print propaganda in 1642 as the compiler of *The tears of Ireland*, a graphically visceral anti-Catholic account of the 1641 massacre of Irish protestants.[107] The use of Cranford's *imprimatur* by a small group of authors and publishers in the city would become notorious by the mid- to late-1640s as the London presbyterians gained a near-dominance over the city's official religious press. The London ministers had sought controls over the licensing of books since March 1641 when they petitioned the House of Lords to allow a number of them to act as the sole licensers of religious works.[108] The ministers were granted their wish in June 1643 when a majority of presbyterians were appointed as licensers of religious books.[109] However, it was Cranford, above all other licensers, who recognised the crucial link between licensing and the organisation of religious propaganda. Cranford's alliances with pro-presbyterian authors, printers and publishers would be key to the emergence and public projection of a partisan presbyterianism from 1643 onwards.[110]

Cranford's use of his *imprimatur* to further the presbyterian cause would become most apparent in 1644–5. In late 1643, however, he used his powers as a licenser to circumvent Parliament's delaying tactics on the issue of antinomianism. Cranford's realisation of the role of the press in the emergence of religious politics in this regard is shown by his licensing of works against antinomianism written by non-assembly authors such as the anonymous *The second part of the un-deceiver* and *A short view of the antinomian errors*, a work by the Fleet Street baker and later presbyterian ruling elder Thomas Bakewell. More prophetic of the descent into the *ad hominem* polemic of 1644 was the publication, licensed by Cranford, of John Goodwin's 1639 letter to Thomas Goodwin bemoaning Thomas's adoption of congregationalism. In the context of 1643, this letter was designed to cause deep embarrassment to both Thomas and John Goodwin by tarring the former with the brush of separatism and the latter with that of hypocrisy.[111] The publication of such works shows how acutely aware presbyterians such as Cranford were becoming of the role of printed propaganda in advancing their agenda to establish presbyterianism as the government of a reformed Church of England.

A further development in 1643 was the London presbyterian ministers' capture of the institution of Sion College. Situated in a dissolved medieval hospital in the parish of St Alphage, London Wall, Sion College had been founded in 1626 by the will of Thomas White, the moderate puritan vicar of St Dunstan-in-the-West.[112] Like London's parishes, the college was purged in favour of the godly when in October 1643 the committee for plundered ministers sequestered its leadership, forcing the election of the prominent London presbyterians Andrew Janeway, of All Hallows, London Wall, Edmund Calamy and Henry Roborough as the president and two assistants respectively. From the October 1643 election until 1661, Sion College would be controlled by the London presbyterian clergy and it replaced Calamy's house as the organisational headquarters of presbyterianism in London.[113] Such was the association between the presbyterian ministry and Sion College that John Goodwin would sarcastically identify 'the sacred conclave of Sion College' as the institution most associated with presbyterianism in the city.[114]

Late 1643: sectary agitation and the London ministers' counter-attack

By late 1643 the growing rift between the presbyterian and congregationalist clergy again threatened to unleash a public dispute on the issue of church polity. On 17 September *Mercurius aulicus* noted that the 'spirit of discord which moves so powerfully at London, hath been guilty of great difference wrought betwixt the [...] Brownists and anabaptists on the one part, and the craftsmen of the new assembly on the other'.[115] *Aulicus* was alluding to a petitioning campaign initiated by the general baptists Edward Barber and Thomas Nutt challenging the assembly to a public debate on the validity of infant baptism, the Church of England and its ministry.[116] Nutt had scattered printed copies of the petition throughout London together with a broadsheet of instructions for followers to 'go to all in your parishes, and desire their hands' to the petition.[117] This brazen challenge to the Westminster assembly represented only one of a number of attacks by sectaries on the project of national reformation in late 1643.

In light of these challenges to the Westminster assembly's deliberations, London's parish ministers mobilised to call for the settlement of what amounted to an ad hoc presbyterian system in the city. On 17 November, a group of London ministers sent a letter to the Westminster assembly arguing the 'deepe sence of the distractions of the Church'.[118] The letter requested that the assembly find ways to prevent the gathering of churches and the spread of heresies, and to promote moral reformation. In addition, the ministers wanted the establishment of regular catechising and the power to bar communicants judged unworthy from the sacrament of the Lord's supper.[119] More controversially, the assembly was asked to turn its attention to establishing a presbytery to ordain ministers. The issue of ordination had been highlighted as a problem in late October 1643 when the town of Harwich had petitioned the House of Commons about a Mr Wood, an unordained preacher, who had been intruded into the town's pulpit.[120] Wood's case was followed in early November by the scandal of a Mr Anderson, a 'plundered minister' who had been declined by the assembly for a parish living because he lacked ordination.[121] After being turned away, Anderson returned with a certificate confirming that he had, indeed, been ordained. It was reported to the assembly that John Goodwin and Nathaniel Holmes were responsible for this clandestine ordination.[122] The assembly's congregationalist members countered this accusation by bringing letters from Holmes and Goodwin stating that, while the two of them had certified Anderson's godly conversation, they had not ordained him. The issue highlighted that, with the removal of the episcopal system, no official mechanism for the ordination of parish ministers existed within England.[123]

The London ministers' letter of 17 November demonstrates how the city ministers and their brethren in the assembly were working together to advance their agenda.[124] Those pushing for satisfaction of the London ministers' demands included William Gouge, the venerable minster of St Anne, Blackfriars, whose long career looked back to the Elizabethan presbyterian movement. Gouge complained that, as the law stood, suspension from the Lord's supper could only be imposed after presentation of an offender to the ecclesiastical courts. As these courts no longer functioned, the system of ecclesiastical discipline was in chaos. Gouge's suggestion was to petition Parliament to give parish ministers 'the power to repel from the Sacrament whom they should think fit'.[125] However, the assembly, mindful of Parliament's fear of such naked clericalism, ultimately decided to take the more cautious path of petitioning Parliament to appoint magistrates to enforce the law in the service of the reformation of manners.[126]

If the creation of an ad hoc presbyterian government was one of the London ministers' primary demands, the problem of the sects and gathered churches was an equally pressing concern. The assembly set up a committee in November to discuss the London ministers' letter and advised on 23 November that measures should be introduced to prevent 'the seduction of the people into sects'. The committee demanded that those members of assembly 'that know who gather churches, take notice of them, and we shall seek redress'.[127] This was an overt threat to the congregationalist churches, and Philip Nye objected that the reference to 'gathered churches' should be changed to 'disorderly gathering'. Nye was answered by the Exeter delegate Henry Painter, who told Nye that gathering churches from 'pagans and heathens' was good and scriptural, but that 'gathering of churches out of churches is disorderly'.[128] Painter had long experience with such arguments, having debated congregationalist practice with his kinsman John Winthrop, the governor of the Massachusetts Bay colony, in the mid-1630s.[129] His argument against Nye would become the stock presbyterian response to the practice of gathering churches throughout the 1640s and 1650s. Unsurprisingly, the majority in the assembly agreed to approve the committee's report and to demand measures against the gathering of churches.[130] Nevertheless, desiring to prevent a further breach with the congregationalists, the assembly left the drafting of its response to Stephen Marshall and 'the cheefe men of the Assemblie, and the chief of the Independents'.[131]

The finished paper, published on 28 December as *Certaine considerations to dis-swade men from further gathering churches*, was not issued in the name of the assembly, but was signed by twenty-one of its leading ministers, including the prolocutor William Twisse and the congregationalist delegates. The paper urged ministers and people to obey Parliament and refrain from any further gathering of churches. The paper pledged to 'preserve whatever shall appear to be the rights of particular congregations' within a national ecclesiastical settlement. It gave the further undertaking that the signatories would 'beare with such whose consciences cannot in all things conforme to the publicke rule, so farre as the word of God would them borne withall'.[132] The publication of the *Certaine considerations* demonstrated that the London ministers could use their compatriots within the Westminster assembly to intervene in and exploit the assembly's deliberations for their own advantage. Nevertheless, the assembly was too cautious of Parliament's disapproval to push the disciplinarian demands of the London ministers too far. The Scottish commissioner Robert Baillie felt that *Certaine considerations* had given too much hope to the sects.[133] In this he was joined by those in the assembly who had attempted to secure an agreement that the existing gathered churches should be disbanded.[134] Conversely, as Joel Halcomb has shown, *Certaine considerations* was met with insecurity by the existing gathered churches, who saw it as a threat to their future survival.[135]

Certaine considerations was challenged almost immediately by the London separatist community. On 28 December a member of a separatist church brought a paper into the assembly decrying the Solemn League and Covenant as tyrannical.[136] The church had been founded in 1630s by the lay preachers John Spencer, a coachman to Lord Brooke, and John Green, a London felt maker.[137] Accompanying the Spencer-Green paper was a tract written by the separatist Leonard Busher demanding religious toleration.[138] The congregationalist leaders Thomas Goodwin and Philip Nye were furious with the separatists' paper, demanding the 'suppressing [of] all such fantastick papers'.[139] This reaction has to be understood in the context of Nye's earlier opposition to 'disorderly gatherings' of churches and the contempt shown by the Spencer-Green church to the congregationalist members' appeal for the continuation of the public silence on matters of polity. In addition, they did not want the 'orderly' gathered churches to be prejudiced by being lumped together with separatist congregations led by lay preachers in an assembly report to Parliament. This episode reveals how, despite the attempts of moderate presbyterians and the congregationalists to maintain intact the outlines of the peace between the godly, forces both outside and inside the assembly were beginning to see that the consensus engineered at Aldermanbury in 1641 was becoming unstable and increasingly incapable of containing the politics of religion.

Conclusion

The ejection of anti-parliamentarian clergy from the parishes of London and its environs, together with the arrival in London of godly ministers fleeing from the war in the provinces or attending the Westminster assembly, saw a caucus of pro-presbyterian ministers installed in the city and its surrounding parishes. This exodus strengthened the presbyterian cause in London so far that, by November 1643, it is possible to talk about the emergence of a presbyterian movement in the city and its surrounding area.

The period also saw the development of the political thought of the London presbyterian movement. The London presbyterians' position can be encapsulated in two main ideas. First, the presbyterian preachers (among others) developed the idea of limited and mixed monarchy. This platform built on and expanded the parliamentarian justification for its defensive actions against Charles I and the projected constitutional settlement that would arise at the end of hostilities. As would become plain in the later 1640s, the notion of mixed monarchy was rife with ambiguity and contradiction, for it anticipated that the king (albeit advised by true counsellors) would exercise executive power in the ordinary course of events, but would ultimately cede sovereignty to Parliament. This would have a knock-on effect on the internecine conflicts that eventually fractured parliamentarianism.

The second political foundation of presbyterian thought to emerge in 1642–3 was the vision that the people of Charles I's three kingdoms were bound both to each other and to God by the Solemn League and Covenant. The Covenant obliged the three kingdoms to maintain mutual political defence and to provide for the security of the British Reformed churches by an ecclesiastical settlement that uncoupled the church from royal administration. Such a position ran contrary to the English Reformation's tradition of the royal supremacy and would meet with a torrent of political opposition in the mid-1640s. Taken together, these positions would form the intellectual bearings by which the London presbyterian movement navigated the ever more treacherous waters of the British revolution.

In addition to developing their intellectual foundations, the presbyterian ministry also advanced their demands for the establishment of presbyterian church discipline within the shattered Church of England. From the London ministers' letter to the Kirk in July 1642, to their letter of demands to the Westminster assembly of 17 November 1643, the ministers signalled their desire for the imposition of a presbyterian system of church government in the parishes of London and beyond. These demands were made more urgent by the increasingly common spectacle of the gathering of congregational churches in the city. Such tensions and ambitions triggered the beginnings of the publishing conflict that would swamp the city presses from 1644. These early print engagements sharpened the presbyterians' understanding of the role of, and the need to control, print in the city.

As we shall see in chapter 4, the presbyterians' political development in 1643 would serve them well in the following years as disagreement over questions of church settlement among the parliamentarian godly could no longer be contained.

Notes

1 The presbyterian output of 1642 included a reprint of [Anon.], *The beauty of godly government*; [Calybute Downing], *An appeale to every impartiall [...] reader whether the prelacie or presbyterie be the better church government* (1642) and *A forme of ecclesiastical government* (1642).
2 Edmund Calamy, *Englands looking glasse* (1642), p. 56.
3 *Acts of the general assembly*, pp. 66–7. Alexander Gordon's entry for Stephen Marshall in the old *DNB* states that Marshall was the leading signatory of this letter, although I have not been able to verify this source.
4 L. Kaplan, 'Steps to war: the Scots and Parliament, 1642–1643', *JBS*, 9:2 (1970), pp. 51–2.
5 *CJ*, II, p. 564; Gardiner, *CD*, p. 252.
6 *CJ*, II, p. 754; *LJ*, V, p. 348.
7 Thomas Welde, *An answer to WR* (1644), pp. 2–3; R. P. Stearns, 'The Weld-Peter mission to England', *Transactions of the Colonial Society of Massachusetts*, 32 (1933–7), pp. 236–46.
8 Episcopacy would not be legally abolished until 9 October 1646.
9 For the purges see I. Green, 'The persecution of "scandalous" and "malignant" parish clergy during the English civil war', *EHR*, 94:372 (1979), pp. 512–14, 522; Argent, 'Aspects of the ecclesiastical history of London', pp. 45–51, 58; Lindley, *Popular politics*, pp. 50–5.
10 LMA JCC40, fo. 42v (the future ruling elders on the committee were William Greenhill, Michael Herring, Edward Hooker, William Kendall and Richard Turner).
11 E. C. Vernon 'The Sion College conclave and London presbyterianism during the English revolution' (Ph.D thesis, University of Cambridge, 1999), pp. 81–7.
12 B. Quintrell, 'Ferne, Henry', *ODNB*. For the royalist propaganda attack on Parliament in winter 1642–3 see M. J. Braddick, 'History, liberty, reformation and the cause: parliamentarian military and ideological escalation in 1643' in *The experience of revolution in Stuart Britain and Ireland: essays for John Morrill*, eds M. J. Braddick and D. L. Smith (Cambridge, 2011), pp. 120–2.
13 Henry Ferne, *The resolving of conscience* (1642), frontispiece, sig. A1v.
14 J. Dunbabin, 'Government' in *The Cambridge history of medieval political thought, c.350–c.1450*, ed. J. H. Burns (Cambridge, 1988), pp. 506–8; Mendle, *Dangerous positions*, pp. 21–37.
15 Mendle, *Dangerous positions*, chs 3 and 4; P. Lake, 'Presbyterianism, the idea of a national church and the argument from divine right' in *Protestantism and the national church in sixteenth century England*, eds P. Lake and M. Dowling (Beckenham, 1987), pp. 201–3.
16 P. Christianson, 'The peers, the people, and parliamentary management in the first six months of the Long Parliament', *Journal of Modern History*, 49:4 (1977), 580–1.
17 M. J. Mendle, 'Politics and political thought 1640–1642', in *The origins of the English civil war*, ed. C. Russell (Basingstoke, 1973), pp. 219–45.

18 Edmund Calamy, *God's free mercy to England* (1642), p. 2; *England's looking glass*, p. 46; G. Burgess, 'Religion and civil society: the place of the English revolution in the development of political thought', in Braddick and Smith, *The experience of revolution*, pp. 273–4.
19 Stephen Marshall, *Meroz cursed* (1642), pp. 5–7, 34–54; J. Downs, 'The curse of Meroz and the English civil war', *HJ*, 57:2 (2014) 343–68, pp. 345–7, 352.
20 Downs, 'The curse of Meroz', p. 357 n. 61.
21 Edmund Ludlow, *A voyce from the watchtower part five: 1660–1662*, ed. A. B. Worden (1978), p. 260.
22 For Herle's political thought see I. M. Smart, 'Liberty and authority: the political ideas of the presbyterians in England and Scotland during the seventeenth century' (Ph.D thesis, University of Strathclyde, 1978), ch. 3.
23 For Herle prior to the outbreak of the first civil war see J. Mawdesley, 'Peers, pastors and the particular church: the failure of congregational ideas in the Mersey Basin region, 1636–41' in *Church polity and politics in the British Atlantic world, c.1635–66*, eds E. Vernon and H. Powell (Manchester, 2020), pp. 38–59.
24 V. Larminie, 'Herle, Charles', *ODNB*; Herle resigned his interest at St Olave on 15 April 1645 (BL Add. Ms. 15669, fo. 55v).
25 H[enry] F[erne], *The resolving of conscience* (1642), p. 5.
26 For the tradition of English protestant 'obedience theory' see R. M. Reeves, *English evangelicals and Tudor obedience, c. 1527–1520* (Leiden, 2014). For the London context of winter 1642–3 see Lindley, *Popular politics*, pp. 337–45 and I. Gentles, 'Parliamentary politics and the politics of the street: the London peace campaigns of 1642–3', *Parliamentary History*, 26:2 (2007), 139–49.
27 For a summary of Ferne's position, see D. L. Smith, *Constitutional royalism and the search for settlement c. 1640–1649* (Cambridge, 1994), pp. 229–31.
28 F[erne], *The resolving of conscience*, pp. 29–30.
29 Burroughes, *A briefe answer to Dr Ferne's booke* (1642), p. 3; Stephen Marshall, *A plea for defensive armes* (1643), p. 13.
30 Herle, *A fuller answer*, pp. 2–3, 7; J. Greenberg, *The radical face of the ancient constitution: St Edward's 'laws' in early modern political thought* (Cambridge, 2006), p. 207.
31 S[amuel] C[larke], *Englands covenant proved lawfull* (1643), p. 15. This tract was a defence of Parliament's June 1643 Vow and Covenant.
32 Burroughes, *A briefe answer*, pp. 2–3, 7–8; Marshall, *A plea for defensive armes*, pp. 12–16.
33 Herle, *A fuller answer*, p. 3; J. Franklin, *John Locke and the theory of sovereignty: mixed monarchy and the right of resistance in the political thought of the English revolution* (Cambridge, 1978), pp. 28–9.
34 Herle, *A fuller answer*, pp. 7–8.
35 Burroughes, *A briefe answer*, pp. 2–3; Marshall, *A plea for defensive armes*, p. 14; William Bridge, *The wounded conscience cured* (1643), pp. 5–7; [Anon.], *Scripture and reason pleaded for defensive armes* (1643), p. 20.

36 R. D. Bradley, '"Jacob and Esau struggling in the womb": a study of presbyterian and independent conflicts, 1640–48' (Ph.D thesis, University of Kent, 1975), p. 55; D. Wootton, 'From rebellion to revolution: the crisis of the winter of 1642/3 and the origins of civil war radicalism', *EHR*, 105:416 (1990), 663–9.
37 Herle, *A fuller answer*, pp. 22–3; C. C. Weston and J. R. Greenberg, *Subjects and sovereigns: the grand controversy over legal sovereignty in Stuart England* (Cambridge, 1981), pp. 57–8.
38 Herle, *A fuller answer*, p. 18.
39 *Ibid.*, pp. 18, 25.
40 *Ibid.*, pp. 14, 17; Marshall, *A plea for defensive armes*, p. 22.
41 R. Foxley, *The Levellers: radical political thought in the English revolution* (Manchester, 2013), p. 34.
42 Herle, *A fuller answer*, p. 25; Charles Herle, *An answer to Dr Fernes reply* (1643), p. 14.
43 Herle, *A fuller answer*, p. 10; Smart, 'Liberty and authority', pp. 57–8.
44 Burroughes, *A briefe answer*, p. 7; [Anon.], *A few propositions shewing the lawfulness of defence* (1643), sigs Blr–v; G. Burgess, 'Was the English civil war a war of religion? The evidence of political propaganda', *Huntington Library Quarterly*, 61:2 (1998), 173–201; G. Burgess, *British political thought, 1500–1660* (Basingstoke, 2009), pp. 193–8.
45 Marshall, *A plea for defensive armes*, p. 3; Burroughes, *A briefe answer* (1642), p. 6; C[larke], *Englands covenant proved lawfull*, p. 9.
46 G[eorge] L[awrence] and C[hristopher] L[ove], *The debauched cavalleer* (1642), p. 8.
47 *Scripture and reason*, pp. 19–20.
48 C[larke], *Englands covenant proved lawfull*, p. 14.
49 *Scripture and reason*, p. 20; Burroughes, *A briefe answer*, pp. 3, 6.
50 Herle, *A fuller answer*, pp. 7–8.
51 Franklin, *John Locke and the theory of sovereignty*, pp. 29–30.
52 Wootton, 'From rebellion to revolution', p. 661.
53 *Ibid.*, pp. 663–4.
54 For a useful survey, see R. Tuck, *Philosophy and government, 1572–1651* (Cambridge, 1993), pp. 221–53.
55 *A letter of dangerous consequence from Sergeant Major Ogle to Sir Nicholas Crispe* (1643), pp. 6–7; Lindley, *Popular politics*, p. 305.
56 Brenner, *Merchants*, pp. 440–8, 452–6.
57 Lindley, *Popular politics*, pp. 311–14; Como, *Radical parliamentarians*, pp. 158, 325–8. As Lindley demonstrates, Brenner overplays his argument about the radicalism of the Salters' Hall committee.
58 Brenner, *Merchants*, pp. 452–9. A balanced review of the evidence can be found in Lindley, *Popular politics*, pp. 307–16.
59 For Watkins see Lindley, *Popular politics*, p. 308; Como, *Radical parliamentarians*, pp. 146–7, 159, 164–5.
60 *CJ*, II, p. 695; NA SP 28/5, fos 204, 206–7; J. Adair, *Roundhead general: the campaigns of Sir William Waller* (Stroud, 1997), pp. 128, 190, 193–4.

61 For St Stephen Walbrook see T. Liu, *Puritan London* (1986), pp. 60–1.
62 Lindley, *Popular politics*, p. 317.
63 M. Mullet, 'Case, Thomas', *ODNB*; M. Reynolds, *Godly reformers and their opponents in early modern England: religion in Norwich, c.1560–1643* (Woodbridge, 2005), pp. 171–2.
64 LMA MS P69/STE1/B/001 (St Stephen's, Coleman Street, Vestry Minutes), fo. 147.
65 Braddick, 'History, liberty, reformation and the cause', p. 119.
66 Kaplan, 'Steps to war', pp. 60–1.
67 *A&O*, I, pp. 175–6; Lindley, *Popular politics*, pp. 348–9.
68 C[larke], *Englands covenant proved lawfull*, p. 11.
69 *Ibid.*, pp. 4–5; Edmund Calamy, *The noble man's patterne* (1643), p. 45; Stephen Marshall, *The song of Moses* (1643), pp. 40–1.
70 Calamy, *Noble man's patterne*, p. 46.
71 C[larke], *Englands covenant proved lawfull*, pp. 14–16.
72 LMA P69/MRY9/B/001/MS02597/001 (St Mary Magdalen, Milk Street, Vestry Minute Book), fos 66–7. Ted Vallance provides examples of the Vow and Covenant being taken with reservations: Vallance, *Revolutionary England*, p. 118.
73 Scott, *Politics and war*, pp. 61–2.
74 The path to the negotiation of the Solemn League and Covenant has been well trodden by historians; see, e.g., D. Stephenson, *The Scottish revolution 1637–44: the triumph of the covenanters* (Newton Abbot, 1973), pp. 283–90; Paul, *The assembly*, pp. 90–96.
75 Thomas Case, *The quarrell of the Covenant* (1644), p. 44; Thomas Coleman, *The hearts ingagement* (1643), p. 38; S. W. Curruthers, *The everyday work of the Westminster assembly* (Philadelphia, PA, 1943), pp. 18–20.
76 A. MacInnes, *The British revolution, 1629–1660* (Basingstoke, 2005), p. 150; Vallance, *Revolutionary England*, p. 84.
77 MacInnes, *The British revolution*, p. 160.
78 Vallance, *Revolutionary England*, p. 87–100.
79 Coleman, *The hearts ingagement*, p. 30.
80 Lightfoot, *Journal*, pp. 11–13; Paul, *The assembly*, pp. 93–4.
81 *CJ*, III, p. 225, 242; Paul, *The assembly*, pp. 90–5.
82 *The Covenant with a narrative of the proceedings* (1646), p. 19.
83 *Foure speeches delivered at Guildhall* (1646), p. 19.
84 *A&O*, I, pp. 180–4.
85 Baillie, *L&J*, II, p. 20.
86 A succinct summary of what the 'orthodox' thought antinomians taught can be found in Thomas Bakewell, *A short view of the antinomian errors* (1643), frontispiece, verso. For historical discussions see T. D. Bozeman, *The precisianist strain: disciplinary religion and antinomian backlash in puritanism to 1638* (Chapel Hill, NC, 2004); Como, *Blown by the spirit*, p. 40, ch. 6; D. Parnham, 'The humbling of "high presumption": Tobias Crisp dismantles the puritan *ordo salutis*', *JEH*, 56:1 (2005), 50–74; R. J. McKelvey, '"That

error and pillar of antinomianism'": eternal justification' in *Drawn into controversie: Reformed theological diversity and debates within seventeenth-century puritanism*, eds A. G. Haykin and Mark Jones (Göttingen, 2011), pp. 223–62; W. Gamble, *Christ and the law: antinomianism and the Westminster assembly* (Grand Rapids, MI, 2018).

87 For a case study of these problems see van Dixhoorn, 'Strange silence of Prolocutor Twisse', pp. 395–418.

88 *CJ*, III, p. 201; *MPWA*, V, pp. 22–3.

89 *MPWA*, II, p. 122; the committee was composed of Edmund Calamy, Lazarus Seaman, Thomas Goodwin, Francis Cheynell, Thomas Gataker, Herbert Palmer, Charles Herle, Thomas Temple and Daniel Featley. See C. B. van Dixhoorn, 'Reforming the reformation: theological debate at the Westminster assembly, 1643–1652', 7 vols (Ph.D thesis, University of Cambridge, 2005), II, appendix A: 'John Lightfoot, "A briefe journal of passages in the assembly of divines", a transcript of CUL Dd.XIV.28.4 fos 1r–62v (1 July 1643 to 12 October 1643)', especially pp. 31–4, 38–9, 44, 53–4; Thomas Gataker, *Mysterious cloudes and mistes* (1648); Gamble, *Christ and the law*, pp. 56–84. I am very grateful to Professor Whitney Gamble for email discussions on this issue.

90 The report was ordered on 12 September 1643 and delivered on 23 September: *CJ*, III, pp. 237, 252; *MPWA*, V, p. 25; BL Add. Ms. 18778 (Walter Yonge's *Parliamentary Diary*, vol. 2) fos 39r, 53v (I am grateful to Christopher Thompson for letting me consult his careful transcript of this document). See also Paul, *The assembly*, pp. 83–4; J. Peacey, *Politicians and pamphleteers: propaganda during the English civil wars and interregnum* (2004), p. 149.

91 *MPWA*, II, pp. 145–8.

92 *CJ*, III, pp. 271–2; *MPWA*, V, p. 26; BL Add. Ms. 18778, fo. 62v.

93 Edwards, *Antapologia*, p. 242. Cotton's works published in 1642 were *A modest and cleare answer to Mr Balls discourse of set formes of prayer* (1642) and *The true constitution of a particular visible church, proved by Scripture* (1642).

94 Thomas Goodwin and others, *An apologetical narration* (1644), pp. 15–16; [Nathaniel Holmes?], *A coole conference* [1644], p. 10; [John Goodwin], *M S to A S* (1644), p. 25.

95 Samuel Rutherford, *A peaceable and temperate plea for Pauls presbyterie in Scotland* (1642), pp. 20–5.

96 Ibid., pp. 52–63.

97 *Jus divinum regiminis ecclesiastici*, p. 97. This book (and its authorship) are discussed in chapter 4, note 13.

98 'Gather' describes ministers or congregations setting up their own church meetings, without observing parish boundaries. *Mercurius aulicus* (9–16 April 1643), p. 184.

99 Coffey, *John Goodwin*, p. 105; J. Halcomb, 'A social history of congregational religious practice during the puritan revolution' (Ph.D thesis, University of Cambridge, 2009), pp. 28–32.

100 BL Sloane Ms. 922, fo. 140r.
101 Lightfoot, *Journal*, p. 50.
102 W. L., *The bramble berry* (1643); *Satisfaction concerning mixt communions* (1643). These tracts were answered in October by *Satisfaction concerning mixed communion unsatisfactory* (1643).
103 [Richard Mather], *Church-government and church covenant discussed* (1643).
104 Charles Herle, *The independency on scriptures of the independency of churches* (1643), pp. 4–5.
105 Welde, *An Answer to WR*, p. 63.
106 Simeon Ashe and William Rathband, *A letter of many ministers in old England* (1643), 'To the Reader', sig. A2.
107 James Cranford, *The tears of Ireland* (1642).
108 PA HL/PO/JO/10/1/54 (12 March 1641, petition of ministers including Edmund Calamy, Stephen Marshall, Lazarus Seaman, George Walker and Thomas Edwards, for a godly system of licensing).
109 Peacey, *Politicians and pamphleteers*, pp. 144, 148.
110 Ibid., pp. 149–50.
111 John Goodwin, *A quaere concerning the church covenant practiced in the separate congregations* (1643).
112 E. H. Pearce, *Sion College and library* (Cambridge, 1913) pp. 3, 7.
113 LMA CLC-198-SICA-008-MS33445-00 (Sion College court minute book), fos 66, 69; Pearce, *Sion College*, pp. 1–10.
114 John Goodwin, *Sion-colledg visited* (1648), p. 26.
115 *Mercurius aulicus* (17–23 September 1643), pp. 519–20.
116 Thomas Nutt, *To the right honourable [...] the house of Commons* (1643).
117 Thomas Nutt, *The humble request of certain Christians* (1643); S. Wright, *The early English baptists, 1603–1649* (Woodbridge, 2006) pp. 127, 164.
118 *MPWA*, II, pp. 341, 343.
119 Lightfoot, *Journal*, pp. 56–7; Baillie, *L&J*, II, p. 111; Edwards, *Antapologia*, pp. 5–6.
120 *CJ*, III, p. 281; *Mercurius aulicus* (15–21 October 1643), pp. 594–5.
121 *MPWA*, II, pp. 181, 282.
122 *MPWA*, II, pp. 289–90; Lightfoot, *Journal*, pp. 42, 46.
123 *MPWA*, II, p. 292; Lightfoot, *Journal*, pp. 42–6; Paul, *The assembly*, pp. 183–4; Coffey, *John Goodwin*, pp. 102–3.
124 *MPWA*, II, p. 371.
125 Lightfoot, *Journal*, p. 62; *MPWA*, II, pp. 361; B. Usher, 'Gouge, William', *ODNB*.
126 *MPWA*, V, pp. 27–8; Lightfoot, *Journal*, pp. 62, 66; *CJ*, III, p. 326; *LJ*, VI, p. 319.
127 Lightfoot, *Journal*, p. 61.
128 *MPWA*, II, p. 381; Lightfoot, *Journal*, p. 62.
129 R. C. Winthrop, *Life and letters of John Winthrop (1630–49)*, 2 vols (1867), II, p. 417.
130 Lightfoot, *Journal*, pp. 62–3.

131 Baillie, *L&J*, II, p. 118.
132 William Twisse and others, *Certaine considerations to diss-wade men from further gathering churches* (1643), p. 3; Bremer, *Congregational communion*, p. 137.
133 Baillie, *L&J*, II, p. 121.
134 Lightfoot, *Journal*, p. 92.
135 Halcomb, 'A social history of congregational religious practice', p. 33.
136 Lightfoot, *Journal*, p. 93.
137 Wright, *The early English baptists*, pp. 65–8, 124–6; C. Burrage, *The early English dissenters*, 2 vols (Cambridge, 1912), II, p. 304; Tolmie, *The triumph of the saints*, pp. 26–7, 67.
138 Lightfoot, *Journal*, p. 93; Baillie, *L&J*, II, p. 121; Mark Busher, *An exhortation unto the learned divines assembled at Westminster* (1643).
139 Baillie, *L&J*, II, p. 121; Lightfoot, *Journal*, p. 93; Paul, *The assembly*, pp. 191–2.

4

London presbyterians and the fracture of parliamentarianism, 1644–5

The events of 1644 would finally shatter the fragile godly alliance that had emerged at Aldermanbury in 1641. In January 1644, the publication of the congregationalists' *Apologeticall narration* made public debate on church government unavoidable. This debate ran alongside the majority in the Westminster assembly coalescing around a presbyterian position that stressed the independence of the church and the central role of collective presbyteries in ecclesiastical government. Working against the realisation of this presbyterianism, however, was the fracturing of the alliance of the Solemn League and Covenant, as 'war party' parliamentarians at Westminster and Scottish covenanters divided over the political and religious settlement of the three kingdoms. The Scots' insistence that they should share power with the English in any post-war settlement, the continuing problem of the organisation of the parliamentarian armies and the conflict over the nature of the future ecclesiastical settlement served to push the covenanters and their English war party allies apart. This political reconfiguration would recast the London presbyterians as religious partisans in the emerging, disjointed coalition that contemporaries and historians alike have termed the 'presbyterian party'.

This chapter explores the emergence of partisan religious presbyterianism in London during 1644. The first section explores the collapse of the Aldermanbury Accord in the aftermath of the publication of the *Apologeticall narration* in January 1644. The second section provides an analysis of the intellectual development of presbyterian church polity during the Westminster assembly and in the London presbyterians' published treatises. The final section investigates the position of the London presbyterian movement in the transformation of parliamentarian politics in the last months of 1644, as the Westminster 'war party' jettisoned its alliance with the Scottish covenanters. These developments would see the emergence in the later 1640s of political constellations of political 'presbyterian' and 'Independent' factions at Westminster, with the London presbyterian movement representing an organised 'Scotified' interest within English parliamentarian politics.

The *Apologeticall narration* and the end of the Aldermanbury Accord

The *Apologeticall narration*, published by the leading congregationalists in the Westminster assembly around 3 January 1644, was an intentionally equivocal pamphlet. Its authors sought to keep open the possibility of accommodation with their presbyterian brethren, while defending themselves against the threat that their voices might be drowned out by the presbyterians' supremacy within the assembly.[1] The *Apologeticall narration* has long been seen as one of the critical documents in making public the inexorable divisions between Independents and presbyterians. William Hetherington saw the *narration* as acting 'instantaneously like a declaration of war' which prevented 'the probability of an amicable arrangement' within parliamentarian puritanism. For Hetherington, the document left in its wake an 'irreconcilable rivalry' between presbyterians and Independents.[2] On the other hand, the Anglo-American liberal tradition, exemplified by W. K. Jordan, saw the *narration* as heralding the principal of toleration in English political culture against the pre-modern bigotry of the presbyterians.[3] Such interpretations have been criticised, particularly by Avihu Zakai and Hunter Powell, who both see the *narration* as essentially an attempt to reconcile with presbyterians while retaining a distinctive 'middle way' congregationalist position.[4]

The date of the *Apologeticall narration*'s publication reflected a timely choice by its authors.[5] As we have seen, during 1643 presbyterian feeling had hardened against gathered churches, and the assembly was soon to turn its attention to the question of church government. This made it imperative for the congregationalists to show their nearness to the presbyterians and stress that they were not separatists.[6] As Zakai notes, these aspects of the *narration* disappointed William Walwyn, the London war party activist and future Leveller, who considered it to be 'a remonstrance of the nearness between them and the presbyterians'.[7] In addition, the *narration* stressed that the 'toleration' sought by its authors was limited in scope, being only for a 'latitude to some lesser differences' if accommodation could not be reached on church government in the assembly.[8]

There was, nevertheless, much in the *Apologeticall narration* to upset presbyterians. Presbyterian church government was criticised for failing to advance 'the power of godliness and the profession thereof' in the people.[9] The presbyterian arguments for synodic authority were censured as being based on the unscriptural 'additiment' of human reason.[10] Finally, the *narration* appealed to the widespread aversion against presbyterian clericalism in English political culture. An example of this can be found in comments made in 1643 by the Earl of Northumberland, who feared that presbyterianism put the clergy 'above all humaine laws, law-makers, and Parliam[en]ts', and who claimed that clericalist demands to control the power of excommunication was the 'rod by w[hi]ch the ecclesiastical gover[n]m[en]t is by Clergie men [...] kept up'.[11] Pandering to this sentiment, the *Apologeticall narration* declared that the congregational way gave 'as much, and (as we think) more [to the magistrates' power], than the principles of the presbyterial government will suffer them to yield'.[12] It is unsurprising, therefore, that the document left many presbyterians smarting.

Despite these barbs, the *narration* was licensed and introduced by the prominent presbyterian minister Charles Herle and even 'rigid' presbyterians later accepted that it distinguished the authors from the separatists.[13] Presbyterians were thus divided over how to take the *narration*. Herle told the assembly that he had licensed it to free its authors from the charge of 'anabaptism'.[14] It was later reported that Herle had 'incurred the odium of some of his hotter brethren' for this act of licensing.[15]

According to Robert Baillie, the Scottish commissioners' initial reaction to the *Apologeticall narration* was to consider it an attack on 'all the Reformed churches, as imperfyte' and a 'slie and cunning' plea to Parliament to obtain toleration.[16] Despite Baillie's privately expressed opinion, the Scottish delegates' response, *Reformation of church government in Scotland cleered from mistakes*, was couched in an irenic register.[17] The stated aim of the Scots' reply was to 'unite and not to divide' and to provide 'a simple and innocent manifestation and defence' of Scottish presbyterianism.[18] The Scottish commissioners argued that, contrary to the *narration*'s charge that the Reformed churches were based on the 'additiment' of human reason, church government had evolved in the apostolic period as the needs of the church had expanded. At the height of the apostolic age, the church had settled on a presbyterian model of polity, more fitted to national reformation than the protean congregations of the earliest church foundations.[19]

Alongside this official conciliatory path, the 'hotter' sort of presbyterians in London used the *Apologeticall narration* to escalate the propaganda battle against Independency.[20] In the six months after the publication of the *narration*, four presbyterian authors penned pamphlet responses. The two English respondents, William Rathband and Thomas Edwards, had long been suspicious of the congregational way as a Trojan horse for separatist ideas.[21] Rathband and Edwards were joined by two Scottish interlopers. The first and most incendiary was Adam Steuart, a 'sawcey-turbulent spirit' who had formerly been professor at the protestant academy of Saumur. Finding himself temporarily in London in 1644 before taking the chair of physics at the University of Leiden, Steuart was quick to join the fray.[22]

Steuart was joined in this venture by a Mr Forbes of Delft, who published a tract narrating the scandals in Sydrach Simpson's gathered church in the late 1630s.[23] Behind the publication of these works was the London presbyterian propaganda machine that had emerged in 1643 with James Cranford acting as licenser for most of the works, and the presbyterian stationers John Bellamie, Robert Bostock, Christopher Meredith and Ralph Smith bringing the works to print.

The *Apologeticall narration*'s boast that the congregationalists 'give as much, and (as we think) more' power to the magistrate in matters of church discipline as the presbyterians was particularly offensive to these polemicists. Thomas Edwards wrote that this comment was 'an odious and dangerous insinuation to prepare King and Parliament to reject the presbyterie'.[24] For Edwards, the strategy behind the *Apologeticall narration* was to obtain for congregationalism the same kind of private toleration that the Arminian Remonstrants had obtained in the Netherlands.[25] Against the charge that presbyterianism rejected the power of the magistrate in the sphere of religion, Edwards argued that the civil magistrate had a 'coercive and coactive power' complimenting the decisions of synods to suppress heresy and error.[26] In addition, both Edwards and Steuart accused the congregationalists of conceding to the civil magistrate ecclesiastical power that was 'intrinsecall to the Church'. In a foretaste of the debates that would erupt between the presbyterians and Parliament a year later, Steuart warned that the congregationalists 'symbolize with *Erastus* in many things' in their position on church and state.[27]

The dispute over the *narration* finally ended the 1641 agreement between the presbyterian and Independent clergy to remain publicly silent over controversies concerning church polity.[28] Thomas Edwards averred in July that a meeting had recently taken place in London at which 'it was openly declared by a full assembly [that] the agreement was broken, and I declared I would be at freedome, and some of them [i.e. the Independents] said the like'.[29] The collapse of the Aldermanbury Accord allowed the more militant London presbyterians to pioneer the use of printed propaganda in their campaign to publicly undermine their opponents. The London ministers seized the polemical high ground by funding a lecture at Christ Church, Newgate for Edwards to preach against heresy and schism.[30] This acted to fan the flames of division as, according to Hezekiah Woodward, 'all the City and Parliament' was shocked by the *ad hominem* methodology deployed by Edwards in *Antapologia*.[31]

Alongside Edwards's pulpit polemics, James Cranford and his coterie of publishers stepped up the technique of printing semi-private correspondence to embarrass opponents. Cranford had been instrumental in scoring a propaganda victory in late 1643 by licensing the embarrassing 1638 letter from John Goodwin to Thomas Goodwin criticising the latter's congregationalism. This was followed up in February 1644 when Cranford licensed and Ralph Smith published a letter from the New England minister Thomas Parker to his brother-in-law, the assembly member Thomas Bayley.[32] Parker, the son of the leading nonconformist ecclesiologist Robert Parker, criticised New England congregationalism for allowing suffrage to the people in decision-making, advising Bayley that 'the ordinary exercise of government must be [...] in the presbyters'.[33] A further letter, by Nathaniel Rogers, sometime minister of Ipswich, Massachusetts, was published in July 1644 by the presbyterian publisher Christopher Meredith, with Edmund Calamy's *imprimatur*. Rogers' letter called for speed in church reformation in England and repentance for previous conformity, and supported the Solemn League and Covenant.[34]

Dan Beaver has argued that print polemic was critical in creating and sustaining the 'symbolic boundaries' by which civil war factional 'communities' were constructed.[35] The replies and rejoinders that often accumulated in 1640s printed debates often served to intensify the demarcation between individuals and groups. The pamphlet debate over the *Apologeticall narration* established much of the lexicon of intra-parliamentarian religious partisanship for the remainder of the 1640s and 1650s. Hetherington's description of the *Apologeticall narration* acting as a 'declaration of war' finds a contemporary resonance in the pro-tolerationist city merchant Henry Robinson's November 1644 description of the debate over the *narration* as a 'clergie-warr'.[36] In defending the *narration*, works such as John Goodwin's *A S to M S* went beyond the *narration*'s notion of a godly forbearance for lesser differences into the fully developed language of liberty of conscience.[37] The debate would see Independents increasingly begin to deploy arguments that classical presbyterian government was just as tyrannical as diocesan episcopacy. Nathaniel Holmes, for example, commented that 'a presbytery is a bishop diffused'.[38] John Goodwin, in particular, began to deploy the early-1640s anti-episcopal language of malignancy against the presbyterian reformers in the assembly.[39] It is clear that this deployment of language formerly used against episcopacy had the effect of blackening the godly credentials of the presbyterian movement. In 1646 the London presbyterian minister George Walker, one of Goodwin's oldest adversaries, complained that 'cunning seducers' had represented 'presbyterian government as a bugbear, and a cruell monster, worse than popery and prelacy, unto which if you submit, you and your children are made slaves forever, to the lusts of proud, peevish, tyrannicall priests'.[40]

The effect of the escalation of printed disputation was to publicly split and demarcate those once regarded as brethren into rhetorically defined religious and political camps.[41] Yet, while the *Apologeticall narration* would trigger open hostilities in public, in 1644 both presbyterians and Independents were still attempting in the relative privacy of the Westminster assembly to find means to accommodate each other's positions. In early 1644 there was still a hope that the Westminster assembly would find an acceptable accommodation, but the development of the assembly's high presbyterian position over 1644 would all but end that expectation.

The Westminster assembly, the London ministers and the development of presbyterian church polity

This section will explore the system of presbyterian church polity as developed by the Westminster assembly and the London presbyterians between 1643 and 1654. Given the existence of competing ecclesiologies and the mid-1640s 'Erastian' debate over the respective powers of church and state, the focus of much of this work was defining the respective rights or power ('*jus*') of the church, the ministry, believers and the civil state.[42]

In February 1644 the majority in the Westminster assembly had unified around three propositions on church government. The first and second propositions, that the New Testament 'holden forth' a presbytery to govern a church and that the presbytery consisted of 'pastors and other church officers', caused no debate with the congregationalists. The assembly's third proposition, that 'many particular congregations may be under one presbyterial government', was immediately controversial. The congregationalist Thomas Goodwin later complained that the 'indeterminate ambiguity' of the words '*may be*' abandoned the search for a scriptural rule and replaced it with 'the greatest latitude and compass' designed to satisfy all parties to the debate.[43] Richard Vines admitted as much, stating that the third proposition had been purposefully drafted to build consensus within the assembly. He said that 'may be' rather than 'must be' had been inserted in the hope that 'each side' may 'bear with [the] other'.[44] Vines suggests that the third proposition's ambiguity was drafted with the intent of accommodating the congregationalists, although this irenicism backfired as the wording potentially undermined the congregationalists' stress on the local gathered church as the primary and normative unit of church government.

The 'third proposition' embodied the concern of the majority in the assembly to preserve the credal unity and catholicity of the church and to oppose the atomising consequences of congregationalism. As we have seen in previous chapters, Elizabethan presbyterian and early Stuart nonconformist thought had tended to view ecclesiastical polity on the basis of an ascending model, beginning with the congregation as the primary unit of church polity.[45] This position had been the assumption behind Smectymnuus's first 1641 tract and had important advocates in the Westminster assembly. For example, Charles Herle had argued for an ascending model of presbyterian government based on the distinction (derived from the French jurist Jean Bodin) between officer and commissioner.[46] Herle argued that a minister was instituted as an officer over his own congregation, but was warranted as a commissioner representing that congregation in higher assemblies. On Herle's analysis, the power of classical presbyteries and synods therefore derived from the combined commissions of particular congregations.[47] Contrary to the assembly's congregationalists, who argued that church power could only be exercised with the common consent of the members of each congregational church, presbyterians such as Herle argued that officers of specific churches, through their commissions, could act authoritatively in wider assemblies as representatives of their particular churches.

A growing number of presbyterians inside and outside the assembly were prepared to break with the idea that 'the church' was primarily to be found in the individual congregation. Instead, their focus was on the oneness and catholicity of the church as the structuring principle of church polity, holding that 'there is one generall Church of Christ on earth, and that all particular Churches and single Congregations are but as similar parts of the whole'. As the Suffolk presbyterian ecclesiologist Samuel Hudson later noted, this stance would become the main position among the London presbyterian ministers.[48] This viewpoint had originated as a minority opinion in the Westminster assembly, most forcefully put by the London minister Lazarus Seaman. He had maintained that the unity and catholicity of the church as the mediatorial kingdom of Christ meant that single congregations could never be 'entire' if they failed to associate with their neighbour congregations.[49] This idea was fully explored in print by Samuel Hudson who, using an Aristotelian distinction, argued that while the catholic visible church was not an actual political church, as Roman Catholics argued, it still existed 'habitually' by the presence of the totality of visible believers professing the same faith and having the same covenantal seals of baptism and the Lord's supper.[50] It was this church that was the primary object of the keys of doctrine and discipline as it was the only emanation of 'the church' that, in the words of in Matthew 16, would prevail against the gates of Hades.[51] Individual congregations, along with classes and synods, were all branches issuing from the original ecclesiastical root of the general visible church founded by Christ.[52] Particular congregational assemblies, therefore, were not primary manifestations of 'the church', as they could fall away or dissolve, but were branches of one general visible church.[53]

It followed from this argument that a congregation's officers derived the power to use the keys from their ordination into the catholic, visible church and not from the gathering of believers for worship nor from the taking of a congregational covenant.[54] This point would be made forcibly by John Wallis, the mathematician and, in the 1640s, the London presbyterian minister of St Gabriel, Fenchurch, in his 1654 Oxford doctoral thesis. Wallis denied the proposition that 'the power of a gospel minister extends to the members of only one particular church', much to the chagrin of John Owen, Oxford's congregationalist Vice-Chancellor.[55] The development of this presbyterian position was significant in that it achieved the ecclesiological aims of preserving credal unity and catholicity, while justifying both the parity and authority of church officers. It justified an anti-prelatical stance to church polity while avoiding the potentially dissipative effects that resulted from the view that each particular congregational assembly was a primary church unit.

The desire to preserve the unity of the church against the growth of separatist arguments meant that the 'third proposition' gained acceptance from the assembly's majority.[56] Despite the protests of the congregationalists, the majority found scriptural proof for the proposition from the example of the apostolic-era church of Jerusalem. The presbyterians argued that the Jerusalem church had grown rapidly from the 120 disciples mentioned in Acts 1:15 to the multitude in Acts 6, a growth which required the apostles to institute the election of seven deacons for the better care of the faithful. It was argued that the multitude of believers in the early Jerusalem church could not practically meet in one place and thus worshipped in various house congregations existing in Jerusalem.[57] Despite such exponential growth the church of Jerusalem continued to be referred to as a single church, not a collection of separate congregational assemblies. Drawing on the gathering of apostles and elders in Acts 15:6 to determine the extent to which gentiles should follow Jewish purity requirements, the majority in the assembly concluded that the church of Jerusalem provided scriptural proof for the 'third proposition'.[58] The assembly's argument was expanded by the London presbyterians, who found the pattern of consistorial rule over multiple congregations in the biblical churches of Ephesus, Antioch, Galatia, Philippi and Corinth.[59]

The stress on the warrant of divine right and the manner by which that right operated in the church looked to theological discussions as to who wielded 'the power of the keys', understood from the scriptural constellation of Matthew 16, Matthew 18 and John 20 and 21. Medieval and early modern theology had, with some variation, divided the keys between the keys of order and of jurisdiction, explaining how 'the church' (variously understood) had the jurisdiction to declare in doctrinal matters and excommunicate unrepentant sinners.[60] The assembly debated the issue of the keys in late October 1643, just prior to the Scots joining it.[61] The discussion began as part of a discussion of the nature and power of the apostles in the New Testament church. On 27 October 1643 Lazarus Seaman introduced the proposition 'that the apostells did immediately receive the keyes from the hand of Jesus Christ and did use and exercise them in all churches of the world on all occasions'.[62] This proposition had a respectable pedigree in Reformed thought and was largely uncontentious to the extent that it applied to the apostles as apostles. However, as has been seen earlier, it was not the only interpretation of Matthew 16, with an alternative reading seeing Peter as a representative of all confessing believers.[63] The congregationalist delegates saw in Seaman's proposition a trap for their own position. If Peter had received the keys from Jesus as the representative of the apostles, it was only a short step for presbyterians to assert that the keys were held in the post-apostolic age by the ordained clergy as the successors to the apostles. Indeed, both Seaman and Cornelius Burges revealed that this was the thinking behind the proposition, with Burges declaring 'Peter, as is generally held, represents the pastors'.[64]

The Westminster assembly debate on the power of the keys ended inconclusively, however. It fell to the London presbyterian ministers to flesh out Seaman's initial contentions in their various treatises published after the assembly's debate on the matter had ended. The London presbyterian position was that presbyters, as the successors to the apostles, were the only persons designated by Christ to wield the keys to the kingdom of heaven. This was most clearly seen in the office of preaching. The London Provincial assembly asserted that as God had 'not revealed any other way in Scripture' to 'call home his elect' than by the preaching of the Word 'the Ministry is perpetually necessary to bring in and build up those that belong' to the body of Christ.[65] Consistent with the position that the power of the keys descended from Christ to the universal visible church, rather than upwards from the individual congregation, the London authors of *Jus divinum regiminis ecclesiastici*, one of the leading presbyterian works on the location of power in the church, maintained that, as the apostles had received the keys from Christ before the church had come into existence, the power of the keys had passed through the apostles to the regular ministry.[66] The London ministers made the argument that the apostles and their presbyter successors were therefore the *subject* of Christ's donation of church power and the visible church was the *object* to which this power should be applied.[67] The ordained ministry was Christ's gift to the church with each minister holding a 'double relation' to it, being 'primarily seated in the Church generall visible' and 'secondarily' as a pastor of a particular congregation.[68]

The office of ruling elder was a contentious addition in the projected parliamentarian reformation of the Church of England. One historian has noted the 'considerable lack of detail' as to the function of the ruling elder in the parliamentary ordinances of the mid-to-late-1640s, as well as a 'notable' lack of definition as to where the ruling elder sat on the lay/ecclesiastical spectrum.[69] The debate on the scriptural warrant for the ruling elder took place in the assembly between November and December 1643. Those speaking in favour of the ruling elder as a church officer included Matthew Newcomen and Charles Herle as well as the London presbyterians Edmund Calamy, Lazarus Seaman and George Walker.[70] The debate ended in a stalemate when the future 'Erastian' minister Thomas Coleman brokered a compromise whereby the office of ruling elder was agreed to be 'agreeable and warranted by the word of God' but not essential by divine right.[71]

The London presbyterian theorists outside the Westminster assembly rejected its 'prudential' formulation and issued a strenuous defence of the office of ruling elder as a scripturally warranted ecclesiastical office.[72] For this reason, the London Provincial assembly rejected the term 'lay elder' as a misnomer since those who were elected to the office (which, in London at least, was for life) 'are no longer lay-men, but ecclesiastical persons'.[73] The justification for the office of ruling elder was culled from references to elders who ruled or governed the congregations in Romans 12:6–8, Hebrews 13:24, 1 Corinthians 12:28 and 1 Timothy 5:17.[74] In practice, a ruling elder was meant to assist the ministers (whose office, according to 1 Timothy 5:17, also included ruling) in examining members of the congregation for worthiness to attend the Lord's supper, catechising the young and investigating immoral activity by parishioners such as drinking in taverns on the Lord's day.[75] As such the ruling elder was seen to blend the functions of the parish churchwarden and the officials of the old ecclesiastical courts, albeit without the power to inflict physical punishments or order the payment of fines.[76] The assembly's consideration of the office of ruling elder therefore revealed a deeply clericalist desire among some delegates to protect the authority of the ordained parish ministry from encroachment by the laity, but also the increasing penetration of 'high' presbyterian ideas.[77]

The stress on the parish presbytery made up of ministers and ruling elders holding the power of the keys was also fuelled by the presbyterians' desire to protect the authority of the ordained ministry from separatist arguments for parochial democracy. The London presbyterian ministers argued that a consequence of the ordained ministry being the subject of the keys was that the members of a congregation held little or no formal ecclesiastical power.[78] This satisfied one of the primary desires of the presbyterians, which was to lock out the separatist argument that the ministry derived its authority from the people as their agents or representatives. Following a long tradition dating back at least to Thomas Cartwright, the London presbyterians argued that scriptural references to 'the church' exercising the power of the keys (as in Matthew 18) was a reference to the 'ruling church' or the 'political church', that is, the consistory of elders, and not the body of believers in general.[79] Nevertheless, the London presbyterians accepted that in most cases the members of a congregation should have the ability to elect their pastors, although there was a disagreement as to whether this amounted to a 'right' of election. In the assembly debates, the Scottish minister George Gillespie had argued that the members did, indeed, hold such a right. Lazarus Seaman disagreed, arguing that the members' election of their minister amounted only to 'a measure of liberty'.[80] The London presbyterian theorists, following Seaman's argument, argued that the popular election of ministers was a 'circumstantial' matter of church government, which, while desirable, was not a formal part of church government. The authors of *Jus divinum regiminis ecclesiastici* stated that the congregation's election of a minister was generally to be observed as it laid 'a foundation of love between pastor and people'.[81] However, such election was to be seen as a privilege that should only be afforded by the presbytery to a congregation if the congregation was 'constituted and well-ordered in truth, godliness and peaceableness'.[82] Lazarus Seaman argued that even in the earliest years of the church the people had often preferred false teachers to true apostles. Therefore, candidates for the position of a pastor should first be examined and approved by the local classis before being deemed eligible for election by a congregation.[83] The London Provincial assembly considered that those congregations dominated by profane, factious or heretical parishioners ought to have their ministerial candidates chosen for them by the local classis until the congregation was sufficiently godly and united to be trusted with the privilege of election. Likewise, a classis or synod had the power to annul the election of a doctrinally unsound minister and regulate new elections by choosing a panel of candidates for the peoples' choice.[84]

Although governance of the church by clergy and ruling elders was central to presbyterian church order, the presbyterians were keen to impress that presbyterianism was not oppressive. The London Provincial assembly complained that their opponents had represented the system as 'lordly [and] domineering' as well as 'tyrannical and cruel' and had spread the view that that presbyterianism replaced a diocesan bishop with hundreds of 'parish popes'.[85] In response to such accusations George Walker stressed that the power wielded by the ministry under presbyterianism was akin to that of a steward's benign management of a household.[86] In addition, the presbyterians declared that they made no claim to any of the financial or physical penalties that the episcopate had formerly inflicted on the people through the church courts.[87] Unlike the old prelacy, which Matthew Poole likened to 'government by forreigners', the members' election of their ruling elders and, where appropriate, their pastor, meant that presbyterian churches offered a form of government that matched Polybian ideals of a mixed constitution in the civil state. For this reason, the presbyterians argued that their system was a perfect 'spiritual republic' being composed of the monarchy of Christ, the aristocratic senate of the clergy and the members' representatives through their elected elders.[88] Even if the members of the congregation held no formal church power, some London presbyterians argued that, as a matter of practice, a local presbytery should not act to excommunicate a member without the consent of the whole congregation.[89] In distinction from the oligarchic or populist rule of gathered churches, the classis acted as a 'pillar to uphold and support congregational government' preventing the congregational eldership from abusing their power over the congregation.[90]

The London presbyterians therefore saw the congregational presbytery under the supervision of the local classis as the normative model on which the church would function. The oft-repeated view, first advanced by Alexander Gordon, that English presbyterians held that the individual congregation was the primary body of church government, is therefore untenable, at least with regard to the Westminster assembly and the London presbyterians of the mid-seventeenth century.[91] Beyond these local emanations of the church were synods. These were theorised as meeting relatively irregularly and served, like the assembly in Acts 15, to declare on wider controversies of faith, pronounce against heresies and preserve doctrinal orthodoxy.[92] Synods were also to act as appellate tribunals in matters of church censure and excommunication.[93] The London minsters held that the authority of synods derived from the unity and universality of the general visible church, which was best represented by conciliar decisions made in church assemblies covering a wide number of individual congregations.[94]

In viewing the power of synods as deriving from the general visible church, the London presbyterians' treatises rejected the 'ascending theory' position that saw synods as deriving their power from the commission of individual congregations. Hunter Powell has argued that this model of presbyterian polity advanced by the London ministers was 'unique in the reformed orthodox tradition' for its avoidance of granting any right in church polity to the members of a particular congregation.[95] However, Powell somewhat overstates the case for the uniqueness of this position. Some Scottish presbyterians, for example David Calderwood, made similar arguments to Lazarus Seaman and the London ministers.[96] Likewise, the sixteenth-century French Reformed theologian Antoine de Chandieu, in his controversy with the French 'congregationalist' Jean Morély, had argued that church power resided by divine right in the consistory of church officers.[97] Nevertheless, as critics at the time noted, the London presbyterians' development of the Westminster assembly's model of church polity set out a 'high', even clericalist, presbyterian position, albeit one tempered by a stress on locality. While the clericalism of the London presbyterians' position on polity could accommodate those ministers who leaned towards a reformed episcopacy, in many respects it moved away from the direction in which the 'brethren of the congregational-way' were heading. These differences would become most apparent in the debates of Parliament's committee for accommodation, a body meeting from September 1644.

The reconfiguration of parliamentarian politics and the failure of accommodation

The end of 1644 marked a turning point in the parliamentarian politics of religion. The jettisoning of the Scottish alliance by the 'war party' group around Viscount Saye and Sele and Sir Henry Vane Jr at Westminster led to the divine right pretensions of the Westminster assembly's presbyterianism being reined in by Parliament.[98] The Scots, smarting from their rejection by their former allies, found themselves chasing *rapprochement* with the Earl of Essex and his old 'peace party' advisers.[99] The London presbyterian clergy would follow their Scottish brethren towards Essex's party. This was a natural move as the London ministers' closest English patrons, particularly the Earls of Warwick and Manchester, were also emerging as prominent figures in Essex's new coalition.[100] In terms of religion, although accommodation remained a desired goal, by the closing months of 1644 the hope of godly unity had all but disappeared. The public debate sparked off by the *Apologeticall narration* and the divisions in the Westminster assembly had opened up the public gulf that the parliamentarian clergy had hoped to avoid.[101] By the end of the year the perceived elision of the factional struggles at Westminster with the politics of religion in London and the provinces would see the religious terms 'presbyterian' and 'Independent' emerge as labels for new parliamentarian political coalitions.

The opening of the breach with the Saye-Vane group emerged most clearly for the Scots and the London presbyterian ministers as a result of Parliament's debate over the assembly's directory for ordination in September 1644.[102] This directory had been completed in April 1644, but it had gathered dust until it was debated in late August.[103] The Commons removed from it a statement that ordination was an 'ordinance of Christ' and rejected an exhortation to be given to the congregation that their minister was set 'over them in the Lord'. The assembly protested these changes, but on 8 September the Commons rejected the assembly's request to reinsert the offending passages.[104] Parliament's decision was communicated that evening to the Scots and some English Westminster assembly members at a meeting at Worcester House by Sir Henry Vane Jr and Oliver St John. The Worcester House meeting revealed the gap that had opened up between the

Scots and their former political allies over the future religious settlement.[105] At the conference the penny dropped for Edmund Calamy, who complained to the assembly the next day that 'when these things are opposed, what hopes are there of carrying the whole government and directory?'[106]

Parliament's rejection of these passages in the directory for ordination was soon followed by an attempt by the Saye-Vane group to circumvent the Westminster assembly entirely. On 13 September Oliver St John obtained an order from the Commons for a grand committee to attempt to find an accommodation between the presbyterians and the congregationalists.[107] Robert Baillie saw this committee as being instigated by Oliver Cromwell, who Baillie believed to be working in collusion with St John, Vane and Stephen Marshall.[108] Ominously, the committee was 'to endeavour the finding out some ways how far tender consciences [...] may be borne with' if accommodation could not be reached.[109]

Parliament's committee for accommodation, which met in the third week of September, initially hoped to avoid the issue of outright toleration. At the instigation of the MPs Zouche Tate and Oliver St John, a sub-committee of six ministers was asked to set out the practical differences between the presbyterian and congregationalists in the assembly.[110] The congregationalists stated that they were clear that the parties to the accommodation could 'jointly agree in one confession of faith, and in one directory of publick worship'. However, their demand that the majority of adult men in a congregation should have a 'power of negative voice' over the decisions of the eldership had become an immovable block to compromise. In addition, the presbyterians wanted to know the extent to which the congregationalists would expect any future forbearance to extend to outright separatist and 'anabaptist' congregations.[111]

With these *impasses* in mind, Saye and Sele and Vane attempted to transform the committee by seeking to establish that its recommendations would go directly to Parliament, thus circumventing the presbyterian dominance of the Westminster assembly.[112] This manoeuvre was successfully resisted by the Scots who were assisted by the religious-presbyterian-leaning MPs Zouche Tate and Francis Rous. The committee also agreed that no forbearance in matters of church practice would be established until the assembly had presented its advice on church government to Parliament.[113] This victory came late in the day for the Scots, who had initially been outplayed by Saye and Sele and Vane. The revival of Scottish fortunes appears to be linked to the renewal of Scottish political credibility after their seizure of Newcastle on 19 October. This victory effectively allowed the Scots to force a general adjournment of the committee.[114]

With the failure of the committee for accommodation, the congregationalists were progressively locked out of the assembly's debates on church government. They would enter their formal dissents against the assembly's presbyterian platform of church government on 15 November 1644, essentially ending their involvement with the assembly on questions of church polity. The presbyterian victory was finally sealed on 7 July 1645 when Stephen Marshall presented the assembly's advice to Parliament to adopt a presbyterian form of church government.[115] The presbyterians' victory was ultimately a pyrrhic one, however, as the working-out of the respective platforms of church government had shattered the irenic spirit pioneered at Aldermanbury in 1641. In any event, the triumph of the assembly's presbyterians was soon dwarfed by the seismic shifts in parliamentarian politics in 1645.

Although the London ministers would ultimately become associated with the political party of the Earl of Essex, their shift towards this political alliance was largely predicated on the collapse of the Scottish alliance with the Saye-Vane group. As we have seen, the presbyterian ministers had played an important role in making the arguments both for Parliament's 'defensive' war and for the parliamentarian vision of a constitutionalist political settlement. Nevertheless, the disputes and developments of 1644 saw the London presbyterians increasingly wedded to the Scots' vision of covenanted uniformity for the three kingdoms. Also, the London ministers were generally unwilling to accept a church settlement that allowed liberty for churches fully separated from the national church.[116] It is therefore unsurprising that one of the leading themes of the presbyterians' public sermons and published output during the winter of 1644–5 was the danger of toleration. In a sermon before the House of Commons on 25 September 1644, Lazarus Seaman linked sectary demands for liberty of conscience with a design for toleration of popery.[117] A closely related theme was the obligation of parliamentarians to remain committed to the terms of the Solemn League and Covenant.[118]

The themes of anti-toleration and presbyterian uniformity naturally cast the London presbyterian preachers as the allies of the Scots in the political transformation of late 1644. However, in late 1644 and early 1645 the London presbyterians demonstrated a degree of ambivalence and ambiguity in relation to the emerging political 'presbyterian' and 'Independent' parties at Westminster. The ministers bemoaned the open divisions in the parliamentarian camp. Reflecting on rumours of secret political deals with royalists, most probably originating from Zouche Tate's accusation that Essex's colonels Boteler, Dalbier and Aldridge had been negotiating with the royalist Lord Mohun, Edmund Calamy told the Commons in a sermon on 22 October 1644 that it was MPs' duty to seek the 'publique good' and not to pursue personal or party ends. He counselled his audience to 'search and try your wayes. And if there should be found any amongst you, that drive the designes of Oxford, and that present at Westminster, onely to betray their countrey, the Lord unmaske such, and the Lord give them repenting hearts.'[119]

The theme of parliamentarian division had been expressed in a discussion in the relative privacy of the Westminster assembly on 9 September, after news had been delivered of Essex's military humiliation at the battle of Lostwithiel a week earlier. Charles Herle noted that many MPs had been distracted by the opportunity for profit and that political power had shifted away from Parliament to committees controlled by faction.[120] In military affairs, Calamy identified the dispute between Cromwell and Crawford as the root of the autumn paralysis of Manchester's Eastern Association army. However, the deepest criticism was reserved for the Earl of Essex who, Herle said, had taught his army 'to think that this war is only defensive, and that they may not assault'. Herle added that 'the war is offensive against those who guard and strengthen themselves against the justice of the state'.[121]

This picture of the London presbyterian ministers still wedded to such 'war party' positions can be seen from their hostile public statements concerning the forthcoming Uxbridge peace negotiations in early 1645.[122] Obadiah Sedgwick preached to the Commons on 22 October 1644 that Parliament would be acquitted before God for refusing the treaty if the king denied Parliament's terms.[123] In separate works, John Vicars and Christopher Love, the latter then chaplain to John Venn's garrison at Windsor Castle, invoked the story of the Trojan horse and the 1572 St Bartholomew's Day massacre in Paris as warnings against making treaties with untrustworthy opponents.[124] Vicars warned against trusting the 'atheisticall crew of impious Oxonian malignants' and counselled parliamentarians to 'put no confidence in popishly affected princes or Machivilianly principled courtiers'.[125] Love, in a sermon preached at Uxbridge on the first day of the negotiations, counselled that the leading royalist advisers to the king should be brought to capital justice before any treaty could be successful. He told the citizens of Uxbridge 'there are many malignant humours to be purged out of many of the nobles and gentry in this kingdome, before we can be healed' and that 'the Lord heals a land by cutting off these distempered members'. For Love, the true ends of Parliament's war were to fight popery, absolutism, monopolies and illegal taxation and to replace these malignancies with an orthodox Reformed confession, a mixed civil constitution and 'just law and native privilege'.[126]

The ministers' private criticism of the personal failings of Essex and their public counsel against the Uxbridge treaty illustrate that the London presbyterians had retained much of the 'war party' spirit shown in 1642–3. Nevertheless, their preaching against the power of committees appears largely as criticism of the political machinery being developed by the Saye-Vane group at Westminster.[127] Despite expressing criticism of Essex after his defeat in Cornwall, the London presbyterian ministers continued to hold the Earl in high honour as one of the leading peers of the godly interest. They were also deeply and increasingly entwined with the religious ambitions of the Scottish covenanters. After the collapse of the Uxbridge negotiations, the London presbyterians increasingly followed the covenanters' *rapprochement* with Essex and his faction at Westminster despite their previous 'war party' inclinations.

Conclusion

By the end of 1644 the acrimonious dispute over the *Apologeticall narration* and the development in the Westminster assembly of a high presbyterian platform of church government had left the fragile godly alliance of 1641 all but shattered. With the threat of Parliament granting both an undefined toleration and state domination of the church, the London presbyterian ministers realised that their goals were best served by joining the Scots in the political alliance coalescing around the Earl of Essex. Within this emerging 'political presbyterian' alliance, the London ministers and their Scottish co-religionists demanded that the establishment of presbyterian church polity in the three kingdoms remain an immovable condition of any settlement with the king. In these demands the London presbyterian ministers were joined by a handful of members of the House of Commons for whom a presbyterian religious settlement was a major goal of any future peace settlement.[128] The necessity, particularly after the new modelling of the English army, of retaining the support of the Scots and their army, as well as that of the city of London, would force Essex and his close allies to pay at least lip service to the demands of the 'covenanted interest'. The London presbyterians would become, as Valerie Pearl has put it, a Scottish 'fifth column' within the political and religious wrangling of the mid- to late-1640s.[129] It is to these events that this book will now turn.

Notes

1 Thomas Goodwin, Philip Nye, Jeremiah Burroughes, Sydrach Sympson and William Bridge, *An apologeticall narration* (1644). George Thomason dated his copy of the tract to 3 January 1644 and *Mercurius Britannicus* No. 20 (4–11 January 1644) reported the *Apologeticall narration* as coming out in the week 4–11 January 1644 (p. 159).

2 W. M. Hetherington, *History of the Westminster assembly of divines* (New York, 1843), pp. 163, 157; Paul, *The assembly*, p. 208.
3 W. K. Jordan, *The development of religious toleration*, 4 vols (Cambridge, MA, 1932–40), III, pp. 369–70; J. Coffey, 'The toleration controversy in the English revolution' in *Religion in revolutionary England*, eds C. Durston and J. Maltby (Manchester, 2006), p. 46.
4 A. Zakai, 'Religious toleration and its enemies: the independent divines and the issue of toleration during the English civil war', *Albion*, 21:1 (1989), 1–33; Powell, *Crisis*, ch. 4; Coffey, 'The toleration controversy', pp. 48–9; J. Spurr, *English puritanism 1603–1689* (Basingstoke, 1998), pp. 104–6; Worden, *God's instruments*, pp. 63–90.
5 This was the view of John Goodwin – see *M S to A S*, pp. 1–2 – and Thomas Edwards: *Antapologia*, pp. 3–6.
6 *Apologeticall narration*, pp. 4–6, 11–12, 17–19, 28–9.
7 William Walwyn, *The compassionate samaritan* in Walwyn, *Writings*, pp. 101–2.
8 *Certaine considerations to dis-swade men from further gathering of churches* (1643), p. 3; *Apologeticall narration*, pp. 30–1.
9 *Apologeticall narration*, pp. 4, 22.
10 *Ibid.*, pp. 10–12, 14–15. The apologists' target here was probably George Gillespie, *An assertion of the government of the Church of Scotland* (Edinburgh, 1641), pp. 153–7, 184–9. See W. D. J. McKay, *An ecclesiastical republic: church government in the writings of George Gillespie* (Edinburgh, 1997), pp. 108, 121–2.
11 Adamson 'Peerage in politics', pp. 84–5, citing Alnwick Castle, Northumberland MS XVI, fos 55–7.
12 *Apologeticall narration*, p. 19.
13 For example, the London ministers behind the 1646 work *Jus divinum regiminis ecclesiastici* describe the congregationalists as 'middle way men' in distinction to Brownists (p. 108). This work was written by four London presbyterian ministers, among whom were Samuel Clarke and a minister who is said to have conformed at the Restoration. A likely candidate for the conforming minister is Francis Roberts. For references to the work's authorship see Clarke, *The lives of sundry eminent persons*, p. 9; [William Barrett], *The nonconformists vindicated* (1679), p. 137.
14 *MPWA*, II, p. 589.
15 Joseph Hall, *A true account and character of the times* (1647), pp. 4–5.
16 Baillie, *L&J*, II, p. 130.
17 *Reformation of church government in Scotland cleered from mistakes* (1644).
18 *Ibid.*, p. 2.
19 *Ibid.*, pp. 11–12, 18.
20 Powell, *Crisis*, p. 97.
21 W[illiam] R[athband], *A brief narration of some church courses* (1644); Edwards, *Antapologia*; Hughes, *Gangraena*, pp. 42–9.

22 M. Stewart, 'Steuart, Adam', *ODNB*; and see also [Anon.], *C. C. the covenanter vindicated from periurie* (1644), p. 8.
23 [Patrick (or Alexander) Forbes], *The anatomy of Independency* (1644). For the problems in identifying Forbes, see K. L. Sprunger, *Dutch puritanism: a history of English and Scottish churches of Netherlands in the sixteenth and seventeenth centuries* (Leiden, 1982), pp. 343, 344 n. 113, 364–5.
24 Edwards, *Antapologia*, pp. 155–6.
25 *Ibid.*, pp. 156, 161.
26 *Ibid.*, pp. 159–61.
27 *Ibid.*, pp. 162, 169; Adam Steuart, *Some observations and annotations upon the apologeticall narration* (1644), p. 52.
28 [Anon.], *C. C. The covenanter vindicated*, frontispiece, verso.
29 Edwards, *Antapologia*, p. 243.
30 Baillie, *L&J*, II, pp. 215–16; Hughes, *Gangraena*, pp. 30–1, 135–6.
31 Hezekiah Woodward, *A short letter* (1644), p. 2.
32 For Thomas Parker see F. J. Bremer, 'Parker, Thomas', *ODNB*; J. F. Cooper Jr, *Tenacious of their liberties: the congregationalists in colonial Massachusetts* (Oxford, 1999), pp. 74–5, 145; for Thomas Bayley, see J. Reid, *Memoirs of the lives and writings of those eminent divines* (Paisley, 1811), pp. 130–1.
33 Thomas Parker, *A true copy of a letter written by T. Parker* (1644), pp. 3–4.
34 Nathaniel Rogers, *A letter discovering the cause of Gods continuing wrath against the nation* (1644).
35 D. Beaver, 'Behemoth, or civil war and revolution, in English parish communities 1641–1683' in *The English revolution, c.1590–1720*, ed. N. Tyacke (Manchester, 2007), pp. 134–5.
36 Hartlib Papers, University of Sheffield, 10/11/1A (Henry Robinson to John Dury, 8 November 1644).
37 Coffey, *John Goodwin*, p. 109; Powell, *Crisis*, p. 102.
38 [Holmes], *A Coole Conference*, p. 13; [Goodwin], *M S to A S* (1644), p. 9.
39 See e.g. [Goodwin], *M S to A S* (1644), p. 83. Goodwin's rhetorical strategy was noticed by Edwards: see *Antapologia*, p. 11.
40 [George Walker], *A modell of the government of the Church under the Gospel* (1646), sig. A3.
41 For a full narrative of the printed debates see R. Bradley, '"Jacob and Esau Struggling in the Wombe": a study of presbyterian and Independent religious conflicts 1640–1648' (Ph.D thesis, University of Kent, 1975), pp. 175–218.
42 *Jus divinum regiminis ecclesiastici*, pp. 5–6; N. H. Mayfield, *Puritans and regicide: presbyterian–independent differences over the trial and execution of Charles (I) Stuart* (Lanham, MD, 1988), pp. 126–7 n. 17.
43 Thomas Goodwin, 'The constitution, right order, and government of the churches of Christ' in Thomas Goodwin, *The works of Thomas Goodwin D.D.*, ed. T. Smith, 12 vols (Edinburgh, 1865), XI, pp. 208–12.
44 Gillespie, *Notes*, p. 9.
45 Nonconformist theories of church polity, deriving from the thought of Robert Parker, often distinguished between *ecclesiae primae*, or churches that were

the primary recipients of Christ's gift of the power of the keys, and *ecclesiae ortae*, the assemblies of the church that derived their power from such primary churches. For discussions of this point, see Ha, *Presbyterianism*, p. 58 and Powell, *Crisis*, pp. 75–80.

46 For a discussion of Bodin's view of office see D. Lee, '"Office Is a Thing Borrowed": Jean Bodin on offices and seigneurial government', *Political Theory*, 41:3 (2013), 420–2.
47 Gillespie, *Notes*, p. 11.
48 Samuel Hudson, *A vindication of the essence and unity of the church-catholick visible* (1649), p. 125; De Witt, *Jus divinum*, pp. 119–20; Paul, *The assembly*, pp. 312–13.
49 *MPWA*, II, pp. 617–19; III, pp. 59–64, 423–4; Lightfoot, *Journal*, p. 217; C. van Dixhoorn, 'Presbyterian ecclesiologies at the Westminster assembly' in *Church polity and politics*, eds E. Vernon and H. Powell (Manchester, 2020), pp. 108, 109–10, 113, 118. A further contribution to presbyterian catholicity was provided by the Dutch Reformed theologian William Apollonius in his *A consideration of certaine controversies at this time agitated in the kingdome of England, concerning the government of the Church of God* (1645).
50 Samuel Hudson, *The essence and unitie of the church catholicke visible* (1644), p. 4; Hudson, *A vindication*, pp. 12, 26–7, 117, 130, 210. For Hudson, see S. Lee, 'All subjects of the kingdom of Christ: John Owen's conception of Christian unity and schism' (Ph.D thesis, Calvin Theological Seminary, 2007), pp. 133–5 and Powell, *Crisis*, pp. 77–9.
51 *Jus divinum regiminis ecclesiastici*, p. 98; Hudson, *A vindication*, p. 220.
52 For discussions of this point see Ha, *Presbyterianism*, p. 48 and Powell, *Crisis*, p. 226.
53 See for example, Gillespie, *Notes*, pp. 9, 56.
54 Hudson, *A vindication*, p. 125.
55 John Wallis, *Mens sobria* (Oxford, 1657); Daniel Cawdrey, *Independency further proved to be a schism* (1658), pp. 129–30; J. Parkin, *Taming the Leviathian: the reception of the political and religious ideas of Thomas Hobbes in England* (Cambridge, 2007), p. 171; J. M. Rampelt, 'Polity and liturgy in the philosophy of John Wallis', *Notes and Records of the Royal Society*, 72 (2018), 511–12.
56 Powell, *Crisis*, p. 228.
57 The 120 disciples in Acts 1:15 were seen by presbyterians as being akin to ministers due to their commission to preach and thus the first manifestation of the ministry of the general visible church. See Gillespie, *Notes*, p. 29; [Thomas Bakewell], *An answer to those questions propounded to the Parliament to the Assembly of Divines touching jus divinum in matter of church-government* (1646), pp. 4–10, Lazarus Seaman, *The diatribe proved to be paradiatribe* (1647), p. 41; Paul, *The assembly*, p. 347.
58 See *MPWA*, II, pp. 534–5; Paul, *The assembly*, pp. 277–374; [Walker], *A modell of the government of the Church*, sig. A3v; *Jus divinum regiminis ecclesiastici*, pp. 196, 200–12.

59 *MPWA*, III, pp. 33–4; *Jus divinum regiminis ecclesiastici*, pp. 186, 202, 212–16; [Bakewell], *An answer to those questions*, p. 10.
60 D. Kernan, 'Jurisdiction and the keys' in *A Companion to Richard Hooker*, ed. W.J. Torrance Kirby (Leiden, 2008), pp. 435–50.
61 De Witt, *Jus divinum*, pp. 67–71; W. R. Spear, 'Covenanted uniformity in religion: the influence of the Scottish commissioners upon the ecclesiology of the Westminster assembly' (Ph.D thesis, University of Pittsburgh, 1976), pp. 136–40; Paul, *The assembly*, pp. 146–54; Powell, *Crisis*, pp. 66–82.
62 *MPWA*, II, p. 231; Lightfoot, *Journal*, p. 30.
63 Powell, *Crisis*, p. 83.
64 *MPWA*, II, pp. 235–8.
65 London Provincial assembly, *Jus divinum ministerii evangelici* (1654), p. 35; Seaman, *The diatribe proved to be paradiatribe*, sig. *1.
66 *Jus divinum regiminis ecclesiastici*, pp. 99, 118, 174–5.
67 Ibid., p. 99.
68 *Westminster confession of faith*, 25.iii; London Provincial assembly, *Jus divinum ministerii evangelici*, pp. 138–9, 145, 151; Matthew Poole, *Quo warranto* (1658), p. 5, 17.
69 W. A. Abbott, 'Ruling eldership in civil war England, the Scottish kirk, and early New England: a comparative study of secular and spiritual aspects', *CH*, 75:1 (2006), pp. 38, 57.
70 Lightfoot, *Journal*, pp. 75–6; De Witt, *Jus divinum*, pp. 79, 81, 83. Seaman, consistent with his emphasis that the basic structure of the 'church' was a consistory governing many congregations, did not see the need for ruling elders to be present in every parish church.
71 *MPWA*, II, pp. 354–461.
72 *Jus divinum regiminis ecclesiastici*, pp. 121–8; London Provincial assembly, *A vindication of the presbyteriall-government and ministry* (1650), pp. 34–54. The London Provincial assembly defended the divine right of ruling elders as late as April 1658 in a letter replying to the queries of some Irish ministers: see RLPA fo. 244r (DWL transcript, p. 176).
73 London Provincial assembly, *Vindication of the presbyteriall-government*, pp. 29–30. See also *Jus divinum regiminis ecclesiastici*, p. 141.
74 *Jus divinum regiminis ecclesiastici*, pp. 123–67
75 See the regulations of the first London classis, 20 December 1647 in *RLPA*, fos 21–3 (DWL transcript pp. 22–3; transcribed in Shaw, *HEC*, II, pp. 144–6). For elders' duties see E. Vernon, 'A ministry of the gospel: the presbyterians during the English revolution' in *Religion in revolutionary England*, eds C. Durston and J. Maltby (Manchester, 2006), p. 120.
76 London Provincial assembly, *Vindication of the presbyteriall-government*, pp. 47–8.
77 Paul, *The assembly*, pp. 169–71.
78 *Jus divinum regiminis ecclesiastici*, pp. 121, 190; [Walker], *A modell of the government of the Church*, pp. 17–19; Hudson, *A vindication*, p. 3.

79 *Jus divinum regiminis ecclesiastici*, p. 104, Seaman, *The diatribe proved to be paradiatribe*, p. 33, Ha, *Presbyterianism*, p. 52; Schneider, 'Godly order', p. 367.
80 Gillespie, *Notes*, p. 59; Van Dixhoorn, 'Presbyterian ecclesiologies', pp. 110–11.
81 *Jus divinum regiminis ecclesiastici*, p. 99.
82 *Ibid.*, pp. 98–9, 116.
83 Seaman, *The diatribe proved to be paradiatribe*, pp. 27, 30.
84 *Jus divinum regiminis ecclesiastici*, p. 99, 224; London Provincial assembly, *Vindication of the presbyteriall-government*, p. 26 and *Jus divinum ministerii evangelici*, pp. 126–8.
85 London Provincial assembly, *Vindication of the presbyteriall-government*, p. 14; [Walker], *A modell of the government of the Church*, sig. A3.
86 *Ibid.*, pp. 4–6. N.B. Walker's work uses a combination of signatures and page numbers.
87 *Jus divinum regiminis ecclesiastici*, pp. 57–8; London Provincial assembly, *Vindication of the presbyteriall-government*, p. 23.
88 [Daniel Cawdrey], *Vindiciae clavium* (1645), sig. A3v, p. 28; [Walker], *A modell of the government of the Church*, pp. 7, 20; Poole, *Quo warranto*, pp. 37–8; London Provincial assembly, *Vindication of the presbyteriall-government*, pp. 26, 28, 43–4, 47. This had roots in Elizabethan and early Stuart presbyterian thought: Ha, *Presbyterianism*, p. 80.
89 Thomas Bakewell, *The ordinance of excommunication rightly stated* (1646), sigs A2r–v.
90 London Provincial assembly, *Vindication of the presbyteriall-government*, p. 25; *Jus divinum regiminis ecclesiastici*, p. 99.
91 A. Gordon, 'English presbyterianism', *The Christian Life* (15 December 1888), p. 597. Gordon's position was comprehensively critiqued by Michael Watts in M. R. Watts, *The dissenters from the Reformation to the French Revolution* (Oxford, 1978), pp. 90–1.
92 *Jus divinum regiminis ecclesiastici*, pp. 224–6.
93 *Ibid.*, pp. 198–9, 238–9, 246; London Provincial assembly, *Vindication of the presbyteriall-government*, p. 21.
94 *Jus divinum regiminis ecclesiastici*, pp. 225–6, 245.
95 Powell, *Crisis*, pp. 77, 148–73.
96 Baillie, *L&J*, II, p. 505; Powell, *Crisis*, pp. 216–17.
97 Powell, *Crisis*, pp. 77, 173; R. M. Kingdon, *Geneva and the consolidation of the French protestant movement, 1564–1572: a contribution to the history of congregationalism, presbyterianism, and Calvinist resistance theory* (Geneva, 1967), pp. 76–81; Sunshine, *Reforming French protestantism*, pp. 84–90, 130–7; T. Sarx, 'Reformed protestantism in France' in *A companion to Reformed orthodoxy*, ed. H. Selderhaus (Leiden, 2013), pp. 235–6.
98 Scott, 'Party politics in the Long Parliament, 1640–1648', pp. 42–3.
99 Mahony, 'The presbyterian party', pp. 106–12; Scott, *Politics and war*, pp. 86–7.

100 Kaplan, *Politics and religion*, pp. 33–95; Scott, *Politics and war*, pp. 83–5.
101 For an overview of the pamphlet debate from late 1644, see Bradley, '"Jacob and Esau"', pp. 364–429.
102 Kaplan, *Politics and religion*, pp. 62–3.
103 For the first and second drafts of the directory for ordination (respectively 19 April 1644 and 26 August 1644) see *MPWA*, V, pp. 63–9, 78–86.
104 *MPWA*, V, pp. 66–7, 83, 86; BL Add. Ms. 3116 (Diary of Laurence Whitaker), fos 159r–v. The exhortation to the congregation was formally removed on 1 October, with Oliver St John and the younger Sir Henry Vane Jr leading the division to have the offending phrase excised: *CJ*, III, pp. 622, 647. The opposing tellers were the religious presbyterian MPs Sir Gilbert Gerrard and Sir Anthony Irby.
105 Baillie, *L&J*, II, pp. 230–1, 235–7; Mahony, 'The presbyterian party', p. 106; Adamson, 'Peerage in politics', pp. 86–7.
106 Gillespie, *Notes*, p. 67.
107 *CJ*, III, p. 626.
108 Baillie, *L&J*, II, pp. 230, 235.
109 *CJ*, III, p. 626.
110 The ministers were Stephen Marshall, Charles Herle, Richard Vines, Thomas Temple, Thomas Goodwin, Philip Nye and possibly Herbert Palmer. Gillespie, *Notes*, p. 104; [Anon.], *Papers given in to the honorable committee [...] for accommodation 1644* (1648), p. 2. For the September 1644 committee see Shaw, *HEC*, II, p. 35; Spear, 'Covenanted uniformity', pp. 81–2, 86; and Y. Chung, 'Parliament and the committee for accommodation, 1644–6', *Parliamentary History*, 30 (2011), pp. 289–308.
111 Gillespie, *Notes*, pp. 104–5; *Papers ... for accommodation 1644*, pp. 4–9; Bodleian Library, Oxford, MS Carte 80, fos 192–5.
112 Gillespie, *Notes*, pp. 105–6.
113 *Ibid.*, p. 106–7; Spear, 'Covenanted uniformity', p. 82; *cf.* Chung, 'Parliament and the committee for accommodation, 1644–6', pp. 289–300.
114 *CJ*, III, p. 684; *LJ*, VIII, p. 43; Baillie, *L&J*, II, p. 240; Spear, 'Covenanted uniformity', p. 82; Chung, 'Parliament and the committee for accommodation, 1644–6', p. 300.
115 *CJ*, IV, p. 199; *MPWA*, III, p. 628.
116 Gillespie, *Notes*, p. 67.
117 Lazarus Seaman, *Solomon's choice* (1644), p. 41; Obadiah Sedgwick, *An arke against a deluge* (1644), p. 26.
118 Seaman, *Solomon's choice*, p. 45.
119 Edmund Calamy, *England's antidote against the plague of civil warre* (1645), p. 25; John Adamson, 'The triumph of oligarchy: the management of war and the committee of both kingdoms, 1644–45', in *Parliament at work: parliamentary committees, political power, and public access in early modern England*, eds C. R. Kyle and J. Peacey (Woodbridge, 2002), pp. 119–20.
120 Gillespie, *Notes*, pp. 67–78.
121 *Ibid.*, pp. 67–78.

122 For Uxbridge see Kaplan, *Politics and religion*, pp. 104–10; Scott, *Politics and war*, pp. 91–2.
123 Sedgwick, *An arke against a deluge*, p. 29.
124 Christopher Love, *England's distemper* (1645), p. 4; [John Vicars], *The danger of treaties with popish spirits* (1645), p. 2.
125 [Vicars], *The danger of treaties*, pp. 7–8.
126 Love, *England's distemper*, pp. 32, 36.
127 Baillie, *L&J*, II, pp. 226–7, 230–31. For the Saye-Vane group's management of Parliamentary committees see generally J. S. A. Adamson, 'Parliamentary management, men of business and the House of Lords, 1645–9', in *A pillar of the constitution: the House of Lords in British politics, 1640–1784*, ed. C. Jones (2010), pp. 29–50.
128 Notable among this group were Sir Gilbert Gerard, John Swynfen, Sir Anthony Irby, Sir Robert Harley, Zouche Tate, Francis Rous and Sir William Waller.
129 See V. Pearl, 'London puritans and Scotch fifth columnists: a mid-seventeenth century phenomenon' in *Studies in London history presented to Philip Edmund Jones*, eds A. E. J. Hollander and W. Kellaway (1969), pp. 317–31; Mahony, 'The presbyterian party', pp. 474–80.

5

The campaign for presbyterian church government, 1645–6

At the end of chapter 4 we saw the emerging 'political Independent' parliamentary faction jettison the disappointed Scottish covenanters. This reconfiguration of political alliances at Westminster saw the political Independents look increasingly to home-grown political and religious militants. It was hoped that this shift would allow Parliament to win the war against the king without conceding the constitutional and religious demands made by the Edinburgh regime.[1] The effect of this was to push the Scots, together with the 'Scotified' pro-presbyterian interest in the city, into the arms of the faction that had coalesced around the Earl of Essex. Essex's 'party' was an alliance composed of those personally loyal to the Earl, the old 'peace party' of 1643 and formerly hawkish parliamentarians, such as the Earl of Manchester or Sir William Waller, who had become concerned by the latitude given to extremist elements within the parliamentarian camp. Despite Essex's initial animosity towards the Scots, his group had accommodated their demands for a peace settlement based on the Solemn League and Covenant. Among parliamentarians in the city, this emerging 'political presbyterian' coalition completed the polarisation that had begun over issues of church government and liberty of conscience during the first civil war.[2]

This chapter and chapter 6 explore the role of London's presbyterians within the 'political presbyterian' alliance. The period 1645–7 witnessed a struggle within parliamentarianism to control and define the terms of settlement with the king, ending ultimately in the unintended consequence of the army becoming an ever-present factor in the politics of the period. This chapter analyses the presbyterian clergy's dispute with Parliament in 1645 over the authority and jurisdiction of the projected settlement of the church. The reluctance of Parliament to ratify the Westminster assembly's model of presbyterianism triggered the London clergy to mobilise a campaign for presbyterianism. In so doing, the London ministers encouraged a body of pro-presbyterian, 'covenant-engaged' citizens in London to seize key city institutions to pressurise Parliament into establishing presbyterian church polity. This campaign would ultimately end in disappointment and compromise. However, in 1646 and 1647 the London presbyterians' sophisticated campaigning network and control of important city institutions would prove critical to the wider political presbyterian gambit to take control of the politics of settlement.

Church and state: two kingdoms or one?

The year 1645 saw the London presbyterian clergy engage in a struggle to attempt to shape Parliament's ecclesiastical legislation for a post-civil war settlement. The significance of this struggle would be twofold: first, it delayed the settling of parochial presbyteries in London, as the presbyterian ministers refused to obey Parliament in establishing parish elderships. Second, because the Westminster assembly was limited in its scope to oppose Parliament, the campaigning talents of the Sion College ministers and, especially, the pro-presbyterian citizens came to the fore.

The debate over the autonomy of the church in matters of ecclesiastical discipline was largely couched in theoretical terms. This took the form of a clash between the Calvinist two-kingdoms theory and 'Erastian' notions of the civil supremacy over the church.[3] The presbyterian two-kingdoms theorists saw church and state as separate but co-ordinate jurisdictions, each operating in different spheres. From this perspective, presbyters possessed direct from Christ, as the king of the church, a ministerial jurisdiction to exercise spiritual discipline.[4] Those dubbed 'Erastians', on the other hand, perceived that to establish such a dualist model of church–state relations would lead to either theocratic tyranny or political instability.[5]

The dispute over ecclesiastical power also looked to the pressing political question of preventing the church in England from returning to being an arm of royal power. For its supporters, presbyterianism represented a means to reform the church so that it was both responsive to local needs of reformation and freed from its dangerous relationship with royal government. Historians have sometimes become fixated on the threefold description of presbyterianism as 'rigid, hierarchical and intolerant' and as such they have tended to miss the radical political potential of a presbyterian settlement for the Church of England. This potential was not lost on Charles I, however, who perceived that a presbyterian reformation was a 'pretext to take away the dependency of the Church from the Crowne'. For Charles, the establishment of presbyterianism was 'of equal consequence to that of the militia, for people are governed by pulpits more that the sword, in times of peace'.[6] The clash over the question of the proper location of authority in the church therefore exposed the rift between differing visions of reformation and post-civil war political settlement within parliamentarianism.

These theoretical positions made a substantial intrusion into politics in March 1645. During that month, the Westminster assembly presented a number of papers to Parliament seeking a full jurisdiction for presbyteries to exclude 'ignorant and scandalous' persons from the sacrament of the Lord's supper.[7] After initially seeking clarification of the assembly's proposals, the Commons' grand committee debated the matter on 24 April. While it was ultimately decided that presbyteries should have a power of suspension, a number of MPs voiced their discomfort with affording the projected presbyterian settlement disciplinary powers that were independent of the supervision of Parliament. The initial debate centred on the legal issue of allowing presbyteries to examine parishioners regarding sins that could also be treated as secular criminal offences. The MPs feared that that this would afford presbyteries a judicial power that would clash with local justices of the peace.[8]

These concerns about conflict between the secular and ecclesiastical jurisdictions raised wider questions about the theoretical justifications for the assembly's demands. Such concerns were amplified by those parliamentarians who tended towards a 'single sphere' model of a Christian commonwealth against the dualism of the presbyterians' two-kingdoms theory. This 'single sphere' position, associated with the Zurich theologians Zwingli and Bullinger and most clearly expounded by Thomas Erastus, held that, in a Christian commonwealth, the disciplinary functions of church and state were unified in the Christian magistrate.[9] This perspective cohered with the royal supremacy over the church established in English law by the Henrician Reformation. As Diarmaid McCulloch and W. J. Torrance Kirby have recognised, the Zurich tradition had been blended in the Tudor period with English legal-constitutional thought to provide the dominant intellectual paradigm of church–state relations in England.[10] In the 1640s the single sphere position, with the supremacy firmly residing in Parliament, remained the dominant model of a state–church settlement to those at Westminster.

In 1645 this opposition to the presbyterian theory of church–state jurisdiction would be dubbed 'Erastian' by the Scottish ministers in London. The term appears to have been coined by Robert Baillie in April 1645.[11] Baillie and other presbyterian thinkers deployed the term 'Erastian' to slur various opponents who advanced arguments against the independent jurisdiction of the church in matters of discipline. The initial target of Baillie's ire was the lawyer John Selden, who had applied his prodigious scholarship to challenge the assembly's presbyterians.[12] Selden used his almost unparalleled knowledge of Hebrew learning to marshal effective arguments against the assembly's claims of a scriptural warrant for the autonomous jurisdiction of the church. In April, Baillie claimed that Selden had told the Commons 'as the Jewish state and church was all one and that so in England it must be, that the Parliament is the Church'.[13] Selden, and those like him, thus challenged the theoretical basis of the Scottish covenanters' religious revolution against Charles I.[14]

Despite the scholarship of Selden and other constitutionalists, doubts remained in Parliament about challenging the advice and learning of the Westminster assembly on matters of ecclesiastical jurisdiction.[15] Parliament had, after all, convened the assembly to give it expert advice and in May had even consulted with the London ministers on how the presbyterian system should be structured in the city.[16] However, persuasive support for Selden's arguments was provided by the assembly divine and London minister Thomas Coleman. On 30 July 1645 Coleman preached a sermon before the Commons advising it to resist claims for an independent jurisdiction for the church.[17] Directly contradicting presbyterian two-kingdoms theory, Coleman told the Commons '[a] Christian magistrate, as a Christian magistrate, is a governour in the Church'.[18] In common with Selden, Coleman would deny that the church had any intrinsic disciplinary jurisdiction, arguing that church government was 'merely doctrinall: the corrective or punitive part being civill or temporall'.[19] He therefore provided clerical backing for the arguments of those, like Selden and Whitelocke, who were sceptical of the presbyterians' divine right theory. In September 1645 Selden would refer to Coleman's sermon in a Parliamentary debate as proof that the godly clergy were not *ad idem* on the issue of ecclesiastical jurisdiction and that Parliament held legislative competence in such matters.[20]

The quarrel between the assembly and Parliament over church discipline would break out during the late summer of 1645. On 13 May, contrary to the assembly's advice, the Commons' grand committee decided that a final appeal against suspension from the Lord's supper would lie with Parliament.[21] After the assembly made a request on 4 June for Parliament to address the issue of excluding the scandalous and sinful from the Lord's supper, the assembly was asked the next day by Parliament to draw up a directory of those sins which warranted such exclusion.[22] The refusal of Parliament to ratify an independent jurisdiction for the church became increasingly unacceptable to the assembly. As will be explored in this chapter, presbyterians within and outside the assembly began a campaign to put pressure on Parliament to grant the projected presbyterian settlement a jurisdiction free of state interference.[23]

Throughout the rest of 1645 the assembly presbyterians raised the temperature of the dispute. On 12 August the assembly warned that unless Parliament submitted to its advice, the presbyterian clergy were resolved 'to choose affliction rather than iniquity'. According to Baillie, the Commons were 'highly inflamed' with the assembly's response and retorted with the first major presbyterian ordinance of 20 October, which, while empowering parish presbyteries to suspend parishioners for a substantial number of sins, settled a Parliamentary committee as the final court of appeal in matters of church discipline.[24] The clash between Parliament and the presbyterian clergy was exacerbated when the London presbyterian ministers refused to implement the ordinance in the parishes. Relations between religious presbyterians and Parliament worsened on 21 January 1646 when the Commons proposed a system of lay county commissioners to decide the issue of suspension for sins not enumerated in Parliament's directory of excommunication.[25] This scheme, a revival of Sir Henry Vane Jr's proposals from summer 1641, and rightly described by George Yule as 'clumsy', was enacted on 14 March to the disapproval of an increasingly organised body of lay and clerical presbyterians in London and elsewhere.[26]

The struggle over suspension from the Lord's supper in 1645–6 demonstrated the dominance of the constitutionalist-legalist mindset in Parliament against the British presbyterian vision of further reformation of church and state. As shall be explored below, this dispute would contribute to parliamentarian factional politics as religious presbyterians in London mobilised to pressure Parliament into ratifying their projected two-kingdoms model in law. Presbyterian discontent would increase in late October and November when Parliament re-established the committee for accommodation of the previous year.[27]

The revival of the committee for accommodation

The revival of Parliament's committee for accommodation on 31 October 1645 appears to have been a consequence of the victory of the New Model Army at Naseby and its seizure of Bristol in September 1645.[28] With the war looking to be in its closing stages, the Army's victories reminded Parliament of its long-standing promise that it would provide for dissenters in any post-war settlement.

The committee reconvened on 24 November to discover that the congregationalists were no longer willing to find accommodation within a presbyterian Church of England. Instead, they sought a liberty of practice for dissenters outside the national church. Thomas Goodwin declared that he wished to explore the second limb of Parliament's order of September 1644 to find 'how farre tender consciences [...] may be borne with according to the Word'.[29] Contrary to the usual image of presbyterians as rigid anti-tolerationists, the majority of the presbyterians on the sub-committee were willing to find ways to accommodate dissent that lay within the boundaries of Reformed orthodoxy. On 4 December the dissenting brethren presented a paper setting out their demand for a 'forbearance' in matters of church polity. The paper stated that they agreed on the 'substance' of worship set out in the Westminster assembly's *Directory for public worship* and would submit to the assembly's as yet unfinished confession of faith.[30] This was seized upon by the presbyterians on the sub-committee as setting a limit to the liberty demanded by the congregationalists. On 15 December the committee's presbyterians offered those gathered churches which accepted the assembly's doctrinal standards liberty to practise in their own churches. Those that were outside the assembly's confessional boundaries, however, would 'not have the benefit of this indulgence'.[31]

It was clear that the presbyterian rejoinder was designed to isolate the assembly's congregationalists from other gathered churches, particularly the otherwise doctrinally orthodox congregations that practiced believer's baptism.[32] The congregationalist response on 23 December declared that they were not prepared to 'exclude other tender consciences from this forbearance and to impose on them [... the] directory and confessions'. The congregationalists rejected the presbyterian offer of limited toleration, stating that churches which held to the protestant faith 'in fundamentals' should also receive the benefit of the indulgence.[33]

The presbyterian clergy saw their offer of a limited liberty of practice as a means of settling the boundaries of acceptable dissent from the national church. On 20 January 1646 the ministerial sub-committee recommended that those who dissented on matters of church polity but 'which agree in the substance of the worship of God in the directory, according to the preface, and agree in the confession of faith' should 'have the benefit' of an indulgence to worship according to their conscience.[34]

While the Scots and many English presbyterian ministers were opposed to the committee's offer of a 'forebearance', the committee for accommodation shows that a proportion of the leading English presbyterians were willing to accommodate confessionally orthodox dissenters. This position was expressed by Edmund Calamy in an August 1647 sermon to the city fathers. He stated that 'I am not, nor ever was, against a liberty that is not destructive to church and state, but for a generall toleration, which is distructive to both, that is abominable'.[35] Calamy was not a lone voice among London's presbyterians. In 1646 Captain John Jones, a presbyterian activist, ruling elder and, later, a MP in the Cavalier Parliament, stated that 'all due care' should 'be taken that we persecute not piety and peaceable men, who cannot through scruple of conscience come up in all things to the common rule: but that they may have such a forbearance' necessary to accommodate their consciences.[36] Likewise, in 1669 one English presbyterian remembered that during the mid-1640s the presbyterians had offered that 'they would take the establishment, and allow their brethren of the congregational-way a well-regulated toleration'.[37] These sentiments represent an important countermelody in the English presbyterian attitude to orthodox dissenters and one that historians, often fixated on the bombastic details of Thomas Edwards' *Gangraena*, have often missed.

Nevertheless, it is also clear that less-than-liberal tactical considerations were at play in the sub-committee's decision to offer a forbearance to the congregationalists. Baillie stated that the presbyterians on the sub-committee thought that to deny the congregationalists an indulgence 'would bring on them [i.e. the presbyterians] ane unsupportable odium' and that they were 'persuaded that their offers would not be accepted; and if they were, they would destroy Independencie'.[38] Perhaps more pertinently, the offer of a limited religious indulgence was also an attempt to bargain with Parliament into granting the national presbyterian church full jurisdiction over suspension and excommunication. This rather blatant presbyterian attempt at a *quid pro quo*, however, was summarily dismissed by the Commons on 4 February 1646.[39]

London presbyterian mobilisation 1645–6

The Westminster assembly's demand that Parliament legislate an independent jurisdiction for the presbyterian system was supported by a campaign of mobilisation in London and elsewhere. The London campaign sought to use the city's substantial political influence to force Parliament into accepting the assembly's demands concerning church discipline. The London presbyterian campaign would prove significant in the politics of religion of the mid-to-late-1640s, transforming partisan politics within post-first civil war London. This section will explore London presbyterian mobilisation by examining the relationship between lay and clerical campaigners, the institutional bases from which presbyterian partisanship could operate and the campaigning techniques deployed to force Parliament to legislate the divine right of church government.

The main paradigm for studying the presbyterian campaigns of the 1640s was established by Michael Mahony in an important 1979 article.[40] Mahony's article utilised a prosopographical study of the seventy-three signatories of two lay presbyterian petitions, presented in October 1645 and March 1646, to analyse the network of lay activists in the city. He demonstrated that while the London clergy were central to presbyterian organisation they were joined by the 'repeated involvement' of a select network of lay activists, who would form the backbone of the presbyterian 'covenant-engaged' cause.[41] These activists, who largely came from the western parishes of the city, demonstrated the importance of 'organisation rather than numbers' in the 1640s presbyterian movement.[42] Politically, the vast majority of the 1645–6 petitioners had been supporters of the parliamentary war party during the first civil war and had been zealous in the assault on Laudian and royalist clergy in the city's parishes.[43] Socially, the majority of presbyterian activists were composed of city merchants and wealthier shopkeepers who, by the mid-1640s, held office on their parish vestries and the city's common council. Many were 'new' men who held such positions as a result of the disturbances to the city's institutions caused by the calling of the Long Parliament.[44] The presbyterian petitioners were therefore fully intertwined with what has been called the 'unacknowledged republic' of local office holding.[45] This is significant in that London presbyterian lay-activists tended to be sufficiently well connected socially to be able to direct their mobilisation through established institutions of city power, such as vestries or the common council. Such institutional power can be contrasted with the more covert and impromptu means favoured by 'radical parliamentarians' who in the 1640s, with some exceptions, generally lacked access to the various levels of the city's governing institutions – this has recently been explored by David Como and Gary De Krey.[46] Yet in many respects so-called 'radical parliamentarians' and presbyterian activists shared the same tradition and experiences of mobilisation, drawn from the tradition of London political culture and the war party politics of the early civil war.[47]

The tactics of presbyterian mobilisation accord with more general arguments that historians have made about the nature of urban partisan politics during the seventeenth century. Paul Halliday has argued that such urban politics was based on the paradoxical aim of restoring political and religious unity by obtaining factional control of institutions and purging opponents from office.[48] In the latter half of the 1640s, the city presbyterians would develop a programme based on political exclusion as a means of obtaining their objectives. A key feature of this political strategy was religious identity, focused on the visible and public engagement made by the taking of the Solemn League and Covenant.

The urban politics of the mid-to-late-seventeenth century required partisans to organise locally in order to achieve their objectives. This factor has been explored by Michael Braddick, who has argued that a focus on specific mobilisations demonstrates the social depth of civil war politics. Braddick draws attention to the importance of networks of individuals using local institutions, as well as print, to create the open, dynamic and shifting politics of the period.[49]

Developing the tactics learned and deployed by parliamentarian activists in the early 1640s, the London presbyterian movement of the mid-1640s emerged as a key development in the partisan politics of the 1640s and 1650s. Indeed, as Philip Baker and Gary De Krey have argued, opponents of city presbyterianism, such as those who would later become Levellers, developed similar mechanisms of mobilisation in reaction to the apparent grip that the London presbyterians had on the political processes in the city.[50] The London presbyterian movement of the 1640s, therefore, was a key catalyst in the development of the partisan politics of the mid-seventeenth century.

The campaign to put leverage on Parliament to establish presbyterian church government began in 1645, initially as an exclusively clerical affair. For example, the Westminster assembly's draft of the *Directory for public worship* was supported on 10 March 1645 by a low-key petition from a mere seven London ministers demanding the establishment of parochial measures to control admission to the sacrament of the Lord's supper.[51] A similar petition, presented on 29 August and signed by seventy-four ministers, supported the assembly's attempts to convince Parliament to ratify an independent jurisdiction for presbyterian discipline.[52]

Contemporary opponents of the London presbyterian movement perceived that the most important institutional base for the mobilisation of the presbyterian campaign in the city was Sion College. In 1646 the Leveller William Walwyn complained of the 'private juncto's and councels' at the College and accused ministers of 'framing Petitions for the easie and ignorant people'. He was dismayed at the clergy's 'ability to worke' 'our presbyterian lay-brethren' 'by the smoothnesse of phrase and language to what they please'.[53] Walwyn was not alone in perceiving the influence of the presbyterian clergy in the organisation of the city campaigns. The city militia captain Thomas Juxon saw the clergy as using their pulpits to launch a 'citizen's petition' at the ward election of December 1645.[54] Likewise, the royalist agent Nicholas Oudart had intelligence that a March 1647 presbyterian petition had been 'framed at Sion Collegde' before being presented by a group of citizens.[55]

The main connection between the Sion College clergy and their lay allies was through the city parishes where, as a result of the parliamentarian purges of the early 1640s, presbyterian ministers and the godly laity had day-to-day contact. The clearest example of this can be seen in the London ministers' campaign of opposition to Parliament's March 1646 county commissioner scheme. The co-ordination of the skirmish with the Commons over the county commissioners lay with the Scottish minister Robert Baillie and Francis Roberts, the minister of St Augustine, Watling Street. Baillie gave Roberts the task of convincing Simeon Ashe, the Earl of Manchester's chaplain, to use his influence with the Earl to amend the Commons' ordinance in the Lords. Baillie also recommended that Roberts arrange a citizens' petition to the common council to get the city to oppose the institution of county commissioners.[56] Roberts appears to have followed Baillie's advice, Juxon recording that '[t]he ministers [...] sent to their several agents in the City to bring in their reasons against' the proposals.[57] Consequently, on 9 March a somewhat hastily put-together petition containing the signatures of a mere twenty-four citizens was presented to the common council.[58] The signatories suggest that Roberts was working locally, with at least half of the signatories of the petition coming from parishes surrounding his parish church in Watling Street.[59] Such local organisation demonstrates how ministers and activists used their personal connections to act swiftly in the campaign for the establishment of their goals.

Beyond the parish, webs of interpersonal connections existed within the city at large that made concerted action by the presbyterian citizens possible. Alongside the networks of kinship, commerce, friendship and piety that existed among the London godly, a plethora of social spaces where citizens met to share gossip and news were also used to organise political action. These included public spaces, particularly the Exchange, where merchants and tradesmen gathered daily.[60] In June 1645 James Cranford had caused a near-panic when he had sought out presbyterian citizens such as John Jones, Richard Venner and Thomas Gower to inform them of Viscount Saye and Sele's apparent betrayal of the parliamentarian cause.[61] Such social spaces also included quasi-public venues such as shops and taverns. Bookshops, especially the shops of the presbyterian activists John Bellamie and Christopher Meredith, acted as hubs in the city around which news and rumours were disseminated, theological positions discussed and campaigns facilitated.[62] It was the manipulation of these increasingly politicised relationships and spaces that gave the presbyterian citizenry significant organisational reach in the city in the mid-1640s.

One of the earliest of the citizen's petitions, the ill-fated September 1645 petition, provides a case study of the religious presbyterian movement in action.[63] As seen in the previous section of this chapter, in September 1645 the Commons had discussed limiting the parochial elderships' jurisdiction of suspension from the Lord's supper to those sins contained in the Westminster assembly's catalogue. Supporting the protests of the presbyterian ministry against this measure, a group of London citizens led by the colonial merchant Lawrence Brinley began the circulation of a petition among the citizenry.[64] By 1645 Brinley, a hot parliamentarian activist since the early 1640s, was a member of William Prynne's committee of accounts and a close supporter of Thomas Case's presbyterian reforms at Brinley's parish of St Mary Magdalen, Milk Street.[65] Prynne's committee included in its membership an identifiable bloc of London presbyterians, including Brinley and the future ruling elders Walter Boothby and Christopher Packe.[66] Brinley's petition was sent to agents within the London area including the bookseller George Thomason and Thomas Alle of Stepney, a regular frequenter of John Bellamie's bookshop, to gain the signatures of all those who had taken the Solemn League and Covenant.[67] These tactics caused immediate division within the London area, with many congregationalists and separatists actively speaking against the petition.[68] In light of this commotion, the petition was declared scandalous by the Commons and ordered to be suppressed.[69] Despite being silenced in their petitioning measures, the presbyterian activists were not to be undone. On 23 September the Exchange was plastered with handbills calling for a tax strike until the church was settled according to the Covenant.[70] While ultimately stifled, the September petition demonstrates the reach and techniques of the presbyterian activists in promoting the cause of a covenanted church settlement.

London householders had a long tradition of using the local wardmote inquest and the annual 21 December common council elections to present petitions setting out their grievances to the city's government.[71] Gaining access to the common council for petitioning had become more critical since January 1644 when the common council ordered that no citizens' petitions should be presented to Parliament without its prior consent and approval.[72] It comes as no surprise, therefore, that one of the principal tactics of presbyterian mobilisation was canvassing at the annual ward elections for the common council. In 1645 the Sion College ministers used the election pulpit to attempt to influence voting. Juxon recorded that the sermons from presbyterian ministers 'drove one and the same way: not to choose men of erron[eo]us opinions'.[73] Following the elections, presbyterian representatives of the wards presented local petitions to the alderman and the newly elected common councillors desiring that city policy focus on the settlement of presbyterian government and take steps against those who refused the Solemn League and Covenant.[74] Similar electioneering took place in the run-up to the December 1646 elections, with presbyterians gathering signatures to a petition for a purge of those who refused to retake the Covenant and calling for the disbandment of the New Model Army.[75]

The aim of this presbyterian mobilisation was to influence the city's common council, a critical institution in parliamentarian politics owing to its control over the city's finances and its right to speak for the city corporately. Presbyterian support on the common council, however, never led to total control, making up no more than about 50 per cent of the membership of the council in the later 1640s.[76] Religious presbyterians, therefore, could never claim hegemony over the common council's business or debates. Nevertheless, the Sion College ministers and citizen petitioners could look to a well-organised minority of religious presbyterian partisans who sat on the common council.[77] Thomas Juxon reckoned that these activists were a 'few engaged men': 30 or 40 out of a total of approximately 237 common councillors, who dominated the discussions on religious issues. Against this activist core, Juxon estimated that only five councillors regularly spoke against the presbyterians, the remainder either acquiescing by silence or too afraid to take on such a vocal bloc of partisans.[78]

The City presbyterians also recognised that strong representation on the common council's committees was essential to controlling the city's access to Parliament. Once selected, these committees tended to have a degree of permanency, being asked repeatedly to conduct city business of a similar nature. Robert Brenner has noted that of seven important committees established between 1645 and 1647 the majority were supporters of a presbyterian settlement.[79] The most important city committee for presbyterian mobilisation was that set up in October 1645 to debate the ministers' protests against the election of elders according to Parliament's 'Erastian' model.[80] On 20 October, after a conference at Sion College, the ministers stated to the Lord Mayor that they were not content to establish elderships on Parliament's pattern and returned a series of queries about the parliamentary ordinance of September 1645. The common council directed that the committee, a majority of which were religious presbyterians, should review the ministers' grievances. Juxon detected foul play in the selection of this committee and it seems likely that Sion College had instigated its creation so that the clergy could use the committee as a vehicle within the city government for their own campaign.[81] This was the view of a handful of political Independents on the common council, who used the gravity of challenging Parliament to successfully argue that the ministers' queries should be returned to Sion College to be signed by those ministers who had raised the objections.[82]

Although the Sion College ministers' attempt at anonymity was blown by the decision that they should reveal their names, the ministers were not willing to let the opportunity to utilise a favourable common council committee pass. On 12 November they returned their report, endorsed by eighty-eight ministers, and accompanied with a petition signed by fifty-nine lay presbyterian activists.[83] The presbyterian response was effective, for on 17 November the common council voted that its committee should prepare a petition to Parliament to reform the church 'according to our Solemne Covenant'.[84] This petition was presented to the Commons on 19 November, supported by a clerical petition from the London clergy delivered by George Walker.[85] This committee and others appointed after it would retain its presbyterian majority. Presbyterians, or those sympathetic to a presbyterian settlement, made up about 63 per cent of the total number of common council members of religious committees between 1645 and 1648.[86] These common council committees provided a useful and generally reliable vehicle for presbyterian campaigns to cajole Parliament to accept an authoritative presbyterian settlement.

How effective was the presbyterian mobilisation? The clear aim of the London presbyterian movement was to turn the institutions of the city's government into tools for the campaign to pressurise Parliament into accepting a divine right church settlement. Although the presbyterians failed in their goal of convincing Parliament to establish presbyterianism on a two-kingdoms model, they were largely successful in utilising the city to mobilise for their aims. Even the 9 March 1646 petition against the county commissioners, signed by a mere twenty-four citizens, provided a sufficient pretext for presbyterian partisans on the common council to present a petition to Parliament. When compared with other examples of 'popular' pressure, for example the body of militants who would later become the Levellers, the London presbyterians had greater political and organisational reach. The presbyterian representation in parishes and the common council allowed their mobilisations to be effective in using the institutional resources of the city government to put substantial pressure on Parliament.

Nevertheless, the London presbyterian tactics of using the city to petition Parliament to go against its own recent decisions had clear limitations. Such divisive tactics ultimately affected the relationship between the city and Parliament in a way that was potentially detrimental to the city's wider interests. This is seen clearly in the 9 March petition against the county commissioner scheme.[87] Despite support from ten peers led by Essex and Manchester, the city's petition was condemned in both houses as a breach of privilege.[88] On 16 or 17 March the Commons sent a delegation to chastise the common council for its campaigning strategy and to demand the names of the petitioners who had initiated the city petition.[89] In face of such pressure from Westminster, the presbyterian militants were isolated on the common council and, at least temporarily, side-lined. The result was that the city conceded the issue of divine right church government as it sought to rebuild its relationship with Parliament.[90]

The clashes over the issue of church government between the city and a Parliament dominated by political Independents caused substantial resentment in London. One manifestation of this was the attack on Francis Allein over his disclosure in the Commons of a letter sent on 11 February by the Scottish Parliament to the city.[91] Allein, both a common councillor and a recruiter MP who owed his seat to the patronage of the Earl of Northumberland, was lambasted for this disclosure in a statement drafted by the eldership committee. According to Juxon, the Allein incident led to vocal criticism of Parliament in the common council.[92] This was not the only source of disaffection between the city and Parliament. The House of Commons' handling of the city's March petition, according to the French diplomat Jean de Montereul, caused the city government to be 'very angry' with Parliament.⁹³ This irritation was also shared by the Sion College ministers. William Sancroft, a future archbishop of Canterbury, recorded in May 1646 that Edmund Calamy had preached that 'God would shew them [the House of Commons] what a horrible sin it is to break covenant with him'. Richard Vines had complained that 'the church had power of jurisdiction in it before the supreme magistrate was Christian; and why it should lose that under Constantine which it had under Nero, I know not'. The result, according to Sancroft, was that the presbyterian ministers prayed 'very zealously for his majesty, and began to fumble and botch in their mention of the parliament'.⁹⁴

The presbyterian ministers' renewal of prayers for the king appears to have been part of a wider strategy to support the Earl of Essex's 'party' in its machinations to take control of the settlement process. Rumours that the king was going to surrender to either the city or the Scots had abounded throughout the spring of 1646. With the king's surrender in mind, Essex's party at Westminster had strengthened its ties with the Scots and the city presbyterians. Following the incident over Francis Allein in February, Juxon recorded that a political alliance of 'the Lords, the Scots, the assembly and now the City' had formed against the political Independents in Parliament.⁹⁵ This observation was confirmed by Montereul in March, who recorded that 'the Scottish party' had been 'marvellously strengthened'.⁹⁶ Charles's surrender to the Scots in May meant that Essex's party, backed by the Scottish covenanter army and the finances of the city, appeared to be the parliamentarian faction most likely to broker a future restoration settlement. On 21 May, Essex's allies in the House of Commons led a successful attack on the county commissioner legislation.⁹⁷ On the suggestion of the political Independent grandee Samuel Browne, a compromise was reached whereby Parliament effectively returned to its November 1645 position that a Parliamentary committee should constitute the final court of appeal in matters of church discipline.⁹⁸ On the advice of the Scots and the Westminster assembly, the London ministers accepted this compromise, issuing a face-saving declaration agreeing to establish Parliament's presbyterian settlement in the hope that a better settlement would be reached in the future.⁹⁹ Although this was a victory of sorts, it stopped short of the presbyterian hopes to coerce Parliament into accepting a two-kingdoms model of church–state relations.

Conclusion

The struggle over church government in 1645 revealed the rift that had grown between the presbyterian ministers' project for further reformation and the majority of those in Parliament. Although the fault-lines between the two-kingdoms model of church–state relations and the magisterial single sphere position now seem totally unbridgeable, they both emerged from the Reformed tradition and both aimed at solving the problem of the monarch's control of the Church of England as a tool of royal government. In addition, divisions emerged among presbyterians as to the extent to which they were willing to countenance a forbearance for confessionally orthodox dissenters to worship outside the national church. Nevertheless, none appeared willing to accept the wider liberty demanded by their congregationalist brethren.

The battle with Parliament over the issue of the divine right of church government, while ultimately a battle that could not be won, was significant in that it saw Sion College mobilise lay supporters for a presbyterian settlement in the city. This would provide a core group of well-connected citizens who would use their political connections and the tactics learned during the first civil war to attempt to steer the city into supporting a 'Scotified' presbyterian settlement. While these activists never held control of the city's government, their high level of representation on London parish vestries, the common council and in key trades such as the Stationers' Company, meant that London's religious presbyterians could often direct city policy in favour of a presbyterian settlement.

This alliance of London ministers and citizens, together with the struggle against Parliament's refusal to establish presbyterianism on a two-kingdoms model, would provide a crucial building block for the London presbyterian movement, both in the crisis of 1646–7 and beyond. Despite the bulk of the London presbyterians having been supporters of the parliamentary war party during the first civil war, their commitment to a covenanted settlement and against the emerging political Independent coalition would lead them to be an integral component in Essex's party at Westminster. Throughout 1646 and 1647 this composite faction would attempt to force a settlement with the king. It is to these events that chapter 6 turns.

Notes

1 In this study, when referring to factions within Parliament, I use the terms 'political Independents' and 'political presbyterians', terms which are fully and succinctly explored by David Scott in 'Party politics in the Long Parliament, 1640–8', pp. 32–54.
2 As with previous chapters, David R. Como's *Radical parliamentarians*, particularly chs 10–12, tracks the other side to my exploration of the London presbyterians in politics.

3 See further E. Vernon, '"They agree not in opinion among themselves": presbyterian divine right theory, Erastianism and the Westminster assembly debate on church and state c.1641–1648' in *Church polity and politics in the British Atlantic world, c.1635–1666*, eds E. Vernon and H. Powell (Manchester, 2020), pp. 130–54.
4 *Jus divinum regiminis ecclesiastici*, pp. 65–70.
5 Although not himself an 'Erastian', Philip Nye stated the general objections to the presbyterian position during the debates: see Gillespie, *Notes*, p. 27; *MPWA*, II, p. 530.
6 *Cal. Clarendon SP*, I, p. 325; see also pp. 330, 332.
7 *LJ*, VII, pp. 265–7; *CJ*, IV, pp. 70–1, 85; *MPWA*, V, pp. 176–7, 183–5; Shaw, *HEC*, I, pp. 258–9; De Witt, *Jus divinum*, p. 180; G. Yule, *Puritans in politics: the religious legislation of the Long Parliament* (Sutton Courtenay, 1984), pp. 150–51.
8 *CJ*, IV, pp. 85, 89, 90, 95, 105, 113–14, 118, 122, 127, 131–2, 134; BL Add. Ms. 3116 (Parliamentary diary of Lawrence Whitaker), fos 200v, 201v–203r, 204v, 205v, 207r–v; BL Add. Ms. 18780 ('The journal of Walter Yonge', vol. 3), fo. 8r (I am grateful to Christopher Thompson for allowing me to use his transcript of this manuscript); Shaw, *HEC*, I, pp. 259–62; De Witt, *Jus Divinum*, pp. 181–2.
9 For a summary of the single sphere position, see E. Campi, *Shifting patterns of reformed tradition* (Göttingen, 2014), pp. 60–3. In practice, the 'two-kingdoms' and 'single sphere' stances often manifested as tendencies in thought rather than hard positions.
10 D. MacCulloch, *The later Reformation in England, 1547–1603*, 2nd edn (Basingstoke, 2000), pp. 58–60; D. MacCulloch, 'The Church of England, 1533–1603', in *Anglicanism and the western Christian tradition*, ed. Stephen Platten (Norwich, 2003), pp. 34–40; W. J. Torrance Kirby, *The Zurich connection and Tudor political theology* (Leiden, 2007), pp. 3–4.
11 Baillie, *L&J*, II, pp. 265–6. For Erastus see C. D. Gunnoe, *Thomas Erastus and the Palatinate: A renaissance physician in the second Reformation* (Leiden, 2011).
12 For Selden see M. A. Ziskind, 'John Selden: humanist jurist' (Ph.D thesis, University of Chicago, 1972); R. Barbour, *John Selden: measures of the holy commonwealth in seventeenth-century England* (Toronto, 2003), chs 5 and 6; O. Haivry, *John Selden and the western political tradition* (Cambridge, 2017), pp. 454–6.
13 Baillie, *L&J*, II, pp. 265–6.
14 Haivry, *John Selden*, pp. 376–7.
15 J. T. Cliffe, *Puritans in conflict: the puritan gentry during and after the civil wars* (1988), pp. 128–9.
16 BL Add. Ms. 7005 (Harley Papers), fos 69–70.
17 T. Coleman, *Hopes deferred and dashed* (1645), pp. 24–5. For Coleman's troubles following this sermon, see Paul, *The assembly*, p. 514.
18 Coleman, *Hopes deferred*, pp. 24, 27.

19 Coleman, *A brotherly examination re-examined* (1646), p. 11.
20 BL Add. Ms. 18780, fo. 112r.
21 *Ibid.*, fo. 19r; *CJ*, IV, pp. 114, 140–4; Shaw, *HEC*, I, pp. 263–4.
22 *MPWA*, III, pp. 611–12; V, p. 197.
23 De Witt, *Jus divinum*, pp. 182–6; Paul, *The assembly*, pp. 497–9.
24 *LJ*, VII, pp. 534–5; *A&O*, I, pp. 789–97; *MPWA*, III, pp. 643–4, Baillie, *L&J*, II, p. 307; De Witt, *Jus divinum*, p. 185; Yule, *Puritans in politics*, p. 158.
25 De Witt, *Jus divinum*, pp. 191–3.
26 *A&O*, I, pp. 833–8.
27 *CJ*, IV, pp. 327, 342; *LJ*, VII, pp. 670, 703; Chung, 'Parliament and the committee for accommodation', pp. 301–8.
28 *CJ*, IV, pp. 327, 342.
29 Westminster assembly, *The papers [...] for accommodation at the reviving of that committee 1645* (1648), pp. 13–14. These papers are included in Westminster assembly, *The grand debate concerning presbitery and Independencie* (1652), sigs Aaaa–Qqqq2. The clerical committee consisted of Stephen Marshall, Cornelius Burges, John White, Joshua Hoyle, Thomas Temple, Peter Smith, Herbert Palmer, Lazarus Seaman, Charles Herle, Thomas Goodwin, Philip Nye, William Bridge, Thomas Hill, Edward Reynolds, John Arrowsmith, Thomas Young, Richard Vines, Anthony Tuckney, Matthew Newcomen, Sydrach Simpson, Jeremiah Burroughes and John Dury.
30 Westminster assembly, *Papers [...] for accommodation*, p. 15.
31 *Ibid.*, pp. 18–19.
32 Baillie, *L&J*, II, p. 343.
33 Westminster assembly, *Papers [...] for accommodation*, pp. 26–7, 29–03 (N.B. irregular pagination).
34 *Ibid.*, p. 43; Baillie, *L&J*, II, p. 346.
35 Congregational Library, London, Ms. I.f.18, p. 293.
36 [John Jones], *Plain English, or the sectaries anatomized* (1646), p. 25.
37 [Anon.], *An humble apology for non-conformists* (n.p., 1669), p. 129.
38 Baillie, *L&J*, II, pp. 341, 344, 346.
39 *CJ*, IV, p. 428; Chung, 'Parliament and the committee for accommodation', p. 305.
40 M. Mahony, 'Presbyterianism in the city of London 1645–1647', *HJ*, 22:1 (1979), 93–114.
41 *Ibid.*, pp. 100–11.
42 *Ibid.*, p. 111.
43 Lindley, *Popular politics*, pp. 60–73; K. Lindley, 'London's citizenry in the English revolution' in *Town and countryside in the English revolution*, ed. R. C. Richardson (Manchester, 1992), pp. 19–45, esp. p. 30; Nagel, 'The militia of London', pp. 115–34.
44 Survey of the laity who would become presbyterian activists in the city can be found in Lindley, 'London's citizenry'; Tai Liu, *Puritan London: a study of religion and society in the city parishes* (Newark, NJ, 1986), pp. 51–102; for an important qualification see J. D. Alsop, 'Revolutionary puritanism in

the parishes? The case of St Olave, Old Jewry', *London Journal*, 15:1 (1990), 29–37, esp. p. 32.
45 M. Goldie, 'The unacknowledged republic: office holding in early modern England' in *The politics of the excluded, c.1500–1850*, ed. T. Harris (Basingstoke, 2001), pp. 153–94.
46 Como, *Radical parliamentarians*; G. de Krey, *Following the Levellers*, vol. 1: *Political and religious radicals in the English civil war and revolution, 1645–1649* (London, 2017), pp. 15–37.
47 For the often-overlooked medieval heritage of citizen politics see C. D. Liddy, *Contesting the city: the politics of citizenship in English towns, 1250–1530* (Oxford, 2017), esp. chs 2, 4, 5 and 6.
48 P. Halliday, *Dismembering the body politic: partisan politics in England's towns, 1650–1730* (Cambridge, 1998), pp. xiii, 3–6, 15.
49 M. Braddick, 'Mobilisation, anxiety and creativity in England during the 1640s' in *Liberty, authority, formality: political ideas and culture, 1600–1900*, eds J. Morrow and J. Scott (Exeter, 2008), pp. 175–92.
50 See P. Baker, 'London's liberty in chains discovered: the Levellers, the civic past, and popular protest in civil war London', *Huntington Library Quarterly*, 76:4 (2013), 566.
51 *LJ*, VII, pp. 268–9; PA HL/PO/JO/10/1/182 (10 March 1644/5). The ministers were Immanuel Bourne, Timothy Dod, Thomas Blake, Charles Offspring, James Nalton, Elidad Blackwell and Francis Roberts.
52 *CJ*, IV, p. 253; *LJ*, VII, pp. 558–9.
53 William Walwyn, *Tolleration justified* (1646) in Walwyn, *Writings*, pp. 156–7, 160.
54 Juxon, *Journal*, p. 97; [Anon.], *To the right worshipfull, the alderman, and common counsell-men of the ward of Farrington* (1645).
55 *Nicholas papers*, I, pp. 80–1; Juxon, *Journal*, pp. 150–1.
56 Baillie, *L&J*, II, p. 359.
57 Juxon, *Journal*, p. 108.
58 LMA, JCC40, fo. 174; Lindley, *Popular politics*, p. 365.
59 Juxon, *Journal*, p. 108; Mahony, 'Presbyterianism', pp. 100, 102–5.
60 For the Exchange as a place of news and rumour see R. Cust, 'News and politics in early seventeenth-century England', *P&P*, 112 (1986), 70 and A. Fox, 'Rumour, news and popular political opinion in Elizabethan and early Stuart England', *HJ*, 40:3 (1997), 603–4.
61 Pearl, 'London puritans and Scotch fifth columnists', pp. 317–34; M. Mahony, 'The Savile affair and the politics of the Long Parliament', *Parliamentary History*, 7:2 (1988), 213–27.
62 Eales, 'A road to revolution', pp. 198–9; Hughes, *Gangraena*, pp. 148, 308, 412.
63 Hughes, *Gangraena*, pp. 307–8.
64 Juxon, *Journal*, p. 85.
65 Lindley, *Popular politics*, p. 357; Brenner, *Merchants*, pp. 365, 397–8.
66 J. Peacey, 'Politics, accounts and propaganda in the Long Parliament' in C. R.

Kyle and J. Peacey, *Parliament at work: parliamentary committees, political power and public access in early modern England* (Woodbridge, 2002), pp. 59–78, esp. p. 66. For Boothby see Lindley, *Popular politics*, pp. 197 n. 196, 230, 375 n. 101, 376. For Packe, see K. Lindley, 'Packe, Christopher, appointed Lord Packe under the Protectorate, 1599–1682', *ODNB*.

67 Thomas Alle, *A brief narration of the truth of some particulars* (1646), pp. 3–4; Edwards, *Gangraena*, I, pp. 109–10. The petition can be found in BL 669.f.10 (37). Thomason wrote on his copy 'Sent to Mr. Geo: Thomason to gett hands to it about 20 Sept'.

68 Edwards, *Gangraena*, I, pp. 109–10; *Perfect passages* (17–23 September 1645), p. 380; Henry Burton, *Truth shut out of doors* (1645), sig. A2; K[atherine] C[hidley], *Good counsell to the petitioners for presbyterian government* (1645).

69 *CJ*, IV, p. 280; Juxon, *Journal*, p. 86; *Perfect occurrences* (19–26 September 1645), sig. r1v; *The moderate intelligencer* (18–25 September 1645), p. 997.

70 *CJ*, IV, p. 282; *A lybell 23 September 1645* (1645); Shaw, *HEC*, I, pp. 274–5.

71 I. W. Archer, *The pursuit of stability: social relations in Elizabethan London* (Cambridge, 1991), p. 52.

72 Brenner, *Merchants*, p. 466.

73 For further analysis of the December 1645 elections see Lindley, *Popular politics*, pp. 359–61.

74 Juxon, *Journal*, p. 97; *To the right worshipfull [...] Farrington*.

75 Baillie, *L&J*, II, p. 413.

76 Farnell, 'Politics of the city of London', pp. 349–69.

77 Lindley, *Popular politics*, p. 377.

78 Juxon, *Journal*, p. 106; Pearl, *London*, p. 56; Farnell, 'Politics of the city of London', pp. 341–2.

79 Brenner, *Merchants*, pp. 481–2, 491–2. The future ruling elders were John Bellamie, Walter Boothby, George Dunn, John Gace, Maurice Gething, Richard Glyde, Thomas Gower, Nathaniel Hall, Michael Herring, Edward Hooker, Alexander Jackson, William Jesson, John Jones, William Kendall, Robert Mainwaring, Christopher Meredith, Peter Mills, Christopher Packe, James Russell, James Story, Richard Turner, Richard Venner, Thomas Vyner, John Warner and George Witham.

80 *CJ*, IV, p. 300; LMA, JCC40, fo. 148; Juxon, *Journal*, p. 89; Brenner, *Merchants*, pp. 491–2.

81 Juxon, *Journal*, p. 89.

82 LMA, JCC40, fo. 149; Juxon, *Journal*, p. 89 (Juxon's entry, which is for 25 October, seems to compound the meetings of 20 and 27 October). Juxon identified the independents as Thomas Andrews, John Fowke, Roland Wilson, Robert Tichbourne, Francis Allein and Richard Waring.

83 LMA, JCC40, fos 150v–53v; Mahoney, 'Presbyterianism', pp. 93–114.

84 LMA, JCC40, fo. 151; Juxon, *Journal*, p. 95. The five extra members of the committee were William Gibbs, John Bellamie, William Hobson, Francis Allein and Michael Herring. With the exception of Bellamie and Herring, who can be

identified as presbyterians, the majority of the additional committee members would become political Independents.

85 *CJ*, IV, p. 348.
86 Brenner, *Merchants*, pp. 491–2.
87 LMA, JCC40, fos 173v–4v.
88 *LJ*, VIII, pp. 207–8; *CJ*, IV, p. 479; Juxon, *Journal*, pp. 108–9. The city's petition of 11 March, ordered to be expunged from the Parliamentary and city records, can be found at PA HL/PO/JO/10/1/202, fos 143–6.
89 Juxon, *Journal*, pp. 109–11; Edwards, *Gangraena*, II, p. 8.
90 Brenner, *Merchants*; p. 474; Lindley, *Popular politics*, pp. 365–7.
91 *CJ*, IV, pp. 437, 439; Baillie, *L&J*, II, pp. 352–3.
92 LMA, JCC40 fo. 172; Juxon, *Journal*, p. 103; Lindley, *Popular politics*, pp. 363–4; J. Adamson, 'Of armies and architecture: the employments of Robert Scawen' in *Soldiers, writers and statesmen of the English revolution*, eds I. Gentles, B. Worden and J. Morrill (Cambridge, 1998), p. 52.
93 *Montereul*, I, pp. 174, 176.
94 Cary, *Memorials*, I, pp. 17–18. For an analysis of Sancroft's accusations of presbyterian royalism see Hughes, *Gangraena*, p. 358.
95 Juxon, *Journal*, p. 104.
96 *Montereul*, I, pp. 174, 176.
97 *CJ*, IV, p. 552.
98 Adamson, 'Peerage in politics', pp. 146–7.
99 Baillie, *L&J*, II, p. 377; The ministers of London, Westminster and within the lines of communication, *Certain Considerations and Cautions Agreed by the Ministers of London* (1646).

6

The political presbyterian moment, 1646–7

The campaign to convince Parliament to ratify an independent jurisdiction for parish discipline ended in a compromise that ultimately heralded the defeat of high presbyterian ambitions for a national church settlement. The London presbyterians had established a sophisticated activist network in the city and beyond. However, they realised that they would need greater influence in national political processes to further their objectives in the religious sphere. This pushed the London presbyterians to follow their Scottish friends towards a closer alliance with the Earl of Essex and his 'party' at Westminster. This chapter examines the London presbyterian movement's connections with the wider 'political presbyterian' coalition in 1646 and 1647. These two years, which might be called the 'presbyterian moment' in the history of the British revolutions, would see the political presbyterians attempt to seize and control the politics of settlement. This strategy focused on restoring the fractured parliamentarian consensus by vilifying political rivals and seeking to exclude them from the projected post-civil war political settlement.[1] In the spring of 1647 the presbyterians would ultimately overplay their hand, leading to the revolutionary politicisation of the New Model Army and the defeat of presbyterian hopes to engineer a settlement with the king.

London presbyterians and the Earl of Essex's 'party'

This section looks at the role of London's religious presbyterians in the 'political presbyterian' alliance. In so doing, it considers the London presbyterians' adoption of a political strategy of exclusion aimed at achieving control of the settlement of church and state after Parliament's victory in the first civil war. The perspective and aims of Essex's 'party' were encapsulated by the Earl himself in May 1646, when he is said to have declared that Parliament had been 'bound by the Covenant to defend the king's just rights' and that the civil war had been fought to separate the king from his evil counsellors. Essex reasoned that, given that the king had deserted those advisers by surrendering to Parliament's Scottish allies, there was 'nothing now to be done but to disband the armies and conclude a peace'.[2] Although the majority of Essex's party in Parliament were probably not committed religious presbyterians, they would increasingly take the name 'presbyterian' due to their association with the Scots and the London presbyterian activists.[3]

The connections between London's religious presbyterians and Essex's interest at Westminster were largely by way of the peerage than through alliances with members of the House of Commons. As we have noted, many of the London presbyterian ministers had connections with godly peers, particularly the Earls of Warwick, Manchester and Essex himself. The presbyterian citizenry had similar connections. Many had been officers in the London militia and held Essex in high esteem as a military commander. This was particularly true among those Londoners, led by Colonels Thomas Hooker and Thomas Underwood, who had served under Essex as part of the city's military contingent in the 1643 campaign to relieve Gloucester.[4] This view is exemplified by the publications of Josiah Ricraft, a London merchant and signatory of the November 1645 citizens' petition for presbyterian church government, which championed Essex's military achievements during the first civil war. Ricraft cast Essex as a military and parliamentarian hero, a view shared by many of London's presbyterian citizens, who saw in devout protestant peers such as Essex the model of godly counsel to the king in a post-civil war settlement.[5] London presbyterians had other connections to grandees in Essex's circle. As we have seen, Jeremiah Baines, a Southwark ruling elder, had seen combat as an officer in the armies of both Essex and Sir William Waller.[6] The polemicist John Bastwick, who would be elected a ruling elder for the parish of St Michael, Wood Street, had been supported by Warwick in his unsuccessful attempt to be elected as recruiter MP for Rye.[7] These connections meant that London's religious presbyterians, with their power bases in the Westminster assembly, Sion College and the city's common council, were well connected to political presbyterian partisanship at Westminster.

The representatives of the Scottish covenanter regime in London added a further component to the political presbyterian alliance, with the Scots acting to organise political action between Westminster and London in the furtherance of the presbyterian interest.[8] An example of how city presbyterians could be mobilised by the Scots in support of 'political presbyterian' partisan aims can be seen in the 'Cranford incident' of June and July 1645.[9] Robert Baillie, having learned information about potentially treasonable secret negotiations for the surrender of Oxford between royalists and a Parliamentary sub-committee chaired by the Independent grandee Viscount

Saye and Sele, went to James Cranford's house in the city to see what could be gained from spreading the rumour. Cranford went to great lengths to disseminate Baillie's rumour with the aim of undermining Saye and Sele and his committee as betrayers of the parliamentarian cause. The incident demonstrates how Scottish and London ministers could deploy the politics of gossip for their own factional interests. Upon learning of Saye and Sele's betrayal, Cranford's first thought was to inform prominent lay presbyterian activists with connections to the London common council, who he hoped would raise questions about this apparent treachery.[10] Cranford's lay presbyterian associates proceeded to broadcast the report at the Exchange, a *locus* for informal news in the city. The rumour soon led to near hysteria in London, which was only halted by the intervention of the Lord Mayor and firm action from Parliament. Although Cranford was rewarded with a spell of imprisonment and a substantial fine, the incident demonstrates the utility of the London presbyterian citizenry for the wider purposes of the political presbyterian interest. The value of London presbyterian activists would become plain in 1646–7, when the political presbyterian alliance attempted to gain control of the post-civil war settlement process through measures designed to exclude their opponents from the political sphere.

The politics of exclusion

The common council elections of December 1645 saw London's presbyterians mobilise a campaign aimed at excluding their sectary and Independent opponents from the political arena. As the year progressed, the 'politics of exclusion' would come to define the main strategy of the wider 'political presbyterian' coalition. Although political Independents would ruthlessly master the political art of purge and exclusion in 1648, the London presbyterians attempted to achieve similar results in the period 1645–8. The politics of exclusion was predicated on obtaining religious uniformity among those holding political office, with subscription to the Solemn League and Covenant and confessional Reformed orthodoxy acting as the test for participation in the city's government.

The first shot in the presbyterian campaign was fired during the ward petitions of 22 December 1645, discussed in chapter 5, which sought to convince London voters to reject those who opposed the Covenant and a presbyterian church settlement. These petitions were followed by meetings at Sion College and Cornelius Burges's house, where Francis Roberts argued that his comrades should take action to counter the committee of accommodation's proposal to offer a forbearance to doctrinally orthodox gathered churches.[11] On 1 January 1646, a body of presbyterian ministers meeting at Sion College drafted a letter to the Westminster assembly protesting the committee's concessions.[12] This letter was published by Samuel Gellibrand, Robert Baillie's London publisher, whose family included a number of lay presbyterian activists. Reacting to the letter, William Walwyn noted that it had been published, rather than sent to the Westminster assembly, the intent being to stir up the wider body of presbyterian partisans to action. Given that many of the ministers behind the 1 January letter were also members of the Westminster assembly, Walwyn reasoned that it was 'not made for the information of the Sinod but the misinformation of the People'.[13]

Walwyn was correct in seeing the 1 January letter as part of a wider campaign to stir up action against the proposals for the toleration of gathered churches. The letter was followed by sermons preached at St Paul's Cathedral by James Cranford and the Smectymnuan Matthew Newcomen to condemn toleration. In addition, Robert Baillie reissued his anti-sectary work *A dissuasive from the errours of the time*. Baillie's republication of this book served to preface Thomas Edwards' publishing of the first part of his infamous *Gangraena* in February.[14] As well as registering protest at the committee for accommodation's willingness to grant a forbearance for gathered churches, this high presbyterian salvo of sermons and publications sought to vilify and marginalise sectaries and other refusers of the Solemn League and Covenant.

The principal object of the campaign to revile opponents of presbyterianism was encouraging the city government to take action. The common council obliged when it considered the December 1645 ward petitions on 8 January 1646. The 1645 'eldership' committee was reconstituted and put to work drafting a petition in favour of presbyterian church government and against granting toleration to the sects. In addition, the common council decided that the Solemn League and Covenant should be readministered to the members of the corporation on 14 January, which had been appointed by Parliament as a day of humiliation to contemplate the sins of the nation. This retaking of the Covenant was seen as a means of delineating the acceptable political boundaries of the city.[15] To highlight the partisan nature of this event, the leading presbyterian ministers Edmund Calamy and Simeon Ashe were invited to preach sermons before the city at St Michael Bassishaw, stressing the need to remain loyal to the cause of the Covenant and warning that those who were unfaithful to it would be condemned.[16] The retaking of the Covenant was thus an act designed to expose those who opposed the Covenant and to mark them as outside the boundary of the 'well-affected' citizenry.[17] The ritualism of the 14 January reswearing of the Covenant was followed up in February when the common council charged the 'eldership' committee to investigate and expose those on the common council who had refused to retake the

Covenant. In addition, the committee was to consider what action to take against preachers who had used sermons to criticise the city over the issue of church government.[18] The presbyterians' efforts to establish the Solemn League and Covenant as a test to outline the boundaries of loyalty signalled the beginning of a partisan attempt within the city to exclude both royalists and parliamentarian opponents. As will be seen, the politics of exclusion would become one of the general strategies deployed by the wider 'political presbyterian' alliance in seeking to gain control of the post-civil war quest for settlement.

The City Remonstrance and the political presbyterian alliance

London's presbyterian activists recognised the need for greater co-ordination with Essex's faction at Westminster. For his part, Essex needed the financial, political and potential military influence of the city, and the Scottish covenanter army, to counterbalance his rivals in Parliament. It is important to recognise that for all but a small minority of parliamentarians, politics after the first civil war aimed at finding a way back to a form of royal government.[19] The dynamics of such politics required not only limiting Charles I's room to manoeuvre until the terms of settlement could be reached, but also excluding opposing interests within the parliamentarian camp from being able to offer alternatives to the politically capricious king. This section will analyse how the political presbyterian alliance rallied to advance a politics of exclusion designed to prepare for a favourable restoration of Charles I.

The vehicle for the political presbyterian mobilisation for control of the settlement process was a Remonstrance from the city of London, ultimately presented on 26 May 1646. The idea for this Remonstrance emerged from meetings in April between representatives of Essex's interest at Westminster and a group of presbyterian activists on the London common council. The purpose of the Remonstrance was to put pressure on Parliament to steer it to adopt the Essex party agenda for a political settlement with the king. Thomas Juxon alleged that a number of city presbyterians had met the MPs Lionel Copley and Edmund Harvey, both allies of Essex, on 13 April. Copley and Harvey carried 'instructions' from Sir Philip Stapilton, Essex's close political counsel in the Commons, to 'put forth a remonstrance' and threaten Parliament with a city-wide tax strike if London's demands were not met.[20] This strategy was advanced by presbyterians at a meeting of the common council the next day.[21] Consequently, the common council ordered a committee, composed of a substantial number of presbyterian activists, to draft a remonstrance to be delivered to Parliament.[22]

The political presbyterian moment, 1646–7

Given the nature of its inception as a political presbyterian manifesto, the City Remonstrance was a highly divisive document, with common councillors who leaned towards 'political Independency' opposing it at all stages.[23] Nevertheless, the presbyterians ultimately prevailed in passing the Remonstrance through the common council, which took the rare step of recording in its official journal that 'every particular clause and point' of the Remonstrance was 'twice read and after debate was put to vote, and the remonstrance and petition beeing againe putt to question was by the Court approved'.[24] Despite the internal opposition, and a 22 May counterpetition against the Remonstrance, the common council decided that it should be presented to both houses of Parliament separately.[25] This decision was to take advantage of Essex's recently acquired majority in the Lords, gained on 18 May through obtaining the Earl of Mulgrave's proxy. The citizens calculated that an easy passage for the Remonstrance through the Lords would block the Commons' predictable response of declaring it a breach of privilege.[26]

The Remonstrance can thus be seen as part of the wider political presbyterian gambit to project the impression that it was Essex and his allies who could close the endgame and settle a lasting peace. On 19 May, a few days before the Remonstrance's presentation, Essex (as commander-in-chief of the city's militia force), together with Major General Edward Massie, called a general muster of London's trained bands at Hyde Park. As a coda to this projection of his military power, the Earl, together with many prominent citizens, kissed the hand of the Duke of Gloucester, the king's youngest son, as a sign of an impending restoration settlement.[27] The Hyde Park muster coincided with a conciliatory letter from the king dated 18 May, offering peace along the lines of the Uxbridge treaty and agreeing to submit to the advice of an assembly of divines reconstituted with the addition of clergy of his own nomination. As John Adamson has noted, the king's letter and the City Remonstrance were timed to be both presented to Parliament on 26 May in order to cast Essex's 'party' as the best hope for a peace settlement.[28] The level of organisation between Westminster and London is again revealed by Thomas Juxon, who reported that the presbyterian citizens John Bellamie and John Jones had met Essex on 22 May to co-ordinate the presentation of the Remonstrance.[29] It is also unlikely to be a coincidence that a petition from 300 or so ministers in Norfolk, Essex and Suffolk for the settlement of presbyterian church government and against toleration was presented to the Commons a day later.[30] The City Remonstrance was therefore part of a wider manoeuvre by the political presbyterian coalition to seize control of the terms of the post-civil war settlement.

The Remonstrance has generally been characterised by historians as differing from previous presbyterian petitions by having a strongly secular character.³¹ Nevertheless, its main clauses followed the original remit of the common council's concerns of 14 April, complaining of the subversive ambitions of the 'swarmes of sectaries' in the city.³² It demanded the suppression of gathered churches, the imposition of a presbyterianism and legislation to prosecute sectaries who refused to submit to the public religion established by Parliament. Indeed, the only aspect of the presbyterians' religious programme from the 1645 campaign that was jettisoned from the Remonstrance was the demand for an independent jurisdiction for presbyteries.

The Remonstrance developed the exclusionist themes of the January 1646 city campaign to use subscription to the Solemn League and Covenant as a test of political loyalty. It demanded that conformity to the national presbyterian church settlement be made a condition for those holding positions of public trust and that all dissenters be barred from public office.³³ The City Remonstrance thus sought to settle England's troubles by achieving a partisan domination of political office-holding. That this was also the policy of Essex and his supporters is shown by the other demands of the Remonstrance: a treaty with the king; continuation of the Scottish military alliance; vesting control of the city and the suburban militias in London's own pro-Covenant hands; and the end of the Parliamentary finance committees that served as power bases for the political Independents.³⁴ Although not part of the manifesto proclaimed in the City Remonstrance, the contemporaneous, and nearly successful, plan by political presbyterians at Westminster to weaken the New Model Army by sending six of its regiments to quell the Irish rebellion has to be seen as part of the same programme.³⁵ The Remonstrance thus envisaged a political settlement with the king based on the prior elimination of political and religious opponents and the control of a substantial military force.

The Remonstrance was presented on 26 May. In the Lords, Essex and his allies made sure that the petition was welcome, despite the dissent of 'political Independent' peers led by the Earl of Northumberland and Viscount Saye and Sele. Predictably, the Commons did not receive the Remonstrance very well and the best that Sir Philip Stapilton could manage was to obtain a decision to take it into consideration when time was 'convenient'.³⁶ The Commons' failure to support the Remonstrance only served to alienate the city further, leading to a June citizens' petition containing an alleged 8,634 signatures, which demanded that the Commons give immediate consideration to the Remonstrance.³⁷

The themes of the City Remonstrance continued to act as a manifesto for London's presbyterians into the later part of 1646. At a meeting with leading city presbyterians in early November, Robert Baillie was told that the London presbyterians would accept a restoration of Charles I on the terms of Parliament's Newcastle Propositions, presented to the king in July 1646. However, he was also informed that the king would never get 'the hearts of the Citie' unless the Solemn League and Covenant was enshrined in the constitution by an act of Parliament.[38] The king's rejection of the Newcastle Propositions, together with the rumour that 'the sectarian party' were willing to abandon the Covenant in return for liberty of conscience, led the city presbyterians to redouble their focus on dismantling the sources of political Independent power, in particular the New Model Army. Baillie reported on 8 December that his London presbyterian friends bargained that 'if peace were settled, and the armie downe [...] the noyse of heresies, which is now very loud, would evanishe'.[39]

The presbyterian alliance, however, suffered two setbacks in the later part of 1646. The first blow was the sudden death of the Earl of Essex on 14 September, a shock that robbed the presbyterians of their most important leader and the newly won dominance of the House of Lords. The second setback was the failure to secure the election of the presbyterian alderman John Langham as Lord Mayor in the September mayoral elections. The vote at common hall went to Sir John Gayer, a solidly pro-peace, perhaps even crypto-royalist, candidate.[40] The presbyterian citizens were therefore mindful that they needed to maintain their position of strength in the city. The December common council elections saw the presbyterians campaign for the dissolution of the New Model Army, a popular measure in the city given that payment of the Army had led to unprecedented levels of taxation. The December campaign, which included the publication of the pronouncedly anti-Army third part of Thomas Edwards' *Gangraena*, can be seen as representing a turning point in the politics of the London presbyterians. With the political fortunes of Denzell Holles and Sir Philip Stapilton, Essex's acknowledged successors, rising after they had successfully brokered a financial deal with the city to pay for the withdrawal of the Scottish army, the London presbyterians found themselves allied to an increasingly powerful voice at Westminster.

The organisation behind the December petition also reveals the atmosphere of fear and mutual distrust that had descended on London's post-civil war parliamentarians. In late November and early December London presbyterian activists promoted a petition to the common council calling for measures against the sects and for the dissolution of the New Model Army.[41] In response, the Commons ordered on 2 December that this London petition be suppressed.[42] This led to the arrest on 4 December of three leading lay presbyterian activists: Valentine Fyge, Patrick Bampford and Nicholas Widmerpole.[43] The arrest of the three citizens was turned by the London presbyterians into a propaganda coup when it was successfully argued that the warrants for their arrest had been defective and were void. The day after the arrests, a crowd of supporters appeared before the Parliamentary committee of complaints to secure the release of the three citizens to the cries of 'one and all'.[44] This was followed by a larger gathering in Westminster on 7 December, when around 200 citizens congregated to protest the treatment of their comrades.[45]

The presbyterian activists behind these protests were also instrumental in spreading the rumour that Sir John Evelyn of Wiltshire, a leading political Independent grandee in the Commons, was about to call on Parliament to order the Army to march into London to crush the city. The rumour had begun at the Ludgate haberdashery shop of Major Walter Lee, who in 1643 had led the smashing of the stained-glass windows in Westminster Abbey and had also been a signatory of the citizens' church government petition of November 1645.[46] The rumour caused panic throughout the city.[47] The news of the political Independent's plan to use a military coup to crush the city illustrates the mutual distrust that had come to infect parliamentarianism. The rumour fed increasingly confrontational politics, with presbyterian citizens casting the Army as the principal threat to a presbyterian settlement and the much-hoped-for return to peace-time conditions.

The environment of mutual distrust led the common council on 10 December to appoint a largely pro-presbyterian committee to draft another petition to Parliament.[48] This petition, which was presented on 19 December, can be seen as a sequel to May's Remonstrance. Like its predecessor, it put the city's religious demands first, calling for adequate maintenance for ministers and renewing the demand for the suppression of heresy and separatist churches. The 19 December petition renewed the demands for a settlement with the king, free Parliamentary elections and the abolition of the political-Independent-dominated finance committees. In addition, it repeated the long-standing demand for city control of its own militia and called for the disbandment of the New Model Army; and requested that the Solemn League and Covenant be deployed as a test of loyalty to Parliament.[49] The petition was accepted by the Lords on 22 December, who used its presentation as cover to pass an order against 'anabaptists and other sectaries' disturbing church services, as well demanding that Lord General Fairfax give an account of those of his officers who had refused to take the Covenant. The Lords' order against lay preachers was confirmed by the Commons on 31 December. More fatefully for events to come, on 29 December the Lords resolved to draw up an ordinance to give the city control of its militia.[50] The city's December 1646 petition thus provided a mission statement for the political presbyterians' programme continuing into 1647.

The evidence suggests that these manifestos set out a programme popular among the city's electorate. Despite strong efforts by militant Independents and sectaries to challenge presbyterian candidates in the December 1646 common council elections, contemporaries considered that the results of the elections provided an overwhelmingly popular mandate for the presbyterian agenda in London.[51] One pamphleteer stated in January 1647 that the 'the sense of the whole body of the City was palpably discovered in the last election, when such as had shewed themselves dis-affected to the [19 December] petition were cast out of that body generally in all wards'.[52] The French ambassador observed that the London electorate had 'turned out all the Independents, so that all is presbyterian in the City'.[53] Juxon also accepted the presbyterian ascendancy, but commented that the ferocity of the presbyterian election campaign had allowed several 'known malignants', or crypto-royalists, to secure election to the common council.[54] The presbyterian victory in the city elections put them in good stead to advance their agenda over the next few months. However, the belligerent campaign to achieve political dominance revealed deep fractures after the spring of 1647, when the Army's revolt unexpectedly threatened to make the feared military intervention against the city a reality.

The presbyterian moment, winter 1646–spring 1647

Between December 1646 and March 1647, the London presbyterians reiterated much of the programme they had set out in the campaign of 1646, targeting both toleration and the Army as threats to political and religious settlement. With the issue of church government compromised in June 1646, their campaign shifted to opposing a general toleration of religious sects and gathered churches. This anti-sectarian drive was connected to their other focus in the early months of 1647: the desire to weaken the political underpinnings of the gathered churches in London by seeing the New Model Army disbanded. This campaign neatly dovetailed with the political presbyterians at Westminster, who strived to remove the New Model Army as the military linchpin of the political Independents' power. The prize for success would be effective hegemony over the negotiations with the king (who, from February 1647, the presbyterians held in check at Holdenby House). This gambit made tactical sense given the New Model's military power and Charles's penchant for playing parliamentarian rivals off against each other. The political presbyterian move against the Army in 1647 involved developing a new array of military assets, including the city militia, to provide at least the appearance of an armed counterforce. The combination of presbyterian attempts to exclude opponents from the political arena and their plans for military expansion raised the political stakes, ultimately leading to physical confrontations in the summer of 1647. This section will focus on the role that the London ministers and citizens played in the early months of 1647 within the wider political presbyterian alliance to determine the terms of settlement with Charles I.

With their allies in the ascendancy at Westminster, in the early months of 1647 the London presbyterian clergy were invited to use the pulpit to set out their agenda for the settlement of peace.[55] These sermons followed the general themes that had been expounded in 1646: the need to settle the kingdom according to the Covenant,[56] the establishment of effective church government[57] and criticism of those who sought to delay further reformation.[58] Two main topics stand out in these sermons: first, the duty incumbent on magistrates to take action against heresy;[59] second, the need to both demilitarise England and subdue the rebels in Ireland.[60] These subjects provided cover for the launch of 'presbyterian' policies in Parliament such as the declaration against lay preachers and the House of Lords' February 1647 attempt to introduce an ordinance to punish schism and heresy.[61] Sermons also supported the policy of reducing the New Model Army's numbers and bolstering Holles's Derby House committee as the principal political vehicle controlling the terms of a future peace settlement.[62]

The agenda set by the ministry in their sermons was also advanced by the city's presbyterian laity in petitions presented to the common council in January and March. A 25 January petition from the 'Covenant-ingaged' citizens called for the silencing of lay preachers and the suppression of sectary publications. Following on from the growing fear of political interference by the New Model Army expressed in December, this petition sought to have the Army remain at a non-threatening distance from the city.[63] The March petition, however, revealed divisions among city presbyterians between those who sought a thorough-going 'Covenant-engaged' settlement and those who wished to treat with the king on more flexible terms. Thomas Juxon reported that the March petition was presented by those he considered to be 'well affected presbyters' and the royalist agent Nicholas Oudart claimed that it had been originally 'framed at Sion colledge'.[64] In terms of religion, the petition desired that presbyterianism be settled throughout the kingdom. Politically, however, it demonstrated that many of the city's religious presbyterians remained committed to the uncompromising peace terms proposed by Parliament in 1646, desiring that the king should be forbidden to come to London for negotiations until he had both sworn the Solemn League and Covenant and assented to the Newcastle Propositions.[65]

The hard-line parliamentarian terms of the March 1647 citizens' petition did not accord well with those political presbyterian grandees within the city who wished to adopt a more pragmatic and less stringent negotiating position with Charles I. On 14 February, the French ambassador wrote of his hopes that the city could be convinced to join with those in the House of Lords who were willing to give up 'the Covenant, and consequently the interest of the Scots'.[66] This most likely referred to secret peace negotiations conducted in January through the turncoat Earl of Holland by parliamentarian peers including the Earls of Northumberland, Warwick and Manchester to convince the king to accept a truncated version of the Newcastle Propositions.[67] Against such sentiment, the presbyterian citizens' March petition represented a statement of the continuing presence of the 'Scotified' element within the political presbyterian alliance. This 'Covenant-engaged' aspect would not survive the petition's passage through the common council, where it was referred to a committee headed by the former Lord Mayor Thomas Adams.[68] According to Juxon, 'malignants' on the committee, identified as Adams and Thomas Skinner, the city's Remembrancer, removed the demands for the imposition of the Newcastle Propositions and Covenant on the king.[69] Juxon thought the finished version, presented to Parliament on 17 March, had been rendered 'very lame and poor, very much to the dislike of the honest party' among London's presbyterians.[70]

Running alongside the presbyterian dominance described above was a period of division and despondency among the city's Independents.[71] John Goodwin's congregation, among the most politically savvy of the city sectaries, were counselling their comrades in Hertfordshire to 'sit still and await the mind and providence of God' and not issue petitions to combat the presbyterian offensive.[72] According to William Walwyn the leading London separatist churches, particularly Goodwin's congregation, 'stood aloof' from the March 'Large Petition' that he and a number of general baptist congregations were organising. The Large Petition outlined the radical understanding of the parliamentarian cause in opposition to the city's 'Covenant-engaged' agenda.[73] This petition was intercepted in the congregation of Thomas Lamb and was presented by John Glynne, the city's Recorder and MP, to the Parliamentary committee for investigating unlicensed preaching. The presbyterian-dominated committee's enquiry into the petition led to an ill-tempered scuffle and the arrest of the sectaries Nicholas Tue and Alexander Tulidah.[74] The radicals' pugnacious conduct before the committee set the Commons, led by Holles, against the petitions of the gathered churches, with the House ordering the burning of the 'Large' petition together with a further such petition presented in May.[75]

The upshot of this presbyterian offensive was that, by late May, Independents in the city found the need to temporarily settle their differences. This led to a series of meetings with members of the Army at Oliver Cromwell's house in Drury Lane to plan a response to presbyterian dominance in politics. Ultimately, this would lead to the invitation of a number of city militants, including Walwyn and the future Leveller John Wildman, to contribute to the Army's debates at its Reading headquarters to advance its own settlement for the kingdom.[76]

The activities of the London ministers and their lay allies in the spring of 1647 demonstrated that they could use the pulpit and the petition to advance a common programme that largely accorded with their allies at Westminster. However, as Valerie Pearl notes, the political presbyterian coalition was an 'alliance of dissimilar groups' and the Covenant-engaged March petition suggests that the political presbyterian coalition's level of coherence should not be overestimated.[77] In the spring of 1647 these divisions were not so apparent while the presbyterians scented victory; however, the fault-lines within the political presbyterian alliance would surface again in the summer of 1647 as the hopes of a settlement faded.

London's solemn engagement

The 'political presbyterian' attempt to establish political dominance began to derail from March, as the New Model Army became politicised over the issues of arrears and indemnity.[78] This politicisation accelerated further after Denzell Holles imprudently caused Parliament to issue a 'declaration of dislike' against the Army's protest of its treatment on the evening of 31 March.[79] From May onwards the New Model and the 'political presbyterian' alliance were locked in a war of words that ultimately led to the Army's bloodless coup in late July and August. This section will explore London's religious presbyterians' role in the events that culminated in apprentices invading Parliament on 26 July and the Army entering London in force.

From early 1647, the primary goal of the Westminster political presbyterians was to raise the necessary funds to disband the bulk of the New Model Army and send its remaining forces to Ireland. Holles also sought to build the foundations of a military force to threaten and perhaps even engage the New Model should his planned disbandment and dispersal of the Army fail.[80] Valerie Pearl has seen this policy as a largely coherent one, drawing together an alliance of the 'political presbyterians' at Westminster, 'Scotified' religious presbyterians in the city and crypto-royalists to effect a 'counter-revolution'. Historians such as Austin Woolrych and Ian Gentles, who have studied the era from the perspective of the Army, have largely confirmed Pearl's analysis. However, other historians have questioned the extent to which the 'political presbyterian' coalition either was united in its actions or made common cause with outright royalists. Mark Kishlansky, the most strident critic of Pearl's thesis, views her analysis as 'circumstantial and open to question'. He argues that the lack of cogent and united action by the 'political presbyterian' alliance belied any genuine 'counter-revolutionary' design in 1647.[81] In addition, Ann Hughes, Patricia Crawford, Barbara

Donegan and Paul Seaward have all, to a lesser or greater degree, challenged both the argument that the London and Westminster presbyterians were willing to make common cause with outright royalists, and the notion that the presbyterians sought merely to return to the constitutional gains obtained by the Long Parliament in 1641–2.[82] The account presented here shares much with these studies, arguing that the events of summer 1647 were not so much an attempted 'counter-revolution' as the culmination of the long-running factional struggle to control the direction of the shattered parliamentarian cause and the politics of settlement.

To understand the London presbyterians' attitude to the rise of the New Model in 1647 it is necessary to consider the conspiracy narrative through which city presbyterians understood the Army's place in the political struggle within parliamentarianism. Probably drawing on memories of the events in Germany during the Thirty Years War, Nehemiah Wallington believed the rumours circulating in the city that the Army intended to 'plunder our houses [...] fier our houses and lay the City levell and waste [... and that] they would deflower and ravish the daughter[s]'. This narrative connected the Army to the London sects, with Wallington adding that the sectary supporters of the Army in the city spoke 'filthy reprochfull words and terrible threatenings [... about] the best of our Ministers'.[83]

An equally pressing fear, which has already been seen at work in the Cranford incident in 1645, was the suspicion that the political Independents were conspiring to join with the king's party to betray the parliamentarian cause. In February 1647, Robert Bostock, the leading London printer of Scottish covenanter material, wrote a satirical dialogue narrating a conversation between the characters 'Independent' and 'Malignant' and their agreement to join forces to prevent a presbyterian settlement.[84] Presciently, Bostock's dialogue imagined plans being laid for Charles I to be rescued by the Army from his presbyterian 'captors' at Holdenby House. He imagined a committee of sectaries and royalists, with John Lilburne as the Independents' 'grand commander', settling a secret treaty with the king. In the dialogue, the character of 'Malignant' strikes a deal with 'Independent', promising that in return for 'blow[ing] the bellows now of dissension' against the Scots and the English presbyterians, the king would grant the Independents liberty of conscience.[85] Wallington's fears of plunder and rapine and Bostock's satire, with its theme of a sectary-royalist conspiracy and collusion, would encapsulate the viewpoint of many city presbyterians in relation to the Army and the sects in the late spring and summer of 1647.[86]

The political presbyterians aimed to utilise a number of key city institutions to lay the foundations to build a counterforce to challenge the New Model's military dominance. In particular, control of the city's militia committee and the finance treasuries set up to pay 'reformardoes', unpaid soldiers from Parliament's disbanded armies, would be key elements of the presbyterian strategy. Control of the London militia committee was won on 16 April, when an ordinance passed in Parliament gave the city the right to constitute a committee of its own choosing. Acceding to London's long-term demands, the new committee would direct both the city militias and the previously autonomous suburban forces.[87] On 27 April, the common council, after once again reaffirming the Solemn League and Covenant and hearing a sermon from the presbyterian minister Anthony Burgess, elected a new militia committee of thirty-one members. All of these members of the committee were of a 'political presbyterian' complexion, although only twelve can be definitely placed as religious presbyterian activists.[88] Controversially, all of the members of the previously constituted militia committee who supported 'political Independency', including Isaac Pennington the former Lord Mayor, were purged.[89] One critic thought that the purged committee members were marked out because they had opposed the May 1646 Remonstrance 'by which means they discovered themselves opponents to their Scotch design of presbyterie'.[90] An analysis of pay warrants signed by the new militia committee suggests that the committee's main activities were conducted largely by the aldermen Adams, Langham, Bunce and Thomas Cullum, all former supporters of the Earl of Essex and now leading allies of Holles, as well as the religious presbyterian militia officers John and Edward Bellamie, Edward Hooker, Thomas Gower, Richard Venner and John Jones.[91] The first act of the new committee was a purge of political and religious Independents from the militias of the city and the suburbs.[92] In addition to the capture of the London militia committee, prominent presbyterian citizens were appointed in June as treasurers for the city committees set up to organise the payment of the reformado soldiers.[93] The city's religious presbyterians were thus central to the management of the institutions that Holles and his Westminster allies captured in their attempt to raise a counterforce to the New Model Army.

While many of London's presbyterian activists were prepared to contemplate the development of the city's trained bands as a potentially offensive militia, this design did not have uniform support, even among 'Covenant-engaged' citizens. As we have noted from Nehemiah Wallington, many citizens feared that the city would be subject to rapine and destruction. The theatrics of Major General Edward Massie, who on 6 June exhorted the citizens from his coach 'to defend themselves against the madd men in the Army', perhaps suggest that the political presbyterian architects of the city's military counterforce were driven to desperation born from the opposition of many citizens to military action.[94] This was revealed during a joint meeting of the city's militia committee and Holles's reconstituted

Parliamentary committee of safety on 11 June after the Army's seizure of the king from his presbyterian captivity at Holdenby House. At this meeting John Dalbier, Sir Thomas Essex and Edwin Sandys, former officers under Essex's command, sought the militia committee's authority to raise a force from among the reformadoes to present 'a vigorous opposition to the army'.[95] The attempt to conscript reformadoes to lay the cap stone to a counterforce to the New Model was met by opposition from John Bellamie, one of the leading 'Covenant-engaged' presbyterian activists. Bellamie 'made a motion that all ways might be taken to avoid the shedding of blood and to prevent the ruin of the City, which would follow if the reformadoes were entertained'. He suggested that instead of commissioning Essex's former officers to prepare for military confrontation, commissioners should be sent to the Army 'to know their desires and see if it might not be reconciled'. Although the majority on the militia committee, including some of Bellamie's religious presbyterian friends, defeated his motion, it was raised in a meeting of the common council the following day, which voted to reverse the militia committee's refusal to send commissioners to the Army.[96] These votes point to divided opinions among the London presbyterians in the face of a pending military engagement with New Model Army.

Despite these protests the militia committee's recruiting of reformadoes throughout the summer contributed to the growing tensions between the city and Army. The issue reached crisis point when the New Model presented demands for the impeachment of its chief political opponents on 9 July and for the restoration of the pre-April 1647 militia committee.[97] The Commons, frightened by clear threat of a military *Putsch*, debated the issue on 22 July and granted the Army's request.[98] Alarmed by Parliament's capitulation to the Army, a crowd of citizens and apprentices gathered at Skinners' Hall on 21 July where a 'solemn engagement' had been printed and brought for subscription. This document called for the king come to Parliament without the Army to confirm the peace terms that he had offered on 12 May in reply to the Newcastle Propositions and to enter into a personal treaty with Parliament and the Scottish commissioners according these terms.[99] The king's 12 May terms were those secretly negotiated by the presbyterian peers in January and included Parliamentary control of the militia for ten years, the establishment of presbyterian church government for three years and further deliberation by a reconstituted Westminster assembly.

Thomas Juxon considered the Londoners' 'solemn engagement' to be a last-ditch attempt by the Westminster 'political presbyterians' to reverse the Army's political ascendancy. He believed that it had been 'procured' in secret meetings organised by Holles and the other MPs 'secluded' from Parliament as a result of the Army's threats.[100] Credence is given to Juxon's suspicions by the royalist agent Joseph Bampfield who reported that, after withdrawing from Parliament on 19 July, the secluded members were engaged in secret meetings with city allies to find ways to revive their political programme.[101] Evidence of collusion between the secluded members and the city presbyterians over the London solemn engagement is also suggested by an anonymous pamphlet that claimed that it was brought to print on the night of 21 July by John Bellamie. The author alleged that the printed copies of the document were later delivered by Bellamie to presbyterian 'agitators in the severall wards, to get hands to it'; a fact confirmed by Juxon, who identified 'many of the trained band officers' as the persons dispersing it.[102] These officers, probably including many of the presbyterian activists of officer rank in the trained bands, were using the same tactics that the city presbyterian petitioning network had used in 1645–6. It therefore appears likely that the same network of presbyterian citizens that had previously organised the city petitions for parish presbyteries was behind the mobilisation to get London to enter into the solemn engagement. Given the political connections between this group and the wider political presbyterian network throughout 1647, the suspicions of Juxon and Bampfield that the secluded members were working with London's religious presbyterians appears highly plausible.

The failure of the political presbyterian gambit

The Army's seizure and securing of the king in June 1647 placed the political Independents again in the ascendancy at Westminster. On 23 July the republican MP Henry Marten penned a declaration charging all who had signed the city's solemn engagement with high treason. Marten's declaration, a parallel to Holles's March declaration of dislike against the Army, only served to focus the anger and resolve of the city engagers.[103] The common council, aggrieved at the loss of its hard-won control of the London militia, prepared a petition to be delivered on 26 July. This section looks at the fateful consequences of that petition for the political presbyterians' attempt to control the terms of political settlement.

The events of 26 July are well known to historians of the mid-seventeenth-century crisis. After the city's petition was presented to Parliament, both houses were stormed by rioting apprentices who demanded that Parliament put into effect the terms of the solemn engagement, restore London's 'presbyterian' militia committee and, at the tail end of the riot, bring the king to London. The threat from the apprentices caused many MPs and Lords to flee to the Army, finally giving the New Model the pretext to march on the city in order to restore Parliament.[104] The events of this day have been the subject of sustained historiographical controversy. For Valerie Pearl and the majority of historians after her, the violence against Parliament on 26 July was a 'counter-revolution' orchestrated by Denzell Holles and the other secluded members, aided by an alliance of city presbyterians and royalists.[105] Other historians, most notably Mark Kishlansky, have dissented from Pearl's analysis, seeing the events of 26 July as an eruption of crowd violence resulting from the collapse of Parliamentary authority and the 'tide of anxiety, righteousness, and exuberance' that followed the political clashes of the middle months of 1647.[106] A moderating interpretation can be found in the work of Michael Mahony who, while seeing the forcing of Parliament on 26 July as the result of collusion between the secluded members and London presbyterians, considers that the apprentices went beyond their brief, especially in their call for the king to be brought to London.[107]

What role did the city's religious presbyterians play in preparing and aiding the tumult of 26 July? Thomas Juxon alleged that the apprentices were ordered into action by alderman James Bunce after Parliament had rebuffed the city's petition. Bunce is alleged to have stated to the apprentices that the city government 'had done what they could and that now it rested in them [the apprentices] to play their parts'. This led the apprentices to storm Parliament, while Bunce stayed behind with his associates 'to give direction for the management of this business'.[108] The secluded members were also implicated in the organisation of the riots. They were dining at the Bell in nearby King Street, ostensibly to settle their financial affairs, although Pearl interpreted this meeting as the 'cockpit' from which the secluded members controlled the riot.[109] John Glynne, the city's Recorder, is said to have given refreshments to the rioters from his apartment near Westminster Hall.[110] In addition, the later Parliamentary investigation of those accused of organising the riot gathered evidence that the presbyterian activist William Drake and Thomas Papillon, an apprentice of the presbyterian militia officer and common councillor Thomas Chamberlain, were among those instrumental in instigating the riots.[111] An eye-witness to the events claimed that one of the rioting apprentices had stated that 'what they did they were advised by a member of the House of Commons'.[112] Put together, these connections plausibly suggest that the apprentices had been stirred up in advance, possibly by those connected to the political presbyterian alliance. On the other hand, the earliest accounts of the riot, those of Gilbert Mabbot, *A Perfect Summary* and John Rushworth, all state that the city delegates withdrew before the rioting broke out in the afternoon. These accounts do not condemn the city presbyterian fathers for directing the riot, but rather criticise them for their studied failure to come to Parliament's aid when the apprentices began to force the Commons.[113] On balance, while arguments for the secluded members and the city presbyterians actively controlling the riots appear somewhat overstated and overly coherent in the historiography, it is difficult to escape the conclusion that political and religious presbyterian leaders were involved in instigating the events of 26 July.[114]

It is also possible, however, that the rioting got out of hand due to the apprentices being targeted by *agents provocateur*.[115] Pro-royalist handbills calling for action had been distributed to apprentices throughout July 1647.[116] Sir William Waller, one of the secluded members, recorded that a group of apprentices came to him before the riots disclosing their intention to act against Parliament on 26 July.[117] If royalist instigation can be detected, the backbench MP Clement Walker also accused sectaries of provoking the rioters. According to Walker's account, most of the apprentices had departed from Westminster after obtaining the city's demands but 'some disorderly persons [...] instigated by divers sectaries and friends of the Army', including the Southwark separatist Samuel Highland, remained in Parliament to provoke the mob.[118] As Michael Mahony notes, the rioters' final demand, to bring the king back to London, went against the policy of the city and political presbyterians who only sought that the king negotiate with Parliament (and stay at his palace in Richmond) to enact the 12 May peace propositions.[119] According to Walker this final phase of the riot 'was cunningly and premeditatedly contrived, to encrease the scandal upon the City' and forced it to finally intervene to suppress the riot.[120] Walker's account raises the possibility that the apprentices, who, as noted above, had been courted by those making overtly royalist demands, went further than the political presbyterians in the city considered desirable.

What role did the Sion College ministers play in the crisis of summer 1647? There is little doubt that the ministers' sermons of the summer months had been critical of the Army. A sectary newsletter of 3 July informed the Army that 'the preists' had 'rail[ed]' against it.[121] Although one might be rightly sceptical of such information, the tone is confirmed by a pamphlet published on 23 July by Christopher Love, which touched on many of the themes of the presbyterian narrative of an Army-sectary conspiracy to pervert the parliamentarian cause. Love censured the New Model for its mutinous refusal to obey Parliament's orders, as well as its role in instigating a 'design' for universal toleration.[122] Love's printed pamphlet probably reflected his sermon oratory, as Love, together with Thomas Edwards, was singled out as preaching against the Army in May grievance lists presented by three New Model regiments.[123] However, although the Commons summoned William Jenkyn, Cornelius Burges and Thomas Edwards on 2 October 1647 to be examined for allegations of stirring up the mob on 26 July, there is little evidence that the presbyterian clergy were directly involved in the tumult. No charges followed the questioning of the ministers, and descriptive accounts most contemporary to the events of 26 July do not mention the clergy's direct involvement in the riot.[124]

The apprentices' forcing of Parliament set the city on a collision course with the Army. Following the riots, the restored 'presbyterian' militia committee, dominated by the former Lord Mayor Thomas Adams and supported by a group of core religious presbyterian citizens, met to attempt to find a solution to the problem of the New Model.[125] Many of the city's presbyterian ministers had been appointed to preach on 28 July, which had been set aside as a city-wide day of humiliation.[126] According to pro-Independent sources, the sermons of 28 July were used to kindle the city for imminent conflict with the Army. John Price, the leading polemicist of John Goodwin's gathered church, later asserted that the Sion College ministers had preached 'go out to meet with that proud and blasphemous Army; the Lord hath delivered them into your hands'.[127] In similar vein, the Earl of Leicester recorded that 'Mr Edwards and divers other ministers in London stirred up the people in theyr sermons to rayse armes to suppress the Army'.[128] The presbyterians were quick to deny these charges. An anonymous tract published by the presbyterian bookseller Thomas Underhill stated that the collective opinion expressed by the city ministers on 28 July was that mob violence was in 'no ways justifiable'.[129] Cornelius Burges, while accepting that the Sion College ministers had been ordered by the forced Parliament 'to stirre up the people', had made clear their protest 'against any desires of a new war'. Burges admitted that the ministers had used the pulpit to encourage the people of the city 'to their own just and necessary preservation' but had 'never purposely or wittingly done anything to ingage the City against the Army, or the Army against the City'.[130] Burgess' comments are borne out by manuscript notes of the 28 July sermon preached by Edmund Calamy. Warning the city that 'we are all going into a huge abisse of misery', Calamy blamed the situation on the rule of Parliamentary factions and the breach of the Covenant. While he advised the city to 'take heed of a universall toleration', he nevertheless championed a 'liberty' for doctrinally orthodox dissenters who were 'not distructive to church and state'. While Calamy's sermon held to the usual themes of London presbyterian polemic, his text did not call for military engagement against the Army.[131]

It is also apparent that many citizens' attitude towards any military engagement with the Army was lukewarm at best. Nehemiah Wallington recorded that everyone he knew 'were either for the Army or eles their hearts failed them' so that 'our case was desperate and feeres increased'.[132] On 31 July Thomas Adams and Thomas Skinner penned a defiant declaration refusing to concede the city's right to appoint its own militia and pointing out the threat posed by the Army's actions to constitutional government.[133] Adams and Skinner's declaration was divisive even among city presbyterians. Juxon recorded that it was 'too low' for supporters of the immediate restoration of Charles I and 'too high for the honest party' among the presbyterians.[134] This lack of common resolve and the impending threat of a military showdown soon caused the city's collective determination to crack, with many in the trained bands failing to attend a muster of London's forces at St James's Field. In addition, the presbyterian militia officer Colonel Nathaniel Campfield, together with other militia officers, resigned their commissions rather than engage the Army.[135]

With disaster approaching and naked royalist sentiment being expressed throughout the city, the presbyterian ministry called time on the preparations for a military confrontation with the Army.[136] The emergence of openly royalist sentiment may have been a factor in quelling presbyterian resolve against the Army. Even Christopher Love had couched his criticisms of the Army with the caveat that 'I would have none of you conceive as if I were a malignant royalist (I hate arbitrary power and tyranny in princes as much as any)'.[137] On 2 August, a troop of reformadoes under the command of Edward Massie and Sednham Poynts charged on a crowd meeting at Guildhall to present a petition against engaging the Army, resulting in some of the protestors being killed.[138] Shocked by the escalation of events, the Westminster assembly voted to draft letters to the city, Army and Parliament counselling immediate reconciliation. At the same time the assembly sent a messenger to the London presbyterian ministers to ask them to use their influence to avert the impending showdown.[139] This measure produced a letter from twenty London presbyterian ministers 'professing our abhorrency from the shedding of any blood on either side'. Edmund Calamy, Simeon Ashe and Thomas Case went in person to the joint meeting of the militia committee and the committee of safety to advise that peace should be swiftly settled with the Army.[140] The ministers' actions had the effect of breaking the resolve of the militia committee to resist the Army further. On 3 August the city sent a submissive letter to Thomas Fairfax reversing Skinner's and Adams' declaration of 31 July and by 4 August London had been encircled in preparation for the soldiers' triumphant march through the city on 7 August.[141] This, quite understandably, led many presbyterians to fear reprisals, with Thomas Edwards fleeing the city to exile in the Netherlands.[142] However, the city was to be spared Army violence. Nehemiah Wallington commented on the 'civill and modest deportment' of the Army as it progressed in a humiliating show of strength through the city, but recorded that rank and file soldiers had told him that they 'did intend to have plundered the Citie', but had been prevented from doing so by their officers.[143] While fighting had been averted, it came at the cost of the loss of presbyterian influence in the city and Parliament.

The period directly after the Army's march into the city saw the Army grandees and their political Independent allies attempt to achieve what the presbyterians had failed to accomplish in the first half of 1647: a negotiated settlement with the king, according to the *Heads of proposals*.[144] When this attempt failed, the Independent alliance became divided over how to deal with the recalcitrant king. The Parliamentary investigations into those responsible for the actions of the summer led to the incarceration of a number of key presbyterian activists involved in the 1645–7 mobilisation.[145] Following the logic of exclusion that was rapidly coming to define parliamentarian politics in the later 1640s, the city's militia regiments were purged of their presbyterian officers.[146] In a final measure to attenuate the ability of city presbyterians to mobilise, Parliament issued an ordinance on 17 December barring all those who had signed the city's solemn engagement from holding civic office.[147] Backed by the Army, the political Independents were able to impose the politics of exclusion on the city in a way that the presbyterians had failed to do in 1646. One presbyterian broadside, using language that in other places might be described as 'Leveller', complained that the ordinance excluding presbyterians was designed to prevent free elections in order 'to bring in a new pack' of Independents 'to overtop and ruin the City'.[148] In practice, the ordinance's application appears to have been limited and based on the willingness of local wardmotes to co-operate with it. While presbyterians such as John Bellamie, George Thomason and Edward Hooker were returned to the common council, the 17 October ordinance did manage to inflict some electoral casualties, with Major Walter Lee, the publisher Christopher Meredith and the imprisoned Captain John Jones being excluded from the common council.[149] The effect of the defeat of the presbyterian struggle to control the terms of settlement in the first half of 1647 and the political Independents' follow-up policy of purge and exclusion was that the city's religious presbyterians fell largely silent in the later part of 1647.

Conclusion

The events of late summer 1647 marked the passing of the presbyterian 'moment' in civil war politics. The 'political presbyterian' coalition contained mismatches of vision that would lead to fractures within the alliance as it came under pressure. This was particularly true among London's presbyterian citizens, the majority of whom had been 'war party' activists in the first civil war and who still sought the imposition of a vigorous settlement according to the Solemn League and Covenant as the condition for the king's restoration. The London presbyterians had used their alliance with Essex's 'party' to seize substantial control of city institutions. By the early months of 1647 the main goals of the political presbyterian alliance had become the control of negotiations with the king and the dismantling of their parliamentarian rivals' sources of power. In the spring of 1647 presbyterian dominance appeared complete. However, the presbyterians overplayed their hand, largely by treating the Army roughly. In the face of a strong external military force and internal differences, the presbyterian design collapsed. Nevertheless, London's religious presbyterians remained within the parliamentarian fold and, as we shall see in chapter 9, regained position in 1648 as the political Independent coalition diverged over the question of the right way to conclude the 'intestinal' conflict of the 1640s.

Notes

1 The most detailed narratives of the mid-1640s political presbyterian moment can be found in Mahony, 'The presbyterian party' and Kishlansky, *New Model Army*.
2 Cary, *Memorials*, I, p. 30.
3 Adamson, 'Peerage in politics', pp. 68–107; Scott, 'Party politics in the Long Parliament, 1640–8', pp. 42–5.
4 Nagel, 'The militia of London', pp. 115–34; William Marshall, *The true mannor and forme of the proceeding to the funerall of the right honourable Robert Earl of Essex and Ewe* (1646), p. 2.
5 Ricraft's pro-Essex broadsides were collected together in *A survey of Englands champions, and truths faithfull patriots* (1647).
6 BL Add. Ms. 18780 (Notebook of Jeremiah Baines); D. Scott, 'Baines, Jeremy (1611–78)', *History of Parliament 1640–1660* (forthcoming).
7 F. M. Condick, 'The life and works of Dr John Bastwick, 1595–1654' (Ph.D thesis, University of London, 1983), p. 166.
8 Pearl, 'London puritans and Scotch fifth columnists', pp. 317–31; Brenner, *Merchants*, pp. 464–5; A. Hughes, '"The remembrance of sweet fellowship": relationship between English and Scottish presbyterians in the 1640s and 1650s' in *Insular Christianity: alternative models of the Church in Britain and Ireland, c.1570–c.1700*, eds R. Armstrong and T. Ó hAnnracháin (Manchester, 2013), pp. 170–89.
9 For the Cranford incident, see PA HL/PO/JO/10/1/189 (House of Lords' Main Papers, June–July 1645), fos 198–263; Pearl, 'London puritans and Scotch fifth columnists'; P. Crawford, 'The Savile affair', *EHR*, 90:354 (1975), 76–93; Mahony, 'The Savile affair', pp. 211–27.
10 These included the future ruling elders Captain John Jones, Colonel Thomas Gower, Richard Venner and Robert Lant.

The political presbyterian moment, 1646–7   161

11 Baillie, *L&J*, II, pp. 344–6.
12 *A letter of the ministers of the City of London [...] against toleration* (1646). The letter was passed by the assembly to the committee of accommodation (*MPWA*, III, pp. 730–1).
13 William Walwyn, *Tolleration justified*, reprinted in Walywn, *Writings*, pp. 156–7, 172; [Anon.], *Several letters from the Parliament and [...] Kirk of Scotland* (1646).
14 James Cranford, *Haereseo-machia* (1646); Matthew Newcomen, *The duty of such as would walke worthy of the Lord* (1646); Robert Baillie, *A dissuasive from the errours of the time* (1645); Thomas Edwards, *Gangraena* (1646); Baillie, *L&J*, II, p. 352.
15 LMA, JCC40, fo. 160; *Mercurius civicus* (8–15 January 1646), pp. 2005–6; Baillie, *L&J*, II, p. 337.
16 Simeon Ashe, *Religious covenanting directed* (1646); Edmund Calamy, *The great danger of covenant-refusing and covenant-breaking* (1646).
17 *Cal. Clarendon SP*, I, p. 298.
18 LMA, JCC40, fo. 166v; Lindley, *Popular politics*, pp. 362–3.
19 Scott, 'Party politics in the Long Parliament, 1640–8', p. 33.
20 Juxon, *Journal*, p. 114.
21 LMA, JCC40, fo. 176; Baillie, *L&J*, II, pp. 365, 368.
22 The drafting committee for the Remonstrance contained a large number of the 1645 eldership committee, with presbyterians being represented by the aldermen John Langham and James Bunce and the common councillors John Jones, John Bellamie, Edward Hooker, Michael Herring, Richard Venner, Richard Glyde, John Gace and William Kendall.
23 Juxon, *Journal*, pp. 119, 122; C[ornelius] B[urges], *Sion college, what it is and what it doeth* (1648), pp. 9–10.
24 LMA, JCC40, fo. 178v. The political Independents Stephen Estwicke, John Fowke, Thomas Andrews and Robert Tichborne demanded to be permitted to formally enter their dissent to the Remonstrance.
25 *Ibid.*, fos 181–2v; Juxon, *Journal*, p. 123; *A petition [...] to the common council* (22 May 1646).
26 *LJ*, VIII, p. 319; Adamson, 'Peerage in politics', pp. 135–6.
27 *Cal. Clarendon SP*, I, p. 318; Mahony, 'The presbyterian party', pp. 220–1, 268.
28 Adamson, 'Peerage in politics', pp. 142–4.
29 Juxon, *Journal*, p. 123.
30 *CJ*, IV, p. 556; *The weekly account* (27 May–3 June 1646), sigs Z1r–v; *A perfect diurnall* (25 May–1 June 1646), p. 1190.
31 V. Pearl, 'London's counter revolution' in *The Interregnum: the quest for settlement 1646–1660*, ed. G. E. Aylmer (1972), pp. 35, 40; Mahony, 'The presbyterian party', p. 217.
32 *To the right honorable the house of Commons [...] the humble remonstrance and petition of the [...] City of London* (1646), p. 2. The City Remonstrance is discussed by Pearl, 'London's counter revolution', pp. 38–40; Kishlansky, *New*

Model Army, pp. 85–9; Lindley, Popular politics, pp. 367–8; and Hughes, Gangraena, pp. 347–8.
33 The humble remonstrance, p. 7.
34 Ibid., pp. 7–8; Adamson, 'Peerage in politics', pp. 139–40.
35 The attempt to send the New Model regiments to Ireland failed by only one vote: CJ, IV, pp. 631–2.
36 LJ, VIII, pp. 331–4; CJ, IV, pp. 555–6.
37 For fuller discussions see Kishlansky, New Model Army, pp. 86–7; Lindley, Popular politics, pp. 367–70; and Scott, Politics and war, p. 120.
38 Baillie, L&J, II, pp. 407–8.
39 Ibid., II, pp. 413, 391.
40 Ibid., II, p. 400; Juxon, Journal, p. 137; Hughes, Gangraena, p. 361; R. Ashton, 'Gayer, Sir John', ODNB.
41 Juxon, Journal, p. 141. The key activist in this petitioning had been William Drake, a signatory of the November 1645 petition.
42 CJ, IV, p. 735, Baillie, L&J, II, p. 412.
43 The humble remonstrance, p. 9. Bampford and Widmerpole were both militia officers, while Widmerpole, of the presbyterian-led parish of Christ Church, Newgate and Fyge, a ruling elder of St Bride, Fleet Street, had been signatories of the November 1645 petition calling for *jure divino* presbyterianism.
44 Juxon, Journal, p. 141; Lindley, Popular politics, pp. 371–3.
45 CJ, V, p. 17; Montereul, I, pp. 352–4; BL Add. Ms. 37344, fos 71–2. The organisers of the 7 December protest were the presbyterian activists William Drake, Josiah Ricraft, Lawrence Brinley, William Barton and Thomas Browne.
46 Nagel, 'The militia of London', p. 115.
47 CJ, V, pp. 15–17; Mahony, 'The presbyterian party', pp. 332–3; Lindley, Popular politics, pp. 370–1.
48 LMA, JCC40, fo. 199; Juxon, Journal, p. 141.
49 The humble remonstrance; Mahony, 'The presbyterian party', pp. 325–8; Ashton, Counter-revolution, p. 64; Lindley, Popular politics, pp. 371–3.
50 LJ, VIII, pp. 617–18, 621, 635; CJ, V, pp. 20–1, 29–30, 32–3; Lindley, Popular politics, p. 372; Ashton, Counter-revolution, p. 154.
51 A summary of the sectary response to the December 1646 elections can be found in de Krey, Following the Levellers, I, pp. 91–2.
52 [Anon.], England's remembrancer of London's integritie, No. 1 (1647), p. 3.
53 Montereul, I, p. 372.
54 Juxon, Journal, p. 144, esp. n. 144; Lindley, Popular politics, pp. 372–3.
55 For discussion of these sermons see Hughes, Gangraena, pp. 379–81.
56 Francis Roberts, A broken spirit, God's sacrifices (1646), p. 32; William Jenkyn, A sleeping sicknes the distemper of the times (1647), p. 29.
57 Jenkyn, A sleeping sicknes, sig. A3; Roberts, A broken spirit, sig. A4v, 69 (N.B. both Jenkyn's and Roberts's work use a combination of signatures and page numbers); Lazarus Seaman, The head of the Church, the judge of the world (1647), p. 27; Richard Vines, The authours, nature and danger of Haeresie (1647), p. 69.

58 Vines, *The authours, nature and danger*, p. 3; Jenkyn, *A sleeping sicknes*, pp. 28–9.
59 Obadiah Sedgwick, *The nature and danger of heresies* (1647), pp. 37–9; Seaman, *The head of the Church*, p. 27; Vines, *The authours, nature and danger*, pp. 9, 14, 17, 66.
60 Jenkyn, *A sleeping sicknes*, sig A3v, p. 28; Seaman, *The head of the Church*, sig. A4v.
61 *CJ*, V, pp. 34–5; *LJ*, VIII, p. 718.
62 Mahony, 'The presbyterian party', pp. 346–61.
63 *The humble petition [...] of those covenant-ingaged citizens [...] presented 25 January* (1647).
64 *Nicholas papers*, I, pp. 80–81; Juxon, *Journal*, pp. 150–1.
65 The citizens' petition can be reconstructed from: *Nicholas papers*, I, pp. 80–1; *Montereul*, II, p. 35; Juxon, *Journal*, pp. 150–1, BL Egerton Ms. 2533, fo. 417v.
66 *Montereul*, I, p. 451.
67 S. R. Gardiner, *History of the great civil war, 1642–1649*, 4 vols (1901), III, p. 252; Mahony, 'The presbyterian party', p. 465; Ashton, *Counter-revolution*, pp. 15–16.
68 LMA, JCC40, fos 205v–206.
69 Juxon, *Journal*, p. 151.
70 LMA, JCC40, fos 207–10; Juxon, *Journal*, pp. 150–1; Mahony, 'The presbyterian party', p. 365. The London petition was supported by petitions from Essex and Suffolk. Oudart believed these had been by instigated by Holles: *Nicholas papers*, I, pp. 74–5.
71 *Montereul*, II. p. 109; *Cromwell Letters and speeches*, I, p. 252.
72 Hertfordshire Record Office, MS 70556 (letter from Barbor, Turner and Feake to Colonel Alban Cox); John Lilburne, *Jonahs cry out of the whales belly* (1647), pp. 5–6.
73 William Walwyn, *Walwyns just defence* (1649) in Walwyn, *Writings*, p. 390; De Krey, *Following the Levellers*, I, pp. 109–11.
74 William Walwyn, *Gold tried in the fire* (1647) in Walwyn, *Writings*, pp. 276–93; M. Kishlansky, 'The Army and the Levellers: the roads to Putney', *HJ*, 22:4 (1979), pp. 803–4.
75 *CJ*, V, pp. 118, 162, 179.
76 Walwyn, *Walwyns just defence*, pp. 390–3.
77 Pearl, 'London's counter revolution', pp. 29, 56.
78 J. Morrill, 'The army revolt of 1647' in Morrill, *The nature of the English revolution: essays by John Morrill* (Harlow, 1994), pp. 307–31.
79 P. Crawford, *Denzil Holles 1598–1680: A study of his political career* (1979), p. 142.
80 Pearl, 'London's counter revolution', pp. 44–6; Crawford, *Denzil Holles*, pp. 150–52, 155.
81 Kishlansky, *New Model Army*, pp. 269–71, 341 n. 80, 347 n. 216, 348 n. 246.
82 Hughes, *Gangraena*, pp. 404–7; Crawford, *Denzil Holles*, pp. 148–9;

B. Donegan, 'Review of Robert Ashton, *Counter-revolution*', *The Journal of Modern History*, 69:3 (1997), pp. 583–4; P. Seaward, 'Constitutional and unconstitutional royalism', *HJ*, 40:1 (1997), pp. 233–5.
83 Wallington, *Notebooks*, p. 228.
84 [Robert Bostock], *Herod and Pilate reconciled* (1647).
85 *Ibid*., pp. 1–2.
86 A converse conspiracy theory of presbyterian-royalist betrayal informed Independent-sectary polemic during this period: see [Anon.], *The poore wisemans admonition unto all the plaine people of London* (1647).
87 *CJ*, V, p. 145; *LJ*, IX, p. 143. This ordinance granted the city's request presented in its 17 March petition: *LJ*, IX, p. 82.
88 For the election of the committee see LMA, JCC40, fos 215r–v; *CJ*, V, pp. 160–61; *A perfect diurnall* No. 196 (26 April–3 May 1647), pp. 1570–71; Nagel, 'The militia of London', pp. 267–8. The militia committee consisted of John Gayer, Thomas Cullum, Simon Edmonds, John Wollaston, Thomas Adams, John Langham, James Bunce, William Gibbs, Samuel Avery, John Bide, Philip Skippon, Francis West, Christopher Packe, John Jones, John Bellamie, Nathaniel Campfield, Richard Venner, Edwin Browne, Walter Boothby, Robert Mainwaring, Thomas Arnold, Tempest Milner, Maurice Gethin, Thomas Gower, Edward Hooker, Richard Glyde, Richard Turner, William Kendall, Lawrence Bromfield, Edward Bellamie and John Gace. Jones and Mainwaring had signed the November 1645 petition. Those delegated as elders to the London Provincial assembly were Packe, Jones, Bellamie, Venner, Boothby, Gethin, Gower, Hooker, Glyde, Turner, Kendall and Gace. Of these Jones, Venner, Gethin, Hooker, Glyde and Gace would serve on the Provincial assembly's 'executive' grand committee.
89 *A perfect diurnall*, No. 196 (26 April–3 May 1647), pp. 1570–71. Ousted members included Isaac Pennington, John Warner, John Fowke, Kendrick, Colonel Wilson, Thomas Player and Robert Tichbourne.
90 Amon Wilbee, *Plain truth without feare or flattery* (1647), p. 6.
91 NA SP 28/237 (London militia committee pay warrants); Mahony, 'The presbyterian party', p. 471; Nagel, 'The militia of London', p. 318.
92 *Clarke papers*, I, pp. 118, 152–6.
93 NA SP 28/237, fos 23, 46. The Weavers' Hall committee was chaired by James Bunce and included the religious presbyterian activists Richard Glyde and Lawrence Bromfield as its treasurers; see *CJ*, V, pp. 205, 248. The Christ Church treasury for maimed soldiers containing the presbyterian citizens William Greenhill and Thomas Blackwell was expanded on 18 June to include the religious presbyterians Thomas Gower, Anthony Bickerstaffe, James Story and Maximillian Bard. For these treasury committees see Mahony, 'The presbyterian party', pp. 391, 444–5.
94 Mahony, 'The presbyterian party', p. 427.
95 Juxon, *Journal*, p. 159; Denzell Holles, *Memoirs of Denzil Lord Holles* (1699), p. 109; *Fairfax Memorials*, I, p. 367. The same night saw handbills scattered around the streets in distinctly royalist language calling on the apprentices

to rise for the king. See *For the renowned apprentices of this famous Citie* (1647).
96 Juxon, *Journal*, pp. 159–60.
97 [Anon.], *A Particular Charge or Impeachment [...] against Denzill Hollis esq* (1647); *CJ*, V, pp. 250, 252, 253.
98 *CJ*, V, p. 254.
99 *The petition and solemne engagement of the citizens of London* (1647), p. 2.
100 Juxon, *Journal*, p. 161; [Anon.], *The arraignment and impeachment of Major General Massie* (1648), p. 2.
101 *Colonel Joseph Bampfield's Apology 'written by himself and printed at his desire' 1685*, eds J. Loftis and P. H. Hardacre (1993), pp. 61–2. For an opposing view see Kishlansky, *New Model Army*, p. 264.
102 [Anon.], *The arraignment [...] of Major General Massie*, p. 2; Juxon, *Journal*, p. 161; *A petition from the City of London with a covenant* (1647), pp. 3–4; *CJ*, V, p. 254; Pearl, 'London's counter revolution', p. 50. Unlike many of his fellow presbyterian activists who signed the solemn engagement, Bellamie escaped exclusion from holding office under the Rump legislation of 14 December 1649 and 8 October 1652 (*A&O*, II, pp. 319, 620).
103 *CJ*, V, pp. 254–5; Sir Lewis Dyve, 'The Tower letter-book of Sir Lewis Dyve, 1646–47', ed. H. G. Tibbut, *Publications of the Bedfordshire Historical Record Society* 38 (1958), p. 71; Kishlansky, *New Model Army*, p. 265.
104 I. Gentles, *The New Model Army in England, Ireland and Scotland, 1645–1653* (Oxford, 1992), pp. 187–9.
105 Pearl, 'London's counter revolution', p. 52; A. Woolrych, *Soldiers and statesmen: the general council of the Army and its debates, 1647–48* (Oxford, 1987), pp. 171–2; J. S. A. Adamson, 'The English nobility and the projected settlement of 1647', *HJ*, 30:3 (1987), pp. 567–9, 576.
106 Kishlansky, *New Model Army*, pp. 265–7.
107 Mahony, 'The presbyterian party', pp. 467–8, relying on Clement Walker, *The compleat history of Independency* (1661), pp. 39–40 and Sir William Waller, *Vindication of the character and conduct of Sir William Waller* (1793), pp. 101–2.
108 Juxon, *Journal*, p. 162.
109 Holles, *Memoirs*, pp. 153–4; Waller, *Vindication*, pp. 103–6; Pearl, 'London's counter revolution', p. 52; Crawford, *Denzil Holles*, pp. 156–7.
110 Gentles, *New Model Army*, p. 188.
111 *CJ*, V, p. 317; P. Gauci, 'Papillon, Thomas', *ODNB*.
112 PA HL/PO/JO/10/1/239, fo. 23v. For the use of this evidence, see Adamson, 'The English nobility and the projected settlement', pp. 576–7. For an opposing view, see M. Kishlansky, 'Saye what?', *HJ*, 33:4 (1990), p. 931.
113 *Fairfax Memorials*, I, pp. 380–84; *Clarke papers*, I, p. 281; *A perfect summary* (26 July–2 August 1647), pp. 9–13.
114 *CJ*, V, pp. 322–3.
115 Mahony, 'The presbyterian party', pp. 467–8.

116 For example, *The humble petition of many thousand of young men and apprentices [...] 13 July* (1647), p. 5.
117 Waller, *Vindication*, pp. 103–4.
118 Walker, *History of Independency*, I, p. 39.
119 Mahony, 'The presbyterian party', p. 468.
120 Walker, *History of Independency*, I, p. 39.
121 *Clarke papers*, I, p. 150.
122 Tom Tell-Troth [i.e. Christopher Love], *Works of darkness brought to light* (1647), pp. 1, 6, 10–11, 14–16.
123 *Puritanism and liberty, being the Army debates (1647–49) from the Clarke manuscripts*, ed. A. S. P. Woodhouse, 3rd edn (1986), p. 399; Morrill, 'The army revolt of 1647', p. 331.
124 *CJ*, V p. 324; *Clarke papers*, I, p. 281; *A perfect summary* (26 July–2 August 1647), pp. 9–13; cf. Gentles, *New Model Army*, pp. 187–8, 492–3.
125 LMA, JCC40, fos 240–1; Mahony, 'The presbyterian party', p. 469; Kishlansky, *New Model Army*, p. 269.
126 Rushworth, *Collections*, VI, pp. 645–51; Hughes, *Gangraena*, p. 397.
127 [John Price], *The pulpit incendiary* (1648), pp. 9–10; Hugh Peter, *A word for the armie* (1647), p. 6.
128 *Sydney papers, consisting of a journal of the Earl of Leicester*, ed. R. W. Blencowe (1825), p. 26; HMC, *Report on the manuscripts of Lord De L'Isle & Dudley* (1925), vol. VI, p. 569; Hughes, *Gangraena*, p. 397.
129 [Anon.], *A word to Mr Peters and two words for the Parliament and kingdom* (1647).
130 B[urges], *Sion college*, pp. 22–3; [Anon.], *Anti-Machiavel, or honesty against policie* (1647), p. 18.
131 Congregational Library, London Ms. I.f.18, fos 254, 273–5, 276, 293.
132 Wallington, *Notebooks*, p. 228.
133 Thomas Adams and Thomas Skinner, *A declaration of the [...] City of London* (1647).
134 Juxon, *Journal*, p. 164.
135 *Ibid.*, p. 165; *Clarke papers*, I, p. 221.
136 Woolrych, *Soldiers and statesmen*, p. 182.
137 [Love], *Works of darkness*, p. 10.
138 Juxon, *Journal*, pp. 166–7; Hughes, *Gangraena*, p. 400.
139 *MPWA*, III, pp. 662–3; V, p. 331; Baillie, *L&J*, III, p. 17.
140 B[urges], *Sion college*, pp. 22–3.
141 Woolrych, *Soldiers and statesmen*, pp. 182–3; Gentles, *New Model Army*, pp. 192–4.
142 Hughes, *Gangraena*, pp. 416–18.
143 Wallington, *Notebooks*, p. 230.
144 *The heads of proposals agreed on by his excellency Sir Thomas Fairfax* (1647).
145 Along with the aldermen Gayer, Adams, Langham, Cullum and Bunce, the London presbyterian activists who were incarcerated by the Commons were Edward Hooker, John Jones, William Drake, Jeremiah Baines, Joseph Vaughn

and Lawrence Bromfield (*CJ*, V, pp. 274, 283, 292, 315–17). These activists would have to wait until 23 May 1648 for their liberty: *CJ*, V, p. 570.

146 [Anon.], *A pair of spectacles for the City* (1647) pp. 8–12; Nagel, 'The militia of London', pp. 291, 318–19. The purged officers included religious presbyterians Laurence Bromfield, Walter Lee, Nicholas Widmerpole and Henry Potter. Religious presbyterian activists purged from other regiments included Joseph Vaughn, Thomas Gellibrand, Edward Hooker and John Lane.

147 *A&O*, I, pp. 1045–6.

148 [Anon.], *A just and solemn protestation of the free-born people of England* (1647).

149 James Farnell estimates that the London electorate returned a common council in 1648 with 'political presbyterians' making up two-thirds of its number: see Farnell, 'Politics of the city of London', pp. 98–9.

7

Presbyterian church government in the Province of London, 1646–60

From June 1646 the London presbyterians devoted considerable collective energy to constructing and maintaining a working presbyterian church polity. Although frustrated by difficulties from the outset, the longing aspiration of the presbyterian ministers was to win hearts and minds to the new discipline. These attempts were hampered by the growing political divisions within parliamentarianism, the novelty of presbyterian polity and the historical weaknesses of what remained of London's ecclesiastical infrastructure. Presbyterian church government in the mid-seventeenth century was, in essence, a voluntary association, relying on godly citizens and ministers for its being, rather than the national or local magistrate.[1] Parish elderships and classical presbyteries were established in the second half of 1646 and in May 1647 the London Provincial assembly, which would act as the central governing body for London presbyterianism, met for the first session of a series of continuous biannual meetings until 1660.[2]

London's presbyterian polity has quite rightly received a negative verdict from church historians. As far back as 1881, C. A. Briggs noted that the Province was 'paralyzed in its beginning'.[3] Gerald Strauss's negative appraisal of the effectiveness of the Lutheran Reformation in Germany has informed more modern historiographical arguments for the failure of godly rule in the mid-seventeenth century.[4] While such a conclusion is unsurprising given the short period of time and the chaotic nature of mid-seventeenth-century crisis, a number of historians, most notably Ronald Hutton and Bernard Capp, have argued that examples of limited successes can be found.[5] In regard to London presbyterianism, Tai Liu argues that the Province of London was 'by no means a historical nonentity' and sees the long-term structural problem of ecclesiastical finance and the immediate lack of assistance by the civil magistrate as the fundamental reasons why presbyterian discipline failed to take root.[6] For Philip Anderson, on the other hand, London's presbyterian polity was genetically flawed in its theoretical and legislative beginnings.[7] Nevertheless, he concludes that the presbyterians' commitment to Reformed ideals of pastoral care was the Provincial assembly's 'greatest legacy'.[8]

This chapter seeks to reassemble the history of the Province of London between June 1646 and August 1660. While accepting the judgement of historians that presbyterian government failed to effectively fill the space left by its episcopal predecessor, it does not seek to rehearse the question of success or failure. Instead, it argues that the critical factor in understanding the history of the Province of London was not institutional, but rather personal. The true backbone of London presbyterian government was not institutional foundation or authority, but the collective dedication of the London presbyterian laity and clergy to the cause of further reformation.

The election of ruling elders

The Province of London, at least according to the Parliamentary ordinances, covered 'London' in the widest sense of the word used in the seventeenth century.[9] Along with the parishes of the city proper, the Province extended to the west through Westminster and Middlesex as far as Knightsbridge. To the north and east of the city it stretched from the Tower Hamlets into Stepney and Hackney. South, across the Thames, it covered the parishes of Southwark, Bermondsey, Rotherhithe and Lambeth.[10] This section looks at the election and institution of parish ruling elders, the first step in the construction of London presbyterian polity.

Following the *Certain considerations and cautions* of 19 June 1646, the ministers abandoned their collective refusal to comply with the Parliamentary ordinances and set about establishing elderships in the parishes of London. One of the main problems of the Parliamentary ordinances of 1645–6 was that they were vague as to the procedure that a parish should take in choosing its eldership. Prior to June 1646, while maintaining the general policy of refusing to institute presbyterian government, some London ministers agreed in the interim to examine parishioners for entry to the Lord's supper.[11] Some went so far as to elect lay assistants to assist the minister. For example, on 23 January 1645 Edmund Calamy asked the vestry of St Mary, Aldermanbury to choose three men 'to asist him in exammining and preparing the people of the parish for their admittance to the sacrament of the Lords' supper'.[12] Likewise, in 1645 the vestry of St Stephen, Coleman Street, which had facilitated the ejection of John Goodwin for denying the Lord's supper to all but members of his own gathered congregation, chose the presbyterian William Taylor in Goodwin's place. On 20 January 1646 the parish met in a general meeting and agreed that the Lord's supper should be administered and that a committee of thirteen parishioners should join with Taylor 'to judge of persons whether they are such as may be admitted to the sacrament or no'.[13]

The Parliamentary ordinance of 19 August 1645 set out a skeletal directory for the election of ruling elders. Only men who were 'of good understanding in matters of religion, sound in faith' and 'of unblameable conversation' were to be selected. The ordinance specified that only those parishioners who had taken the Covenant, were of legal age and were not in service were permitted to elect their elders.[14] In practice the London vestries generally used the same local mechanisms for the election of elders as they did for other parish officers. For example, at St Olave, Old Jewry a vestry of twenty-five of the parish's leading men elected the eldership for the congregation. The same process was followed at St Peter, Westcheap, with a vestry of twenty-eight electing four elders from a pool of seven candidates.[15] In July 1646, a vestry of thirty-six parishioners of St Michael, Cornhill had the *Considerations and cautions* read to them and then resolved 'to putt the presbyteriall government in execution upon the ordinance of Parliament'.[16] At the end of July, the vestry gave notice to the whole congregation (the parish had around 723 communicants) that elders were to be elected. The election took place on 16 August at a meeting of a mere forty-one parishioners.[17] A similar procedure can be seen in the neighbouring parish of St Peter, Cornhill. The vestry minutes of 30 December noted that after 'the publique exercises were finished', thirty-seven men of the parish went into the vestry and, after prayers, debated how many elders to choose. The number agreed upon was six and the meeting decided to put thirteen in nomination. Although the parish had about 600 communicants, only the 37 chose the eldership 'by every man setting a strook to the names of them whom they desired should be chosen upon a peece of paper'.[18]

The process of using the vestry or substantial parishioners as an 'electoral college' for the eldership, while common in conducting parish business, did not always go unchallenged. At the impoverished parish of St Bride, Fleet Street this method of choosing elders led to an acrimonious dispute.[19] On 7 July the vestry hotly debated the number of elders needed and, after prayers led by the curate John Dicks to calm the situation down, it was resolved that twelve men would be put into nomination and that the congregation would select six elders from among them. However, when on 19 July this decision was brought before the congregation, the parishioners demanded that they should choose eight elders from a pool of sixteen nominees. Ultimately the parish was unable to agree which elders to elect.[20] To resolve the problem the parish sought arbitration from the triers appointed by Parliament for the fifth London classis.[21] In August, the triers selected twelve candidates, five of whom had not been on the original list selected by the vestry. Despite this intervention, some of the new elders refused to serve and, in face of this trouble, the vestry had to conclude that any of those chosen could hold the office 'more or less'.[22] Although a rare example, this conflict between the general congregation and the vestry demonstrates how vestry decisions did not always cohere with the other members of a parish.[23]

The godly and moral standing of the newly elected elders was not taken for granted by Parliament. To make sure that elders were aware of the gravity of their office, committees of triers were appointed in each classis to be 'judges of the integrity and ability' of those elected.[24] The triers were given power to test the religious acumen of the eldership, as well as to hear any complaints made against those elected. The triers were appointed from local ministers and laity, many of whom would become elders themselves. The election of elders seems to have begun relatively smoothly. Robert Baillie, in one of his happier moments, wrote to David Dickson on 18 August 1646 stating that the London parishes had 'chosen many very gracious and able elders' and that 'the tryers publicklie hes taken accompt of them, both of their life and knowledge, with their own consent; none hes refused to be tryed: they are all chosen for life; they will be a great help and strength to the Government'. By 7 December 1647, however, the London Provincial assembly was complaining about 'the negligence of some tryers in confirming and approving of elders elected'. This complaint had to wait for reform until 12 September 1648, when Francis Rous's committee for scandals bolstered the London triers with a larger number of presbyterian ministers.[25]

Between 1647 and 1660 around 125 ministers and approximately 199 ruling elders were elected to the Provincial assembly from around 94 of a possible 140 parishes. In reality, however, the core membership of the Provincial assembly derived from about sixty-four parishes. This was because some parishes only sent delegates once or twice and ministers and elders from the four unformed classes attended the Provincial assembly in the later 1650s only in an informal capacity.[26] More individuals were involved at the parish or classical level than were delegated to the meetings of the Provincial assembly: for example an additional five ministers and twenty-two elders attended meetings of the fourth classis.[27] Nehemiah Wallington, who served his parish of St Leonard, Eastcheap, the fourth classis and was delegated fifteen times to the London Provincial assembly, provides a rare insight into the personal disposition of a ruling elder. In a letter written to his neighbour Thomas Player, who leaned towards political and religious Independency, Wallington said he had 'used means and freends' to prevent his election as an elder. Although Wallington had 'this thirty yeers [lived] under the gospel' he believed he was still unworthy to be an officer of the church. He told Player 'I have more need to be taught my selfe than to instruct others'. In his 'own thoughts', Wallington was 'the weakest and unfittest' man to be elected to the eldership.[28] Wallington's acceptance of the office, despite his reticence, illustrates the sense of duty to serve the church that must have been characteristic of many of the new elders. The reason for Wallington's letter was that Player had also been chosen a ruling elder at St Leonard's, but was refusing to serve since he was opposed to presbyterianism. Wallington reminded Player of his Christian obligation to the visible church and upbraided him: 'I intreat you as you tender the glory of God and love to the Church of God stand to this place which God hath called you to by the free choyce of his children'.[29]

Evidence for the role of ruling elders at the parish level is somewhat sparse. According to a set of rules adopted by the first classis, ruling elders were charged with visiting parishioners' houses to encourage the catechising of the young and to provide 'holy watch' for older parishioners.[30] Elders also carried out 'tavern hunting' to report to the civil authorities parishioners attending alehouses on the Lord's day.[31] Although elders were theoretically empowered to judge in cases of church discipline, there appears to be no evidence from the parish, classis or Provincial assembly records in London that any cases were heard that led to suspension from the Lord's supper or excommunication.[32] This was almost certainly due to the London presbyterians' reticence to be subject to Parliament's committee to hear appeals against wrongful suspension. The main function of ruling elders was to act with the parish minister in approving congregants to partake of the Lord's supper.[33] It appears that this system of vetting was used to keep scandalous and sinful parishioners away from the sacrament in the first place, rather than resorting to suspension or excommunication.[34]

The eldership generally had success in the task of screening parishioners for admission to the Lord's supper when they formed part of the controlling group on the parish vestry. For example, at St Mary, Aldermanbury the vestry supported the minister Edmund Calamy and the eldership against complaints from a minority of parishioners who bemoaned the requirement of appearing before the eldership in order to be permitted admission to the Lord's supper.[35] Parish records suggest that the congregational eldership continued to operate to maintain the standards for admission in the parishes into the 1650s. For example, in 1652 the ruling elder and bookseller John Bellamie wrote a letter to the prospective minister Anthony Harford on behalf of the parish of St Michael, Cornhill demanding that Harford conform to the presbyterian practices of the parish and admit all parishioners to the Lord's supper who had previously been vetted by the parish presbytery.[36] In July 1652, the vestry of St Bride, Fleet Street recorded that Samuel Fisher, who had acted as essentially a 'locum' minister since 1651, would hold communion with 'such who have been admitted of formerly by the eldership and to such that will come to give an accompt to the minister and elders of their faith'.[37] Likewise, upon Richard Vines's election to St Lawrence, Old Jewry in 1654, the vestry agreed that only those parishioners who came before the congregational eldership for examination should be admitted to the Lord's supper.[38]

The refusal to admit parishioners to the Lord's supper was always controversial and, where the vestry was not supportive of presbyterian government, ministers and elders could find a harder time maintaining the policy of barred admission. At the wealthy parish of St Paul's, Covent Garden, Thomas Manton was determined as late as 1657 that parishioners should be tested before admission in accordance with the Parliamentary ordinances.[39] Discontent within the parish could lead to a vestry withdrawing support for parish presbyterianism. By August 1649 a substantial number of parishioners refused to pay tithes as a result of being required to come before Thomas Cawton and the eldership of St Bartholomew-by-the-Exchange in order to obtain admission to the Lord's supper. The vestry sided with the parishioners and on 27 August required Cawton to revert to the pre-civil war system of open communion and to not require ruling elders.[40] There is no indication that Cawton changed his practice and the parish elders would still attend the London Provincial assembly into the mid-1650s. After Cawton's flight to the Netherlands in 1651 due to his role in Christopher Love's plot, the vestry, with some controversy, elected as their minister George Hall, the son of Bishop Joseph Hall and himself the future Bishop of Chester. Hall's tenure at St Bartholomew would be reversed during the Protectorate, when Oliver Cromwell used his powers of patronage to impose the rigid congregationalists Sydrach Simpson and John Loder on the parish, essentially unchurching the bulk of the parishioners from the religious life of their parish entirely.[41]

The election of elders and, more so, the testing of parishioners for admission to the Lord's supper, were controversial and often unwelcome changes from the practice of the pre-civil war Church of England. Where successfully implemented, they relied on the close co-operation of a parish minister willing to work with the wider presbyterian system, and a vestry leadership prepared to set up and support the discipline. These conditions were not present in the majority of London parishes, either due to the poor financial state of many parishes, or because of parochial resistance to the imposition of presbyterianism. The result was that presbyterian government was set up in only a substantial minority of parishes. This weakened presbyterian government in London from the outset and even parishes supporting presbyterianism could change as the composition of the vestry altered over time.

The London Provincial assembly

The London Provincial assembly met for the first time at the convocation house of St Paul's Cathedral on 3 May 1647, where it would meet for five sessions until being permitted by Parliament to move to Sion College.[42] The assembly's first task was to agree on rules of order and create a managing grand committee of seven ministers and fourteen ruling elders 'to consider the whole buisinesse being to this province'.[43] The assembly then proceeded to diagnose the structural problems afflicting London presbyterian government.[44] It was agreed that parishes under the supervision of the Provincial assembly should insist on ruling elders joining with ministers in examining those who sought admission to the Lord's supper. In addition, a petition to Parliament, presented on 11 and 12 January 1648, was put in train to complain about the defective state of the polity.[45] The assembly sought Parliament's consideration on the issue of excommunication, ministers who performed clandestine marriages, the absence of the Reformed office of deacons and the role that parish officers such as churchwardens and overseers for the poor held in relation to presbyterian government.[46]

The assembly determined that the most pressing structural weakness of the Province was that four of the twelve classical presbyteries had failed to form.[47] In the January 1648 petition, the assembly claimed that the reasons for the classes not forming were 'want of settled ministers to join with the people in chusing elders, or want of triers to approve those who are chosen, or because some elders and triers are removed'.[48] Three of the unformed classes were outside the city's walls. They included the ninth classis, which covered the large, impoverished parishes of the Tower Hamlets, Wapping, Whitechapel and Stepney. The other two extra-mural classes were the eleventh classis, comprised of the parishes of the political centre at Westminster and the twelfth classis, which encompassed the western and north-western suburban townships of Middlesex.[49] The parishes in these extra-mural precincts were geographically dispersed and had less chance of regular contact with each other. Although the tenth classis, comprising Southwark and the area to the south of the city, had formed, the scattered nature of the extra-mural parishes in this area made meeting on a regular basis difficult, leading the classis to cease to meet regularly by 1656.[50] Inside the city, the second classis had failed to form. This area encompassed the riverbank wards of Queenhithe and the Vintry. Although the second classis area contained a number of presbyterian ministers such as Charles Offspring at St Antholin, Budge Row and Matthew Haviland at Holy Trinity, Queenhithe, it also contained many of the most impoverished parishes within the city. Of the fifteen parishes in the classis area, a stable ministry was not fully settled in twelve.[51] The problem of vacant benefices, however, was not limited to the second classis and plagued the entire London region during the mid-seventeenth century.

The London Provincial assembly realised that the Province's power to enforce presbyterian government would be limited unless it had a majority of parishes acting with it. At the end of 1648 the assembly called for a survey to be made into the condition of London's parishes. The result led the assembly to conclude that forty of the Province's parishes had 'the defect of an able & faithfull ministry'.[52] This problem was conceived by the assembly to be primarily financial: parishes were unable to afford to employ permanent ministers after the purges of the 1640s. The assembly also conceded that there was a reticence to set up the presbyterian system, with the assembly complaining in the 11 January 1648 petition 'that divers churchwardens [...] set themselves to oppose both the government and the power of godliness'.[53] Examples of this problem abound throughout the records of city parishes: for example, the fourth classis vestries of St Botolph, Billingsgate and St Benet, Gracechurch refused to elect elders, despite having presbyterian stalwarts as ministers.[54] The assembly's solution was to ask Parliament to take short-term action by imposing civil sanctions against churchwardens who refused to set up presbyteries. The assembly's ultimate aim was for Parliament to abolish the parish offices of churchwarden and overseer for the poor altogether and to establish the system of elders and deacons found in the continental Reformed churches.[55] Such a request was never seriously entertained by Parliament as the offices of churchwarden and overseer of the poor played critical functions in the civil administration of early modern England.[56]

The Provincial assembly also realised that the Parliamentary ordinances had not done enough to establish the presbyterian system with any authority in London. The assembly complained that many conceived the presbyterian polity 'to bee settled for three yeares, and in most parts of the kingdome not settled at all, and so not probable long to continue'. As a result, presbyterian ministers intruded into parishes by Parliament's committee for plundered ministers had been forcibly removed or had left London discouraged.[57] Furthermore, Parliament's failure to give the presbyterian system any real authority had allowed people to attend the services of clandestine 'Prayer-Book' ministers, who administered services in private enclaves or took the opportunity to fill the pulpits of vacant parish churches as locum ministers.[58] The assembly complained bitterly that 'there are some ministers who baptize children in private houses; the same or others marry without publishing the purpose of marriage betweene the parties [...] and others who admit all sorts to the sacrament of the Lords supper without taking in the elders to joyne with them'.[59] Taken together, these problems would render presbyterian church government in London an essentially voluntary system, effective only where an alliance of minister and godly laity were prepared to operate the system.

The Provincial assembly took advantage of the *détente* between religious presbyterians and Westminster Independents in the summer of 1648 against the Hamiltonian engagers to present another petition to Parliament.[60] This petition, presented to the Lords on 29 June, asked Parliament '[t]o resume the consideration of the [... former] Petition, and to grant the humble and necessary requests contained therein'.[61] When this petition received a favourable response from the Lords and Parliament started to debate what would become the presbyterian ordinance of 29 August 1648, the assembly's grand committee ordered the classical presbyteries to make a survey of the vacant parishes in the Province.[62] On 6 October this was presented to the city government as *A representation of the sad condition of the Province of London*. This document complained that heresy and disorder was multiplying in the city and called on income from former episcopal estates to be used to augment the livings of the poorer parishes in London.[63]

With both the Lord Mayor John Warner and Sheriff Thomas Vyner being favourably disposed to presbyterian government, the assembly's suggestions were taken up by the city government. A committee of largely religious presbyterians was elected to consult with the Provincial assembly and on 16 October a petition was presented to Parliament desiring that action be taken to improve the livings of London parochial ministers.[64] This bore some fruit, as on 27 October an ordinance enforcing the payment of tithes was issued.[65] Parliament also ordered that a Parliamentary committee join with the London common council to discuss the issue of augmenting impoverished livings. This joint committee ordered that the Province's ministers, common councillors and churchwardens report on the value of dean and chapter lands in their respective areas.[66] It is doubtful whether augmentations, had they been enforced, would have resolved the financial problems in the London parishes, although they might have meant that some vacant parishes would have been able to provide for a settled parish minister. In any case, political events intervened to prevent this scheme from having effect. The death of John Warner on 28 October and the presbyterians' loss of influence following the Army's occupation of the city on 1 December ended the hope that the Province of London's structural problems would be addressed by Parliament and the city government.

Classical presbyterianism in action

One area where the London classes attempted to impose what little authority the classical system possessed was attempting to stop unsuitable and heterodox preachers from taking up parish livings. The few case studies that we possess demonstrate that the authority of the classes relied, in practice, on the will of local parish vestries and ministers to enforce classical jurisdiction.

Although the records for the practical work of the London classes are sparse, two case studies can be derived from the records of the surviving fourth classis. The first concerns William Blackmore, who had been elected to the ministry of St Peter, Cornhill in June 1646.[67] He had received only deacon's orders under the episcopal system. This was unacceptable to the presbyterian view of the ministerial order, which held that the 'care of souls, the preaching of the word, the administration of the seals' belonged only to those that had received ordination 'by prayer, fasting and imposition of hands'.[68] According to presbyterian theory, Blackmore should not have been administering the sacraments to his congregation until he had received full ordination.[69] To correct this problem, the fourth classis ruled that if Blackmore wished to continue, he was required to receive ordination from the classis. On 19 April 1647 Blackmore was ordered to present himself for ordination and was assigned a telling thesis: *an cui competat ex officio praedicare, competat Sacramenta administrare* ('if a person's office gives him the ability to preach, does it make him competent to administer the sacraments?')[70]

The other case study to be found from the fourth classis demonstrates that presbyterian government had similar problems to the pre-civil war episcopal Church of England in ensuring the orthodoxy of lecturers. In early December 1646, twenty-one parishioners of St Michael, Cornhill approached the parish's vestry desiring to replace its recently deceased lecturer, congregationalist Jeremiah Burroughes. The parishioners' choice was Joseph Symonds who, like Burroughes, was a former exile of congregationalist persuasions.[71] Symonds had a good puritan pedigree, having been a former student at Thomas Gataker's seminary, but after being deprived from his living at St Martin, Ironmonger Lane in 1639 had settled in Rotterdam.[72] Here he had joined Sydrach Simpson as co-pastor of Simpson's gathered church.[73] Symonds had fallen ill in the Netherlands and, fearing death in a foreign land, had returned to England in 1646.[74] Upon his return, he was offered one of the expository lectures sponsored by a group led by the former 'war party' activist and religious Independent Richard Shute.[75] These sponsors had recently caused trouble at St Mary, Aldermanbury by funding a lecture for Henry Burton, who had attempted to gather members for his congregation out of Calamy's parish. In response the Aldermanbury vestry had decided to no longer permit the lecture, causing Burton to cry foul, claiming that Calamy had locked 'truth' out of his parish.[76] Returning to Symonds' case, on 3 December the vestry of St Michael, Cornhill resolved that three of its ruling elders – John Bellamie, Francis Mosse and James Maslyn – were to present the details of the Independents' request to the fourth classis.[77] On 7 December the classis inquired as to Symonds' doctrinal orthodoxy and moral character. Symonds was generally well liked by London presbyterians, with even Thomas Edwards describing him as 'one of the moderatest and modestest of [the Independents]'.[78] Henry Roborough, the curate of St Leonard's, Eastcheap, told the classis that he knew Symonds personally and could commend him to be a good preacher. Nevertheless, Roborough warned about Symonds's views on liberty of conscience.[79] As a result of this discussion, the classis ordered that Symonds could not be settled until the classis had determined him to be 'orthodox in judgement'. Joseph Caryl, a member of the classis who can be safely identified as a congregationalist, attempted to use the dispute to assert the authority of the classis. Caryl moved that, until Symonds's orthodoxy was determined, any supply lecturers were to be approved by the congregational eldership five days in advance: a ruling that the vestry agreed to follow.

On 22 December, the fourth classis decided that, as it was negotiating with the parish vestry and not the congregational presbytery alone, its orders would 'bee but advice'. This decision was designed to prevent any accusations from Independents that the presbyterians were acting in a tyrannical and autocratic manner and also probably fitted Caryl's understanding of the extent of the authority of a classis.[80] The fourth classis vindicated its power and decision to verify Symonds' orthodoxy on the basis of a particularly loose interpretation of the ordination ordinance of 28 August 1646.[81] While the ordinance gave classical presbyteries the power to determine the orthodoxy of local incumbents, the jurisdiction over lecturers was not specified. Because of the weakness of its legal position, the fourth classis also invoked two precedents from recent ecclesiastical cases. The first came from the example of the committee for plundered ministers, who sent lecturers to a sub-committee of the Westminster assembly in order to confirm their orthodoxy. It was argued that the practice of the committee for plundered ministers gave the classis authority to test lecturers entering into their precinct.[82] The second precedent, a recent decision of the seventh London classis, was more direct. The seventh classis had intervened to stop a Mercers' Company lecture at St Bartholomew-by-the-Exchange being filled by an unsuitable candidate.[83] The desperation that the fourth classis had in finding precedents to help determine Symonds's case demonstrates the incomplete nature of Parliament's presbyterian legislation. It also reveals that, from the outset, London's classical system was plagued by a crisis of authority.

On 4 January 1647, the classis sent John Ley, Edward Hooker and John Bellamie to meet Symonds. The purpose of this meeting was to determine his position concerning the toleration of papists. Symonds initially adopted a policy of avoidance, but the committee finally met with him on 15 January. Symonds told the delegates that he did not agree with a universal toleration and added that, although he did not feel the classis had authority over lecturers, he would 'give the right hand of fellowship to his brethren of classis' if he ever held a pastoral position.[84] Three days later, the committee reported Symonds's statement to the fourth classis, which ordered that it would be happy to authorise his lecture on condition that he commit what he had said to writing.[85] The classis seems to have been on the verge of a precedent-setting victory over the subscribers filling presbyterian parishes with congregationalist lecturers. However, rather than allowing the classis this triumph, the subscribers moved Symonds's lecture to the parish of St Mary, Abchurch in the unformed third classis, a living which he ultimately received in March.[86] Symonds's ministry at St Mary, Abchurch proved the concerns of the fourth classis right, as the parish became a haven for the gathered churches of John Goodwin and Vavasour Powell.[87] Although the fourth classis could claim a victory in Symonds's case, it demonstrates that classical authority rested on local vestries acting with, and abiding by, the decisions of the classis. In addition, the presence of areas within London but outside the reach of functioning presbyterian supervision essentially undermined the jurisdiction of the presbyterian system to control the parish churches in the Province of London.

Another incident which demonstrates that the whole weight of presbyterian government was powerless to act if it lacked the support of the local minister or parish vestry was the dispute that arose between the vestry of St Michael, Crooked Lane and their minister Joseph Browne in January 1647.[88] It appears that the parish had split into factions over Browne's religious and political position and these were no longer co-operating with each other.[89] The godly faction at St Michael desired to establish presbyterian government but, as a Mr Fauster explained to the classis, they were 'but a part of the parish' and needed Browne's reconciliation to make the parish 'accord one with another'.[90] The 400 or so communicants of the parish were divided, with Browne and his supporters probably advocating the use of the Prayer Book, whereas the vestry leaders were, at least nominally, presbyterian and declared their willingness to the classis 'to submitt to the present government'.[91] By the summer of 1648 some parishioners were becoming impatient and tried to get the vestry to allow the congregationalist Thomas Goodwin to use the parish church for his gathered congregation.[92] Goodwin's invitation could have been due to two reasons. It is likely that an Independent faction existed within the parish. Certainly, Thomas Edwards noted that sectaries had hindered the election of parochial ruling elders at St Michael.[93] It is also possible that many of the parishioners who had refused to co-operate with Browne were desperate for a godly minister and the failure of the classis to resolve their difficulties led them to look elsewhere. In an attempt to show authority, the fourth classis declared to the parish on 31 January 1648 that the vestry should 'proceed to the setting up of the presbyteriall government, which wee hope may be done in love'.[94] Despite the ruling of the classis the dispute was still continuing in April 1648 and the fourth classis, no doubt at the end of its collective tether, appealed to the London Provincial assembly for assistance.[95] The Crooked Lane incident thus put the Provincial assembly's power to the test. The assembly decided that it would determine the issue by calling a provincial fast at St Alphage, London Wall to address the issue. The result of its deliberations was to order the London classes to report on the state of the presbyterian government in parishes.

The results of the Provincial assembly's survey demonstrated how tenuous classical government was in the city.[96] At all levels presbyterian government was entirely reliant on the co-operation of the local minister and the parish vestry. Because the system of presbyterian government was utterly devoid of any formal authority and was gradually losing support from the national and civic magistrate, the Provincial assembly was powerless to resolve the problems at the level of classes and parishes. The fourth classis, therefore, chose to quietly ignore the problems at St Michael, Crooked Lane, a testament to the Province's lack of authority over unco-operative parishes.

The Province of London and the struggle for presbyterian discipline 1651–60

Despite the London presbyterians' best efforts, the polity would rapidly collapse after the political revolution of 1649. Their opposition to the Commonwealth regime and the new republic's commitment to a degree of liberty of conscience meant that it offered the Province of London little by way of support and protection. Even Sion College itself was used to quarter soldiers garrisoned in London from 1651 and the Provincial assembly was thus expelled from its favoured meeting place. From 1651 until the Protectorate, meetings of the Provincial assembly took place at St Anne, Blackfriars, St Mary, Aldermanbury and at Stationers' Hall and Painter Stainers' Hall.[97] Throughout the last ten years of its life, the Provincial assembly attempted to fight a rear-guard action against the decline of presbyterian government by focusing on what it considered to be the basic functions of a presbyterian provincial assembly: the ordination of ministers and the revitalisation of parochial presbyteries.

The ordination of new ministers was considered a critical function of the Provincial assembly and London classes. It has been calculated that around 700 presbyterian ordinations took place in England in the period 1646–60, with the fourth London classis accounting for 82 of those ordinations.[98] The fourth classis appears to have rejected only nine candidates, largely due to late applications or the failure to produce testimonials on time.[99] It is unfortunate that there is little qualitative evidence of ordination in London. The procedure followed by the fourth classis was to obtain testimonials from candidates proving that they were of the appropriate age, had taken the Solemn League and Covenant, were of godly 'life and conversation' and were suitably qualified academically. The candidate was then interviewed by the classis, which sought to determine 'the grace of God in him', the presence of a calling and skill in biblical languages, arts and divinity. After this interview the candidate was given a Latin thesis on a topic of divinity and was required to preach at a church in the area of the classis. The process would take roughly ten days with ordination taking place at a day of fasting and prayer by the laying on of hands by the ministers of the classis in the presence of its ruling elders and people.[100]

Ordinations by the London classes had begun in the spring of 1647 and on 30 November 1648 the Provincial assembly agreed a set of propositions based on the Westminster assembly's directory to be sent to the eight formed classes, which were directed to conduct ordinations on a rotating monthly basis.[101] While the Provincial assembly accepted that the London classes were permitted to ordain ministers for congregations outside London, it warned that great care should be taken in ordaining ministers from parts of the country where the presbyterian system was already in operation.[102] An example is that of Adam Martindale's ordination in July 1649. Martindale was due to be ordained by the Manchester classis, but this had been delayed because he expressed scruples regarding presbyterian church government and was opposed by some parishioners at his intended parish of Rostherne in Cheshire. Having travelled to London, Martindale met with Elidad Blackwell, the minister of St Andrew Undershaft, and convinced Blackwell of his need for swift ordination. On Blackwell's recommendation, the eighth classis agreed to examine Martindale and ordained him in two days without apparently taking into account that a more appropriate, local classis was in operation.[103]

The desire to prevent inadequate candidates being ordained was of utmost importance to the Provincial assembly which, on 13 August 1649, ordered that the moderator of each classis should put together a register of the names of candidates who had been denied ordination, together with the reason for the refusal. On 25 February 1651 the assembly resolved to keep a record of the time and place of each monthly ordination so that it could better inform candidates from Oxford, Cambridge or other parts of the country where they could obtain ordination. On 11 March the Provincial assembly decided to keep a central register of those rejected for ordination by the London classes. This register acted to co-ordinate ordination between the classes and on 14 June 1652 the Provincial assembly ordered that the classes should send information of those candidates who only spoke English, so they could be prevented from receiving ordination within the Province.[104]

As well as ensuring that only appropriate candidates were ordained, the Provincial assembly also ensured that its orders as to correct procedure were maintained. On 7th October 1658 it was revealed that an ad hoc presbytery consisting of John Fuller, William Whitaker, William Cooper and Thomas Manton had met to conduct ordinations outside the timetable set by the assembly. These ministers were chastised by the assembly, who informed them that it was necessary to keep to the established rules as to rotation, so that the register of unsuitable candidates could be maintained.[105] On the other hand, on 3 March 1656 the Provincial assembly authorised the ministers of the unformed second classis area to form as a presbytery without ruling elders for the purposes of assisting in the work of the province's monthly rotation of ordaining classes.[106]

If the presbyterians maintained ordination to promote an educated ministry in the nation and to find encouragement and *raison d'être* for the classical system, the Provincial assembly also frantically sought to develop policies to prevent presbyterian government in London from collapsing. The first concerted drive to preserve and revitalise the presbyterian system in the post-regicide period came in the aftermath of Christopher Love's execution. In December 1651, the assembly ordered its managing grand committee to meet at Edmund Calamy's house and work on 'rules' for revitalising the presbyterian government. These rules, which were sent out on 22 January 1652, ordered the ministers and elders to attempt to convince their fellows and neighbouring parishes to reconstitute the discipline at the local level. The assembly warned that if the Province's government was allowed to decline further there would be 'an utter dissolution of the whole frame of presbiterial government'.[107]

To effect this policy of revitalisation another survey into the state of the parochial presbyteries in their respective precincts was ordered at the beginning of 1652.[108] Although the survey returns were hurried and incomplete (with returns being received from a total of fifty-six parishes), they suggest that the presbyterian system had suffered losses as a result of the upheavals of the early 1650s.[109] Of the parishes that sent in returns thirty-two (57 per cent) had ministers that continued to act with the classical system. The ratio for parishes with at least some operating ruling elders was higher, with thirty-nine parishes (70 per cent) sending delegates to the classis. However, it was clear that the sum total of serving ruling elders had substantially fallen since 1646–7, with some parishes having only one or two serving elders. As in 1648, the main reason for the failure of a minister to join with the presbyterian government was the inability of many parishes to afford or find a minister to permanently fill the living. Of the parishes surveyed, sixteen (28 per cent) were destitute of a minister altogether. The problem of vacant livings in London appears to have become increasingly dire during the 1650s, although this was rooted in the problems of the 1640s and earlier; for example, seven of the parishes recorded as destitute of a minister in 1652 had also recorded vacant livings in the Provincial assembly's October 1648 survey of parishes.[110] The revolution had done little to address these fundamental structural problems in London parish churches.

Where the Provincial government had sway over its own members, it did its best to prevent parishes becoming destitute of a minister. One example can be found in September 1657 when the Provincial assembly decided the case of Thomas Wills, the minister of St Botolph, Billingsgate. Wills had desired to leave St Botolph to take up the post at the less urban and more financially lucrative parish of St Mary, Stoke Newington. The parishioners of St Botolph appealed to the Provincial assembly for Wills to remain as their minister. After a committee of the assembly met the parishioners of both churches, it held that Wills should stay at St Botolph as he had not been released from his pastoral charge by his flock to 'the g[rea]t danger of the utt[e]r ov[e]rthrow of the good work begun' in establishing presbyterian government in the parish.[111]

In addition to vacant parishes, eight (14 per cent) of the parishes in the 1652 survey had ministers who refused to co-operate with the presbyterian system in London. This number was roughly equally divided between congregationalists and episcopalians. At least three parishes had beneficed congregationalist ministers, including John Cardell of All Hallows, Lombard Street. Cardell and his ruling elders had acted with the presbyterian classical and provincial government in 1647–8. However, the parish had moved progressively towards stricter congregationalist principles so that by 1652 it no longer acted in fellowship with the classis or Provincial assembly.[112] Four parishes contained episcopalian ministers, such as Robert Gell at St Mary, Aldermary and William Sclater at St Peter le Poer. I should also include the parish of St Peter, Paul's Wharf, described by Tai Liu as 'the most recalcitrant Anglican parish in London', where Robert Mossom provided Prayer Book services. In May 1658 a petition was presented to Cromwell, signed by, among others, Thomas Underhill and John Wynne, both ruling elders of St Benet, Paul's Wharf, seeking to merge St Peter, Paul's Wharf with their parish. The petition, supported by a recommendation from Calamy, Ashe, Jenkyn and Bartholomew Beale, the lay presbyterian auditor of the Exchequer, requested that John Jackson, the presbyterian minister of St Benet, be given the living to prevent the use of the Prayer Book by 'disaffected persons' at St Peter. This business appears to have failed only due to the death of Oliver Cromwell in September.[113]

The political conflict between the Commonwealth regime and the Sion College conclave from 1649 to 1651 was the main source of losses to the number of presbyterian-controlled parishes in the survey. The former presbyterian stronghold of Christ Church, Newgate Street had been sequestered from William Jenkyn in July 1650, with Jenkyn being replaced with the fifth monarchist preacher Christopher Feake. However, it was episcopalian ministers who generally benefited from the Rump's moves against presbyterians. At St Bartholomew-by-the-Exchange, Thomas Cawton's flight to Holland in 1651 for his involvement in Love's plot allowed a pro-Prayer Book faction in the parish to elect George Hall, as mentioned earlier. Thomas Case's removal from St Mary Magdalen, Milk Street in 1650 left the parish destitute of a settled minister. This derailed the dominant presbyterian faction that had aggressively reformed the parish in the 1640s, in favour of a 'Prayer Book' protestantism led by William Laud's nephew John Robinson.[114]

The comparison between the 1648 and the 1652 surveys show that the problems of the Province of London in 1652 looked back to the failure of Parliament to settle presbyterianism in 1647–8. The economic difficulties experienced by smaller parishes, a factor that had often been solved by pluralism and the use of curates in the pre-civil war episcopalian period, was a major reason for the failure of presbyterianism to attain the necessary level of parochial saturation in the London region. The problem of impoverished London parishes was both a long-term issue and a result of the upheavals of the 1640s, and therefore cannot entirely be seen as a failing of the presbyterian system.[115]

Nevertheless, the fact that the Province's government was taking measures to ascertain the dangers that the polity faced must have been born from the realisation that presbyterian government was in decline. The Provincial assembly and the classes were certainly having difficulties obtaining sufficient delegates to attend meetings. For example, of the twelve sessions of the eleventh provincial assembly (May–November 1652), Simeon Ashe, the assembly's aging moderator, attended five and the assessors John Rawlinson and Robert Abbott attended only four and two sessions respectively. John Crodacott, one of the scribes, attended two meetings and Thomas Jacombe, the other scribe, attended only one meeting, leaving others to record the minutes.[116] Despite attempts to make rules to counter such inattentiveness, some of the weaker classis began to collapse due to non-attendance by the laity, prompting the assembly to set up a 'committee for the preservation of the government' to try to rectify the problem.[117] In November 1654, the third classis stopped delegating ruling elders, a problem that, despite conferences by leading ministers from the other classis, continued until the Restoration.[118] By 1655 the eighth and tenth classes were also having difficulty sending sufficient delegates to the meetings of the Provincial assembly.[119]

The Province's solution to this problem was to attempt to make up for lost numbers by trying to convince the unformed classes to establish themselves. On 19 May 1652 the Provincial assembly ordered its grand committee to assist the ministers of the second classis in forming a classical presbytery for the purposes of ordination.[120] This was followed up on 27 September 1653, when ministers were sent by the assembly to confer with the ministers of the second and ninth classes to discuss forming clergy-only presbyteries.[121] These measures slowly came to fruition and on 13 September 1655 the Provincial assembly directed that the ministers of the four unformed classes should start ordaining candidates for the ministry.[122] In early February 1656 Arthur Jackson was delegated to meet to meet with ministers in Westminster to discuss establishing the eleventh classis and the members of the Provincial assembly were sent to meet newly settled ministers to try to convince them to join the presbyterian system.[123] In July 1657 ministers from the unformed classes were invited to attend provincial meetings without elders 'to help carry on the government'.[124] This measure brought in ministers from all four unformed classes.[125] The following November, clerical delegates from the second, eleventh and the now-collapsed third classes attended the Provincial assembly as well as a full delegation of ministers and ruling elders from the twelfth classis.[126]

While during the 1650s the London presbyterians did not manage to establish the unformed classes with any degree of consistency, nor stem the decay of the presbyterian system, they were rewarded with occasional minor victories. The 1652 drive to revitalise the parochial elderships in the parishes had little success overall, although at St Peter, Westcheap, Roger Drake convinced the parish in February 1652 to reconstitute its diminishing eldership by electing the 1640s presbyterian activist and Restoration nonconformist leader Maximillian Bard as a ruling elder.[127] Similar occasional achievements followed the Provincial assembly's mid-1650s efforts to revitalise the government. In response to attempts to establish the eleventh classis, Thomas Case reported on 28 April 1656 that the measure had not been successful. As consolation, he could offer 'news that rejoyced the Assembly', that he had managed to get the congregational eldership fully running at St Giles-in-the-Fields. Valentine Fyge, the ruling elder of the parish of St Bride, Fleet Street, added that since his parish had finally acquired a settled minister in John Herring, the presbyterian discipline was operating successfully at St Bride's.[128] These minor successes suggest that the laity were not always entirely opposed to working with their minister in establishing parochial church government, even if presbyterian government was diminishing overall.

One possible reason for the rapid decline of London presbyterianism after the establishment of the Cromwellian Protectorate may have been simply the result of progressive disenchantment and fatigue. The fact that the Cromwellian regime and its parliaments failed to reach any legislative conclusion in matters of church administration may well have increased the despondency in all but the most committed lay members of the Provincial government. Another reason contributing to the decline of the eldership must also be attributed to the fact that under the Parliamentary system elders were elected for life. If many of the elders were at the pinnacle of their office-holding career when elected in 1646, they were beginning to become age noticeably by the mid-1650s. Thomas Wadsworth, who obtained the living of the tenth classis parish of St Mary, Newington Butts in 1655, recounted this problem to Richard Baxter, stating that upon taking charge of the parish's ministry he found that the eldership was 'all but one dead'.[129]

A further possible reason for the decline in lay participation is suggested by the Provincial assembly's decision on 31 October 1653 to set out an order of business for each following meeting of the Provincial assembly. That such an order was necessary may suggest that a reason for the decline in numbers was the absence of any useful business for the laity to conduct at classical and provincial meetings. An explanation for the decline of the London classis may therefore be that there was little need for the laity's participation in classical or provincial business.[130] The same may also have been true of the parochial presbyteries. There does not appear to have been a single case of excommunication in the Province of London's history. By the mid-1650s, the work of the ruling elders, therefore, would have diminished to examining adolescents or newcomers to the parish.

It is possible, therefore, that the limited functions of the English ruling elder contributed to the endemic non-attendance that so plagued the classical and provincial government of London in the 1650s. By the latter half of the decade the decline could not be reversed. The fourth classis conducted its final business on 17 November 1659, and the other classes probably collapsed around the same period.[131] The London Provincial assembly conducted almost no business after the fall of Richard Cromwell, although its last meeting came as late as 15 August 1660.[132]

Conclusion

In December 1655 Robert Baillie wrote to the London minister Simeon Ashe bemoaning that English 'presbyterians are either restrained or not carefull to use your libertie' in matters of church government. The result was that the London ministers sat in a 'powerless provinciall synod' that did little to advance presbyterianism in England. Ashe replied defensively, stating that while matters conspired 'to overthrow the power and practise of presbyteriall government', yet, 'through God's mercy, many act presbyterialie in London, and in many counties, both in reference to ordination and admission to the sacrament, notwithstanding of discouragements'.[133] Throughout this chapter we have explored the constitution of the Province of London and charted its decline. In theory, an English presbyterian church was meant to fulfil the godly desire for an ecclesiastical polity that united both disciplinary and pastoral functions into a representative and federal structure. In practice, London presbyterian government was rendered institutionally impotent from the outset. Nevertheless, as Ashe noted, the Province of London provided an association of like-minded ministers and laity that continued the discipline despite its many-fold troubles.

Two main reasons stand out for the Province's failure. The first of these was the restrictive 'Erastianism' of Parliament's legislation. The ordinances that brought the presbyterian church into existence both denied it the power to act as a Reformed ecclesiastical polity and failed to make up that deficit with magisterial support. The English presbyterian system was therefore reliant on the voluntary support of local office holders. In the factionally charged environment of the English revolution, the political reticence of the magistrate to support presbyterian polity meant that the Province of London quickly floundered. After 1649, with the magisterial vacuum in ecclesiastical affairs, the Province was often little more than an ecclesiastical club operating church government under a veil of questionable legality.

These political problems were not the only reason why the Province failed to establish itself. Structural problems, such as the general economic problems of the church in England, particularly in the London parishes, acted to deprive many parishes of a settled ministry. The consequence was that the Province of London never attained the critical mass of parishes necessary to operate authoritatively. While a more enthusiastic magistracy might have solved these problems, the financial difficulties of London parishes were deep and endemic and the failure to address them left presbyterianism exposed in the city.

The defective state of the classical presbyteries was also partly a symptom of the relative unpopularity of the presbyterian government. The Province of London relied on the voluntary support of the vestries and parish ministers to apply discipline. Although presbyterians held the livings of a substantial number of parishes, they were never hegemonic and had only achieved this incomplete position of strength as a result of the parochial and magisterial coup of the early years of the civil war. In light of irreligion, the continuing presence of 'Prayer-Book protestants' in parish vestries and the resistance of congregationalists and religious radicals, parishes and parishioners opposed to presbyterian rule were easily able to find spiritual comfort elsewhere. With the city an effective religious market place, most inhabitants were able to successfully defy the authority of the presbytery.[134]

As the events of the English revolution struck home, the presbyterian polity in London was rendered a voluntary affair and is perhaps better seen as a confederation of parish churches operating in a manner not unlike that of a congregationalist association. Reading back to works like the Smectymnuus tracts of 1641, or Simeon Ashe's reply to Baillie cited above, such an association is perhaps not substantially less than what London's presbyterian ministers wanted.

Notes

1. E. Vernon, 'Godly pastors and their congregations in mid-seventeenth-century London' in Davies, Dunan-Page and Halcomb, *Church life*, pp. 56–61.
2. The records of the London Provincial assembly are located at Lambeth Palace Library, London Ms. ARC.L40.2/E17. A typescript of the manuscript by Charles Surman, together with a volume of Surman's notes on the membership of the Provincial assembly, can be found in the Dr Williams Library: DWL Ms. 201.12–13. The manuscript records of the Westminster assembly also contain some scribal minutes of the meetings of the London Provincial assembly, together with attendance registers (DWL Ms. 38.3, fos 383–426).
3. C. A. Briggs, 'The Provincial assembly of London', *The Presbyterian Review*, 2 (1881), 79. See also A. H. Drysdale, *History of the presbyterians in England: their rise, decline, and revival* (1889), pp. 304–15; Shaw, *HEC*, II, pp. 98–100; and *The English presbyterians: from Elizabethan puritanism to modern unitarianism*, eds C. G. Bolam, J. Goring, H. L. Short and R. Thomas (1968), pp. 43–5.
4. G. Strauss, 'Success and failure in the German Reformation', *P&P*, 67 (1975), 30–63; D. Hirst, 'The failure of godly rule in the English republic', *P&P*, 132:1 (1991), 33–66; C. Durston, 'Puritan rule and the failure of cultural revolution, 1645–1660' in C. Durston and J. Eales, *The culture of English puritanism, 1560–1700* (Basingstoke, 1996), pp. 210–33.
5. R. Hutton, *The rise and fall of merry England: the ritual year 1400–1700*

(Oxford, 1994), pp. 213–26; B. Capp, *England's culture wars: puritan reformation and its enemies in the Interregnum, 1649–1660* (Oxford, 2012).
6 Tai Liu, 'The founding of the London Provincial assembly, 1645–47' in *The English civil wars: local aspects*, ed. R. C. Richardson (Stroud, 1997), pp. 43–55.
7 P. J. Anderson, 'Presbyterianism and the gathered churches in old and New England 1640–1662: the struggle for church government in theory and practice' (D.Phil thesis, University of Oxford, 1979), pp. 3–4.
8 P. J. Anderson, 'Sion College and the London provincial assembly 1647–1660', *JEH*, 37:1 (1986), 90.
9 For the extent and various geographical meanings of 'London' see V. Harding, 'The population of London, 1550–1700: a review of the published evidence', *London Journal*, 15:2 (1990), 111–15; R. Weinstein, 'London at the outbreak of the civil war' in *London and the civil war*, ed. S. Porter (Basingstoke, 1996) pp. 31–44.
10 For the list of parishes in the province of London see *A&O*, I, p. 750.
11 See for example, LMA P69/LAW1/B/001/MS02590/001 (St Mary Magdalen, Milk Street vestry minutes – in this chapter V. M.), fo. 83; LMA P69/STE1/B/001/MS04458/001 (St Stephen, Coleman Street V. M.), fo. 147; LMA P69/MTN1/B/001/MS 01311/001/001 (St Martin, Ludgate V. M.), fos 143, 193.
12 LMA P69/MRY2/B/002 (St Mary the Virgin, Aldermanbury V. M.), fo. 52.
13 LMA P69/STE1/B/001/MS04458/001/001 (St Stephen, Coleman Street V.M.), fo. 147; Shaw, *HEC*, II, pp. 143–4. The eldership included the leading parliamentarians Isaac Pennington, Samuel Avery and Owen Rowe.
14 *A&O*, I, pp. 749, 1189.
15 LMA P69/OLA2/B/001/MS04415/001 (St Olave, Old Jewry V. M.), fo. 132v; LMA P69/PET4/B/001/MS00642/001 (St Peter, Westcheap V. M.), no foliation, 19 July 1646.
16 LMA P69/MIC2/B/001/MS04072/001 (St Michael, Cornhill V. M.), fo. 177v.
17 Ibid., fo. 178; Tai Liu, *Puritan London: a study of religion and society in the City parishes* (1986), p. 220.
18 LMA P69/PET1/B/001/MS04165/001 (St Peter, Cornhill V. M.), fos 286–7. The composition of the vestry at St Peter appears generally to have been a body of seventeen men: see e.g. *ibid.*, fos 283, 286. Other parishes that left records in their vestry minute books of the election of elders include St Mary Magdalen, Milk Street V. M., fo. 85; St Bartholomew by the Exchange (*The vestry minute book of the parish of St Bartholomew-by-the-Exchange*, ed. Edwin Freshfield (1890)), p. 19; St Margaret, Lothbury (*The vestry minute book of the parish of St Margaret Lothbury*, ed. Edwin Freshfield (1887)), pp. 88–9 and St Mary, Colechurch (LMA P69/MRY8/B/001/MS00064 (St Mary, Colechurch V. M.)), fo. 42.
19 St Bride had about 3,000 communicants; Tai Liu, *Puritan London*, p. 223.

20 In January 1644 St Bride moved to a select vestry whose membership was based on those who had served as parish scavenger; see LMA P69/BRI/B/001 (St Bride, Fleet Street V. M.), propositions written of front flyleaf, fo. 1r.
21 These were John Conant, Anthony Tuckney, Simeon Ashe, Sir John Wollaston, Edward Honeywood, William Hart, John Johnson, Richard Flood and John Sherman. See A&O, I, p. 798.
22 LMA P69/BRI/B/001 (St Bride, Fleet Street V. M.), fos 35, 36v, 37.
23 On the lack of legal status of the congregation, see A. E. McCampbell, 'The London parish and the London precinct, 1640–1660', *Guildhall Studies in London History*, 11:3 (1976), 124.
24 A&O, I, p. 793.
25 Baillie, L&J, II, p. 390; RLPA, fo. 16 (DWL transcript, p. 17); *An order of the committee of the Lords and Commons of Parliament [...] for supply of tryers* (1648).
26 These figures are based on my calculations from RLPA; *cf.* Anderson, who counts 190 ministers and 205 elders (Anderson, 'Sion College', p. 73).
27 *The register booke of the fourth classis in the province of London 1646–1659*, ed. C. E. Surman (London, 1953), pp. 1–3.
28 BL Sloane Ms. 922 (letters of Nehemiah Wallington), fo. 153.
29 *Ibid.*, fo. 154.
30 A&O, I, p. 1198; RLPA, fos 21–3 (DWL transcript pp. 22–3); Shaw, HEC, II, p. 142. The London Provincial assembly recommended (but did not require) the use of the Westminster assembly's *Shorter catechism*: London Provincial assembly, *An exhortation to catechizing* (1655), pp. 11–12.
31 *The register booke of the fourth* classis, p. 6; Vernon, 'A ministry of the gospel', pp. 119–30 and 'Godly pastors', pp. 54–61.
32 A&O, I, pp. 1206–7, 1211–15.
33 A&O, I, p. 1198.
34 Vernon, 'Godly pastors', pp. 54–6.
35 St Mary the Virgin, Aldermanbury V. M., fo. 58v; Vernon, 'Godly pastors', pp. 59–60.
36 St Michael, Cornhill V. M., fos 198r–v.
37 St Bride, Fleet Street V. M., fo. 127v.
38 LMA P69/LAW1/B/001/MS02590/001 (St Lawrence, Old Jewry V. M.), fo. 431; Vernon, 'A ministry of the gospel', pp. 128–9.
39 CCRB, I, pp. 269–70, 272–3; J. F. Merritt, *Westminster 1640–60: a royal city in a time of revolution* (Manchester, 2013), pp. 241–2; A. Richardson, 'Thomas Manton and the presbyterians in interregnum and Restoration England' (Ph.D thesis, University of Leicester, 2014), p. 12.
40 *Vestry minute books of [...] St Bartholomew Exchange*, pp. 26, 28; Vernon, 'A ministry of the gospel', p. 127.
41 *Vestry minute books of [...] St Bartholomew Exchange*, pp. 40, 59, 61–2, 70, 72–4; Shaw, HEC, II, pp. 132–4, 149. The parish would, however, elect the presbyterians John Crosse and Zachary Crofton as weekly lecturers during this period. For Cawton's ministry in Amsterdam, see C. Cotter, 'Going Dutch:

beyond black Bartholomew's day' in *'Settling the peace of the church'*: *1662 revisited*, ed. N. H. Keeble (Oxford, 2014), ch. 6.
42 RLPA, fos 5–6 (DWL transcript, pp. 6–7); *CJ*, V, p. 190; *LJ*, IX, p. 215. The Provincial assembly was initially composed of two ministers and four ruling elders from each classis but this was increased by Parliament to three ministers and six ruling elders on 29 August 1648.
43 RLPA, fo. 5 (DWL transcript, p. 6); Anderson, 'Sion College', p. 76.
44 RLPA, fos 7–12 (DWL transcript, pp. 6–12).
45 RLPA, fos 18–20 (DWL transcript, pp. 19–20); PA HL/PO/JO/10/1/250, fo. 118; *CJ*, V, p. 427; *LJ*, IX, pp. 658–60; Shaw, *HEC*, II, pp. 98–9.
46 RLPA, fos 10–11 (DWL transcript, pp. 11–12).
47 For the most comprehensive discussion of the unformed classes see Tai Liu, *Puritan London*, pp. 85–8.
48 *LJ*, IX, p. 659; RLPA, fo. 18 (DWL transcript, p. 19).
49 Tai Liu, *Puritan London*, pp. 85–8; E. Jones, 'London in the early seventeenth century: an ecological approach', *The London Journal*, 6:2 (1980), 123–33.
50 Richard Baxter's correspondent Thomas Wadsworth, of St Mary, Newington Butts, noted that the tenth classis was meeting 'scarcely' by June 1656: *CCRB*, I, pp. 173, 214.
51 Tai Liu, *Puritan London*, pp. 86–8, 102 nn. 169–71.
52 The Provincial assembly's October 1648 report, *A representation of the sad condition of the province of London*, listed forty parishes in the province that had 'the defect of an able and faithfull ministry': RLPA, fos 34–5 (DWL transcript, pp. 36–7). This diagnosis was confirmed by the Laudian Peter Heylin, who estimated that forty parishes had been left permanently vacant in the period by Parliament's sequestrations: see Anderson, 'Sion College', p. 74.
53 *LJ*, IX, p. 659.
54 The ministers of these parishes were William Harrison and Jacob Tice respectively. LMA P69/BOT3/B/001/MS00943/002 (St Botolph, Billingsgate V. M.) fo. 62; LMA P69/BEN2/B/001/MS04214/001 (St Benet, Gracechurch V. M.), fo. 23v.
55 *LJ*, IX, p. 690. The Provincial assembly began to work on a report concerning churchwardens, but this was set aside on 11 December 1648: RLPA, fo. 42 (DWL transcript, p. 48).
56 For a mid-seventeenth-century discussion of the legal status and function of churchwardens, overseers for the poor and other parish offices see William Sheppard, *The office and duty of churchwardens* (1652).
57 *LJ*, IX, p. 659.
58 A point later made by the congregationalist leader Philip Nye in *Beames of former light* (1660), pp. 158–9. Examples include St Clement, Eastcheap, which employed Thomas Fuller, George Hall, John Pearson and Nathaniel Hardy (LMA P69/CLE/B/001/MS00978/001, fos 58–99); St Gregory by St Paul, which employed Richard Goddard and Jeremy Taylor (LMA P69/GRE/B/001, fos 30–58).
59 *LJ*, IX, p. 659; RLPA, fo. 18 (DWL transcript, p. 20).

60 *A&O*, I, pp. 1117–18; RLPA, fo. 31 (DWL transcript, p. 31).
61 *LJ*, X, pp. 353–3; RLPA, fo. 31 (DWL transcript, p. 32).
62 RLPA, fo. 33 (DWL transcript, p. 34); *A&O*, I, pp. 1188–215.
63 RLPA, fo. 34 (DWL transcript, p. 36).
64 *The humble petition of the [...] City of London [...] October 17* (1648).
65 *A&O*, I, p. 1226.
66 BL Thomason Broadsheets 669, fo. 13 (38) and (39).
67 St Peter, Cornhill V. M., fo. 285.
68 William Wickins, *A plea for the ministry* (1650), pp. 1–9.
69 London Provincial assembly, *Jus divinum ministerii evangelici* (1654), I, p. 156; J. L. Ainslie, *The doctrine of the ministerial order in the Reformed churches of the sixteenth and seventeenth centuries* (Edinburgh, 1940), pp. 180, 195–6.
70 *The register booke of the fourth classis*, p. 33.
71 St Michael, Cornhill V. M., fo. 178v.
72 Bremer, *Congregational communion*, pp. 37–8.
73 For Symonds's principles in the Netherlands see Sprunger, *Dutch puritanism*, pp. 169, 173–4.
74 *Ibid.*, p. 349; The fourth classis of the province of London, *A full and faithfull accompt of the passages betwixt the parish of Michaels Cornehill [...] the ministers and elders of the fourth classis [...] and Mr. J. Symonds* (1646), p. 11.
75 For Richard Shute see Brenner, *Merchants*, pp. 430–1, 435, 447, 616; Como, *Radical Parliamentarians*, pp. 140–8, 158–9.
76 Henry Burton, *Truth shut out of doores* (1645).
77 St Michael, Cornhill V. M., fo. 178.
78 *Register booke of the fourth classis*, p. 6; Thomas Edwards, *The third part of Gangraena* (1646), p. 243; Hughes, *Gangraena*, p. 111.
79 *A full and faithfull accompt*, p. 2.
80 *Register booke of the fourth classis*, p. 6; *A full and faithfull accompt*, pp. 3, 5; St Michael, Cornhill V. M., fo. 179.
81 *A&O*, I, pp. 865–70.
82 *A full and faithfull accompt*, pp. 3–4.
83 *Ibid.*, pp. 3–4; *Register booke of the fourth classis*, p. 8.
84 *A full and faithfull accompt*, pp. 10–12.
85 *Register booke of the fourth classis*, p. 9.
86 *A full and faithful accompt*, p. 15; Shaw, *HEC*, II, p. 338; *LJ*, IX, pp. 71, 73.
87 J. Coffey, *John Goodwin*, pp. 152–3.
88 *Register booke of the fourth classis*, p. 9.
89 Such factional struggles were common. One such incident took place at the parish of St Martins in the Field during the April 1648 election of churchwardens. During the election an anti-presbyterian faction in the parish confronted the parish ruling elders with cries of 'no roundheads, no eld[er]s' and threatened to resume the use of the Book of Common Prayer (Bodleian Library, University of Oxford, Clarendon Ms. 31, fos 44r–v). For further examples of parish factionalism see J. A. Dodd, 'Troubles in a City parish under the Protectorate', *EHR*, 10:37 (1895), 41–54; A. E. McCampbell, 'Studies in

London parish history 1640–1660' (Ph.D thesis, Vanderbilt University, 1982), chs 3–4; Vernon, 'Godly pastors', pp. 57–61.
90 *Register booke of the fourth classis*, pp. 11, 12, 15, 16, 18, 29, 30.
91 Tai Liu, *Puritan London*, pp. 114, 141, 220; *Register booke of the fourth classis*, p. 9.
92 *Register booke of the fourth classis*, pp. 54–5, 59.
93 Edwards, *Third part of Gangraena*, p. 222.
94 *Register booke of the fourth classis*, p. 49.
95 RLPA, fos 25–6 (DWL transcript, p. 26).
96 RLPA, fo. 31 (DWL transcript, pp. 31–32); for the *Representation of the sad condition of the province of London* see RLPA, fos 34–5 (DWL transcript, pp. 36–7).
97 RLPA, fos 133v–134r (DWL transcript, pp. 130–31).
98 Anderson, 'Sion College', p. 80.
99 H. Smith, 'Ordinations by the fourth classis of London', *EHR*, 41:161 (1926), 103–08.
100 *Register booke of the fourth classis*, pp. 81–7. This process tallies with Philip Henry's recollections of his ordination by the fourth Shropshire classis: see Matthew Henry, *The life of the Rev. Philip Henry A. M.*, ed. J. B. Williams (1834), pp. 23–7; B. Coulton, 'The fourth Shropshire presbyterian classis, 1647–1662', *Transactions of the Shropshire Archaeological and Historical Society*, 73 (1998), 33–43.
101 Westminster assembly, *Propositions concerning church-government and ordination of ministers* (Edinburgh, 1647); RLPA, fos 41–2, 124 (DWL transcript, pp. 46–7, 116–17).
102 RLPA, fos 22–23 (DWL transcript, p. 23); Anderson, 'Sion College', pp. 79–80.
103 *The Life of Adam Martindale, written by himself*, ed. R. Parkinson (Manchester, 1845), pp. 67–9, 84–7.
104 RLPA, fo. 57 (DWL transcript, p. 61).
105 RLPA, fo. 245 (DWL transcript, p. 179).
106 RLPA, fo. 235 (DWL transcript, p. 152).
107 RLPA, fos 117–18 (DWL transcript, pp. 102–7); *Register Booke of the fourth classis*, pp. 99–102; Shaw, *HEC*, II, pp. 104–8.
108 RLPA, fo. 118 (DWL transcript, pp. 103–7).
109 Shaw, *HEC*, II, pp. 108–10.
110 RLPA, fo. 35r (DWL transcript, p. 37). These parishes were St Mildred, Bread Street, St Botolph, Aldersgate, St John Zachary, St Olave, Silver Street, St Alphage, London Wall, All Hallows the Less and St Mary Abchurch.
111 RLPA, fos 241v–242r (DWL transcript, pp. 169–70).
112 In 1648 the parish had elected William Greenhill as its lecturer and permitted Thomas Goodwin to use the church for his gathered church: see LMA P69/ALH4/B/001/MS04049/001 (All Hallows, Lombard Street V. M.), fos 27r–v; Tai Liu, *Puritan London*, p. 112.
113 Tai Liu, *Puritan London*, pp. 139–40; NA SP 18/181, fos 30–5; *CSPD, 1658–9*,

pp. 13–14, 145. A counterpetition in favour of the antinomian John Simpson was also presented.
114 Vernon, 'Godly pastors', pp. 58–9, 61.
115 For the financial problems of London parishes see C. Hill, *Economic problems of the Church from Archbishop Whitgift to the Long Parliament* (Oxford, 1956), esp. chs 4, 10, 12 and 13; and McCampbell, 'Studies in London parish history 1640–1660', ch. 3.
116 DWL MS 35.3, fos 425v–426.
117 RLPA, fos 128, 132, 133 (DWL transcript, pp. 121, 127, 129–30).
118 RLPA, fos 228r, 229r (DWL transcript, pp. 141, 146).
119 RLPA, fos 233–4 (DWL transcript, pp. 149–50).
120 RLPA, fo. 124 (DWL transcript, p. 116).
121 RLPA, fo. 133 (DWL transcript, p. 129).
122 RLPA, fo. 229 (DWL transcript, p. 148).
123 RLPA, fo. 234 (DWL transcript, p. 151).
124 RLPA, fo. 240 (DWL transcript, p. 166).
125 RLPA, fos 240–41 (DWL transcript, pp. 166–7).
126 RLPA, fo. 243 (DWL transcript, p. 173).
127 St Peter, Westcheap V. M., no foliation, 20 February 1652.
128 RLPA, fo. 236r (DWL transcript, p. 154); Shaw, *HEC*, II. pp. 111–12.
129 *CCRB*, I, pp. 172–3.
130 For a survey of the role of elders in England, America and Scotland see W. M. Abbot, 'Ruling eldership in civil war England, the Scottish Kirk, and early New England: a comparative study of secular and spiritual aspects', *CH*, 75:1 (2006), 38–68.
131 *Register Booke of the Fourth Classis*, p. 131.
132 RLPA, fo. 255v (DWL transcript, p. 196); Shaw, *HEC*, II, pp. 111–16.
133 Baillie, *L&J*, III, pp. 303, 306–7.
134 A. Hughes, 'Religious diversity in revolutionary London' in *The English revolution c.1590–1720: politics, religion and communities*, ed. N. Tyacke (Manchester, 2007), pp. 111–12.

8

The London presbyterians and the projected settlements of the British civil wars, 1647–9

In early 1649, after the Army's *coup d'état* of the previous December, Christopher Love set out his understanding of what defined the parliamentarian cause. These were a 'regulated monarchy, a free Parliament, an obedient Army, and a godly ministry'. These objects stood in opposition to 'tyranny, malignity, anarchy and heresie'.[1] Love was not alone in his opinion. The city's 'Covenant-keeping' citizens declared that they had engaged for Parliament to protect England against 'arbitrary and tyrannical government'. Their wealth and blood had been ventured to ensure the reformation of religion and the liberties of the subject against the predations of a misguided monarch.[2] Despite new wars and the rise of a radical parliamentarian counternarrative, this presbyterian vision of Parliament's aims was almost attained in the period from September 1647 to the revolution of early 1649. This chapter will analyse how the London presbyterian ministers, nudged by their Scottish counterparts, rebuilt the religious presbyterian cause in London and, indeed, the nation. It will be argued that, although there were substantial divisions among London presbyterians over the direction to follow in the second civil war, many religious presbyterians remained loyal to Parliament and their vision of what the parliamentary cause entailed. The chapter concludes by addressing the London presbyterian response to the Army's forceful repudiation of the Isle of Wight treaty and the trial and execution of the king.

The projected settlement of 1647 and *A testimony to the truth of Jesus Christ*

The failure of the political presbyterians to seize control of the peace process in the summer of 1647 left the now dominant political Independent grandees, described by the radical printer John Harris as 'the royal Independents', in a position to impose a settlement on Charles I.[3] The grandees laid the groundwork for their settlement, including proposals for the church, in October 1647. These would form the basis of the religious propositions included with the 'four bills', which were sent to the king in December for a restoration settlement.[4] Parliament would adopt the suggestion, first suggested by the revived committee for accommodation, of a two-tier ecclesiastical system of a national church running alongside a forbearance for voluntary gathered churches. On 13 October, propositions were presented by Parliament's committee of religion to both houses for discussion. Parliament confirmed the existing Parliamentary ordinances for presbyterian government, adding provisions 'for tender conscience of such as are godly' and bills for the abolition of episcopacy and the sale of bishops' lands.[5] Parliament's propositions threatened to render the as yet unfinished Westminster confession of faith a dead letter by establishing a truncated version of the Church of England's thirty-nine Articles approved by the Westminster assembly in 1643 as the confessional basis for the future Church of England. Although Roman Catholics were not to be afforded toleration, the House of Lords' initial draft would have left devotees of the Book of Common Prayer free to use it in private congregations.[6] This liberty, however, was removed by the Commons who, responding to complaints that the Prayer Book was being used in the chapels of the universities of Oxford and Cambridge, ordered that it should not be used 'in any place whatsoever'.[7]

The main source of dispute in the Commons was the length of time for the trial run for presbyterian polity as the government of the national church.[8] The initial suggestion was that Parliament would adopt the three-year period offered by the king in his 12 May 1647 answer to the Newcastle Propositions. This was unacceptable to religious presbyterians, who sought the establishment of presbyterian polity for an indefinite period. This proposal was defeated by a mere three votes, with Sir John Evelyn of Wiltshire and Oliver Cromwell acting as tellers against the proposition. Cromwell and Henry Lawrence, nevertheless, offered a compromise to presbyterians in the Commons, proposing that presbyterian polity should be established as the polity of the national church for a period of seven years. This proposal was defeated by eight votes, with the unlikely pairing of Evelyn and the religious presbyterian Sir Walter Erle acting as tellers against the suggestion.[9] With the Cromwell and Lawrence compromise measure defeated, the presbyterian church settlement was voted to continue to the next session of Parliament, a period expected to last as little as six months.[10]

Parliament's projected settlement of religion was unacceptable to those presbyterians who remained committed to the covenanted reformation of the Church of England. The protests against the proposals initially issued from Scotland. On 18 December the Scots presented a long complaint to the House of Lords bemoaning the English Parliament's lack of consultation over the four bills and Parliament's apparent abandonment of the Solemn League and Covenant.[11] The Scots objected that the religious proposals contained 'nothing but a mere shadow of presbyterial government' which amounted in practice to 'no more than a toleration of it'.[12] The liberty of conscience granted to dissenting protestants gave 'an unlimited toleration' to errors and heresies and opened 'a door to atheism'.[13] The English Parliament's proposals, the Scots alleged, were fundamentally defective as they set out no penalties against those, such as anti-trinitarians, who were proscribed by its terms.[14] The Scottish commissioners concluded by desiring the English Parliament to adopt the platform of church government drawn up by the Westminster assembly. They also demanded that the 1646 proposals for an ordinance against blasphemy and heresy, stalled since 1647, be revived and brought into law.[15]

The Scottish commissioners' complaint to Parliament coincided with a gradual return to campaigning by London's religious presbyterian activists.[16] On 1 December, the day the four bills were sent down from the Lords to the Commons, the city delivered a petition to Parliament seeking the removal of the Army to a further distance from London and renewing the call for a settlement in accordance with the Covenant.[17] The Scots took the city's rediscovery of its presbyterian voice as a signal that London had regained its nerve in the cause of the Covenant. Agents from the Kirk were instructed to deliver letters to both the Westminster assembly and the London ministers at Sion College. The purpose of these letters was to mobilise English religious presbyterians to assist the Scots in their protest against the English Parliament's projected religious settlement. Although the Westminster assembly obediently handed over its letter, on 10 December, to the Commons, the Sion College ministers were not so cautious. After a meeting at Sion College on 14 December it was decided that the Kirk's letter should be made public. It was given to Ralph Smith, Thomas Edwards' publisher, to print, with James Cranford's *imprimatur*.[18] Implicitly referring to Parliament's October proposals, the Kirk's letter complained of the 'wayes of errour, schisme, heresies, self interest, and carnall policy fathered by many upon Christ, under the names of tender consciences, saints and the like'. It called on the London ministers 'to stand fast in the truth of Christ' by giving 'a good testimony for it, even when it is opposed and persecuted'. The Kirk advised the London ministers that they had 'the clearer call from God to give testimony' against the heresies of the times.[19]

The London ministers took their Scottish brethren's advice literally, hastily compiling and publishing a pamphlet entitled *A testimony to the truth of Jesus Christ* at the Sion College meeting. This work, subscribed by fifty-two London presbyterian ministers, set out a list of contemporary doctrinal errors and heresies drawn from recently printed works. This catalogue of errors was loosely categorised according to the pattern of the Reformed confessions, beginning with heresies concerning the theological fundamentals of the authority of scripture, the nature and essence of God and the trinity, before moving on to soteriological and Christological errors and then heresies concerning the use of church ordinances. The pamphlet concluded with theological errors concerning the civil state, such as the doctrine of divorce and 'the errour of toleration, patronizing and promoting all other errours, heresies, and blasphemies whatsoever, under the grossely abused notion of liberty of conscience'.[20] Following the Scots' direction, the London ministers' *Testimony* called on Parliament to settle the presbyterian government and, alluding to the stalled blasphemy ordinance, to enact measures to punish idolatry and blasphemy.[21]

The publication of the *Testimony* was the signal for a national campaign, leading to similar pamphlets being published from thirteen counties, containing the signatures of 902 ministers.[22] These county documents generally followed the London ministers in calling for a more doctrinally limited church settlement than Parliament's October propositions envisaged. The Essex and Cheshire ministers, however, included calls for liberty of conscience to be extended to doctrinally orthodox Christians who differed only on matters of ecclesiastical polity.[23] Although there appears to be no direct evidence to prove the point, it is likely that the national *Testimony* campaign was arranged through the communication network that existed between the London ministers and their comrades in the counties. Central to this national campaign were the London presbyterian booksellers and publishers who acted as the publishers of the county responses.[24] The *Testimony* campaign demonstrated that despite the crackdown on the mobilisation of presbyterians by Parliament in the months after August 1647, they were still able to organise for the Covenanted interest.

The campaign around the *Testimony* demonstrates the continuing commitment of the London presbyterians to the cause of the Solemn League and Covenant. These efforts would reap rewards as Parliament became alarmed at the potential for a new civil war in 1648. It is clear that the Scots were heartened by the campaign of their English presbyterian brethren in giving testimony to the presbyterian cause. In a tract of May 1648, the Kirk considered it a 'door of hope to us' that godly ministers had joined together to give 'a fair publike testimony for the truth of Jesus Christ, for the Covenant, for the presbyterial government, and against that abominable toleration of most dangerous errors, heresies and schismes'.[25] In addition, by the end of December 1647 it was reported that political presbyterians were beginning to return to the Westminster Parliament.[26] As will be seen in the next section, divisions among parliamentarians over the nature of the endgame with the king would lead to a revival of presbyterian fortunes in the quest for settlement.

The Hamiltonian engagement and parliamentarian *rapprochement*

The Kirk's timing in using their English presbyterian allies to register their protests through the *Testimony* campaign proved to be fortuitous for religious presbyterian interests in both Scotland and England. The national support for the *Testimony*, together with the resurgence of political presbyterian demands, demonstrated that the Covenant-engaged interest retained the ability to mobilise despite the events of summer 1647. Nevertheless, there were fundamental splits within the presbyterian camp. Two weeks after the London ministers issued their *Testimony*, the Duke of Hamilton agreed an engagement with the king at Carisbrooke. This treaty, kept secret until 21 January 1648, engaged the Scots to invade England to restore Charles's monarchy in return for a 'British' court policy that would benefit the Scottish nobility.[27] Hamilton's engagement, which would propel Britain towards a second civil war, would divide presbyterians in all three kingdoms.

It has often been asserted that most English presbyterians were complicit in supporting and making preparations for the 'Scots' invasion under Hamilton. It has also been argued that English presbyterians made a *rapprochement* with royalists to complete the so-called 'counter-revolution' begun in 1647.[28] Even the bout of obnoxious apprentice behaviour in London in the winter of 1647 and the spring of 1648, which was both fiercely anti-puritan in expression and royalist in content, has been laid at the feet of London's presbyterians.[29] However, against this view, there has been a growing recognition that the politics of 1648 was complex and chaotic and that the question of allegiance does not always yield to simple binary reductions.[30] This more nuanced view has been at the fore in recent Scottish historiography, which has pointed out that a monolithic notion of 'the Scots' in these events does not withstand scrutiny. Even the covenanters in this period were divided and fractured over the Hamiltonian engagement.[31] Similar criticism of seeing English presbyterians in monolithic terms has been voiced by historians.[32] This section addresses the activities of London's presbyterians in the early months of 1648 and asks whether a *détente* emerged with royalist elements in the city and questions the extent to which London's presbyterians were willing to support Hamilton's invasion.

The main evidence for London religious presbyterian political activity in the early months of 1648 comes from the pamphlet reportage of the sectary propagandist John Price. A member of John Goodwin's Coleman Street separatist church, Price attended the presbyterian morning exercises between February and May 1648 digging for evidence to question the loyalty of the presbyterian clergy to the parliamentary cause. Although he managed to extract from these sermons what he considered to be sufficient proof of presbyterian infidelity to Parliament, he had to admit that the ministers spoke 'so covertly, and with such caution, warinesse and circumspection' that his evidence was limited.[33] Although regularly taken at face value by historians, Price's diatribe against presbyterian perfidy was not without its contemporary critics.[34] One such asserted that Price had perverted the ministers' 'words as well as their meaning' so that he could 'wrest, and misconstrue, to carp, and cavil at every word and expression' so that his 'false glosse might admit of a misconstruction'.[35] Such a contemporary response counsels caution against a simplistic use of Price's reports as historical evidence. Reading his accusations against the grain of his propagandistic purpose, however, suggests that the presbyterian ministers were reiterating many of the themes that had characterised their position between 1645–7, rather than proclaiming a new-found royalism. As might be expected, a dominant theme of the 1648 sermons was criticism of the Army's military interference in the spheres of politics and religion.[36]

With regard to the king, Price's evidence was rather weak. He could report the complaint of John Wall, minister of St Michael, Cornhill, at the Army's seizure and captivity of the king, but could find only one minister, Peter Witham of St Alban, Wood Street, who prayed for Charles I's unconditional restoration.[37] Overt presbyterian royalism, therefore, was a rare catch for Price. Criticism of Parliament was more common, but such criticism had been part and parcel of the relationship between Parliament and the ministers throughout the 1640s.[38] Indeed, most of the presbyterian critiques of Parliament discovered by Price were nothing new, going no further than what ministers had said in the fast sermons before Parliament itself in 1646–7.[39]

Price contended that the London ministers had preached in support of Hamilton's engagement and the Scottish invasion of England. He accused William Jenkyn of praying for Scotland, thanking God for the Scots' influence in English religious affairs and praying to God to 'blow up those sparks into a flame'. Likewise, Thomas Cawton is alleged to have prayed for 'our brethren of Scotland to settle Reformation in their own kingdom', hoping that God would 'quash all those that rise up against them'.[40] In order to assess whether this was support for Hamilton, it is necessary to understand the position of the London presbyterians with regards to Scottish politics in the run-up to, and during, the second civil war. As noted above, historians have often deployed an overly simplistic notion of a 'Scottish–royalist' axis in 1648 and have failed to recognise the deep divisions within Scotland over Hamilton's engagement. One aspect of this division was religious in nature, with the 'Kirk party' ministers opposing the engagement on the basis that the king had refused to swear the Solemn League and Covenant and had opposed the Kirk's presbyterian ambitions outside Scotland.[41] In this context, it is entirely possible that Price was purposely misrepresenting the London ministers' advocacy for their fellow presbyterians in the Kirk party as support for Hamilton's invading army.

The evidence of the London ministers' activities during this period tends to suggest that Price was indeed twisting the message of their sermons. Certainly, the more moderate political Independents at Westminster, perceiving the utility of exploiting internal presbyterian divisions, began to make overtures to the 'Covenant-engaged' interest in both Scotland and England to neuter the threat posed by Hamilton.[42] As a result, the English Parliament sent a delegation to Scotland led by the pro-presbyterian MP William Ashhurst and accompanied by the ministers Stephen Marshall and Charles Herle. While in Scotland, the English delegation courted the Marquess of Argyll and the Kirk party in an attempt to scupper Hamilton's political and military manoeuvres.[43] The political *rapprochement* between parliamentarians over the threat from Scotland also extended to London's religious presbyterians. In February, the Earl of Lanerick's London agent reported that the Westminster Independents were attempting to find ways to rebuild the parliamentarian alliance by appealing to religious presbyterians.[44] By the end of March, the same informant reported that the London ministers Cornelius Burges and Edmund Calamy, together with John Glover, a lawyer and member of the presbyterian-led committee of accounts and now described by Clement Walker as Cromwell's 'solicitor', were acting as brokers between Parliament and the city in an attempt to effect 'a right understanding betweene the Army, two houses, and the Citty'.[45] These discussions had initially centred on the city declaring its support for Parliament against the Hamiltonians. In return, it was proposed that the aldermen and citizens imprisoned for the disturbances of summer 1647 would be released, along with restoring control of the Tower and the militia committee to the city government.[46] It is not clear to whom Burges, Calamy and Glover were talking, but their overtures on behalf of Parliament were rebuffed, with the ministers' counterparts demanding a restoration of Charles I in return for an act of indemnity for parliamentarians.[47] Nevertheless, the deployment of Calamy, Burges and Glover on behalf of Parliament tied in with the *détente* reached at Westminster between the leading political Independents and former 'war party' religious presbyterians led by the Earl of Manchester and John Swynfen in the late spring and early summer of 1648. This *détente* focused on revoking the 'vote of no address' in favour of a personal treaty with the king, with the settlement of presbyterian church government, Parliamentary control of the militia and the revocation of the king's declarations against parliamentarians as conditions for any final treaty.[48] By cultivating Argyll and the Kirk party in Scotland and making concessions to the likes of the Manchester and other religious presbyterians in England, the Parliamentary Independents also attempted to quell any sympathy that 'Covenant-engaged' religious presbyterians had in London (and elsewhere) for Hamilton. By April, Lanerick's informant was reporting that English presbyterians considered that 'Argyll's partie and intentions' were the 'more laudable and honest' of the Scottish factions, and Nehemiah Wallington was writing that Hamilton's appeal to presbyterian unity was a hypocritical 'pretence'.[49]

Wallington's suspicions were shared by many of the most committed London presbyterian ministers, including those alleged by Price to be preaching in favour of the engagement. In May Stanley Gower, James Cranford and William Jenkyn (who, as we have seen, had been singled out by Price as pro-Hamilton) wrote to Major General Edward Massie to advise him to refuse to have any dealings with the Hamiltonian faction in Scotland. While the ministers were critical of the New Model Army, they counselled Massie that the Hamiltonians could not be considered brethren and pleaded with him to oppose the efforts of royalist 'malignants' in stirring up conflict. The ministers informed Massie that the 'Kirk party in Scotland are the honest and well affected party to our Covenant. The noble Earle of Argile is theyr head.'[50] The ministers' advice seems to have influenced Massie. In July he rejected Queen Henrietta Maria's invitation to command a royalist army in support of Hamilton, stating that 'he would never betray his Countrey so much, as to aid a forrein Nation, to assist them against England'.[51]

One of the measures of *rapprochement* between the Westminster Independents and religious presbyterians was for Parliament to press ahead with the settlement of presbyterian polity in the English national church.[52] Legislation enabling the construction of the parliamentary presbyterian system in the counties was passed, some of the problems of ecclesiastical finance were addressed and concerns raised by English and Scottish presbyterians as to the doctrinal orthodoxy of Parliament's projected religious settlement were answered.[53] The concerns raised by the Scottish commissioners in their letter of 18 December 1647 were addressed by Parliament in a joint declaration of the Lords and Commons on 4 March.[54] The joint declaration has received little attention by historians and, although carefully worded for the immediate political situation, reveals much of the thinking of the political Independent grandees on the issue of the settlement of the church. One of the key points that the joint declaration sought to counter was the Scots' complaint that the religious settlement did little more than tolerate presbyterian polity in England. The joint declaration replied that presbyterianism was to be protected, 'owned and countenanced' as the public ecclesiastical polity in England and that Parliament had allotted 'the publike maintenance and places of Worship unto it'.[55] Nevertheless, it maintained the 'Erastian' thrust of the 1647 proposals, stating that in return for public support, the national presbyterian church would 'receive also rules from the State which others do not'.[56] As to the Scots' complaint that the use of the truncated thirty-nine Articles was inadequate to counter heresy, Parliament stated that it could not adopt the Westminster assembly's confession of faith as it had not yet been passed into law, hinting that the Westminster confession would be established as the national confession in the future. Further, the joint declaration considered that the truncated version of the thirty-nine Articles, as approved by the Westminster assembly, was sufficient to exclude from the indulgence granted to tender consciences the heresies and errors, such as Arminianism and antinomianism, complained of by the Scots.[57] Parliament unapologetically declared that its indulgence was specifically aimed at benefiting particular baptists, who merely held 'a difference about a circumstance of time in the administration of an ordinance' and congregationalists who were 'godly and learned men of known integrity and fidelity to the State' who had 'been very faithful' to Parliament 'in the common cause'.[58]

According to William Rosse, Parliament's agent in Edinburgh, the joint declaration 'did so much good here, amongst some honest minded men, though others are not yet convinced'.[59] One reason for Scottish and English presbyterian scepticism was the view that the October 1647 proposals provided no penal sanctions against blasphemers and heretics. Parliament replied that it was neither within the 'scope nor work' of the October 1647 proposals to provide penalties against heretics or blasphemers. The punishment of public outbursts of blasphemy and heresy would be dealt with by the magistrate according to already adequate existing laws, although it was hinted that the topic would be the subject of future legislation.[60] In dropping this hint, Parliament was perhaps alluding to its order, made on 28 January 1648, that the draft bill against blasphemy and heresy should be revived.[61] The blasphemy and heresy bill had been largely the product of Zouche Tate and Nathaniel Bacon, both religious presbyterians, and its revival has often been seen as a sign of the rising fortunes of the presbyterians in Parliament. Its progress from late January into law on 2 May would suggest that the ordinance was part of the package of concessions offered by the political Independents to secure the support of English and Scottish religious presbyterians and prevent them being tempted by the Hamiltonian engagement.[62] In June Parliament approved the Westminster assembly's confession of faith, albeit a version stripped of the chapters that gave voice to divine right presbyterianism.⁶³ This would be followed on 29 August with an ordinance consolidating and perfecting Parliament's votes for presbyterian church government in England.⁶⁴ With hindsight the blasphemy ordinance, which was never substantially put into practice, looks, at least in part, like a sop to appease the Kirk party in Scotland and the Covenant-engaged presbyterians in England. The progress of the ordinance and other legislation for presbyterian government appears to have been taken by London's religious presbyterians as a sufficient answer to their *Testimony* campaign and a reason to oppose conspiring with Hamilton in Scotland and royalists at home. Certainly, by 27 May Lanerick's informant could inform his master 'the [London presbyterian] clergy is very jealous of all your proceedings and appears much more friendly to Indep[endent] principles then formerlie', a view shared in other royalist intelligence of the time.⁶⁵

The second civil war

Despite the concessions to Scottish and English religious presbyterians, the outbreak of local insurrections throughout England and Wales in the late spring of 1648 and the threat of Hamilton's invasion from Scotland put Parliament on a crisis footing. With the Army fighting these uprisings, Parliament felt compelled to make concessions to a broad range of parliamentarians and neutrals to retain political control.⁶⁶ This section will analyse the role of the London presbyterian ministers and citizens in the politically divisive atmosphere of the second civil war.

An influential line of historical argument has seen the city's government and London's presbyterians as heading in an increasingly royalist direction during this period. Robert Brenner sees the city presbyterians entering a 'closer alliance with the old forces of royalism in the City'.⁶⁷ Ian Gentles frames his analysis as the continuing struggle between the forces of revolution and counter-revolution, seeing a partnership of 'high presbyterianism' with royalists in the crisis of 1648.⁶⁸ Consequently, he sees the city magistrates as paying only 'lip-service' and showing a 'pretended' loyalty to Parliament. His study credits Major General Philip Skippon, together with the leading members of John Goodwin's gathered church, with preventing the city from switching its allegiance to royalism.⁶⁹

This line of argument can be criticised for its broad-brush approach to the politics of 1648. As argued above, any analysis that equates 'the Scots' with the Hamiltonian engagers is untenable, given the deep divisions in Scottish politics in 1648. This is particularly so, given that the anti-engager faction in Scotland was driven by the 'high presbyterian' counterparts to the religious presbyterians in London and elsewhere in England. Ann Hughes has argued that equating the position of Westminster Independents, or the Army, with 'parliamentarianism' provides too simplistic a picture of the chaotic politics of 1648.[70] Her analysis tallies with David Underdown's argument that Parliament's retreat from the vote of no addresses in April 1648 divided the political Independents at Westminster between those who sought a negotiated restoration settlement with Charles I and those requiring more radical solutions to Britain's troubles.[71] Underdown's position has been modified by David Scott, who argues that the Independent grandees sought to rebuild a parliamentarian consensus by prising those presbyterians for whom a godly religious settlement was a central concern away from those who privileged a return to constitutional normality.[72]

From April, the city government seized on the crisis to demand a number of political goals aimed at achieving a national settlement favourable to London's interests. Unsurprisingly, these aspirations harked back to the political presbyterian programme of 1646–7. The city's aims can be summarised as three objectives. The first was the release of and dropping of all charges laid against the aldermen and citizens imprisoned for the events of summer 1647. This goal was achieved by 3 June, when the proximity of the Earl of Norwich's royalist insurgents to London forced Parliament to release the last of the incarcerated aldermen as a token of goodwill to the city.[73] London's second aim was to regain control of its militia and unite the city's forces with those of the suburbs and, more ambitiously, the surrounding counties. This was partially achieved by the end of May, when the city regained the power to nominate its militia committee (albeit subject to Philip Skippon's overall command) and to appoint the Lieutenant of the Tower, a position that was given to the political presbyterian Francis West.[74] London's ambition to amalgamate the militias of the suburbs and, beyond them, the home counties, was unsurprisingly less successful as it clearly aimed at providing a military counterbalance to the Army.[75] The final objective was a personal treaty between Parliament and the king, significantly stated to be 'according to the Covenant', to be signed in London or its environs. This step was encouraged by presbyterian sermons throughout the late spring and summer of 1648.[76]

As noted above, the city's strategy during the second civil war has often been seen as a joint presbyterian and royalist venture. It is clear that its strategy was predicated on the Army being mired in conflict in the provinces and thus out of the way of Westminster politics. It cannot be doubted that there were many in the city who hoped that Hamilton and the royalist insurgencies would be, at least partially, successful, if only to bring Parliament to negotiate with the king. Nevertheless, as we have seen above, the London presbyterian ministry, along with presbyterian citizens such as Nehemiah Wallington, opposed Hamilton as a hypocrite and opponent of the Covenant. A number of contemporaries perceived that the city government's objectives in the spring and summer of 1648 were not so much support for Hamilton or royalist forces but the building of the conditions for controlling a settlement with the king free from interference by either cavaliers or Fairfax's army. In May, the Earl of Lanerick's London agent thought that the city's objective in its militia policy was to secure for itself a zone of neutrality in order to stage a treaty between king and Parliament.[77] This strategy, as the newspaper *Mercurius pragmaticus* observed, was an attempt to turn the political clock back to the situation when Charles I had been imprisoned at Holdenby House and thus to regain control of the king in order to force a political presbyterian settlement.[78] That such a strategy would benefit from the success of Hamilton in the north cannot be doubted, but the city did not come out in support of Hamilton or English royalist insurgents. As such, London's policy is best seen as an attempt to resurrect the old Essex-Holles group's approach for a settlement between king and Parliament, rather than support for a royalist resurgence.

Analysis of the committees drafting the city's five main petitions to Parliament in the summer of 1648 suggests that the dominant voices driving London's policy were the political presbyterian aldermen John Langham and James Bunce, who were selected for all five petition committees.[79] In 1648 Langham's and Bunce's variety of political presbyterianism appealed to an emerging 'neo-royalist' accent in city politics associated with the wider demands of a body of wealthy citizens identified by opponents as 'common hall men'.[80] This term derived from attempts in June to use the more exclusive, livery-only membership of common hall to put pressure on the common council for a treaty with the king and a return to pre-civil war normality. Unsurprisingly, the common council resisted this attempt to subvert its authority.[81] Joining Langham and Bunce on all five committees were Edwin Browne, William Chamberlain and Philip Chetwynd, a draper turned publisher, who would emerge as Philip Skippon's most vocal opponent within the city.[82]

Although Langham and Bunce appear to have favoured a presbyterian church settlement, they were not religious presbyterian activists, having never signed any of the city petitions nor served as parochial ruling elders. Langham, Bunce and the former Lord Mayor Thomas Adams were singled out in June 1648 by the Earl of Lanerick's London informant as those in the city most likely to fund Hamilton's invasion if it ever gathered steam.[83] Bunce would flee to the Netherlands to join the Stuart court in exile in 1649, and Langham, although a leading guardian of presbyterian nonconformity at the Restoration, is said to have protected sequestered godly episcopalian ministers throughout the 1650s.[84] Religious presbyterian activists did not dominate the crucial city committees of the second civil war period.

Of the thirty people selected for the city drafting committees in summer 1648, only ten were connected to previous religious presbyterian activism. Five religious presbyterians would be selected for the relatively non-partisan committee that drafted the well-received petition of 27 June for a personal treaty and seven would be selected for a 31 June petition against the taxation of Newcastle coal. By contrast, only four of the eighteen people involved in drafting the two petitions opposing Philip Skippon's continuation as the commander of the city's forces would serve as presbyterian ruling elders.[85] Skippon had come to be seen by many among the city leadership as the Army's Trojan horse within the city militia's command structure, and was criticised for surreptitious enlistments without the knowledge of the militia committee. Nevertheless, the city's opposition to Skippon appears to have been divisive. For example, the religious presbyterians William Webb and Robert Minwaring were supporters of Skippon and were appointed treasurers for Skippon's enlisted forces.[86] In addition John Bellamie and William Jesson, described by *Mercurius elenticus* as wavering politically between Independency and presbyterianism, were conspicuous by their absence from the anti-Skippon drafting committees, as well as the poorly-received 8 August city petition for a personal treaty. Only one religious presbyterian activist (Edward Hooker) was selected for the committee drafting the 8 August petition, which was led by Bunce and Langham and was mainly composed of early 1640s opponents of parliamentarian militancy in the city.[87]

Langham's and Bunce's attempt to use the City of London's government to force a swift political settlement with the king ended with the Army's defeat of both Hamilton's invasion and royalist resistance at Colchester on 28 August. A day later, the common council adopted a petition that had been circulating in the city for a couple of weeks appealing for parliamentarian unity.[88] Although probably originating from moderate political Independents, the petition appealed to many religious presbyterians by stressing covenanted reformation, the preservation of the mixed constitution and calling on the Army to declare its submission to the terms of any treaty negotiated between the king and Parliament. The city's leadership under Bunce and Langham was criticised for its apparent support for the Hamiltonian Scots and for having receded from its 'zeale for the reformation of religion'.[89] The entourage of aldermen and common councillors selected to accompany the city's sheriffs to Parliament to present the petition embodied these objectives, including prominent political Independents as well as 'Covenant-engaged' religious presbyterians who had been absent from the city's drafting committees in the summer.[90]

The evidence presented here suggests that, in tune with the research of David Scott and Gary de Krey, London's presbyterians were divided in 1648 between those who were committed to a Parliamentary settlement with the king 'according to the Covenant' and those who had come to favour a restoration merely on the basis of the king's promises to address grievances.[91] The city, dominated in the summer of 1648 by the political presbyterian leadership of 1646–7, had attempted to use the chaos of provincial insurrection to settle a peace that was favourable to a return to pre-civil war normality. On the other hand many religious presbyterians in London were committed to working with Parliament to achieve a more robust settlement with the king. While these differing directions did not cause London's lay religious presbyterians to split into distinctive factions, the differing choices and tendencies would have repercussions throughout the 1650s.

The English revolution and the execution of Charles I

The opening of the treaty negotiations between the king and Parliament at Newport on 15 September represented a victory for those presbyterians who had sought a robust parliamentarian settlement with the king, without a descent into revolution. Although the presbyterians failed to have the talks held in the London region, the Newport negotiations represented the opportunity to reach a settlement that matched the war aims contained in Parliament's various declarations, oaths and covenants that presbyterians saw as definitive of the parliamentarian cause. It was the near-success of that opportunity that would trigger the Army to revolution, the trial and execution of the king and the establishment of the English Commonwealth. This section looks at the role of the London presbyterians in the English revolution of 1648–9.

Charles's early concessions in the Newport discussions to Parliament's demands for reducing his power in civil affairs, particularly his concession regarding control of the militia, raised hopes that a genuine settlement could be obtained. The main sticking point in the negotiations was the settlement of the Church of England.[92] The king, playing for time in anticipation of either a chance to escape or the Duke of Ormonde making a military alliance with the Catholic confederation in Ireland, remained committed to episcopacy, refusing to concede the terms of his coronation oath.[93] The Parliamentary commissioners, joined by five ministers led by Stephen Marshall and Richard Vines, sought to convince the king to adopt presbyterianism. The king's conscience concerning episcopacy could be satisfied, the ministers argued, through his adopting the presbyterian understanding of what the term 'bishop' signified in scripture. The debate, essentially couched in terms of the 1641 argument between Bishop Hall, Archbishop Ussher and the Smectymnuans, saw the parliamentarian clergy maintain a presbyterian two-office model of church polity, where those called 'bishops' were synonymous with the pastors of a single church. In response, the king argued that scripture held out an order of bishop that had oversight over both the flock and other presbyters (*'episcopi gregis et pastorum'*).[94] This issue proved to be the source of the *impasse* between the king and the parliamentarians. As Richard Vines later told Richard Baxter, while Charles was willing to accept the possibility of a fixed president over a collection of individual churches, he was not willing to accept that such an individual should have additional jurisdiction or a power of negative voice.[95] This disagreement concerning the power that the presidential bishop would wield remained the stumbling block for any settlement based on 'primitive' or 'reduced' episcopacy. While the king was willing to concede that bishops should consult with panels of local presbyters in acts of jurisdiction, he insisted that the bishop should ultimately retain the powers of a prelate. The presbyterian ministers, on the other hand, were unwilling to concede any power to a reduced bishop that went further than that held by a presbyterian moderator. The problem of jurisdiction would remain a sticking point, one which would render the apparently attractive compromise of a 'reduced episcopacy' a dead end throughout the 1650s and into the early 1660s.

The king's concessions at Newport raised the hope for most religious and political presbyterians that a presbyterian settlement beyond its initial three-year trial period, or at the very least some form of 'presbytery in episcopacy', could be obtained in a peace settlement. In addition, the king's concessions in civil affairs satisfied those parliamentarians whose primary objectives remained the limiting of royal power without abolishing monarchy. The majority in the Commons therefore voted on 5 December that the king had given enough away for a viable settlement, a vote that triggered the Army, buoyed by support from the city's gathered churches and the resurgent Leveller movement, to carry out its long-threatened *Putsch* of Parliament, which became known as Pride's purge after Colonel Thomas Pride who commanded the New Model Army soldiers involved.[96]

Following Pride's purge, Parliament, assisted by leading London political and religious Independents largely from John Goodwin's gathered church, wasted no time in neutralising the presbyterian voice on the city's common council.[97] This was effected by Parliament passing ordinances on 18 and 20 December disabling all who had signed the city's engagements and petitions for a treaty with the king from holding civic office.[98] The purged Parliament's ordinances garnered complaints from the city that the documents supporting a personal treaty were so widely signed that London could not fill the seats on the common council.[99] For example, the parish of St Bride, Fleet Street recorded on 21 December 1648 that 'all or most' of those elected for city office by the parish had been disabled from taking their places.[100] Such was the extent of support for a personal treaty that Abraham Reynardson, the crypto-royalist Lord Mayor, burned the books of signatures urging a treaty to protect citizens against the possibility of facing trial under martial law.[101] Historians have confirmed the city's complaints, estimating that between half and three-quarters of those routinely returned to the common council were prevented from holding office by the two Parliamentary ordinances.[102] The political *Putsch* at the end of 1648, therefore, removed many of the presbyterian activists of the mid-1640s from a key institutional base in the city government.

Pride's purge inevitably unleashed a wave of protest from the disenfranchised presbyterian citizens. In a declaration of 24 January, the citizens complained that the parliamentarian cause had been betrayed. The citizens had supported Parliament 'for the defence of our liberties by Law, that our English spirits might not be intimidated or beslaved'. The revolution had set about replacing the ancient constitution with the 'headlesse confused arbitrary and tyrannical government' represented by proposals to settle the constitution by one of the various agreements of the people then in circulation. The ordinances of 18 and 20 December, the citizens argued, were key examples of the new military tyranny, their 'franchises and priviledges, as freemen' to elect their own common council being extinguished at the Army's *Diktat*. Even the Army's justification for demanding these ordinances, the signing of an engagement for a personal treaty, the citizens pointed out, offended the ancient common law principle against retrospective legislation, it being imposed 'after this supposed crime was acted'.[103]

Similar complaints about the 6 December purge and its immediate aftermath issued from the London ministers. On 27 December, Thomas Watson, the minister of St Stephen, Walbrook, used his invitation to preach to the Commons to accuse those sitting of hypocrisy and to warn of divine judgement for breach of the Covenant.[104] Similar protests came after 7 January, when the Army commanded the common council to instruct the London clergy to inform their parishes that the city must raise £19,000 to pay the Army or face military reprisals. The presbyterian ministers' reaction was understandably unenthusiastic. It was reported that some ministers refused to convey the Army's demands and others 'grievously rayl'd' that the Army and those sitting in the purged common council were 'covenant breakers'.[105]

With the London ministers' pulpits ringing out against the illegality of the Army's revolution, Lord General Thomas Fairfax took steps to find ways to accommodate the presbyterians to the new state of affairs and the proceedings against the king. On 11 January one of two inconclusive meetings took place between Fairfax and senior city ministers including Edmund Calamy, Jeremiah Whitaker and Obadiah Sedgwick. It appears from the confused reports of these meetings that the presbyterian ministers protested against Pride's purge, but nevertheless received a courteous reception from Fairfax.[106] On 14 January the leading presbyterian ministers refused to take part in the Army's Whitehall debates after an altercation between Edmund Calamy and Hugh Peters, who had been sent as the Army's messenger, but used the meeting to insult Calamy. When invited to attend the following day for a conference at the house of Robert Tichbourne, a City linen-draper and leading political Independent, to discuss the matter, Simeon Ashe refused, instead offering Tichbourne a debate on whether the Army's *Putsch* was legitimate.[107] These actions suggest that despite their opposition to the military purge of Parliament and the abandonment of the Newport treaty, the London presbyterians were maintaining a degree of dialogue with their former parliamentarian allies. Sean Kelsey has argued that the willingness of leading presbyterian ministers to talk with the Army in the second week of January 'revealed some of the hairline cracks' within the London presbyterian camp as to what direction to take as the king's trial approached.[108] He draws attention to a report in *The Moderate* newspaper which claimed that Edmund Calamy, William Jenkyn and Cornelius Burges had preached on 14 January that the king 'might be convicted and condemned, but not executed'.[109] This report was likely an exaggeration, but was probably not entirely inaccurate. *The Moderate*'s rival publication, the *Moderate Intelligencer*, reported the following week that Calamy and Jenkyn had complained that they were 'wronged by what hath been said in print of them' the week before.[110] Burges, whose sermon was later printed, said, with reference to the king's trial: 'O ye citizens; have no hand, nor joyn with any, in such a wicked act'. However, he did go on to say 'I deny not but Kings may, in some cases, be called to account, matters of fact may be examined, and course taken to prevent tyranny, and slavery: yet if such a thing should follow as the taking away of a Kings life, it is enough to make a dumb man speak'.[111] The role that London presbyterian clergy such as Calamy and Burges had played throughout 1648 in maintaining parliamentarian unity gives credence to Kelsey's argument that they may have been willing to see whether the revolutionary turn of events could still lead to a final settlement with the king. John Adamson has argued that this was the position of the Earl of Warwick in late December. As Edmund Calamy's most important parishioner and the patron of many of the city ministers, where Warwick led the London clergy were possibly following.[112] The more constitutionalist opinions being expressed by some of the Army's leaders, particularly Fairfax and Skippon, may have convinced the leading London presbyterian ministers that the excessive language of soldiers bent on settling popular government was not representative of the Army's ultimate aims.[113] Perhaps more importantly, the mixed messages coming from the covenanter regime in Scotland until the last week of January possibly acted to cause the presbyterian ministers to wait on the northern winds before fully forming their judgement of the Army's actions.[114] The London Provincial assembly, with Calamy as its moderator, entered into a period of self-reflection and fasting, ordering on 11 December (the day of the meeting with Fairfax) that 'the businesse [of the Provincial Assembly] be kept secret' for the time being.[115] Mary Love, the wife of Christopher Love, remembered that fasts were held between 28 December until 29 March to 'find out some way to disappoint [... the Regicides'] bloody intentions'. Mary Love's statement may not tell the whole story, however. As with the Army's better-known prayer meetings at the Putney debates or Windsor, it is possible that the Provincial assembly's fasts were held to discern the will of God and to heal the damaged consensus among the ministers themselves.[116]

The majority of London's religious presbyterians, however, did ultimately respond critically to the Army and the regicide court, which sat between 18 January and 27 January. This position was set out in three pamphlets issuing from Sion College, the last remaining institutional stronghold of London presbyterianism. It appears that the intention behind these pamphlets was to trigger a national subscription campaign, although events soon intervened to quash that mobilisation.[117] The first of these pamphlets, *A serious and faithful representation*, was not signed by the leading ministers nearest to the discussions with the Army, such as Calamy, Ashe, Whitaker and Burges, and it is likely that they refrained from signing documents critical of the Army while lines of communication were open with Fairfax. By 27 January, when Thomason collected the *Vindication of the ministers of the gospel*, written by Cornelius Burges, the signatures of the leading London presbyterians were present and it is likely that the period of reflection at Sion College had settled near-unanimity among London's presbyterians to oppose the king's trial.

The essence of the London presbyterians' criticism of the Army was that its actions constituted a breach of the 'first engagements' of the parliamentarian cause, as defined by the Protestation and the Solemn League and Covenant, as well as Parliament's declarations that it fought the civil war to preserve the ancient constitution. The Army's recourse to arguments of necessity and providence, the presbyterians argued, provided no respectable political reason. The Army was the creature of a Parliament whose cause was bound up with, and legitimated by, oaths and covenants it had made with God. It was therefore not open to the Army, who individually and collectively were no more than private persons, to adopt a novel political course for the nation without being guilty of rebellion.[118] Against Army apologists such as John Goodwin, the presbyterians insisted that the Army's military victories could not accurately be read as a sign of providential right.[119] Clinging rhetorically to the notion that the war had been fought against the king's evil counsellors, the London presbyterians could refer to the true will of the parliamentarian cause as resting in the Newport treaty. The 'Covenant-keeping' citizens in London published their own declaration, complaining that the Army's *coup d'état* had come just as the 'King and Parliament were in an hopefull way not only of being reconciled, but of settling the Kingdome in a way that would have answered [...] the expense of our blood and treasure, and our Covenant engagement also'. The execution of Charles I as a 'tyrant, traitor and murderer' on 30 January and the establishment of the English republic confirmed the long-term fear of the presbyterian citizens that the Army's actions aimed at an unconstitutional dictatorship. The citizens argued that if the king and the purged members of Parliament, despite the protection of 'so many oaths, covenants, priviledges, laws and engagements' that had been imposed on Parliament's supporters and servants in the 1640s, could be 'tyrannically and barbarously [...] trampled under feet [...] by an imperious military power', the populace was likely to be 'miserably subjected to martiall-law'.[120]

Conclusion

For religious presbyterians the civil war had been fought to re-establish monarchy in its proper place as an estate of the realm, limited by its co-ordination with both houses of Parliament. It had also been a war to reform the Reformation. The settlement almost obtained at Newport, which would establish what cavaliers would later disdainfully call an 'Isle of Wight' monarchy, came close to achieving the war aims of the London presbyterians. There may have been a good deal of wishful thinking in trusting Charles I to abide by that settlement, but given the alternative of an Army coup driven by the ideas of sectaries and Levellers, the presbyterians were willing to risk the king's perfidy rather than military and radical rule. As the ordinances of 18 and 20 December 1648 showed, the sectaries' apparent populist agenda would probably only be achievable by the political disenfranchisement of large swathes of the population, leaving an unrepresentative minority in political control. Pride's purge and the political revolution that followed represented the eclipse of the London presbyterians as a political force until Oliver Cromwell's death in 1658. In the following chapter we will look at the ultimately fatal consequences of the London presbyterians' continued resistance to the English republic.

Notes

1 [Christopher Love], *A modest and clear vindication of the serious representation* (1649), frontispiece.
2 *An apologeticall declaration of the conscientious presbyterians of the province of London* (1649), pp. 4–5.
3 Sirraniho [i.e. John Harris], *The royal quarrel* (1648), p. 5; V. Pearl, 'The "royal Independents" in the English civil war', *TRHS*, 5th ser., 18 (1968), 69–96.
4 J. S. A. Adamson, 'The English nobility and the projected settlement of 1647', *HJ*, 30:3 (1987), 584–6; Gardiner, *CD*, pp. 343–4.
5 A Parliamentary committee for religion had begun to put together the propositions on 6 October; see *CJ*, V, p. 327; Rushworth, *Collections*, VII, p. 834; *The perfect weekly account*, No. 40 (6–13 October 1647), sig. P; *Perfect occurrences*, No. 40 (1–8 October 1647), p. 281. The main sources for the propositions can be found at PA, HL/PO/JO/10/1/241, fos 140–1, 162r–3v; *LJ*, IX, pp. 481, 483–4; *CJ*, V, pp. 332–3, 335; Rushworth, *Collections*, VII, pp. 840–4.
6 Adamson, 'The English nobility', pp. 584–6.
7 *CJ*, V, pp. 331–3; Rushworth, *Collections*, VII, p. 839; *The kingdomes weekly intelligencer*, No. 230 (12–19 October 1647), p. 967; *The moderate intelligencer*, No. 135 (14–21 October 1647), p. 1321.
8 *CJ*, V, pp. 332–3, 339; *LJ*, IX, p. 483.
9 *CJ*, V, p. 332. Erle would be elected a ruling elder in the parish of St Botolph, Bishopsgate and sent as a delegate to the London Provincial assembly in November 1649 (RLPA, fo. 101v (DWL transcript, p. 68)).
10 *CJ*, V, p. 332.
11 *LJ*, IX, pp. 591–601; Bodleian Library, Oxford, Clarendon Ms. 2695, fo. 248.
12 *LJ*, IX, pp. 594, 595.
13 *Ibid.*, p. 594.
14 *Ibid.*, p. 595.
15 *Ibid.*, p. 600.
16 Presbyterian pamphlets began to appear in the book shops around December, e.g. [Anon.], *A word to Mr Peters and two words for the parliament and kingdom* (1647); [Thomas Adams], *Plain dealing or a fair warning* (1647); [Anon.], *A paire of spectacles for the Citie* (1647); [Anon.], *Hinc illae lachrymae, or the impietie of impunitie* (1647).
17 *CJ*, V, p. 374; *LJ*, IX, pp. 550–1; Bodleian Library, Oxford, Clarendon Ms. 2672, fo. 211; *The humble petition of the Lord Major, aldermen and commons of the City of London* (1647); Sharpe, *London*, II, p. 269.
18 *CJ*, V, p. 378; *MPWA*, IV, p. 714.
19 Church of Scotland, *To our reverend and well-beloved brethren the assembly of the divines at Westminster, the ministers of London* (1647), pp. 2, 6–8.
20 London ministers, *A testimony to the truth of Jesus Christ* (1647), pp. 3–23.

21 *Ibid.*, pp. 24–6, 31.
22 Matthews, *CR*, pp. 553–8. The ministers' *Testimony* was also supported by a broadsheet from London's Covenant-engaged citizens: *The hearty concurrence of divers citizens and inhabitants of the City of London* (1648).
23 Hughes, *Gangraena*, pp. 373–8.
24 The presbyterian publishers bringing the county *Testimonies* to print were Thomas Underhill (London, Essex, Warwickshire, Somerset and Shropshire ministers), Luke Fawne (Lancashire and the West Riding of Yorkshire ministers), Christopher Meredith (Cheshire), Ralph Smith (Devon), Michael Sparke (Norfolk), George Calvert (Staffordshire) and Stephen Bowtell (Wiltshire). Two publishers involved in the printing of these tracts cannot be described as presbyterian activists: John Wright (Northampton ministers) and the Army printer John Clowes (Gloucestershire).
25 *The Declaration of the commission of the General Assembly [...] of Scotland* (1648), p. 4.
26 Bodleian Library, Oxford, Clarendon Ms. 92, fo. 232.
27 Scott, *Politics and war*, p. 159.
28 This is one of the main questions addressed in Ashton, *Counter-revolution*, which ultimately concludes that presbyterians and royalists were always too far apart to make a successful *rapprochement*.
29 See e.g. Brenner, *Merchants*, p. 528. For the events of winter 1647 and spring 1648 see I. Gentles, 'The struggle for London in the second civil war', *HJ*, 26:2 (1983) p. 286; Nagel, 'The militia of London', pp. 292–5.
30 See the balanced narrative given by Mike Braddick in *God's fury, England's fire: a new history of the English civil wars* (2008), pp. 529–36.
31 L. A. M. Stewart, *Rethinking the Scottish revolution: covenanted Scotland, 1637–1651* (Oxford, 2016), pp. 256–67.
32 Hughes, *Gangraena*, p. 408; B. Donegan, 'Review of *Counter revolution: the second civil war and its origins, 1646–1648* by Robert Ashton', *Journal of Modern History*, 69:3 (1997), 583–4.
33 J. Price, *The pulpit incendiary* (1648), p. 15.
34 For example, Price's reportage is used extensively and uncritically by Robert Ashton in his *Counter-revolution*.
35 [Anon.], *The pulpit incendiary anatomised* (1648) pp. 3–4, 6.
36 Price, *The pulpit incendiary*, pp. 11–12, 6, 15.
37 *Ibid.*, p. 14.
38 Cary, *Memorials*, I, pp. 17–18.
39 Themes included Parliament's breaches of the Covenant (Price, *The pulpit incendiary*, pp. 12, 14–15), its high-handed governance and corruption (pp. 14, 51) and causing heresy to increase (p. 4).
40 Price, *The pulpit incendiary*, pp. 19–20, 34–5.
41 Stewart, *Rethinking the Scottish revolution*, ch. 6, esp. pp. 263–7.
42 Scott, *Politics and war*, pp. 162–4.
43 *The Hamilton papers*, ed. S. R. Gardiner (1880), p. 177; Ashton, *Counter-revolution*, p. 291.

44 *Hamilton papers*, pp. 163–4.
45 *Ibid.*, p. 169; Walker, *History of Independency*, I, p. 83; [Anon.], *Tricks of state, or more Westminster projects* (1648) pp. 4–7. For Glover see Peacey, 'Politics, accounts and propaganda', pp. 62–3, 68, 70, 75.
46 Walker dates this to a common council meeting of 8 April: *History of Independency*, I, pp. 82–3, although it is not recorded in the common council's own journal: see LMA, JCC40, fo. 268v.
47 *Hamilton papers*, p. 170.
48 *Ibid.*, pp. 202–4, 205–6; Adamson, 'Peerage in politics', pp. 237–8, 240–1; Scott, 'Party politics in the Long parliament', p. 48.
49 *Hamilton papers*, p. 173; Seaver, *Wallington's world*, pp. 172, 178.
50 Gloucester Record Office, Barwick Manuscripts, D678/1 F21, fo. 6.
51 Edward Massie, *The declaration of Major General Massey* (1648), p. 2. Lauderdale reported, however, that Massie had accepted the command of the city's horse in August: see *Hamilton papers*, p. 247.
52 Scott, *Politics and war*, pp. 164.
53 See e.g. *A&O*, I, pp. 1062–3, 1065–70, 1117–18.
54 *A declaration of the Lords and Commons assembled in parliament concerning the papers of the Scots commissioners* (1648).
55 *LJ*, X, p. 89; *CJ*, V, p. 479; *A declaration of the Lords and Commons*, pp. 46–7.
56 *A declaration of the Lords and Commons*, pp. 48–9.
57 *Ibid.*, pp. 51–2.
58 *Ibid.*, pp. 50, 53, 58.
59 *A declaration of the Kirk of Scotland [...] March 7 1647* (1648), p. 6.
60 *A declaration of the Lords and Commons*, pp. 54–5.
61 *Perfect occurrences* (28 January–4 February 1648), p. 396. For the blasphemy ordinance, see J. Coffey, 'A ticklish business: defining heresy and orthodoxy in the Puritan revolution' in *Heresy, literature and politics in early modern English culture*, eds D. Loewenstein and J. Marshall (Cambridge, 2006), pp. 117–18 and Y. Chung, 'Parliament and the heresy ordinance of 1648', *Journal of Church and State*, 57:1 (2015), 119–52.
62 *A&O*, I, pp. 1133–6.
63 *CJ*, V, p. 608; *Articles of Christian religion, approved and passed by both houses of parliament* (1648).
64 *A&O*, I, pp. 1188–215.
65 *Hamilton papers*, p. 202; Bodleian Library, Oxford, Clarendon Ms. 31, fo. 79 (Intelligence of 15 May 1648).
66 Scott, *Politics and war*, ch. 6; Braddick, *God's fury*, ch. 19.
67 Brenner, *Merchants*, p. 486.
68 I. Gentles, 'The struggle for London', pp. 277, 281 n. 1, 284, 292, 295.
69 *Ibid.*, pp. 278, 294, 302, 304.
70 Hughes, *Gangraena*, pp. 406–8.
71 D. Underdown, *Pride's purge: politics in the puritan revolution* (Oxford, 1971), ch. 4.
72 *Hamilton papers*, p. 199; Scott, *Politics and war*, pp. 171–2.

73 LMA, JCC40, fos 275v–77, 280v; *CJ*, V, pp. 570, 583–4; *LJ*, X, pp. 276, 300, 307.
74 LMA, JCC40 fo. 272v; *The humble petition of the Lord Major, Aldermen, and Commons [...] May 9* (1648), p. 4; *CJ*, V, p. 555; *LJ*, X, pp. 249, 254; Sharpe, *London*, II, p. 278; Gentles, 'The struggle for London', p. 292.
75 *LJ*, X, p. 296; *Two petitions presented [...] 5 July* (1648); Gentles, 'The struggle for London', p. 296.
76 For the sermons see John Geree, *Ippos pyros: the red horse or bloodines of war* (1648), pp. 21, 26–30; Stephen Marshall, *The sinne of hardnesse of heart* (1648) p. 25; Samuel Annesley, *A Sermon [...] 26 July* (1648) p. 13; William Gouge, *The right way* (1648), pp. 33–5.
77 *Hamilton papers*, pp. 199–200.
78 *Mercurius pragmaticus* No. 16 (11–16 July 1648), sigs Q–Q2.
79 These petitions were the city petition of 27 June for a negotiated treaty between Parliament and the King, the 31 June 1648 petition against the taxation of Newcastle coal, the petitions of 24 July and 28 July against Philip Skippon and the 8 August petition in favour of a personal treaty.
80 [Anon.], *London's new colours displaid* (1648), sig. A, p. 9.
81 Sharpe, *London*, II, p. 281.
82 Chetwynd had been apprenticed to the father of the presbyterian activists Roger and William Drake. For Chetwynd see H. Farr, 'Philip Chetwind and the Allot copyrights', *The Library*, 4th ser., 15:2 (1934), 129–60; Sharpe, *London*, II, pp. 276, 292–3. For Browne and Chamberlain see Lindley, *Popular politics*, pp. 174, 202.
83 *Hamilton Papers*, p. 206.
84 M. W. Helms and E. Cruickshanks, 'Langham, John', *History of parliament*; B. Dobell, 'Memoirs of Sir John Langham, Baronet', *Notes and Queries* (October 1913); De Krey, *London*, p. 42.
85 The religious presbyterians on the drafting committee of the anti-Skippon petitions were Richard Glyde, Nathaniel Hall, Edward Hooker, Peter Mills and William Vincent, the latter being John Langham's nephew.
86 *At the committee of the militia of London* (1648).
87 Langham and Bunce as well as the former Lord Mayor Thomas Adams and Humphrey Ford can be classed within the category 'Essexians'. Anti-innovatory common councillors on this committee included William Bateman and Peter Jones. In addition, there were a sizeable number of signatories of George Benyon's February 1642 petition against parliamentarian changes to the constitution of London: Edwin Browne, William Chamberlain, Jeremy Sambrooke and Andrew Kendrick. For Benyon's petition, see Lindley, 'London's citizenry in the English revolution', p. 21.
88 *CJ*, V, p. 694; *LJ*, X, pp. 476–80; *To the right honourable, the Lords and Commons* (1648), (BL 699 fo. 12 [106]); *Three petitions [...] to the right honourable, the Lords and Commons [...] August 31* (1648). Thomason thought that the petition issued from 'Independents, Levellers and the rest of the sectaries' but it appears to have originated from the city's political Independents.

89 *Three Petitions*, pp. 7–8.
90 LMA, JCC40, fo. 296. The political Independents presenting the petition included John Fowke, Thomas Andrewes, William Gibbs, Stephen Estwicke, John Dethicke, William Antrobus and Tempest Milner. The presbyterians were Christopher Packe, John Bellamie, Jeremiah Story, John Wallington and Nathaniel Camfield.
91 Scott, *Politics and war*, p. 172; De Krey, *London*, pp. 59–62.
92 Ashton, *Counter-revolution*, pp. 295–7.
93 Scott, *Politics and war*, p. 185; Braddick, *God's fury*, pp. 554–5; A. Milton, 'Sacrilege and compromise: court divines and the King's conscience, 1642–1649' in *The experience of revolution in Stuart Britain and Ireland*, eds M. J. Braddick and D. L. Smith (Cambridge, 2011), pp. 135–53.
94 Francis Peck, *Desiderata curiosa* (rev. edn, 1779), pp. 387–96; 'Perfect copies of all the votes […] held at Newport' in Sir Edward Walker, *Historical discourses* (1705), pp. 38–48; *The humble answer of the divines […] at Newport* (1648).
95 Baxter, *RB*, II, p. 147.
96 De Krey, *Following the Levellers*, I, ch. 6.
97 Farnell, 'Politics of the city of London', pp. 97–8; Coffey, *John Goodwin*, p. 172.
98 *A&O*, I, pp. 1252–3.
99 Gentles, 'The struggle for London', p. 302.
100 LMA, MS P69/BRI/B/001 (St Bride, Fleet Street V. M.), fo. 68.
101 K. Lindley, 'Reynardson, Sir Abraham', *ODNB*.
102 Farnell, 'Politics of the city of London', pp. 98–109; Gentles, 'The struggle for London', pp. 302–3.
103 [Anon.], *An apologeticall declaration of the conscientious presbyterians* (1649).
104 Thomas Watson, *Gods anatomy upon mans heart* (1649).
105 *Mercurius elenticus*, no. 59 (2–9 January 1649), p. 564; *Kingdoms weekly intelligencer*, no. 293 (2–9 January 1649), p. 1216.
106 [Anon.], *A serious and faithful representation* (1649) p. 2; *The moderate*, No. 27 (9–16 January 1649), pp. 257; *The moderate intelligencer*, no. 200 (11–18 January 1649) p. (1838); *Perfect occurrences*, no. 107 (12–19 January 1649), p. 802; E. Vernon, 'The quarrel of the covenant: the London presbyterians and the regicide' in *The regicides and the execution of Charles I*, ed. J. Peacey (Basingstoke, 2011), pp. 203–4.
107 *Clarke papers*, II, p. 72; *Puritanism and liberty: being the Army debates (1647–9) from the Clarke manuscripts*, ed. A. S. P. Woodhouse (1986), p. 125; [Love], *A modest and clear vindication*, p. 10; Walker, *History of Independency*, II, p. 67; C. Polizzotto, 'Liberty of conscience and the Whitehall debates of 1648–9', *JEH*, 26:1 (1975), 74–6.
108 S. Kelsey, 'The death of Charles I', *HJ*, 45:4 (2002), 736.
109 *The moderate* No. 27 (9–16 January 1649) p. (259); *Perfect occurrences* no. 107 (12–19 January 1649), p. 802.

110 *The moderate intelligencer* no. 200 (18–25 January 1649), sig. Rrrrrrrrrr.
111 Cornelius Burges, *Prudent silence* (1660), pp. 31–2.
112 J. Adamson, 'The frightened junto: perceptions of Ireland, and the last attempts at settlement with Charles I' in *The regicides and the execution of Charles I*, ed. J. Peacey (Basingstoke, 2011), pp. 39–43.
113 A. Hopper, *Black Tom: Sir Thomas Fairfax and the English revolution* (Manchester, 2007) pp. 101–4.
114 Kelsey, 'The death of Charles I', pp. 738–40.
115 RLPA, fos 43–4 (DWL transcript, pp. 48–50).
116 DWL MS PP.12.50*.4 (21), fos 85, 87.
117 *The kingdom's faithful scout* (26 January–2 February 1649) reported that the London ministers' *Serious and faithful representation* had reached Pontefract in Yorkshire on 25 January 'for subscription, intimating, that it is dispersed into other parts of the Kingdom for approbation'. The speed of events and fear of the new regime probably prevented the campaign taking off, with the only response being *The humble advice and ernest desires [...] of [...] Banbury [...] and of Brackley* (1649).
118 Vernon, 'The quarrel of the covenant', pp. 212–19; Vallance, *Revolutionary England*, pp. 159–61.
119 John Geree, *Katadynastes: might overcoming right* (1649); Coffey, *John Goodwin*, pp. 173–6.
120 *An apologeticall declaration of the conscientious presbyterians*, pp. 4–8.

9

'Mr Love's case' and the London presbyterian struggle against the English republic, 1649–51

The regicide and the Commonwealth regime that succeed Charles I's monarchy created a new political reality for presbyterians in London, as elsewhere. The cause of the Covenant and the confessional unity of the three kingdoms had been the London presbyterians' principal justification for engaging against the king. With the Essex-Holles faction largely purged from political life, the Scots clear enemies of the new English regime and religious presbyterianism passed over in favour of Independency, the London presbyterians found themselves as an interest without any true political constituency. The period 1649–51 were dark times for the city presbyterians and Christopher Love would pay the ultimate price for the presbyterian challenge to the English revolution. This chapter explores the London presbyterians' resistance to the first three years of republican government in England. It will explore the presbyterians' initial resistance to the new regime, the arguments surrounding the Commonwealth's Engagement and the plot, trial and execution of Christopher Love.

The London presbyterians and 'the first year of freedom'

From its first days, the new republic was plunged into a crisis of legitimacy. This section will explore the London presbyterian challenge to the post-regicide regime. Although a Leveller-inspired crisis in the Army and the alliance brokered by Ormonde and the Catholic confederation in Ireland vexed the Commonwealth during its first months, the 'Scotified' interest in England threatened to create the British presbyterian–royalist alliance that had been avoided in 1648.[1] The Sion College ministers, using their command of many of London's pulpits, capitalised on the Rump Parliament's early problems, so much so that the journalist Marchamont Nedham complained that 'every prayer' among the presbyterians 'is a statagem' and 'most sermons mere plots'.[2] The Commonwealth was forced into taking a measure of retaliation. Mary Love recorded that the council of state was using spies to monitor London presbyterian sermons.³ The republic fired a warning shot at the presbyterians on 6 March, when Thomas Cawton, the minister of St Bartholomew-by-the-Exchange, was arrested on a charge of treason. On 25 February Cawton had preached and prayed for the house of Stuart at Mercer's chapel before the neo-royalist Lord Mayor Sir Abraham Reynardson.⁴ Although intended as a warning, Cawton's arrest and charge provoked the Sion College ministers further. A Scottish agent reported that, despite the arrest, the ministers were 'railing' against the Commonwealth's illegitimacy even though the republic was attempting to 'doe what in them lyes to terrify [the presbyterians], by threatenings and blowes and tumults'. In particular, the Scottish spy reported that Christopher Love, William Jenkyn and Stephen Watkins, of St Saviour, Southwark, were among the most virulent critics of the new republic.⁵

In light of the ministers' denunciations, the Commonwealth regime set about providing the legal apparatus to counter the political potential of presbyterian prayer. On 16 March the Rump revoked James Cranford's publishing licence, probably for agreeing to provide the *imprimatur* to the *Vindication* published by the presbyterian MPs secluded by Pride's purge.⁶ Between 28 March and 4 May, it discussed legislation to prevent ministers from using their ministerial calling 'to meddle with matters of government' and 'prohibiting them to hold correspondence or intelligence with foreign states'.⁷ While discussing this legislation, the Rump seems to have prepared the way by employing the minister John Dury, who had formerly supported the presbyterian position, to inform the presbyterian clergy of the illegitimacy of 'medling with state-matters in their sermons'.⁸ The London ministers had already anticipated Dury's arguments in their tracts against the revolutionary events of winter 1648–9, arguing that ministers were charged 'as ambassadors of Christ' to exercise a prophetic function to preach against sin and the 'illegal actings of these times'.⁹ Adam Martindale noticed in July 1649 'the wrath of rulers against presbyterian ministers in the Citie, which they daily exasperated by their cutting sermons, while in Lancashire pulpits so rang out against the army that soldiers had to keep the peace actively'.¹⁰ On 9 July the Rump received a petition from the parish of St Stephen, Coleman Street complaining that its presbyterian minister, William Taylor, was 'preaching [doctrines] non-conformable to the state'. In response, Parliament issued a series of 'resolves' against clerical interference in politics and referred Taylor to the committee for plundered ministers, who forthwith ordered his sequestration.¹¹

The Rump realised the resilience of the London ministers' opposition to the new regime. With the Irish campaign pressing and the threat of *rapprochement* between the Scottish covenanter regime and Charles Stuart growing in the middle months of 1649, the regime attempted a policy of reconciliation with the more conformable presbyterians. As Blair Worden has shown, the MPs John Gurdon, Miles Corbet, Thomas Atkins and Isaac Pennington, all in some way well disposed to religious presbyterianism, were particularly involved in these attempts at reconciliation.[12] As the royalist newspaper *Mercurius aulicus* contemptuously put it, 'the supreame puppies here are glad to wag their tailes [...] and bark nothing but presbitery, presbitery' in an attempt 'to juggle in the presbyterians'.[13] In April, Cromwell had sought to build bridges with presbyterians by calling on Parliament to settle presbyterian church government. Further overtures were made in June when an act for ministers' maintenance was passed.[14] Although Cromwell's attempt to have presbyterian church polity established in the national church was ultimately lost in Parliamentary business after failing an initial vote on 7 August, the dropping of charges against Thomas Cawton on 14 August further demonstrated the Commonwealth's desire to reconcile with its English presbyterian critics.[15]

It is quite possible that the Rump's concessions were beginning to placate some of the London ministers into, at least, a passive acceptance of the Commonwealth. This seems particularly true of the older generation of ministers. It is noticeable that contemporary sources tell us little of the actions of men like Gouge, Calamy and Ashe. However, younger presbyterian ministers seem to have treated the Rump's offer of peace with outright contempt. One such was Christopher Love. On 29 July, he had preached a sermon at St Lawrence Jewry against millenarianism, which was cast as general criticism of the Commonwealth's 'saints'. Love told his flock '[t]his is not the way to usher in Jesus Christ; to cut off protestant kings, destroy lawes, government and rule, this is not the fruit of saintshipp'. For Love, the true second coming would occur only when 'the people would get Christ to reign in their hearts that they would labour to set up the discipline of Christ in his Church'.[16] These sermons began to attract government attention. On 6 September Love and his fellow presbyterian ministers Peter Witham and Thomas Jaggard appeared before the committee for plundered ministers accused of seditious preaching. Witham, whom we have already seen venting pro-monarchist positions since 1648, was sequestered, but Love and Jaggard were discharged with a caution.[17] No witnesses had attended to give evidence against Love and, according to the *Perfect weekly account*, 'a great company of people' had gathered outside the meeting of the committee and cried out 'not a persecutor durst appear against him'.[18]

The popularity and audacity of men like Love and Cawton led the Parliament to issue its 'Engagement', a declaration of loyalty, to enforce compliance with the Commonwealth regime. The presbyterian clergy were asked to make this declaration early, it being applied to ministers on 12 October 1649.[19] The Engagement thereupon became a banner under which to rally opposition to the Commonwealth. In mid-November, London's churches were daubed with printed broadsheets naming the (mainly Independent) clergymen who 'in diametricall opposition' to the Solemn League and Covenant had taken the Engagement.[20] At the same time, *The man in the moon* newspaper noted the united front of the Sion College conclave against the Engagement. It declared that 'Mr Calamy, Case, Love, Ashe and others stand out, and will not engage'.[21]

The historiography of the political arguments arising from the Engagement controversy has been extensively treated by historians. The debate owes much to an influential article by Quentin Skinner, which drew attention to the *de facto* arguments of pro-Engagers as a context for some of Hobbes's arguments in *Leviathan*.[22] Skinner noted the transition in the controversy from arguments based on scripture and providence (as used, for example by Francis Rous) to more rational, secular political arguments (as deployed by Anthony Ascham and Hobbes). This point has been challenged by Glenn Burgess, who observes that scriptural and providentialist arguments remained a mainstay of the controversy throughout its lifespan. Burgess argues that the anti-Engagers saw the pro-Engagement arguments as deploying 'simplistic, inconsistent and ill-considered attempts to avoid some of the traditionally accepted moral constraints on political life'.[23] This issue has been picked up by Conal Condren, who has argued out that the term *de facto* is somewhat inapposite, as pro-Engagers were seeking to argue that the Engagement demanded a moral commitment to the Commonwealth, rather than mere passive acceptance of the post-coup status quo.[24] Both Burgess and Condren note that the binding nature of previous oaths and promises, particularly the Solemn League and Covenant, was at the heart of the debate.

The London presbyterians' response to the Engagement (together with those of their brethren in Lancashire and elsewhere) demonstrates the continuing influence of the Covenant-engaged political language of the mid-to-late 1640s. Despite the revolutionary events of the winter of 1648–9, most presbyterians continued to argue that the Solemn League and Covenant was the binding statement of the obligations of the three kingdoms and the basis on which Parliament had engaged against the king.[25] The London ministers had already opposed the Army's arguments for the legitimacy of the revolution based on providence and necessity. Having made these arguments then, generally they were not prepared to concede the same point to legitimate the Commonwealth. In any event, the reasoning from *de facto* of the likes of Francis Rous amounted to a rogues' charter that, according to the Essex presbyterian Nathaniel Ward, would be the 'greatest inlet to tyranny in the world' and would provide a continual justification for usurpers to use violence in the political sphere.[26] Anti-Engagers argued that, by forcing a person to proclaim that he or she was 'loyal to the Commonwealth of England [...] without a King or House of Lords', the Engagement required the oath-taker to perjure themselves of former oaths and promises that had been solemnly made before God and that, with the heirs of Charles I still living, were obligations still capable of being met.[27]

The Engagement controversy thus left both the presbyterian clergy and the presbyterian laity of London in a quandary as to how to act and retain a clear conscience. Given their general opposition to the regicide, it is unsurprising that few London presbyterians adopted the position of accepting the Engagement. One exception was Lazarus Seaman, who in 1649 asserted 'the Providence of God in disposing of political government' in the Cambridge disputation for his doctor of divinity degree.[28] In 1650 Seaman preached sermons on Matthew 22:19–21, arguing that Christ's commandment to pay tribute money to the Roman emperor, a usurper in Judea, provided justification for submitting to the Commonwealth regime.[29] Most London presbyterians, however, were not willing to accept the Rump's claim to legitimacy as easily as Seaman. As one put it, they were sworn to the ancient constitution composed of king, Lords and Commons. Even if the principle that final supremacy rested in the House of Commons as the representative of the people was accepted, the post-purge Rump was only 'a companie of men, or a part of the house sitting under a visible force'. Consequently, the Rump's claim to hold 'title to that legislative and supreme power' held in parliamentarian theory by the Commons had to be 'doubted'.[30]

Given the illegality of the revolutionary regime, a number of moderate presbyterians, led by Edward Reynolds, sought a middle way by refusing to take the Engagement, but adopting a stance of passive obedience, promising to 'live quietly' under the new regime and 'submit to such things' that were 'in themselves lawfull and necessarie to the preservation of ourselves and others'.[31] The third choice for presbyterians was to actively resist the Engagement. Christopher Love instructed his congregation 'not to goe contrary to those solemn vowes of God' by taking the 'cursed engagement'.[32] There is evidence that at least some lay religious presbyterians in London heeded their ministers' advice to refuse the Engagement. For example, on 17 May 1650 it was reported that Alderman Michael Herring, the treasurer of Goldsmiths' Hall and ruling elder of St Mary Woolnoth, had refused to subscribe to the Engagement.[33] Nehemiah Wallington commented that the Engagement was 'a great trouble to many honest men'. On 4 January 1650, when the requirement to subscribe to it was extended to all adult men, Wallington recorded the 'heavy judgement of God' had been revealed when a store of gunpowder exploded, causing a conflagration in the city. Wallington felt confident in discerning the message of divine providence when he observed that at the church of St Leonard, Eastcheap the explosion had destroyed the printed Engagement posted on the church wall, but that the copy of the Solemn League and Covenant remained undamaged on the chancel pillar.[34]

The London presbyterian reaction to the Rump Parliament in its first year was largely one of either hostility or resigned acquiescence. While in 1648 the Sion College conclave had failed to support Hamilton's Scottish invasion in response to both the Kirk party in Scotland and Parliament's promises of treaty negotiations with Charles I, the revolutionary coup of December 1648 led to presbyterian resistance. The possibility that Charles Stuart would submit to the covenanters in Scotland (which became a reality in June 1650) meant that the more hot-headed presbyterians in London maintained the quarrel of the covenant with the new regime in England. The Rump's insistence on subscription to the Engagement acted to alienate those presbyterians who were prepared to render passive obedience to the republic. This would have disastrous consequences for the London presbyterians, who would enter into plots with their Scottish brethren and former comrades who had fled to the Netherlands in exile.

Love's plot

The issue of the Engagement returns our discussion to the core basis of London presbyterian politics during the first years of the English revolution: their conscientious attachment to the Solemn League and Covenant. In the first years of the interregnum, the London presbyterians' devotion to the 'Covenant-engaged interest' would disastrously couple them with their Scottish counterparts' ill-fated relationship with the exiled house of Stuart. As we have seen, the London presbyterians had supported Argyll and the Kirk in 1648 against Hamilton's forces. With Charles Stuart signing the Solemn League and Covenant on 23 June 1650 and being crowned Charles II, King of Scots in January 1651, many of London's presbyterians were enticed by the possibility of a Stuart monarchy that rested on the agency of the Covenant-engaged interest in Britain.[35] Presbyterian flirtation with Scoto-royalist politics would receive its tragic climax in August 1651 with the public execution of Christopher Love for treason. Love's conspiracy reveals that the London presbyterian network continued to operate politically after the English revolution in the service of the 'Scotified' interest in British politics.[36]

Love's plot came to the attention of the Commonwealth regime in March 1651 after the discovery of plans for a general uprising. The source of this information was Thomas Coke, the son of Charles I's secretary of state, who was arrested in late March. Coke confirmed evidence recently acquired by Robert Lilburne that the Marquess of Argyll was planning to join forces with north-western English cavaliers for an invasion of England. In addition, Coke related all he knew about Scottish and royalist intrigue in England.[37] His depositions revealed an incredibly coherent network of royalist and presbyterian plotters waiting to strike. These claims appear to be a mixed fabric of hearsay, half-knowledge and truth woven together to link disparate pockets of malcontent into a lucid plot.[38] However, the Rump had experienced similar stratagems before, and with its military forces in almost continual conflict, the Scoto-royalist design appeared a credible threat.[39]

Coke informed his interrogators that while the Scottish invasion was to engage the Army in north-western England, the London ministers would stir up a mob in the city. In what must have appeared as a replay of the events and threats of 1647 and 1648, the mob was either to seize Parliament or join a royalist uprising in Kent.[40] At the same time Charles Stuart and the turncoat parliamentarian commander Major General Richard Browne would triumphantly enter London to place Charles on the English throne.[41] In this plot, Coke implicated the Sion College clergy, as well as leading presbyterian citizens. He identified the bookseller George Thomason and the Blackfriars apothecary Captain Henry Potter as his presbyterian contacts in the city.[42]

Coke's depositions were the lead that the council of state needed to confirm their suspicions that the Sion College conclave was now fully converted to the royalist cause. On 2 May 1651 Christopher Love, William Jenkyn and Thomas Case, and some lay presbyterians, were arrested on suspicion of treason.[43] The reality of 'Love's plot', however, appears far less coherent than Coke's depositions make out. While it is clear that the London presbyterians were involved in treasonable correspondence with Scottish and English presbyterians who had fled abroad, much of Coke's information seems to have originated in the wishful thinking of 'the wandering alderman' James Bunce, who even the anti-presbyterian journalist Marchamont Nedham recognised to be a fantasist.[44]

The 'plot' had apparently begun in early March 1649. The principal protagonist in the affair seems to have been William Drake who, as we have seen in previous chapters, was a leading campaigner in presbyterian electoral campaigns for the common council. At Love's trial, John Jekyll (who, with Drake, had signed the November 1645 city petition for presbyterian discipline and who gave evidence against Love) reported that Drake 'was the actor and agent that moved all'.[45] Drake had retained firm connections with the exiled James Bunce and Major General Edward Massie, and communicated with them via their agent Silius Titus, a former parliamentarian soldier who had turned his coat to support the king.[46] These presbyterian exiles' aim was to convince Charles Stuart that his only effective political constituency in England was the pro-Covenant, pro-Scottish faction alienated by the revolution. In this venture, they sought to obtain written confirmation to support Charles from their brethren still in London.

It is clear that the London presbyterians were not as engaged for Charles as Bunce and Massie hoped. Titus and Drake appear to have been tasked with stirring up London's Covenant-engaged citizens to support a presbyterian restoration of the Stuart monarchy. Drake's *modus operandi* was to peddle the promise of news from exiled friends to city presbyterians; a technique that initially enticed Christopher Love to offer his house as a centre for Drake's cabals.[47] As Major Huntingdon remembered at Love's trial, the first meeting at the Swan tavern in Dowgate consisted of 'only commendations' from friends in exile. Major John Alford added in his evidence that, during this meeting, convened 'to hear news from beyond the sea', Titus had slipped into the conversation overtures to the effect that Charles Stuart would only treat with the covenanters in Scotland if he could be sure of support in England.[48] A fortnight later, Drake convened a rendezvous at the King's Head in Bread Street. Confident that he had gathered a sympathetic audience, Drake introduced Titus, who asked the citizens to sign a petition to Charles Stuart asking him to reject his cavalier court and join the covenanted interest in Scotland and England.[49] It was further related that Titus would go to Jersey to use his influence with the 'Louvre group' of royalist advisers to Queen Henrietta Maria to pressure Charles into accepting the design.[50] The meeting did not go as smoothly as the conspirators hoped. Jeremiah Baines, the Southwark ruling elder, objected that the business was treasonable and that the 'sins of him [Charles Stuart] and his father were so great' that the Stuarts should never be restored.[51] Likewise Colonel William Barton told Drake that he objected to any dealings with the ungodly royalists in the Louvre group.[52] However, despite these protests Drake and Titus managed to get a mandate from other citizens present to proceed with the negotiations with Charles Stuart at Jersey.[53]

While returning from Jersey, Titus learned that the council of state had knowledge of his mission, so he sent word to Drake that he was stranded at Calais. Drake, in a significant move that seems to have involved the London clergy for the first time, contacted Christopher Love to arrange a meeting at Love's house to hear news of the Jersey negotiations. At this meeting Drake related Titus's difficulties and it was decided that Major Alford should go to Calais to collect information from Titus.[54] Upon Alford's return, another meeting was arranged at Love's house, where they were joined by a number of prominent London presbyterian clergymen.[55] The inclusion of the clergy in the conspiracy seems to have been part of Drake's design. Titus's communication contained news that the Jersey negotiations had not gone well for the presbyterian interest, but he also produced a letter of goodwill from Charles Stuart. Alford remembered during the trial that Titus's correspondence had first been read at Drake's house, where it was decided that the signatures of the London clergy would add weight to the representations to Charles.[56] As a further incentive to get the London presbyterians to support the design, Titus related that Charles had 'good inclinations to an agreement with the Scots, but that his bad counsel about him hindered it'.[57]

With Cromwell victorious in Ireland by early 1650, the royalist court looked again to a covenanter alliance. The negotiations for this alliance took place at Breda from 16 March 1650 and agreement was reached on 1 May 1650.[58] In order 'to promote the agreement between the king and the Scots' during the negotiations, William Drake convened another meeting of London presbyterians at Love's house.[59] Drake's plan at this meeting was to get the cabal to authorise a commission for the exiled presbyterian leaders to represent 'the presbyterian party in England' at Breda.[60] As previously, many of those present at the meeting objected to this ploy and even Love argued 'that it was an act of high presumption for private persons to send commission with instructions, and an act of notorious falsehood, to say, this was in the name of the presbyterial party of England'.[61] Despite the dissenting voices, Drake ordered Major Alford to send the commission to Breda.[62] The success of the covenanters at Breda seems to have reinvigorated the Sion College ministers' opposition to the republic. In London the clergy began to disobey the Commonwealth's orders for fasts and humiliations. On 27 June, the committee for plundered ministers questioned James Cranford and William Jenkyn for ignoring a public humiliation. They defiantly replied that they had observed a fast and had 'prayed and preached' 'with high protestations for the privileges of Parliament', albeit 'according to the Covenant'.[63] A few days later Jenkyn was brought before the committee again for not preaching at state fasts and sequestered from his living at Christ Church, Newgate Street.[64]

Throughout the summer of 1650, with the Scots and the New Model preparing for conflict, the communications between the London presbyterian cabal, their comrades in exile and the Scots continued. Love remembered that a meeting at his house authorised William Drake to write a letter of support to the Church of Scotland. This correspondence promised that the English presbyterians would maintain their 'steadfastness to the Covenant'.[65] The next significant meeting of the presbyterian cabal came after the Scots had been defeated at Dunbar in September 1650. The minister Roger Drake (the brother of William, who fled to Holland after Dunbar) wrote and sent a (now treasonable) letter to the Church of Scotland with the intention 'to promote the ends of the Covenant'.[66] In November, another meeting was convened at Love's house to hear the contents of illegally sent intelligence from Massie, Bunce and William Drake. Massie's letter complained of his poverty and requested that the city presbyterians raise £10,000 for a renewed covenanter offensive. Love reported that 'all the company was against sending money on a military account', although they did agree to send £400 for Massey's personal needs.[67] The final meeting of the city presbyterians before Love's arrest took place in February 1651. Henry Potter and John Jekyll had received a packet of papers from Joseph Bampfield, at that point Argyll's agent, containing correspondence from Bampfield, Robert Baillie and the Scottish Lords Argyll, Loudon, Belcarris and Lothian.[68] Baillie's letter, a reply to Roger Drake's September 1650 missive, related that the Scots maintained the covenanted interest and begged the English presbyterians to remain 'firme and zealous to preserve the Covenant'.[69] John Jekyll remembered that Bampfield requested that the London presbyterians attempt to use their influence with the Earls of Manchester and Warwick to lead a presbyterian uprising. The letter from the Scottish lords prompted Massie to renew his November request for £10,000 to purchase arms.[70] Love and his cabal rejected both these demands, although Love and Roger Drake again fell foul of the Commonwealth's treason laws by returning their refusal of assistance to Scotland.

Love's plot points us once again to the twin themes of conscientious adherence to the Solemn League and Covenant and the importance to the wider presbyterian cause of the interpersonal networks of lay and clerical presbyterians in the city. These themes defined the nature of the London presbyterians' negotiations with the revolution. As historians have recognised, the practice of religious covenanting engaged and empowered individuals and bound them in conscience to fulfil the solemn promises made in the oath.[71] For example, Major Alford stated that during the clandestine meetings 'myself, and some others that were there, did think we were bound in duty, and in relation to the Covenant, for the Prince to take it, and to prosecute the ends of it'.[72] Love himself stated to the High Court that:

> I confess the agreement between the king and Scots I desired, and deemed it my duty upon this ground, one clause of the Covenant being to seek the union and good for both nations; and those who endeavour the contrary, are declared by the Covenant to be [...] malignants.[73]

Love's plot also highlights the persistence of the network of clerical and lay presbyterians discussed in earlier chapters. The plot was largely carried out by people who had long-term associations with the cause of London presbyterianism. Of the nineteen lay conspirators named from the city, nine were at some point delegates to the London Provincial assembly and three had signed the presbyterian citizens' petition of November 1645. Bonds of friendship, business and practical piety also functioned to keep the presbyterians together during the conspiracy. Henry Potter related that the meetings took place at Love's house largely 'upon a friendly account, sometimes upon a Christian account, and sometimes to hear news'.[74] Business connections caused William Barton to engage reluctantly with the plotters. Although he disapproved of William Drake's designs, Barton said that Drake 'had been a good customer to me, both for himself and friends, and I was loth to deny him'.[75] Love's plot therefore blended the ideological with the local, religious and commercial networks that were part and parcel of early modern London life.

Love's trial for treason, alongside that of the lay plotter John Gibbons, took place in late June and early July 1651. The trial followed the removal of the last of the London presbyterians' institutional bases in the city, with the order in April 1651 that the building of Sion College should be used to billet soldiers.[76] Despite attempting to deploy the 'free-born' rhetoric of the Leveller John Lilburne, who had been acquitted by a jury in 1649 at a trial Love had attended, Love (who was not afforded a jury trial) was found guilty of treason on 5 July.[77] By communicating with Massie, Bampfield and his Scottish friends, Love's acts were treasonable under the Rump's act of 2 August 1650,[78] although it is clear that the trial and his sentence were designed to set an example to English presbyterians. Sir Henry Vane Jr's statement to Cromwell that Love should be executed because the presbyterians 'do not judge us a lawful magistracy, nor esteem anything treason that is acted by them to destroy us, in order to bring in the King of Scots as the head of the Covenant' graphically exemplifies this point.[79] Love was unrepentant; after his sentence he told Mary, his wife, that:

> I bless my God that, notwithstanding all that is come upon me, I have not forsaken Him, nor dealt falsely in his Covenant, and therefore [...] never had I more joy in my spirit [...] then when the sentence of death was this day read against me.[80]

Despite Love's inclinations for martyrdom, a massive campaign was organised by his wife and friends to save him.[81] The pregnant Mary Love tirelessly campaigned for a pardon for her husband or, failing that, his banishment to preach the Word in America.[82] These petitions were backed up by a campaign from those who saw in pardoning Love the chance to reconstruct the old parliamentarian consensus between presbyterians and Independents.[83] Petitions came in from, among others, the congregation of St Lawrence Jewry, London citizens claiming to be 'cordial friends to this present Parliament', fifty-four presbyterians and Independent ministers, Joseph Caryl's congregation at St Magnus, London Bridge and Richard Baxter and the ministers of Worcestershire.[84] However, the pleas for clemency for Love's life were to no avail. Although his execution was delayed for a month on 15 July, it appears that ardent republicans such as Sir Henry Vane Jr and Francis Allein saw in Love's destruction a warning to presbyterian opponents of the Commonwealth.[85] In a last, desperate attempt to save her husband's life, Mary Love and the London presbyterian clergy sent a petition to Cromwell in Scotland. Arriving on 29 July, the day of the capture of Burntisland, the council of war debated intervening in the affair. The Army council was split down the middle. It was reported that Colonels Goffe and Okey were 'tooth and nayle' for Love's reprieve, but Pride and Lambert spoke 'high against' a pardon. The consequence of this division was that the council advised Cromwell that 'my Lord should not at all ingage or write in the businesse for him'.[86] With the Army's neutrality decided, Love's fate was sealed.

Love's execution and funeral

This section looks at the political drama surrounding Love's execution and funeral, which can be seen as an attempt by the London presbyterians to curse and blacken the Commonwealth regime with the name of tyranny and illegitimacy. Peter Lake and Michael Questier have argued that public executions 'were highly charged, dangerously liminal, even potentially unstable occasions'. Public executions of religious figures opened up rhetorical spaces in which state authority entered into contest with the spiritual charisma of the victim.[87] Lake has shown how the godly clergy were expert in preparing the condemned to be living, public representations of the saint assured of the crown of grace.[88] Love, of course, needed no such coaching, but it is clear that his brethren offered him every opportunity to prepare for the scaffold. In a series of letters published shortly after his death, Love was assured that he would ascend to his heavenly rest as a martyr of the church. Even before his trial Roger Drake congratulated Love on 'the singular honour [that] God hath laid upon [him]' in suffering for the Covenant.[89] Edmund Calamy, Simeon Ashe and Thomas Manton personally spent the days before the execution preparing Love for his martyrdom.[90] As well as coaching him to be resolute as he faced the execution, the support of the London ministers equipped Love with the courage to polemically engage with the Commonwealth regime.

On 22 August 1651 Christopher Love and Simeon Ashe walked calmly to the scaffold at Tower Hill. In the morning, Love had told his friend James Lever that he 'blessed God [that] his heart did not soe much as leape or pant in his breast, but hee was as cheerfull as hee were to live till the day of judgement'.[91] Mary Love remembered that the grim procession to the scaffold 'made the hill ring with [the] bitter-weeping and lamentations' of the crowd gathered to witness his death.[92] According to the 'public transcript' of early modern judicial executions, Love should have received his punishment penitently. On the scaffold he was expected to admit his crimes, confess his sins and vindicate the state's authority in executing him for his treason. Many scholars, following Michel Foucault, have noted that early modern executions were stage-managed dramas that sought to publicly exhibit the inscription of the state's *de facto* power on to the bodies of its citizens.[93] However, as Lake and Questier's work suggests, this type of Foucauldian analysis relies on an abstract and structurally monolithic understanding of 'power' and denies the contesting nature of human agency in the dramas of state domination. When religious victims came to the scaffold, the public theatre of execution was always a symbolically ambivalent drama and carried the risk of becoming a localised contesting of state legitimacy.[94] From his actions on the scaffold, it is clear that Love was prepared to use his final breaths to vindicate the cause of the covenanted interest.

In presenting a critique of the Commonwealth and calling for the completion of the Reformation, Love's scaffold speech was both political and evangelical in intention. By presenting his execution as the providential reckoning of a 'just man made perfect' he drew on the charismatic motif of the martyred saint. In particular, Love invoked the scriptural templates of John and Paul (both of whom died by beheading) and Jeremiah (who was charged with inviting foreign forces to invade Israel).[95] In publicly presenting his gracefully assured state to the crowd, Love made much of his lack of fear and the divine glory of his election. He told his audience that:

> I desire this day to magnifie God, to magnifie the riches of his glorious grace, that such a one as I, born in an obscure country in Wales, of obscure parents, that God should look upon me, and single me out from among all my kindred, single me out to be an object of his everlasting love.[96]

In presenting himself as 'a spectacle unto God, angels and men' and 'a grief to the godly; a laughing stock to the wicked and a gazing stock to all', Love manipulated the role of the martyr to attack the Commonwealth regime.[97] Although he deployed the motif of the meek Christian sacrifice and declared his forgiveness of his persecutors, he made it clear that it was the republic's tyranny that condemned him and not his own guilt. Love proclaimed that his 'charge was high and full but the proof empty and low'. It would appear that this act of impenitence hit the desired political nerve, for it caused a disturbance among some of the crowd who had expected Love to confess his guilt.[98] In declaring his principles, Love proclaimed that he was for the ancient constitution of a mixed monarchy, against the regicide and utterly opposed to the Engagement.[99] He added that the cause of his death was the maintenance of such firm and reasonable parliamentarian principles in the face of tyranny. He warned the Commonwealth that:

> My blood, my body, my dead body, it will be a morsel which I believe will be hardly digested, and my blood it will be bad food for this infant commonwealth [...] Mine is not malignant blood, though here I am brought a grievous and notorious offender.[100]

One eye-witness was impressed by Love's resolve; he wrote in a circular letter, which reached Thomas Fairfax, that 'all men admired [Love's] Christian and cheerful resolution in death. He died not owning the present power. In his speech some passages went high, and became tender.'[101]

The second theme of Love's speech was to defend the cause of godly reformation and, in particular, to further presbyterianism. Love pleaded for the godly to come to agreement in matters of church union in order to stall the spread of libertinism. He warned the crowd that unless the godly united, England would come to fear atheism as much as popery.[102] Following this theme, the last part of Love's speech was a formal exhortation for further reformation. Love pleaded the evangelical cause to the inhabitants of London. Taking on the voice of a Jeremiah, he told the citizens: 'O London, London' 'the symptoms of declension, are here and there', 'thy glory is flying away like a bird'.[103] The only remedies to avoid such decline were for the citizenry to submit to the godly ministry, church discipline and to shun heresy.[104] As well as addressing London's citizens, Love advised the city's ministers to continue the struggle for presbyterian government. In particular, he advised them to keep 'purity and unity' by maintaining both the congregational elderships and the policy of strict admission to the Lord's supper.[105] In making a plea for presbyterian reformation, Love stood firmly for his belief in the cause of the Covenant. Throughout his speech, he singled out the breach of the Solemn League and Covenant as his greatest criticism of the Commonwealth regime. Love told his audience that he was being beheaded 'because I pursue my Covenant and will not prostitute my principles and consciences to the ambition and lusts of men'.[106] He pleaded with the crowd 'take heed [... not to engage] in a war with your godly brethren in the Scotish nation'. It was this defence of the Covenant and the covenanters, the continual feature of London presbyterian discourse throughout the English revolution, that was the most provocative part of Love's speech.[107] Drawing on the political theology that linked the covenant of grace to the national Covenant, Love declared that it was this fidelity that assured him of a martyr's crown. He told his audience:

> I am not only a Christian, and a preacher, but, whatever men may judge me, I am a martyr too, I speak it without vanity: would I have renounced my

Covenant, and debauched my conscience, and ventured my soul, there might have been more hopes of saving my life, that I should not have come to this place: but blessed be my God, I have made the best choyce, I have chosen affliction rather then sin. I tell you all, I had rather die a covenant keeper, then live a covenant breaker.[108]

Love's execution performance resulted from the careful preparation of him by key members of the London presbyterian ministry and can be seen as part of their continuing struggle to demonstrate the illegitimacy of the Commonwealth. Love's death seems to have been a successful, if extreme, protest against the regime and was judged a martyr's death by many observers.

The propagandistic success of Love's performance on the scaffold can be further judged by the state of crisis initiated by the Commonwealth government after the execution. A massive thunderstorm broke out directly after Love's execution and the regime, perhaps frightful that it might be interpreted as a sign of providential displeasure, refused for three days to yield his body for burial.[109] At the same time Fairfax's correspondent noted that printed versions of Love's scaffold speech were being suppressed and that a presbyterian printing press had been broken in order to stop the propagandistic value of its contents spreading.[110]

Love's funeral demonstrates that the presbyterians remained defiant of the council of state's attempts to cower them, although they could only muster symbolic gestures of resistance. As the funeral of the Leveller mutineer Robert Lockier in April 1649 had demonstrated, the public internment of an executed opponent of the regime could be used to fill the streets of London with a message of defiance against the regime.[111] James Winstanley, Love's brother-in-law, whose daughter would later marry Silius Titus, arranged for Love to have a funeral procession through the city on 25 August. The procession would finish with funeral sermons preached at Merchant Taylors' Hall by Thomas Manton and Edmund Calamy. The use of such a large public space was a symbolic challenge to the republican administration's control of the streets and the official narrative of why Love had been executed. The council of state wasted no time in seeking to gain control of both the situation and the meaning of Love's death, ordering the Lord Mayor to forbid Love's public funeral, arguing that '[w]e do not judge it fit that he who was such a notorious traitor [...] should have so a solemn burial'.[112] As a show of force against Love's mourners, a general muster of the city militia was summoned to appear in Islington fields on the day of the funeral.[113] Consequently, Thomas Manton was forced to preach Love's funeral oration at midnight, although Fairfax's correspondent noted that Manton still delivered his sermon to 'a mighty throng of people' who attended in defiance of the Rump's show of domination.[114] Edmund Calamy's sermon, preached at St Mary, Aldermanbury, predictably took as its topic the theme of Stephen's martyrdom, from the text of Acts 7:60.[115] In similar vein, Thomas Manton preached on I Cor. 15:57: 'But thanks be to God, who giveth us the victory through our Lord Jesus Christ'.[116] Applying predestinarian logic to the text's comforting motif of Christ's victory over death for the elect, Manton taught that the text was also a 'terror for wicked men' as 'none but a childe of God can have true and solid courage against death'.[117] Turning this against the Commonwealth, Manton preached that the wicked were typified by the Babylonian King Belshazzar of Daniel 5. Belshazzar had celebrated his military victory over the Israelites, the people of the covenant, by drinking from the vessels of the ransacked Temple. Manton's choice of scripture therefore sought to equate the republic to the Babylonian tyranny. Manton reminded his audience that 'God soon took the edge off [Belshazzar's] bravery and then his joints trembled, his knees smote one against another for fear'.[118]

Love's execution and funeral was therefore an act of final resistance by the London presbyterians to the revolutionary regime. Love and his brethren sought to contrast the republic as an illegitimate, military-backed government resting on force with their fidelity to the cause of the Covenant and the ancient constitution. Love's resistance against the Commonwealth long remained in the presbyterian memory. In 1655 the ailing Nehemiah Wallington would still make causal connections between Love's execution and disasters befalling the city, and Love's memory would continue with the publication of his posthumous sermons in both English and Dutch into the nineteenth century (accruing some spurious prophetic predictions along the way).[119]

Conclusion

Love's execution, as Blair Worden notes, broke the back of English presbyterian opposition at a time when the New Model was preparing to face the covenanter and royalist army at Worcester.[120] Love was a political sacrifice, expedient to quell presbyterian resistance in London at a time of crisis for the Commonwealth. With the defeat of the covenanter regime in Scotland and the flight of Charles Stuart back to the Netherlands, London presbyterian resistance was reduced to throwing oblique scriptural references to their congregations that questioned the regime's legitimacy and prophesied its doom. In the aftermath of Love's execution, six ministers remained incarcerated and James Nalton and Thomas Cawton fled to Holland to avoid prosecution.[121] The direct evidence that at least eight of the Province of

London's ministers had been involved in the presbyterian plot, coupled with Coke's implication of many more, took the political guile out of the presbyterians' actions. Perhaps realising this, on 15 October the Commonwealth, apparently at the behest of Oliver Cromwell, released the ministers, as well as three lay plotters.[122] Freedom did not come cheap, however, and William Jenkyn was required to petition Parliament to state his acceptance of his 'duty to yield to this authority all active and cheerful obedience in the Lord' and to promise 'truth and fidelity to it'.[123] In line with the arguments made by Francis Rous and Lazarus Seaman during the Engagement controversy, and opposed by the majority of presbyterians, Jenkyn accepted submission to the Commonwealth on the basis of divine providence and its possession of power. Jenkyn's acceptance of the providentialist argument could be said to lack full sincerity, and his first sermon after his release counselled the godly to wait 'a few years' for divine vengeance. Nevertheless, Jenkyn's recantation marked the symbolic abandonment of the London presbyterians' principled opposition to the interregnum.[124]

Notes

1 [Anon.], *To Xeifos Ton Marturon, or, a brief narration of the mysteries of state* (The Hague, 1651), p. 94; Worden, *Rump*, pp. 189–90; de Krey, *Following the Levellers*, vol. II: *English political and religious radicals from the Commonwealth to the Glorious Revolution, 1649–1688* (2018), pp. 11–22.
2 Marchamont Nedham, *The case of the commonwealth stated* (1650), p. 63.
3 DWL MS 28.58, fo. 87. This manuscript is contained in a pamphlet collection catalogued under DWL class mark PP12.50*.4 (21).
4 *CJ*, VI, p. 157; [Thomas Cawton Jr], *The life and death of [...] Thomas Cawton* (1662), pp. 25–6; *The moderate*, No. 35 (6–13 March 1649), p. 359. Reynardson would be stripped of his mayoralty on 2 April.
5 *Miscellany of the Scottish History Society* (Edinburgh, 1893), I, pp. 219–20.
6 BL Add. Ms. 70006, fo. 63; *A vindication of the imprisoned and secluded members of the house of commons* (1649); *CJ*, VI, p. 166.
7 *CJ*, VI, pp. 175, 178–9, 183, 199, 201.
8 J[ohn] D[ury], *A case of conscience resolved* (1649). For Dury's previous alliance with Westminster assembly presbyterians see M. Caricchio, 'John Dury, reformer of education against the radical challenge', *Les Dossiers du Grihl: Les dossiers de Jean-Pierre Cavaillé, Libertinage, athéisme, irréligion. Essais et bibliographie, mis en ligne le 18 janvier 2010.* http://journals.openedition.org/dossiersgrihl/3787.
9 Vernon, 'The quarrel of the covenant', p. 205.
10 Adam Martindale, *The life of Adam Martindale: written by himself*, ed. R. Parkinson (Manchester, 1845), p. 87.

11 *CJ*, VI, pp. 256–7; *Resolves of the commons assembled in parliament, concerning such ministers as shall preach or pray against the present government* (1649); Coffey, *John Goodwin*, pp. 188–9.
12 Worden, *Rump*, pp. 191–8.
13 *Mercurius aulicus* (14–21 August 1649), p. 3.
14 Clement Walker, *The compleat history of Independencie* (1661), II, p. 157.
15 *Perfect occurrences* (18–25 May 1649), p. 1059; *CJ*, VI, pp. 275, 278; Worden, *Rump*, p. 207.
16 DWL MS 28.58, fo. 88.
17 *Perfect weekly account* (5–13 September 1649), p. 596; *The man in the moon*, No. 21 (5–12 September 1649), p. 175; *The impartiall intelligencer* (5–12 September 1649), p. 221.
18 *Perfect weekly account* (5–13 September 1649), p. 596; DWL MS 28.58, fos 88–9.
19 *CJ*, VI, p. 307. The rest of the adult male population would be required to take the Engagement on 2 January 1650: see Gardiner, *CD*, p. 391.
20 Thomason collected two such broadsheets, the first on 11 November, the second on 31 November.
21 *The man in the moon*, No. 30 (14–21 November 1649), p. 141.
22 Q. Skinner, 'Conquest and consent: Thomas Hobbes and the Engagement controversy' in *The Interregnum: the quest for settlement 1646–1660*, ed. G. E. Aylmer (1972), especially pp. 80–4.
23 G. Burgess, 'Usurpation, obligation and obedience in the thought of the Engagement controversy', *HJ*, 29:3 (1986), 529–31.
24 C. Condren, *Argument and authority in early modern England: the presupposition of oaths and offices* (Cambridge, 2006), pp. 295–7.
25 Vallance, *Revolutionary England*, pp. 161–2.
26 [Nathaniel Ward], *The grand case of conscience stated* (1649), p. 3.
27 [Nathaniel Ward], *A religious demurrer concerning submission to the present power* (1649), p. 7; I. M. Smart, 'Liberty and authority: the political ideas of presbyterians in England and Scotland during the seventeenth century' (Ph.D thesis, University of Strathclyde, 1978), pp. 127–34; I. M. Smart, 'Edward Gee and the matter of authority', *JEH*, 27:2 (1976), pp. 115–27.
28 William Jenkyn, *Exodus* (1675), p. 52.
29 [Edmund Hall], *Lazarus's sores licked* (1650).
30 [Anon.], *Memorandums of the conferences held between the brethren scrupled at the Engagement* (1650), p. 21.
31 [Edward Reynolds], *The humble proposals of sundry learned and pious divines [...] concerning the Engagement* (1649), pp. 2–3. This position was rejected by the Rump: see Vallance, *Revolutionary England*, p. 161.
32 DWL MS 28.58, fo. 89.
33 *CJ*, VI, p. 413.
34 BL Add. Ms. 1457, fo. 93r–v.
35 D. Stevenson, *Revolution and counter-revolution in Scotland, 1644–51* (Edinburgh, 2003), ch. 4; K. M. MacKenzie, *The Solemn League and Covenant*

of the three Kingdoms and the Cromwellian union, 1643–1663 (Abingdon, 2018), pp. 116–19.
36 L. H. Carlson, 'A history of the presbyterian party from Pride's purge to the dissolution of the Long Parliament', *CH*, 9 (1942), 83–122.
37 S. R. Gardiner, *History of the Commonwealth and Protectorate 1649–1656*, 4 vols (1903), II, pp. 11–14.
38 MacKenzie, *The Solemn League and Covenant*, pp. 119–23.
39 Gardiner, *History of the Commonwealth and Protectorate*, II, pp. 14–15.
40 HMC, *13th Report*, Appendix, Part 1, MSS of the Duke of Portland at Welbeck Abbey (London, 1891), I, p. 584.
41 *Ibid.*, p. 592.
42 *Ibid.*, pp. 586, 597–9; L. Spencer, 'The politics of George Thomason', *The Library*, 5th ser., 14:1 (1959), 18–20.
43 Gardiner, *History of the Commonwealth and Protectorate*, II, p. 15.
44 *Mercurius politicus*, no. 7 (18–25 July 1650), p. 99.
45 *State Trials*, V, p. 115. Jekyll (or Jacquel) later joined Thomas Watson's dissenting congregation and was instrumental in the campaign for nonconformist liberty of conscience. For Jekyll's involvement see Yale University, Beinecke Library Ms. b. 221 (Elizabeth Jekyll's spiritual journal (1643–1652)); Gary S. de Krey, 'The first Restoration crisis: conscience and coercion in London, 1667–73', *Albion*, 25 (1985), pp. 569–71. The position of William Drake as the principal instigator of the affair is backed up by Major John Alford's testimony: see *State Trials*, V, p. 92.
46 This was Henry Potter's opinion: see *State Trials*, V, p. 82.
47 [Anon.], *Mr Love's case* (1651), p. 6; this was also the way Alford was brought into the conspiracy: see *State Trials*, V, p. 89.
48 *State Trials*, V, pp. 89, 98.
49 This is probably the time when the list of eighty citizens, boasted of by Thomas Coke, was gathered: HMC, *13th Report*, MSS of the Duke of Portland, p. 585.
50 *State Trials*, V, pp. 79, 89, 98, 100. For the Louvre group see D. Underdown, *Royalist conspiracy in England 1649–1660* (New Haven, CT, 1960), p. 10.
51 *State Trials*, V, pp. 91, 98–100, 121–2.
52 *Ibid.*, p. 122.
53 *Ibid.*, pp. 78–9, 91, 98, 121.
54 *Mr Love's case*, pp. 6–7.
55 *Ibid.*, p. 7; *State Trials*, V, pp. 93, 115–16.
56 *State Trials*, V, pp. 91–2.
57 *Mr Love's case*, p. 7.
58 Gardiner, *History of the Commonwealth and Protectorate*, I, p. 195.
59 Present were William Drake, Christopher Love, Roger Drake, William Jenkyn, Arthur Jackson, Thomas Cawton, Major John Alford, John Gibbons, Thomas Adams, Ralph Farr and Major Huntingdon; *Mr Love's case*, p. 7.
60 *State Trials*, V, pp. 90, 104.
61 *Mr Love's case*, p. 8. Love's testimony was backed up by Ralph Farr: *State Trials*, V, p. 131.

62 *Mr Love's case*, p. 8.
63 *Mercurius politicus*, No. 4 (27 June–4 July 1650), pp. 50–52.
64 *Mercurius politicus*, No. 5 (4–11 July 1650), pp. 66–70. The fifth monarchist preacher Christopher Feake was appointed at Christ Church in Jenkyn's place.
65 *Mr Love's case*, p. 9; *Mercurius politicus*, No. 6 (11–18 July 1650), p. 81; No. 10 (8–15 August 1650), p. 159; No. 13 (29 August–5 September 1650), pp. 193–4. It was at this time that Thomas Coke contacted George Thomason and Henry Potter. Although Thomason cooled towards Coke, Potter requested that some method of communication be opened with Scotland. HMC, *13th Report*, MSS of the Duke of Portland, p. 598.
66 *State Trials*, V, p. 108; *Mr Love's case*, p. 9. The writing of this letter was treasonable under the Act of 2 August 1650: *A&O*, II, pp. 406–9.
67 *State Trials*, V, pp. 90, 95–6, 108, 129–30; *Mr Love's case*, pp. 10–11. Mary Love and Priscilla Tomson were granted a passport to go to Amsterdam on 18 December 1650: *CSPD, 1650*, p. 568.
68 *State Trials*, V, pp. 84–7; *Mr Love's case*, p. 12; *Colonel Joseph Bampfield's Apology 'written by himself and printed at his desire' 1685*, eds J. Loftis and P. H. Hardacre (1993), pp. 158–60.
69 Baillie, *L&J*, III, pp. 105–8.
70 *State Trials*, V, p. 118; *Mr Love's case*, p. 12. In his depositions, Coke claimed that Manchester and Lord Robartes were engaged with the covenanters; Mary Love relates that Prideaux and Scot offered Love a reprieve if he could implicate a lord or an excluded member: HMC, *13th Report*, MSS of the Duke of Portland, p. 586; DWL MS 28.58, fo. 97.
71 Vallance, *Revolutionary England*, pp. 86–92; Walter, *Covenanting citizens*, pp. 87–8, 111–12.
72 *State Trials*, V, p. 89.
73 *Ibid.*, pp. 164, 199–201.
74 *Ibid.*, p. 82.
75 *Ibid.*, p. 122.
76 NA, SP 25/65, fo. 273.
77 *State Trials*, V, pp. 49–56. For the influence of Lilburne on Love during his trial see S. Wiseman, 'Martyrdom in a merchant world: law and martyrdom in the Restoration memoirs of Elizabeth Jekyll and Mary Love' in *Literature, politics and law in renaissance England*, eds E. Sheen and L. Huston (2005), pp. 209–35.
78 Love later admitted as much. See Christopher Love, *A cleare and necessary vindication* (1651), p. 9.
79 Cited in Worden, *Rump*, p. 244.
80 DWL MS 28.58, fos 115–16.
81 See John Jekyll's letter in [Mary Love], *Love's Name Lives* (1651), pp. 3–5.
82 *CJ*, VI, pp. 599, 604, 622.
83 Worden, *Rump*, p. 244; G[eorge] L[awrence], *Loves advocate* (1651), p. 7; Love, *A cleare and necessary vindication*, 'To the Reverend Fathers and Blessed the Ministers in and about the City of London', n.p.

84 CJ, VI, pp. 599, 603–4; CJ, VII, p. 2; *The humble petition of many cordial friends[...] in behalf of Mr. Christopher Love* (1651), p. 3.
85 Vane, Allein and the Earl of Pembroke appeared constantly as the tellers for the noes in the Rump's debate on Love.
86 *The Clarke papers V: further selections from the papers of William Clarke*, ed. F. Henderson (Cambridge, 2005), pp. 46–7; DWL MS 28.58, fo. 118; *Mercurius politicus*, No. 61 (31 July–7 August 1651), p. 980; [Anon.], *Master Edmund Calamies leading case* (1663), p. 14.
87 P. Lake and M. Questier, 'Agency, appropriation and rhetoric under the gallows: puritans, romanists and the state in early modern England', *P&P*, 153:1 (1996), 104–5.
88 P. Lake, 'Popular form, puritan content? Two puritan appropriations of the murder pamphlet from mid-seventeenth century London' in *Religion, culture and society in early modern Britain: essays in honour of Patrick Collinson*, eds A. Fletcher and P. Roberts (Cambridge, 1994), pp. 321–4; P. Lake, '"A charitable Christian hatred": the godly and their enemies in the 1630s', in *The culture of English puritanism 1560–1700*, eds C. Durston and J. Eales (Basingstoke, 1996), pp. 145–83.
89 [Mary Love], *Love's name lives*, pp. 5–6.
90 DWL MS 28.58, fos 128, 135–6.
91 A. Wallis, 'The diary of a London citizen in the seventeenth century', *The Reliquary*, n.s., 3 (1889), p. 89. James Lever was Edmund Calamy's brother-in-law.
92 DWL MS 28.58, fo. 137.
93 M. Foucault, *Discipline and punish: the birth of the prison* (1979), pp. 3–69; J. A. Sharpe, '"Last dying speeches": religion, ideology and public execution in seventeenth century England', *P&P* 107:1 (1985), 144–67.
94 Lake and Questier, 'Agency, appropriation and rhetoric under the gallows' pp. 66, 68, 77.
95 *Mr Love's case*, p. 15.
96 *Ibid.*, pp. 25–6.
97 *Ibid.*, p. 15.
98 *Ibid.*, pp. 16–17.
99 *Ibid.*, p. 21.
100 *Ibid.*, p. 25.
101 *Fairfax Memorials*, II, p. 131.
102 *Mr Love's case*, p. 20.
103 *Ibid.*, p. 21.
104 *Ibid.*, pp. 22–3.
105 *Ibid.*, p. 24.
106 *Ibid.*, pp. 15–16.
107 For his prayer for the Scots see *ibid.*, pp. 28–9.
108 *Ibid.*, pp. 26, 21.
109 For the storm, see *The weekly intelligencer* (19–26 August 1651), p. 263.
110 *Fairfax Memorials*, II, p. 132.

111 I. Gentles, 'Political funerals during the English revolution' in *London and the civil war*, ed. S. Porter (Basingstoke, 1996), pp. 218–21.
112 NA, SP 25/96, fo. 427.
113 *Fairfax Memorials*, II, p. 132.
114 *Ibid.*, p. 133.
115 Edmund Calamy, *The saints' rest [...] delivered in a sermon at Aldermanbury, London. 24 August* (1651).
116 Thomas Manton, *A sermon preached at the funerall of M. Christopher Love [...] August 25* (1651).
117 *Ibid.*, p. 7.
118 *Ibid.*, pp. 7–8.
119 Wallington blamed the outbreak of a series of fires on the blood guilt incurred from Love's execution: BL Add. Ms. 1457, fo. 100. For Love's posthumous reception see E. Vernon 'Love, Christopher', *ODNB* and *Nederlandse liefde voor Christopher Love (1618–1651): studies over het vertaalde werk van een presbyteriaanse puritein*, eds W. J. Op't Hof and F. W. Huisman (Amstelveen, 2013).
120 Worden, *Rump*, pp. 247–8.
121 The six ministers were William Jenkyn, Thomas Case, Arthur Jackson, Ralph Robinson, Roger Drake and Thomas Watson. For Cawton and Nalton see [Cawton Jr], *The life and death of [...] Thomas Cawton*, pp. 43–52.
122 *CJ*, VII, p. 28; George Bishop, *A rejoinder consisting of two parts* (1658), p. 52.
123 William Jenkyn, *M. Jenkin's recantation* (1651), p. 3.
124 Jenkyn, *M. Jenkin's recantation*, p. 2; William Jenkyn, *Certain conscientious queries from Mr Will Jenkin* (1651?), pp. 1–2; William Jenkyn, *A sermon preached [...] the fifth day of November, 1651* (1651), pp. 9, 12; Worden, *Rump*, p. 248; *cf.* Vallance, *Revolutionary England*, pp. 170–1. Jenkyn later hinted that he had been convinced of the providentialist position by Lazarus Seaman: see Jenkyn, *Exodus or, the decease of holy men and ministers considered* (1675), pp. 52–3.

10

Cromwellian Britain, c. 1653–9

After the execution of Christopher Love, the London presbyterians appear to have largely abandoned their rhetoric of king and Covenant, at least in public, although it was reported in 1655 by the former Hamiltonian engager Lord Balcarres that the London presbyterian ministers would accept a restoration of Charles Stuart on the sole condition that he refer the question of religion to a free parliament.[1] The debacle of Charles Stuart's attempt to masquerade as a covenanted king served to render the idea of supporting an immediate Stuart restoration increasingly distasteful to London's presbyterians. Nevertheless, this did not at the same time manifest as active support for the Rump. Few London presbyterians therefore actively opposed Cromwell's military dissolution of the Rump in 1653, although Edmund Calamy is said to have advised Cromwell against the idea of setting himself up as king in November 1652 on the basis that such a move was 'against the voice of the nation'.[2]

This chapter traces London presbyterian activity from the execution of Christopher Love to the end of the Protectorate. During this period the presbyterians focused their energies on defending Reformed orthodoxy, often in alliance with the 'magisterial' congregationalists at the centre of Cromwellian counsels. By 1654 the London presbyterian ministers were cautiously supporting attempts led by the leading congregationalist John Owen to establish a confessional foundation to the otherwise loose structure of the Cromwellian ecclesiastical administration. This ambition was ultimately frustrated by the chronic instability of Cromwellian politics, although co-operation with the Protectorate ultimately led to the political renovation of London's presbyterians in the mid-1650s.

The defence of Reformed orthodoxy 1651–3

The *de facto* market place of religious ideas during the 1640s meant that by the 1650s Reformed orthodoxy contended with a kaleidoscope of rival theological doctrines.³ The rise of anti-trinitarianism, radical anti-formalism and the 'new Arminianism' associated with John Goodwin and the general baptist congregations led, in John Coffey's phrase, to 'the crumbling of the Calvinist consensus among the godly'.⁴ This in turn inspired a fresh focus for those who held to confessionally Reformed orthodox positions, on the defence of doctrine. The London presbyterian movement actively strove to meet the challenges of the 1650s. In so doing, they found themselves increasingly allied with 'magisterial' congregationalists who, while always being acknowledged as 'brethren', had been opponents in the debates on church polity in the 1640s.

This call for *rapprochement* can be seen in the London Provincial assembly's November 1649 publication, the *Vindication of the presbyterial government and ministry*, a document which served as the London presbyterian manifesto for the early 1650s. The Provincial assembly appealed to congregationalists to unite around doctrinal orthodoxy: 'whilest we have been consulting about the Garment of Christ, others have taken advantage to deny the Divinity of Christ'. The Provincial assembly implored congregationalists and presbyterians to attempt 'all ways of union and accommodation' and declared that London presbyterians 'shall ever be willing to study to find out any scripture way, where we may unite together with them [i.e. congregationalists], for the preservation of the truths of Jesus Christ'.⁵ This process of *rapprochement* had started in the summer of 1651 with some congregationalist ministers offering support for saving Christopher Love's life. A similar olive branch was offered by the Independent Lord Mayor Thomas Andrewes a few days before Love's execution. Andrewes wrote to the Provincial assembly desiring the presbyterians to assist the city magistrate in encouraging observance of the sabbath. Encouraged by this show of godly unity, the Provincial assembly elected a committee to confer with the Lord Mayor. It was agreed that the ministers of the Province should hold, on 19 October, a London-wide day of preaching on sabbath observance.⁶ Lazarus Seaman, then serving as moderator of the Provincial assembly, published a circular letter stating that 'it should be no small incouragement unto us that God have prepared the magistrates' heart to accompany us in our desires and indeavours in this way'.⁷

The political renovation of the London presbyterian ministers in the city would continue between 1652 and 1654 with the election of the presbyterian-leaning Lord Mayors John Fowke, Thomas Vyner and Christopher Packe. This can be seen by the predominance of the presbyterian preachers chosen to give sermons before the city at St Paul's Cathedral, most clearly Richard Vines, who preached the election-day sermon at the successive elections of Vyner, Packe and John Dethick.⁸ Dethick and his successor Robert Tichbourne (who was a congregationalist), continued to favour presbyterian preachers at the cathedral as the 1650s progressed. When the Protectorate relaxed the ban on election to the common council of citizens who had signed calls for a personal treaty with Charles I in the late 1640s religious presbyterians also began to be re-elected to the common council.[9]

Further efforts at reconciliation came in early 1652 with John Owen's presentation of the *Humble proposals* to the Rump's committee for the propagation of the gospel, the scheme that would form the basis of the Protectorate church administration in 1654.[10] Looking back to the religious settlement proposed with the four bills of 1647, the *Humble proposals* envisaged the settling of a state-supervised national ministry coupled with a forbearance for doctrinally orthodox dissenters. The vetting of candidates for parish livings, formerly undertaken by John Ley's now lapsed sub-committee of the Westminster assembly, would be replaced by a panel of state-appointed clergy to act as triers.[11] Theologically, Owen's *Humble proposals* suggested a more narrowly trinitarian and Reformed definition of the boundaries of orthodoxy. This tightening-up of the notion of the necessary doctrinal 'foundation' used the threat of Socinianism as its principal target.[12] However, Sarah Mortimer and Tim Cooper have argued that the real target of the *Humble proposals* was the wilder, anti-trinitarian and anti-formalist ideas of Army-based preachers such as William Erbury.[13] Carolyn Polizzotto has shown that the *Humble proposals* were immediately countered by a sectary and radical Independent campaign led by Roger Williams, John Milton, Sir Henry Vane Jr and William Kiffin.[14] On the other hand, the *Humble proposals* triggered attempts by congregationalists and presbyterians to find ground on which to rebuild godly unity.[15] As Austin Woolrych stated, the *Humble proposals* were designed to be a 'means of rallying the centre against the extremes' by rebuilding the 'Calvinist consensus' that had been shattered in the 1640s debates on church polity.[16] As Sir Henry Vane Jr observed, the embattled magisterial congregationalists were seeking to 'build a tower of defence' on the basis of a Reformed confessional consensus. The reason for this, Vane argued, was 'because there is such confusion of language in church-discipline that that building cannot goe on, therefore it must be attempted by a form of doctrine'.[17]

The attempts to find concord served to ignite presbyterian efforts to defend Reformed orthodoxy. One aspect of this renewed effort was the call in September 1652 by leading London presbyterian stationers for more effective mechanisms for control of the press.[18] The stationers' manifesto, entitled *A beacon set on fire*, noted that the Rump's light touch regarding censorship had allowed a raft of popish books to be published in England, particularly since the lapse of the Rump's 1649 act against unlicensed and scandalous books on 20 September 1651.[19] The strategy of the presbyterian stationers was to use their trade knowledge of average print runs to estimate that 30,000 copies of popish books had come into circulation since the lapse of censorship.[20] This claim was backed up by William Prynne's publisher Michael Sparke, who revealed the depths of the business in popish books in London.[21] While it is the case that illicit Roman Catholic publications had more than doubled in the year since the lapse of the Rump's act, the *beacon*'s pronounced anti-popery was ultimately deployed to seek to censor protestant heterodoxy. Although anti-popery had been an ever-present feature of presbyterian rhetoric, it had tended to take a backstage role in presbyterian publications since the mid-1640s. *A beacon set on fire* deployed the mechanism of cataloguing popish books to appeal to the godly for a stricter licensing system.[22] This is illustrated by the last pages of the *beacon*, which redirected the attack from popery to protestant heresies of equal concern to presbyterians and congregationalists alike. Works cited included John Biddle's Socinianist tracts, Joshua Sprigge's apparent denial of the substitutionary atonement of Christ and the 'statist' civil religion advocated in Hobbes' *Leviathan*.[23]

The beacon tracts' focus on heresies concerning the trinity and the extent of Christ's atonement suggests that the presbyterian stationers were seizing on the concerns expressed about deviant protestant heterodoxy as much as concerned at the resurgence of popish printing.[24] The solution to the problem, the stationers argued, was to return to the 1640s system of giving the licensing of books back to 'faithful able men that are sound in the faith' to act as censors, and handing enforcement of printing back to the Stationers' Company.[25]

The stationers were answered by a collection of soldiers and sectaries in *The beacons quenched*.[26] As Mario Caricchio has noted, this response issued from the collective publishing efforts of Giles Calvert, Henry Hills and William Larner, the presbyterian stationers' commercial and political rivals in the publishing of religious material.[27] These authors complained that, under the cover of complaints about 'popery and blasphemy', the stationers' real motive was to re-establish presbyterian control of the press against the interests of the republican regime. The authors of *The beacons quenched* reminded the Rump that the presbyterian ministry had published works of resistance to the Commonwealth through their close connections with the stationers, so their 'golden characters of zeal and holiness' spelled no 'more than plain presbytery'.[28] Protestants, the authors argued, had little to fear from the particular Roman Catholic publications complained of by the presbyterians, which were little more than works of 'moral divinity'.[29] Indeed, they thought that John Austin's Blackloist tract *The Christian moderator* had been particularly singled out because it attacked both episcopal and presbyterian arguments for ecclesiastical tyranny.[30]

One of the principal points made by the authors of *The beacons quenched* was that the stationers were, in reality, mere 'mercenaries' acting in their own commercial interests as the mouthpiece for 'Mr Calamy, and his party' of presbyterian clergy.[31] The authors perceived that religious presbyterianism in London still operated as a coherent movement encompassing lay and clerical activists. Nevertheless, as Jeffrey Collins has demonstrated, the *beacon* controversy shows that the stationers were acting on behalf of a larger, national presbyterian network. *A beacon set on fire* was, in part, giving voice to recent discussions by Richard Baxter and Thomas Hill over concerns with Hobbes's statist religion and his setting-up of the sovereign as an 'ecclesiastico-civil pope'. This in turn reveals that the presbyterian communication network remained a national one, with London as its centre.[32] The beacon tracts also highlight the importance of the London presbyterian stationers within the workings of this national network. The stationers were essential in linking the presbyterian ministry throughout England together via their commercial role in sourcing and selling books to provincial ministers, acting at the same time as a communication hub for letters from their clients for onward transmission to brethren in the city, the universities and other parts of the country. Given this national presbyterian network, it is likely that Pride and his collaborators were correct in identifying the *beacon* as a joint effort of the stationers and presbyterian clergy.[33] The stationers' reply to *The beacon quenched* was signed by the six stationers themselves, but George Thomason, himself an insider to the workings of the presbyterian stationers, identified its author as the Oxford presbyterian don Francis Cheynell.[34]

In addition to attempting to influence Parliamentary debate on censorship, the London presbyterian ministry also sought to defend Reformed orthodoxy through disputation with opponents. This took the form of print controversies, such as defences of the office of the ordained ministry, an attack on the astrology of William Lilly or Roger Drake's long-running polemics against free admission to the Lord's supper.[35] In addition, London presbyterians entered face-to-face disputations with London opponents. Recent historiography, especially the work of Ann Hughes, has argued that presbyterian ministers were active in advancing a populist defence of orthodoxy against the sects and showed 'a determined concern to compete with radicals for popular support' among the populace.[36] However, Bernard Capp's survey of public disputations in England during the 1650s has argued that the London presbyterians acquired a 'distaste' for public disputation and 'seldom participated' in the disputations that did take place.[37] Capp is correct to point out that the London presbyterians did not engage in many public disputations during the 1650s, but this should not be ascribed to a distaste for disputing with opponents. The importance that the Sion

College ministers attached to disputation is demonstrated by the Provincial assembly's practice, initiated from 31 December 1650, of arranging internal disputations for the ministers to sharpen their arguments against heterodox positions.[38] For example, on 16 January 1654 the Province's grand committee met at James Cranford's house to debate the issues surrounding 'the anabaptisticall controversy'. Cranford was asked to use his contacts to arrange a disputation with advocates of believer's baptism in London. To assist Cranford in preparing for this debate, the assembly arranged an internal disputation on the question 'whither baptisme be a seale of the covenant of grace'.[39] As late as February 1657, when the Province had all but collapsed, the Provincial assembly debated the question 'whether there shall be a more glorious time for the Church of Christ before the end of the world', a proposition designed to arm the presbyterians in controversy with millenarians.[40] A number of other internal disputations followed, which showed that baptists remained an ongoing theological concern for the Provincial assembly. Between May and September 1657, the Province considered Acts 19:1–7, a key proof text used by baptists to justify the rebaptising of members of the Church of England. The debate encompassed whether the apostles were 'rebaptised in Acts 19 by Paul'.[41]

The presbyterian ministers also actively engaged in formal disputations with opponents, making common cause with other clergy holding to orthodox Reformed positions. This can be seen in the three public disputations arranged between December 1649 and February 1650 at St Stephen, Coleman Street and All Hallows the Great with John Goodwin over the issue of universal redemption. Although not a formal disputant, James Cranford moderated two of the three public disputations between Goodwin and Vavasour Powell and John Simpson, both proponents of Christ's limited atonement. These disputations also attracted the input of Cranford's fellow London presbyterian Roger Drake as well as a number of baptists and congregationalists.[42] The disputations attracted full audiences and Cranford, never one to resist a fight, often neglected his moderator's chair to descend into the debate by attacking Goodwin's Arminianism. Indeed, Goodwin, irked by Cranford's interventions, tried to veto his appointment as moderator of the third disputation, a manoeuvre that failed when the congregationalist William Ames demanded that Cranford take the chair.[43]

Alongside old enemies like John Goodwin, new opponents emerged in the 1650s. One such example was the obstetrician and seventh-day baptist lay preacher Peter Chamberlen. In late January 1650 Chamberlen, a resident of William Gouge's parish of Blackfriars, had challenged Gouge to debate the validity of paedobaptism. The elderly Gouge had initially tried to deflect Chamberlen, leading the Fleet Street ruling elder Thomas

Bakewell, a veteran of lay theological disputes since the early 1630s, to reply.[44] In 1652 Chamberlen again entered the lists against the London presbyterians, this time disputing with James Cranford. The topic of debate originated from an argument between William Webb, a ruling elder of St Martin, Ironmonger Lane and his servant John Moore, a member of Chamberlen's gathered church. Moore had become convinced that orthodox Reformed positions were in error and persuaded his master to arrange a semi-private disputation.[45] The debates, which discussed both the validity of the ordained ministry and whether gifted laymen could preach, took place at Webb's house during March and April.[46] Chamberlen's text makes clear that the London presbyterians had been involved in other semi-private household disputations, as he referred to a previous dispute between Cranford and a Mr Rowley at the house of William Williamson, a ruling elder of St Christopher le Stocks.[47]

When the issue of printing the debate came up, Cranford insisted that the disputation should be treated as a mere private conference in the nature of ministerial advice. This was almost certainly a tactical ploy on his part and should be seen as part of the arsenal of tropes and strategies used by presbyterians to deal with disputations with the laity. After pressure from Chamberlen to publish, Cranford maintained that the debate should not be put into print. However, as a past master of printed propaganda, Cranford knew full well that Chamberlen would print the dispute, and so asked Chamberlen to do so truthfully.[48] Such a request can be seen as part of the presbyterian strategy of managing the transition from oral dispute to print. By refusing to acknowledge that Chamberlen's arguments were anything more than the errors of a private man to be confuted in the confines of a house disputation, Cranford was privileging the calling of the ordained ministry. At the same time, Cranford's request for non-publication operated to put the onus on Chamberlen to publish a truthful transcript of the debate, thus nipping in the bud any creativity on the part of his opponent.[49]

While the Sion College ministers avoided full public disputation in the 1650s, the importance of semi-private household disputations should not be underestimated. Such disputations had a long pedigree in London, recalling discussions such as those that took place 'underground' between godly clergy in the early Stuart period.[50] Although such disputations were not physically open to all, they reached a larger audience through the medium of print. As Capp points out, the reasons for avoiding full public disputations in London were inherently linked to the fear of social disorder resulting from public gatherings in the post-civil war city. However, fear of riot was not the only reason for presbyterian ministers preferring household disputations. Gouge's and Cranford's aloofness in their dealings with Chamberlen show the presbyterian desire to cultivate an aura of charisma and dignity for the ordained ministry. Household disputes rarely took place in neutral space. As we have seen, the venue was often the house of a London ruling elder, who was both a substantial citizen and a presbyterian partisan. In such a forum the presbyterian ministers could symbolically maintain the appearance of clerical authority against the lay disputant.

The period between 1651 and 1653 saw the London presbyterians quietly drop the Covenant-engaged public rhetoric that had resulted in the execution of Christopher Love and key ministers such as Thomas Cawton, William Jenkyn and Thomas Case losing their parochial positions. By making this concession to the post-regicide regime, the London presbyterians were able to make common cause with congregationalists in defending the once dominant 'Calvinist consensus'. With the coming of the Cromwellian Protectorate, the London presbyterians were thus able to join attempts to re-establish Reformed orthodoxy at the centre of English religion.

The Cromwellian Protectorate and the quest for a Reformed orthodoxy

In February 1654, after four years of work, the London Provincial assembly published its *Jus divinum ministerii evangelici*, a substantial defence of the presbyterial conception of the ministerial order, attacking both those radicals who denied the need for an ordained ministry and Henry Hammond's theses on early monarchical episcopacy. Introducing this book was a statement from the London presbyterians declaring their willingness to work towards the goal of rebuilding the Reformed consensus. The Provincial assembly offered the hand of fellowship to 'our reverend brethren of New and Old England of the congregational way', declaring that their dispute with such congregationalists was only in 'some lesser things' and those differences 'shall not hinder us from any Christian accord with them in affection'. The Provincial assembly hoped that 'a happy accommodation between' presbyterian and congregationalist was imminent. The presbyterian offer of fellowship was also extended to those episcopalians who held that government by 'a perpetual moderator is most agreeable to scripture' but who conceded that presbyterian orders and government were a valid expression of church government. The Provincial assembly yearned for union 'between all those that are orthodox in doctrine, though differing among themselves in some circumstances about church government' and expressed the desire for godly unity to be restored in English Christianity.[51]

Jeremiah Whitaker, the venerable presbyterian minister of St Mary Magdalen, Bermondsey, took the liberty of sending a copy of the Provincial assembly's new book to Oliver Cromwell to thank him for relieving presbyterians from the legal penalties for non-subscription to the Commonwealth's Engagement.[52] In his accompanying letter Whitaker stressed the need for rebuilding godly unity and asked Cromwell to 'consider seriously how religion is not onely weakened by divisione, but almost wasted by the daily growth of atheisme and the prophane'. Whitaker counselled Cromwell that the onus for action to protect the church now lay with the civil magistrate, as 'the reignes of government' in the church were 'now lost'.[53]

The London presbyterian efforts to re-establish godly unity were, however, more than just platitudes expressed in books and letters. The preface to *Jus divinum ministerii evangelici* represented a policy statement for a series of negotiations between London presbyterians and congregationalists throughout the early months of 1654, designed to establish confessional unity in the new Protectorate.[54] Between February and April meetings took place in Blackfriars between leading presbyterians and congregationalists to attempt to 'find the way of peace'.[55] These talks are likely to have focused on John Owen's plans to seek Parliamentary adoption for a new confessional statement modelled on his 1652 *Humble Proposals*. John Dury, who chaired the meetings, could report on 2 April that the parties were 'in a fair way of composing [their] differences'.[56]

Despite Dury's upbeat prediction of presbyterian–congregationalist *rapprochement*, there was nevertheless a lingering ambivalence among London presbyterians about the congregationalists and the Protectorate in general. In a 1655 letter to Baillie, Simeon Ashe stated that only Stephen Marshall among presbyterians had been enthusiastic about the Protectorate and complained of the continuing political advance of 'Independencie'.[57] Nevertheless, as the letter from Jeremiah Whitaker shows, by 1654 the London presbyterians were willing to work with Cromwell and his Protectorate in the hope of reviving the old alliance between godly magistrates and the ministry.

The willingness of the London presbyterians to look to the new Cromwellian state to rebuild Reformed orthodoxy raises the question of how the London presbyterians viewed alternative proposals to the essentially congregationalist vision of the Protectorate ecclesiastical settlement. From around 1650 Richard Baxter had been advancing an alternative, essentially extra-Parliamentary, approach to Owen's plans through his projected county association scheme.[58] However, the leadership among the London presbyterians initially treated Baxter's association project with ambivalence, although as time went on they warmed to the benefits for godly unity that the association movement generated.[59] An example of this can be seen in correspondence between Baxter's Worcestershire association and the London Provincial assembly in 1654 over which version of the psalms to use. Following a project discussed by Baxter and John Dury in 1653, the Worcestershire association asked the Provincial assembly to state which psalter it recommended. The Worcestershire's association's goal was to use the decision of the London Province to encourage 'a universal acceptance' of a single psalter throughout the association movement.[60] The Provincial assembly's response to Baxter's Worcestershire association was polite but somewhat dismissive. Although the Worcestershire association's letter was first discussed in committee by the London Provincial assembly on 3 July 1654, the assembly did not get around to penning a reply until 21 August.[61] While the response, approved on 11 September, was courteous, the Provincial assembly made it clear that it looked to a Parliamentary solution to the issues of the psalter and the church settlement in general. The letter pointed out that the first Protectorate Parliament, which included a substantial number of pro-presbyterian MPs including the Southwark ruling elder Jeremiah Baines, had resolved to summon an assembly of divines to advise it on matters of religion.[62] It was anticipated by some that the old 1640s approach of a presbyterian establishment with a forbearance for doctrinally orthodox dissent would be instituted by Parliament.[63] The London Provincial assembly made it clear to their Worcestershire counterparts that it was to this Parliamentary approach that the godly should look. A *laissez-faire* solution to the problems of the Church of England would not do as the 'businesse' of making decisions 'in matters of Religion' 'doth properly belong' to a Parliament advised by an assembly of divines.[64]

Despite the reservations of some London presbyterians towards both Oliver Cromwell and his congregationalist advisers, the London presbyterian ministers, along with many pro-presbyterian laity, had come to accept that it was better to work with the Cromwellian state. As at the 1645 committee of accommodation, many London presbyterians recognised the need to concede a degree of latitude to those brethren of differing judgements who held to confessionally Reformed positions. This concession was often dressed in the language of 'healing divisions' by the clergy, but by 1655 even the unyieldingly presbyterian stationers Thomas Underhill and Nathaniel Webb were using the language of 'forbearance'. In a letter to Cromwell, Webb and Underhill acknowledged that it was 'a great mercy that those who hold the foundation of religion in piety and unity, differing in lesser matters, are protected by you, and prevented from injuring each other'.[65] This may appear to be an embarrassing climb-down from the 1640s presbyterian rhetoric of uniformity contained in works such as Edwards' *Gangraena*. To some degree it represented a recognition of the fact that the congregationalists were the leading clergy in Protectorate counsels. Nevertheless, as has been shown in previous chapters, even at the height of the anti-toleration campaign of the mid-1640s many London presbyterians had maintained a language of forbearance for lesser differences within Reformed orthodoxy, without conceding outright toleration. In the 1650s this language could therefore come to the fore without the appearance of an embarrassing *volte-face*.

The hoped-for assembly of divines to accompany the first Protectorate Parliament failed to materialise. Instead a grand committee of MPs, advised by a select number of divines, was established on 5 October 1654.[66] As Patrick Little and David Smith have shown, Parliament's aims were to confirm tithes as the basis of financial support for the established ministry and to seek strict measures for the suppression of extreme heresies.[67] In November, Parliament ordered its clerical advisers to consider what was necessary to establish a confession of faith. The magisterial congregationalists John Owen, Thomas Goodwin, Philip Nye and Sydrach Simpson sought to revive their scheme of 1652 with a statement of Reformed orthodoxy entitled *A new confession of faith*.[68] This was supported by presbyterians on the committee, with Stephen Marshall and Francis Cheynell being enthusiastic for the proposals.[69]

The voice of episcopacy on the committee was to have been represented by Archbishop James Ussher, then perhaps the most respected theologian in England. Ussher refused the nomination and, upon the recommendation of John Dury and Lord Broghill, the place was filled by Richard Baxter. From Baxter's description of the meetings, it appears that Marshall and Cheynell attended having decided to pass Owen's proposals with little debate.[70] Baxter, in part supported by Richard Vines, would be the thorn in the side of this committee, obstructing the passing of the new confession, arguing that the words of any statement of faith should come straight out of scripture.[71] Baxter's obstructions only delayed matters and the *new confession of faith* was presented to Parliament, whose broadly puritan, even 'presbyterian' stance in attempting to restrict the width of liberty of conscience was disappointing to Cromwell. The Lord Protector's decision to dissolve Parliament in January 1655, however, meant that the project of legally establishing a Reformed confessional identity for the Cromwellian church was never realised.[72] Time would show that 1654 represented a critical juncture in attempts to rescue the goals of the parliamentary puritan movement of the early 1640s.

The last years of the Protectorate

John Owen's plan to establish a new confession of faith in February 1654 was to be combined with the establishment of the ecclesiastical administration of the Protectorate, the committees known as the 'triers' and 'ejectors'.

At the same time as the Blackfriars meetings in February 1654, the leading congregationalists were also gathering with fellow ministers at another series of meetings held at Cromwell's lodgings in the Cockpit.[73] These gatherings thrashed out the establishment of the commissioners for the approbation of public preachers, the so-called 'triers' of the Cromwellian ecclesiastical administration.[74] The system was implemented on 20 March 1654, dividing its duties between eleven laymen and twenty-seven ministers. While the congregationalists were numerically the strongest group among the clerical members of the committee, with fourteen magisterial congregationalists and three particular baptists on the commission, the presbyterian ministers were represented by ten ministers, including the London presbyterians William Cooper, Obadiah Sedgwick, Thomas Manton and Samuel Balmford.[75]

The appointment of local 'ejector' commissions on 28 August 1654 to act against 'scandalous, ignorant and insufficient ministers and schoolmasters' shows a similar pattern of rehabilitation for London's religious presbyterians.[76] As with the triers, the lay commissioners were largely former political and religious Independents, although many of these had shown no particular opposition to the presbyterian church system in London. The commission also included presbyterian ruling elders such as Thomas Vyner, Christopher Pack and Maurice Gething.[77] More importantly, presbyterian ministers dominated the list of clerical advisers to the London ejectors, with twelve of the nineteen assistants being presbyterians. A similar pattern can be seen in the list of clerical assistants for neighbouring Middlesex, with William Spurstow and Gabriel Sanger joining other presbyterian ministers such as John Bond, Obadiah Sedgwick and William Bates. This pattern would continue in 1656–7, when the leading presbyterians Edmund Calamy, Thomas Manton and William Jenkyn were added to the ejectors' commission.[78]

As we have seen, the religious presbyterians' political renovation relates back to the London ministers' willingness to find common ground with the magisterial congregationalists and to co-operate with the Protectorate regime. Oliver Cromwell was evidently pleased with the collaborative work of presbyterians and congregationalists on the triers and ejectors committees, and stressed the bi-partisan nature of the collaboration. Speaking to his first Parliament on 4 September 1654, Cromwell praised the work of 'men of as known ability, piety, and integrity' and stressed that the committees contained men 'both of presbyterian and Independent judgments' but 'laboured to approve themselves to Christ, the nation, and their own consciences'. He declared that he was exasperated by the negative attitude of sectaries to the Protectorate efforts to rebuild godly unity and stated that his fears of presbyterian tyranny had proved to be unfounded in practice.[79]

Alongside the ministers' efforts, October 1654 saw a revival of the presbyterian stationers' campaign to establish firmer controls over the printing of heterodox works. Focusing on recent 'blasphemies and errours', particularly 'antimagistraticall errours', the stationers' new tract, *A second beacon fired*, returned to the 1640s attack on the sects. Alongside the obligatory condemnation of John Biddle's Socinianism, old enemies now in political eclipse such as William Dell, John Goodwin and Christopher Feake were catalogued alongside the works of the new threats such as the 'seeker' educationalist John Webster, the quaker Richard Farnworth and the 'ranter' Robert Norwood. Anti-popery, the principal subject of the first *beacon*, received only a passing mention and the main point made by the stationers was that papists had infiltrated the Army disguised as sectaries. The *second beacon* ended with an appeal to impose the stationers' original 1652 proposal for the problem of licensing or, alternatively, for the 'real friends to true religion, the Lord Protector, the Parliament and Commonwealth of England' to use their influence to find means for the suppression of heretical books.[80]

The London stationers were once again probably acting in concert with the presbyterian ministers involved in the efforts to establish the national confession of faith.[81] We have noted the minister Francis Cheynell's involvement in the 1652 *beacon* controversy. Cheynell would be central to the 1654 committee, being disparaged by Baxter as Owen's 'scribe'.[82] John Goodwin, one of the targets of the *second beacon*, saw it as issuing from his clerical enemies at Sion College.[83] Although the influence of the advocates of a free press such as Goodwin or Milton was beginning to decline, Cromwellian policy fell far short of the *second beacon*'s desired return to a 1640s-style licensing system. In line with the Rump's measures, the Protectorate council claimed authority over the press on 28 August 1655, establishing commissioners to control the press and ordering a clamp-down on unlicensed printing.[84] Nevertheless, the presbyterian stationers were prepared to work with the Protectorate's measures. In October 1655 Thomas Underhill and Nathaniel Webb, two of the signatories to the beacon pamphlets, laid information that Isaac de La Peyrère's *Praeadamitae*, a book that had recently been burned in Paris for suggesting that there were human beings on the earth prior to Adam's exile from Eden, had been anonymously published in London.[85] The stationers stated that, despite its anonymity, they recognised the print characters used in the printing of de La Peyrère's work as that of Francis Leech of Shoe Lane.[86] Grateful for the intelligence, the council ordered the Lord Mayor to investigate the accusation and arrest Leech to examine him concerning the publication.

It can be seen that, by 1655, presbyterians had largely re-established themselves politically within the Protectorate, a fact echoed by the increasing preference of sessions of Oliver's second Parliament for stressing Reformed orthodox principles in its policy-making.[87] The membership of the Second Protectorate Parliament included a sizeable bloc of MPs favourable to presbyterianism who sought an anti-militarist return to the ancient constitution. This group included the former religious presbyterian Lord Mayors of London Thomas Foote and Christopher Packe, the latter of whom, as we have seen, was a ruling elder. Packe would present the Humble Petition and Advice, recommending that Cromwell take the crown.[88] The presbyterian group in the Second Protectorate Parliament betrays connections to the London presbyterian ministers, with Edward Reynolds and William Jenkyn being nominated to preach in the Parliamentary pulpit.[89] In addition, Reynolds, Thomas Manton and William Bates were selected alongside Joseph Caryl, Matthew Griffith and Philip Nye to try to convince James Nayler, the 'Quaker Jesus', of his theological errors.[90] The London Provincial assembly paved the way for the Second Protectorate Parliament's ill-fated May 1657 bill for compulsory catechising with its August 1655 *Exhortation to catechizing*, a demand followed up by the publication of a treatise from the London presbyterian cleric Zachary Crofton.[91] The mid-1650s also saw London presbyterians joining numerous committees of Oliver's Protectorate. Manton and Packe, along with Anthony Tuckney and the Essex presbyterian Matthew Newcomen, were part of the committee that heard the proposals of Manasseh Ben Israel for the readmission of the Jews in November 1655.[92] In 1656 Calamy sat on the committee for the foundation of the university college at Durham and Thomas Manton adjudicated on the bid to print the Bible by Henry Hills and John Field.[93] With political and religious presbyterians returning to positions of influence in the Protectorate, London religious presbyterians became an integral part of the Protectorate's counsel in religious matters.

Perhaps the most important contribution of the London ministers to Protectorate policy was their involvement with Cromwellian attempts to settle the rift within the Church of Scotland. This dispute had arisen on 14 December 1650 when the Kirk had passed a general resolution permitting former royalists and engagers, upon repentance of their previous errors, to serve in the Scottish military to defend Scotland against the English conquest. This had led to protests from those who objected to the rehabilitation of anti-covenanters, with these 'protestors' refusing to hold communion with those who had agreed with the 14 December general 'resolution'. In the aftermath of the English republic's conquest of Scotland in 1651, attempts to heal the schism in the Church of Scotland had proved impossible, with Robert Lilburne, the English military governor, favouring the protestors. However, by 1656 Lord Broghill, the president of the post-conquest council of state, had gradually come to prefer the resolutioners, rejecting the protestors as fanatics.[94] The shift in English support effected by Broghill drove a delegation of protestors led by Patrick Gillespie and Lord Wariston to London, to attempt to obtain advantage by interceding with Cromwell directly.[95] Samuel Rutherford, on behalf of the protestors, wrote to Simeon Ashe in October 1656, seeking to obtain the support of the London presbyterians and complaining that the resolutioners had 'deserted us and the Covenant, and joyned [...] with the malignant party' and that they 'do persecute the godly' as much as the old 'prelaticall conformists did'.[96]

Conscious of the protestors' attempt to use a high-profile theologian such as Rutherford to curry favour in London, the resolutioners sent to London James Sharp, the minister of Crail, carrying letters of recommendation from resolutioner clergy including David Dickson and Robert Baillie to the leading London presbyterians Calamy, Ashe and Manton.[97] In February 1657 Sharp had published a pamphlet specifically aimed at English religious presbyterians, explaining the resolutioners' side of the conflict and painting the protestors as schismatics.[98] Sharp's natural charm and his willingness to 'sollicit both friends and unfriends' soon brought the London presbyterians around to the resolutioner cause.[99]

The protestor delegates did not help themselves in London by vocally 'passing their judgment upon' the London presbyterian ministers as 'as carnall formall men' and making alliance with John Owen and numerous anti-presbyterian Army officers.[100] The issue that most divided the English presbyterians from the protestors was their view that the dispute needed the legal intervention of the Cromwellian state to resolve it. The protestors had hoped to convince their English co-religionists that presbyterian theory allowed the Christian magistrate to step in to save a church that had seriously miscarried.[101] The London presbyterians, while accepting the protestors' theoretical standpoint regarding the magistrate, did not see the Church of Scotland as having fallen into such a predicament. On the contrary, the London ministers saw the protestor–resolutioner dispute as essentially political and not ecclesiastical. The protestors' call to the Cromwellian state to settle the dispute was, as William Cooper, Thomas Manton and the Kent MP Lambarde Godfrey, saw it, 'no better then' allowing 'Erastianisme' into a pure church to settle a political schism.[102] Manton had made this clear in speaking to Patrick Gillespie in August 1657, curtly telling him that he 'ought not [...] to profess for presbyterian government and make use of Independents to drive on violently their busines'. Instead, Manton told the protestor leaders that they should take up 'the way of peace and union' with their resolutioner brethren and offered them a conference refereed by leading London presbyterian clergy as an alternative to settlement by the Cromwellian state.[103]

The protestors' rejection of the London presbyterians' offer in favour of an alliance with the Independent Owen and the Army officers can be seen as a substantial tactical error born of their failure to follow the political winds in London. Sharp noted in August 1657 that 'the presbyterians encrease much in England everywhere, and the Independents have much of late declined'.[104] The protestors' alienation of the English presbyterians in London allowed Sharp to convince the London ministers that the resolutioners were the party who most truly held to the presbyterian interest.[105] His success at winning over the London ministers can be seen in Ashe's reply to Rutherford, which upbraided the theologian for supporting the destructive course of the protestors' schism and the 'tartnesse in language' that he had used against his former friends and brethren.[106]

Sharp's alliance with the London presbyterians would yield fruit for the resolutioner cause in July 1657 when a committee for the settlement of the Kirk consisting of English referees, including the London presbyterians Thomas Manton, William Cooper and Samuel Balmford, was set up by Cromwell to mediate the protestor–resolutioner dispute.[107] Manton successfully resisted an attempt by Owen to take advantage of a poorly attended meeting to vote through a recommendation for the protestors' agenda by marshalling his fellow presbyterians and Sharp to attend and enter their dissent against the vote.[108] The presbyterians therefore forced a stalemate in the committee by appealing to Cromwell's ideals of godly unity and healing. The ultimate effect of the presbyterian dissent was that Cromwell, agreeing with the London presbyterian ministers' sentiment, had the dispute returned to Scotland.[109]

As Julia Buckroyd has noted, Sharp's success in London, and thus also that of his London presbyterian allies, was essentially a negative one.[110] They prevented the Scottish protestors from obtaining a victory in London that would secure their advantage in Scotland; yet this in no way assisted the healing of the divisions within the Church of Scotland. As Calamy and Ashe explained in December 1657, the defeat of the protestor delegation in London was a 'happy conclusion' from a presbyterian perspective as it preserved the autonomy of the Church of Scotland from the intruding Erastian jurisdiction of the civil magistrate.[111] More importantly for this study, Sharp's victory was reliant on the London presbyterian delegates' influence within the later Protectorate and illustrates that the London presbyterians had achieved a reconciliation with the Cromwellian administration that would have been unthinkable in 1651.

Richard Cromwell's Protectorate

The short-lived Protectorate of Richard Cromwell continued to improve the position of London's presbyterian ministers in national politics, with

Richard, as James Sharp noted in March 1659, giving 'special notice of those the presbyterial way'.[112] Soon after the death of his father, on 14 September, George Monck advised Richard to call an assembly of divines alongside Parliament to settle religion and to favour presbyterian preachers at court, particularly those who had worked with his father: Calamy, Manton, Cooper and Edward Reynolds.[113] Along with John Owen, these four London presbyterian ministers would preach and pray at the opening of Richard's Parliament on 7 January 1659.[114]

Richard's Protectorate opened with further attempts to find accommodation between congregationalists and presbyterians, the foundations of which had been laid the previous summer.[115] On 14 October 1658 Thomas Goodwin addressed Richard and presented to him the *Declaration of the faith and order* of the congregational churches agreed on 12 October at a conference held at the Savoy. Goodwin stated that the congregationalists had met with the intention of laying 'some foundations of agreement' with the presbyterians.[116] While presbyterians considered that the congregationalists were trying to ingratiate themselves with the new Protector to deflect the possibility of a presbyterian settlement, the congregationalists' desire for accommodation appears to have been genuine.[117] The difficulty for the presbyterians was that the congregationalists' terms of accommodation fell short of their expectations for a national church settlement. The preface to the Savoy *Declaration* made clear that the congregationalists looked back to Owen's programmes of 1652 and 1654; adopting a Calvinist confession of faith as the state confession, but preserving the congregational church as the basic unit of ecclesiastical polity.[118] The congregationalists' declaration on church order, a topic that was purposely kept separate from the doctrinal part of the confession, made only linguistic concessions to the presbyterian position, seeking 'a mutuall toleration' for each party's church way.[119] While not a denial of church association *per se*, the Savoy *Declaration* fell short of presbyterian aspirations for accommodation by continuing its focus on the congregational church. The Savoy *Declaration* therefore sought to maintain the *de facto impasse* on church polity that had arisen between presbyterians and congregationalists since late 1641. Nevertheless, the presbyterians were reluctant to disturb the working *détente* that had emerged under the Cromwellian state. This was especially true in light of the threat to Reformed orthodoxy posed by the quaker movement and Henry Hammond's brand of resurgent episcopalianism.[120]

The London ministers initially appear to have followed a policy of waiting to see what Richard's Protectorate was likely to offer. Around the end of January 1659, the London ministers, led by Edmund Calamy and Matthew Poole, put out feelers to allies as to whether it would be prudent to make a public statement of the critical difference between presbyterians and congregationalists. Writing to Richard Baxter at this time, the London ministers focused on issues that had long divided them from the congregationalists: the nature of schism and the error of gathering churches out of other protestant churches. The peroration of this work, however, was positive, stressing 'the easiness and necessity of an accommodation' between Reformed protestants.[121]

The finished work, *Irenicum*, normally ascribed to the Smectymnuan Matthew Newcomen, can therefore be seen as the collective response by the leading presbyterians to the Savoy *Declaration*.[122] It criticised the limited nature of the congregationalists' concessions and, by the somewhat disingenuous technique of setting quotations from New England authors out of context to make them look more presbyterian in character, argued that the doctrinal agreement offered by the congregationalists should go hand in hand with clerical association on the model of the Cumberland and Westmoreland association.[123] Newcomen recognised, as did Samuel Clarke a month later in a companion piece, that accommodation among those Reformed protestants seen as 'brethren' on doctrinal fundamentals was an essential factor in the search for godly unity.[124] Consistent with their belief that the object of reformation was the national church, the presbyterians opposed outright toleration. However, they had come to accept that a mutual forbearance among Reformed protestants was unavoidable if accommodation was to be achieved. The goal was to preserve something of a national church by the association of doctrinally orthodox congregations.

The composition of *Irenicum* came at a critical juncture in the religious debate in Richard's Parliament. On 5 April, Parliament debated a public declaration for a fast against heresy. More pertinently, on 11 April its committee for religion ordered that the doctrinal parts of the Westminster confession of faith, 'curtailed of what relates to church discipline', should be 'held forth as the public profession of the nation'.[125] James Sharp reported in early April that steps were being taken for establishing the 1640s Parliamentary scheme for a presbyterian church.[126] The settlement was not to materialise. On 14 April, Sharp warned that, with the Army's growing anger at Richard's Parliament, the adoption of the truncated Westminster confession was the 'farthest step' Parliament could take towards the settlement of religion. The matter of church settlement was something that would have to be 'carr[ied] on afterwards'.[127] The Army's ending of Richard Cromwell's Parliament on 22 April and his Protectorate in May 1659 once again alienated the London presbyterians from England's experiment with 'unkingship'. The next four years would see the city's presbyterians take a major role in the politics of the Restoration settlement.

Conclusion

The mid-to-late 1650s, although a period of disappointment for the London presbyterians, was also a time that saw them take part in the rebuilding of the old parliamentarian–puritan alliance. The London presbyterians' return to the political centre was based on the growing recognition that the puritan cause of 1641, of reforming the Reformation itself, had been waylaid by the squabbles and excesses of the 1640s and early 1650s. The presbyterian–congregationalist attempt at *rapprochement*, beginning in earnest from the meetings at Blackfriars in February 1654, went some way to re-establish the old godly alliance that had met at Edmund Calamy's house in 1640–41. That this alliance did not succeed in establishing a national confessional standard was more a matter of the instability of Cromwellian politics than the lack of will or agreement between the leading clerical protagonists.

The willingness of many London presbyterians to actively co-operate with the Cromwellian Protectorate saw the presbyterians shift from being pariahs to participants in the new regime. This is most plainly seen in the victory obtained for the Scottish resolutioners by James Sharp and his London presbyterian allies, particularly Thomas Manton. While it has to be accepted that the London presbyterians were never as close to Cromwell as his congregationalist advisers, from 1654 the presbyterians increasingly had the ear of the Protector and were well established on Protectorate religious committees by the time of Oliver's death in September 1658. This situation would have undoubtedly grown under the more sympathetic administration of Richard Cromwell had the administration survived more than a few months. The renovation of the London presbyterians under the Protectorate, however, would put them in a position of influence during the restoration of the Stuart monarchy.

Notes

1. HMC, *Calendar of the manuscripts of the Marquess of Ormonde*, 3 vols (1902), I, p. 317. The accuracy of this report seems questionable. In any event, as Blair Worden has shown, the presbyterians' understanding of what a 'free parliament' would look like was not on all fours with what royalists understood the idea to mean: B. Worden, 'The campaign for a free parliament, 1659–60' *Parliamentary History*, 36:2 (2017), 167.
2. Isaac Kimber, *The life of Oliver Cromwell, Lord Protector* (1724), p. 225. The meeting between Cromwell and Calamy is sometimes said to have related to

the question of dissolving the Rump, but Kimber, the original source, links it to the November 1652 conversation related by Bulstrode Whitelocke regarding Cromwell taking the crown (see *Memorials of the English Affairs*, 4 vols (Oxford, 1853), III, pp. 468–74). Two presbyterian ruling elders, Lawrence Warkman (or Wahtman) of St Magnus the Martyr and Michael Herring of St Mary Woolnoth, signed the city petition of 20 May 1653 asking Cromwell to reinstate the Rump parliament to prevent further chaos: *To his excellency, Oliver Cromwell, Captain General* (1653).

3 A. Hughes, 'Religious diversity in revolutionary London' in *The English revolution c.1590–1720: politics, religion and communities*, ed. N. Tyacke (Manchester, 2013), pp. 111–28.
4 Coffey, *John Goodwin*, p. 205.
5 London Provincial assembly, *A vindication of the presbyteriall ministry and government* (1649), p. 13.
6 RLPA fos 113v–115r (DWL transcript, pp. 93–7).
7 Lazarus Seaman, *Reverend and beloved* (1651).
8 Richard Vines, *Peitharchia: obedience to magistrates, both supreme and subordinate* (1656). Other presbyterian ministers preaching to the Lord Mayor included Edwarde Reynolds, Samuel Annesley, Thomas Watson and Thomas Jacombe. The only other minister to have repeat invitations was the moderate congregationalist Ralph Venning.
9 This included a number of London ruling elders including Thomas Gower, William Vincent and Maurice Gething: see Farnell, 'Politics of the city of London', pp. 313–14.
10 *The humble proposals of Mr John Owen [...] and other ministers* (1652); Coffey, *John Goodwin*, pp. 233–4.
11 For John Ley's committee see S. W. Curruthers, *The everyday work of the Westminster Assembly* (1943) pp. 148–72; J. Halcomb, 'The examination of ministers' in *MPWA*, I, pp. 217–26.
12 Coffey, 'A ticklish business', pp. 119–20.
13 S. Mortimer, *Reason and religion in the English Revolution* (Cambridge, 2010), pp. 196–200; T. Cooper, *John Owen, Richard Baxter and the formation of nonconformity* (Farnham, 2011), p. 167.
14 C. Polizzotto, 'The campaign against the humble proposals of 1652', *JEH*, 38 (1987), 569–81.
15 See for example Joseph Caryl, *The moderator* (1652); Stephen Marshall, *A sermon preached to the right honourable, the Lord Mayor [...] April 1652* (1653); Giles Firmin, *Separation examined* (1652); Worden, *Rump*, pp. 295–6.
16 Woolrych, *Britain in revolution*, p. 517.
17 [Henry Vane], *Zeal examined* (1652), pp. 45–6.
18 The presbyterian stationers were Luke Fawne, Samuel Gellibrand, Joshua Kirton, John Rothwell, Thomas Underhill and Nathaniel Webb.
19 For a full survey of the controversy see T. H. Clancy, 'The beacon controversy, 1652–1657', *Recusant History*, 9 (1967), 63–4.

20 For the Rump's licensing policy see Peacey, *Politicians and pamphleteers*, pp. 158–9.
21 [Michael Sparke], *A second beacon fired by Scintilla* (1652).
22 On the increase in Roman Catholic publications during this period see P. A. Richardson, 'Serial struggles: English Catholics and their periodicals, 1648–1844' (Ph.D thesis, University of Durham, 2003), pp. 16–18.
23 J. Collins, 'Silencing Thomas Hobbes: the presbyterians and *Leviathan*' in *The Cambridge companion to Hobbes' Leviathan*, ed. P. Springborg (Cambridge, 2007), pp. 478–99.
24 Fawne, Gellibrand, Kirton, Rothwell, Underhill and Webb, *A beacon set on fire* (1652), pp. 6–7.
25 The point was made explicit in the stationers' reply: [Francis Cheynell?], *The beacon flameing with a non obstante* (1652), p. 14.
26 The authors of *The beacons quenched* were Thomas Pride, William Goffe, William Kiffin and Samuel Richardson.
27 M. Caricchio, 'New from the new Jerusalem: Giles Calvert and the radical experience' in *Varieties of seventeenth and early eighteenth-century English radicalism in context*, eds A. Hessayon and D. Finnegan (Farnham, 2011), p. 85.
28 Pride, Goffe, Kiffin and Richardson, *The beacons quenched*, p. 6.
29 *Ibid.*, p. 13.
30 *Ibid.*, p. 12. For Austin see J. R. Collins, 'Thomas Hobbes and the Blackloist Conspiracy of 1649', *HJ*, 45:2 (2002), 329–30 and S. Tutino, *Thomas White and the Blackloists: between politics and theology during the English Civil War* (Farnham, 2008), p. 76.
31 Pride, Goffe, Kiffin and Richardson, *The beacons quenched*, p. 5.
32 Collins, 'Silencing Thomas Hobbes', pp. 485–7.
33 Pride, Goffe, Kiffin and Richardson, *The beacons quenched*, p. 11.
34 [Cheynell], *The beacon flameing*.
35 For London presbyterian works defending the ministerial order see e.g. William Wickins, *A plea for the ministry* (1650); London Provincial assembly, *Jus divinum ministerii evangelici* (1654); Poole, *Quo warranto*. On astrology, see Thomas Gataker, *Thomas Gataker BD his vindication* (1653) and Gataker, *A discours apologetical* (1654). For a detailed summary of the extensive debate on free admission to the Lord's supper see E. Brooks Holifield, *The covenant sealed: the development of puritan sacramental theology in old and New England, 1570–1720* (New Haven, CT, 1974), pp. 109–26.
36 A. Hughes, 'The pulpit guarded: confrontations between orthodox and radicals in revolutionary England' in *John Bunyan and his England, 1628–88*, eds A. Laurence, W. R. Owens and S. Sim (1990) pp. 31–50; A. Hughes, 'Public disputations, pamphlets and polemics', *History Today* (February 1991), pp. 27–33.
37 B. Capp, 'The religious market place', *EHR*, 129:536 (2014), pp. 55–6.
38 RLPA fo. 110v (DWL transcript, p. 86).
39 RLPA fo. 226r (DWL transcript, pp. 136–7).
40 RLPA fos 238v, 239r (DWL transcript, pp. 161–2).

41 RLPA fos 240r–241v (DWL transcript, pp. 165, 168–9). For further debates see RLPA fo. 243r (DWL transcript, p. 172).
42 [Anon.], *Truths conflict with error, or, universal redemption controverted* (1650).
43 Coffey, *John Goodwin*, pp. 205–7; *Truths conflict with error*, p. 72.
44 For the dispute between Bakewell and Chamberlen, see my forthcoming essay 'Puritanism, parish and polemic in civil war London: the case of Thomas Bakewell'.
45 D. S. Katz, *Sabbath and sectarianism in seventeenth-century England* (Kampen, 1997), pp. 48–89.
46 Peter Chamberlen, *The disputes between Mr Cranford and Dr Chamberlen at the house of Mr William Webb* (1652).
47 *Ibid.*, p. 2.
48 *Ibid.*, p. 30.
49 On issues of the need for truthful transcripts, and the literary strategies used by disputants, see Hughes, 'Public disputations, pamphlets and polemics', pp. 31–2.
50 P. Lake and D. Como, '"Orthodoxy" and its discontents: dispute settlement and the production of "consensus" in the London (Puritan) "underground"', *JBS*, 39:1 (2000), 34–79.
51 *Jus divinum ministerii evangelici*, 'To the reader', sigs B1v–B3r.
52 Having matriculated at Sidney Sussex College, Cambridge within three months of each other in 1616, Whitaker and Cromwell were possibly of long acquaintance. Penalties for non-subscription to the Engagement were removed on 19 January 1654: *A&O*, II, p. 830.
53 BL Add. Ms. 4159, fo. 113.
54 G. Nuttall, 'Presbyterians and Independents, some movements for unity 300 years ago', *Journal of the Presbyterian Historical Society of England*, 10:1 (1952) 11–12; *CCRB*, I, pp. 127–8, 133–4.
55 *CCRB*, I, pp. 127, 133; Cooper, *John Owen, Richard Baxter*, pp. 145–6. The presbyterians were Stephen Marshall, Edmund Calamy, Simeon Ashe, Thomas Manton and Richard Vines. The congregationalist ministers included Joseph Caryl, Philip Nye, Sydrach Simpson, Samuel Slater and William Carter.
56 Nuttall, 'Presbyterians and Independents', pp. 11–12; Abernathy, 'The English presbyterians', p. 11.
57 Baillie, *L&J*, III, pp. 306–7.
58 Abernathy, 'The English presbyterians', pp. 8–10; J. Halcomb, 'The association movement and the politics of church settlement in the interregnum' in *Church polity and politics in the transatlantic world, c. 1636–66*, eds E. Vernon and H. Powell (Manchester, 2020), pp. 174–99.
59 For approval of the association scheme, see Matthew Poole's letter to Baxter, 24 August 1658: *CCRB*, I, pp. 334–5.
60 *CCRB*, I, pp. 137–8. The choice was essentially between two versions of the psalms: William Barton's *Book of psalms in metre* (1644) or the Scottish

psalter of 1650 based on Francis Rous' psalter that had been approved by the Westminster assembly.
61 RLPA fos 227r–v (DWL transcript, pp. 138–9).
62 *CJ*, VII, p. 367; P. Little and D. L. Smith, *Parliament and politics during the Protectorate* (Cambridge, 2007), pp. 198–9; D. Scott, 'Baines, Jeremy (1611–78)', in *History of Parliament, 1640–1660* (forthcoming).
63 *Thurloe SP*, II, p. 697.
64 *CCRB*, I, pp. 154–5.
65 NA, SP 18/101, fo. 133.
66 *CJ*, VII, p. 367.
67 Little and Smith, *Parliament and politics*, pp. 199–201; Worden, *God's instruments*, p. 79.
68 John Owen, Thomas Goodwin, Philip Nye and Sydrach Simpson, *A new confession of faith* (1654) in *Reformed confessions of the 16th and 17th centuries in English translation*, ed. J. T. Dennison, 4 vols (Grand Rapids, MI, 2014), IV, pp. 428–31.
69 Baxter, *RB*, II, p. 197. The other presbyterians on the committee were William Reyner, Richard Vines, Thomas Manton and Thomas Jacombe. Daniel Dyke and Henry Jessey, congregationalists who advocated adult baptism, and Joseph Caryl and Samuel Fairclough, were nominated to the committee, but they perhaps did not attend the meetings: see *CCRB*, I, pp. 156–7.
70 Baxter, *RB*, II, pp. 197–9.
71 Cooper, *John Owen, Richard Baxter*, pp. 179–95.
72 R. S. Paul, *The Lord Protector: religion and politics in the life of Oliver Cromwell* (Grand Rapids, MI, 1955), pp. 307–12; Woolrych, *Britain in Revolution*, pp. 613–5; Worden, *God's instruments*, p. 79.
73 *CCRB*, I, pp. 127–8; G. F. Nuttall, 'Presbyterians and Independents', pp. 11–12.
74 NA, SP 25/75, fo. 145; *CCRB*, I, p. 128; *Diary of Sir Archibald Johnston of Wariston*, ed. D. H. Fleming, 2 vols (1919), II, p. 214.
75 *CSPD, 1654*, p. 40; *A&O*, II, p. 855.
76 *A&O*, II, p. 968.
77 *A&O*, II, p. 978.
78 NA, SP25/78, fo. 231; A. Hughes, '"The public profession of these nations": the national church in interregnum England' in *Religion in revolutionary England*, eds C. Durston and J. Maltby (Manchester, 2006), pp. 97–104.
79 *Speeches of Oliver Cromwell*, ed. I. Roots (1989), p. 36.
80 Luke Fawne, Samuel Gellibrand, Joshua Kirton, John Rothwell, Thomas Underhill and Nathanael Webb, *A second beacon fired* (1654).
81 Coffey, *John Goodwin*, pp. 243–4.
82 Baxter, *RB*, II, p. 199.
83 John Goodwin, *A fresh discovery of the high presbyterian spirit* (1655), sigs A3r, A4r; Coffey, *John Goodwin*, p. 243.
84 NA, SP 25/76A, fos 68–9.
85 Isaac de La Peyrère, *A Theological systeme upon the presupposition, that men were before Adam* (1655), republished in 1656 as *Men before Adam* (1656).

86 NA, SP 18/101, fo. 133.
87 Little and Smith, *Parliament and politics*, pp. 205–15.
88 *Ibid.*, pp. 115–17. The 1640s presbyterian activist Captain John Jones was elected for the city, but excluded from sitting.
89 Edward Reynolds, *The peace of Jerusalem* (1657); William Jenkyn, *The policy of princes in subjection to the Son* (1656).
90 *Diary of Thomas Burton*, ed. J. T. Rutt, 4 vols (1828), I, pp. 183–4.
91 *CJ*, VII, p. 535; London Provincial assembly, *An Exhortation to Catechizing* (1655); Z. Crofton, *Catechizing God's Ordinance* (1656). As Patrick Little and David Smith point out, the catechising bill failed only because Cromwell made the sole use of his Protectoral veto: Little and Smith, *Parliament and politics*, pp. 210–11.
92 NA, SP 25/76, fo. 378.
93 NA, SP 18/125, fos 56–7; SP 25/77, fo. 69.
94 K. D. Holfelder, 'Factionalism in the Kirk during the Cromwellian invasion and occupation of Scotland, 1650 to 1660: the protestor–resolutioner controversy' (Ph.D thesis, University of Edinburgh, 1998), pp. 212–23.
95 *Thurloe SP*, V, p. 336; Holfelder, 'Factionalism in the Kirk', pp. 226–8.
96 *Register of the consultations of the ministers of Edinburgh*, ed. W. Stephen, 2 vols (Edinburgh 1921–30), I, p. 232.
97 *Ibid.*, I, pp. 232–9, 276–84.
98 James Sharp, *A true representation of the rise, progress and state of the present divisions of the Church of Scotland* (1657); Baillie, *L&J*, III, p. 354; *Register of the consultations*, I, pp. 292–340.
99 *Register of the consultations*, I, pp. 340–8; II, p. 92.
100 *Ibid.*, I, p. 349.
101 *Ibid.*, II, pp. 114.
102 *Ibid.*, II, p. 112. This had been Sharp's argument before Cromwell: see I, p. 354.
103 *Ibid.*, II, p. 97.
104 *Ibid.*, II, p. 99.
105 Holfelder, 'Factionalism in the Kirk', pp. 236–7.
106 *Register of the consultations*, I, pp. 287–90.
107 Holfelder, 'Factionalism in the Kirk', p. 233.
108 *Register of the consultations*, II, pp. 108–13; NA, SP 18/76, fo. 211. I am grateful to Dr Adam Richardson for pointing out that the calendar misdates this to October 1654 instead of 27 August 1657.
109 Holfelder, 'Factionalism in the Kirk', pp. 241–2.
110 J. Buckroyd, *The life of James Sharp, Archbishop of St Andrews, 1618–1679: a political biography* (Edinburgh, 1987), pp. 39–41.
111 *Register of the consultations*, II, pp. 130–1.
112 *Ibid.*, II, p. 153.
113 *Thurloe SP*, VII, p. 387–8; G. Davies, *The restoration of Charles II 1658–1660* (San Marino, CA, 1955), p. 20; Abernathy, 'The English presbyterians', p. 22.
114 *CJ*, VII, pp. 594–5; *The diary of Thomas Burton*, III, pp. 12, 67; *The*

correspondence of Henry Cromwell 1655–1659, ed. P. Gaunt (Cambridge, 2007), pp. 449–50.
115 Davies, *The restoration of Charles II*, pp. 25–7; T. Barnard, *Cromwellian Ireland: English government and reform in Ireland, 1649–1660* (Oxford, 1975), pp. 128–9.
116 *The publick intelligencer*, no. 148 (18–25 October 1658), pp. 914–15; *Mercurius politicus*, no. 438 (14–21 October 1658), p. 923; 'Memoirs of the life of Dr Owen' in John Owen, *A complete collection of the sermons of the reverend and learned John Owen*, ed. J. Asty (1721), pp. xxi–xxii.
117 *Register of the consultations*, II, pp. 157–8.
118 *A Declaration of the faith and order […] practised in the congregational churches in England* (1659), sigs B1v–B2v.
119 J. Halcomb, 'A social history of congregational religious practice during the puritan revolution' (Ph.D. thesis, University of Cambridge, 2010), pp. 236–8.
120 B. Reay, *The quakers and the English revolution* (1985), ch. 5; J. W. Packer, *The transformation of Anglicanism 1643–1660* (Manchester, 1969), ch. 5.
121 *CCRB*, I, pp. 378–9. The ministers behind this letter were Calamy, Jenkyn, Ashe, Cooper, Wickins, Poole and Thomas Whitfield. However, Poole appears to have been the organising mind behind it.
122 [Matthew Newcomen], *Irenicum, or, an essay towards brotherly peace and union* (1659).
123 *Ibid.*, sig. A2v, pp. 63, 73.
124 Samuel Clarke, *Golden apples* (1659), pp. 16–35.
125 *Diary of Thomas Burton*, IV, p. 402; *Register of the consultations*, II, pp. 164, 171.
126 *Diary of Thomas Burton*, IV, p. 336; *A declaration of the Lord Protector […] for a day of solemn fasting […] the eighteenth day of May 1659*; *Register of the consultations*, II, pp. 164, 168; A. Woolrych, 'The good old cause and the fall of the Protectorate', *Cambridge Historical Journal*, 13:2 (1957), p. 148.
127 *Register of the consultations*, II, pp. 171–2.

11

The Restoration, 1659–60

The fall of Richard Cromwell's Protectorate threw the London presbyterians once again into turmoil. With the general fear of the Army and the sects prevalent throughout the nation, the London presbyterians re-entered the political stage in a manner not seen since 1648. Recent historians of the Restoration have noted, as Tim Harris comments, that 'much of the pro-Restoration sentiment' from late 1659 'was presbyterian in tone'.[1] This chapter explores the London presbyterians and the politics of the restoration of the Stuart monarchy. It examines how they sought to negotiate the re-establishment of order in the English church out of the chaos of the immediate post-Cromwellian period. This ultimately led the presbyterians to make the compromises that would be fatal to both presbyterianism and the reformation of English church order begun in 1640.

The 'good old cause': May 1659–January 1660

The fall of Richard Cromwell's Protectorate began the process that unravelled the London presbyterians' hopes that they could achieve a lasting settlement under republican rule. The Army was again perceived as an illegal clique illegitimately interfering in the political sphere.[2] The removal of Richard and his Parliament all but shattered the willingness of city presbyterians, both lay and clerical, to work with the rapid succession of post-Protectorate regimes.[3] The mayoralty of John Ireton, a member of George Cockayne's gathered church, and the imposition of a militia committee dominated by separatists such as Praisegod Barbon and William Kiffin led many in the city to the fear that a sectary take-over of London government was afoot.[4] In addition, the perception that the Army grandees had been encouraged by John Owen to pull down Richard's Protectorate created an air of distrust of those congregationalists connected with the Army's leadership.[5]

The disdain that London's presbyterians felt for the removal of Richard's Protectorate, however, did not lead them to immediately espouse an outright restoration of the Stuart monarchy. Viscount Mordaunt, Charles's liaison with English presbyterians, appears not to have had direct talks with any of the London presbyterian ministers in 1659, although he was talking to close patrons of the ministers, such as the Earl of Manchester.[6] Booth's uprising in August, while supported by some north-western presbyterian clergy, received a mixed response from the London ministry, despite reports that Booth was 'inflamed with zeal for presbyterianism'.[7] While some ministers who had strong Cheshire connections, such as Zachary Crofton, supported Booth's uprising from the pulpit, letters from the exiled presbyterian-royalist alderman James Bunce to leading city ministers such as Calamy, Nalton and Cawton inciting them to publish support for Booth garnered no response.[8] The Venetian ambassador believed this circumspection was attributable to Lord Mayor Ireton's discovery on 9 August of a common council petition for a free Parliament. As a result of this information Ireton began close co-ordination with the council of state to prevent insurrection in the city.[9] The French ambassador, however, thought that the London ministers' ambivalence to Booth's uprising was due to their being involved in seeking an accommodation with other Reformed protestants for a settlement of religion.[10] On 6 September Edmund Calamy, Lazarus Seaman, Edward Reynolds, William Jenkyn and Thomas Jacombe participated in the first of a series of meetings with leading London congregationalists and baptists. The aim of these meetings was to find reconciliation and co-operation against the quakers and, more positively, agreement on church ordinances. The French and Venetian ambassadors may both have been correct about presbyterian intentions. Gary de Krey and Blair Worden have argued that the call for a free Parliament and accommodation between Reformed protestants owed more to a continuation of the presbyterian strategy pursued under Richard's short-lived Protectorate than the adoption of royalism.[11]

The September meetings, however, betray signs of the beginnings of presbyterian division over the extent to which they were willing to compromise on the national church and the cause of further reformation. Lazarus Seaman appears to have gone out on a limb in calling for Calvinistic proponents of believer's baptism to be included within the unity talks, a step with which other presbyterian ministers were uncomfortable.[12] In his letter of 26 August, Bunce identified William Jenkyn as one who had 'apostatised' from the king's cause.[13] According to Richard Baxter, Seaman and Jenkyn would emerge in 1660 as the leaders of a 'party' within London presbyterianism that 'meddled not' with court negotiations for reconciliation with episcopalians.[14]

The willingness of Lord Mayor Ireton and the restored Rump to interfere with the common council's right to petition triggered a mobilisation of the presbyterian laity in favour of the city's rights. Citizens' anger was compounded in September when the restored Rump attempted to force the city to accept Ireton for a second term as Lord Mayor. This was construed by many as violation of London's independence, and in the event the moderate Thomas Alleyn was elected as Lord Mayor.[15] General John Lambert's ejection of the Rump on 13 October and the placement of political and religious Independents such Henry Brandreth, Robert Tichbourne and John Ireton on the Army's council of safety further sealed the resolve of presbyterians against military rule.[16]

The stirring of George Monck into this political mix, however, provided the catalyst for the city to oppose the Army's haphazard command of politics. The chaos in London between November and December 1659 led the city's presbyterians to the conclusion that national government had effectively dissolved.[17] This sense of anarchy was compounded by street battles between apprentices and soldiers after protesting apprentices were killed by Colonel Hewson's troops on 5 December.[18] The chaos of December 1659 led the city to appoint its own committee of safety under the presbyterian Thomas Chamberlain and the royalist John Robinson.[19] The city-appointed committee symbolised an emerging presbyterian-royalist *détente* in London politics, which was subsequently confirmed by the common council elections on 21 December. This saw the return of a substantial body of 'Covenant-engaged' presbyterians, as well as a powerful bloc of royalists.[20] Around 10 per cent of the membership of the December 1659 common council had served as ruling elder delegates to the London Provincial assembly.[21] The effect of the 1659 election was a purge of republican and sectary elements from the city's committees and, in many respects, a resumption of the politics of 1648. The city's main demand was for a free Parliament, opposing the Army's approach of again restoring the Rump.[22] According to the French ambassador, many presbyterians were moving, albeit with some trepidation, towards considering a restoration of Charles Stuart on the terms of the treaty of Newport.[23]

General Monck and the restoration of the Long Parliament

On 4 January the common council renewed its demand for the election of a free Parliament, and the end of the Rump and military rule.[24] Valentine Fyge, the 1640s presbyterian activist, ruling elder of St Bride, Fleet Street and one of the city's newly elected common councillors, told Samuel Pepys on 5 January that the common council was 'resolved to shake off the soldier; and that unless there be a free parliament chosen, he doth believe there are half the common council will not levy any money by order of this parliament'.[25] By the second week of January this sentiment had led to open conflict. On 12 January, Sir Arthur Hesilrig threatened the city with the loss of its charter for its voting on 4 January in favour of a free Parliament. This move only served to alienate the city further.[26] Fyge informed Pepys that the common council had 'resolved to make no more applications to the Parliament, nor to pay any money, unless the secluded members be brought in or a free parliament chosen'.[27] The activity of the common council was as much a continuation of pre-1648 'presbyterian' parliamentarianism as the emergence of a new royalism.[28] A London broadsheet of 12 January called on the Rump to observe the Solemn League and Covenant, restore the members secluded by Pride's purge, establish presbyterian discipline and to favour the godly party.[29] No mention was made of the restoration of the Stuart monarchy. However, as in 1647–8, some London presbyterians were moving towards such a restoration. For example, the old presbyterian-royalist leaders Major General Richard Browne and John Langham joined a venture with the royalist alderman John Robinson to raise money to bribe London regiments to accept a restoration of Charles Stuart.[30]

With the city and the Rump at loggerheads over the issue of a free Parliament, London's presbyterians cautiously began to look to General George Monck for political resolution. On 19 January the common council extended a vote of thanks to Monck, with Fyge privately expressing the city presbyterians' hopes for Monck to Pepys two days later.[31] On the same day as the city's vote of thanks, a pamphlet was issued calling on the London presbyterian clergy to advise Monck to call for restoring the 'fundamental laws and liberties' and 'true protestant religion' in England.[32] The ministers' request for advice, in the form of a printed *Exhortation*, materialised from the city presbyterian clergy only four days later.[33] This work was signed by sixty-three ministers led by Edward Reynolds, Arthur Jackson, Edmund Calamy and Simeon Ashe. The ministers set out the dangerous state of religion, blaming it on the rise of both overt popery and a 'popish' fifth column to be found within the sects.[34] The exhortation bemoaned the 'unchurching of the nation' and the prejudice against 'all order and discipline in the Church'. These woes were diagnosed as coming from the endless 'pulling down and setting up, setting up and pulling down' of civil government over the past decade.[35] The *Exhortation* included a nondescript call for the healing of divisions among the godly, but made no references to presbyterian government. Its focus was on calling the people to submit to their parish minister and to focus their efforts on family duties, such as catechising, sermon repetition and psalm singing.[36] The *Exhortation* can thus be seen as a tacit, collective admission that the presbyterian experiment in London had come to an end. This left the parochial ministry as the only viable bulwark of Reformed protestant orthodoxy.

The arrival of Monck and his soldiers in the London area on 3 February 1660 and his careful procession to Whitehall along the western borders of the city proper put the inhabitants of the metropolis in turmoil. The Rump had ordered the common council dissolved and had resolved to perpetuate itself through recruiter election. These measures inflamed city presbyterians, who responded by redoubling their demands for a free Parliament.[37] Within hours of Monck's forces occupying London on 9 February with the intention of enforcing Parliament's rule, the general was brought to the realisation that force would not work in reducing the city. His own predilection for the ideals of ministry and magistracy led him to demand that Parliament call immediate elections.[38] Monck's support for London brought with it an alliance with the city presbyterians; Monck and his wife attended presbyterian services in the city on 12 February and on 13 February he declared at Drapers' Hall that he would live and die with the city's government.[39] Monck had summoned the Scottish resolutioner James Sharp to assist him; Sharp entered the city on 13 February to act as a liaison between London and Scotland. He reacquainted himself with his former London allies such as Edmund Calamy, Thomas Manton and William Cooper and this group began to advise Monck on religious policy.[40] They counselled the general to allow the return of the secluded members as 'the only expedient for securing religion, and dashing the designs of both the cavaliers and sectaries'.[41] After some wavering and 'with no small difficulty' Monck was convinced by his advisers to admit the secluded members on 21 February and to restore the city's common council.[42]

The religious policy of the restored Long Parliament

When the Long Parliament was restored on 21 February 1660, the London presbyterians found themselves in the best position to direct a religious settlement since the last months of Richard's Parliament. On 1 March the London ministers presented a list of *Desires of the City ministers* to the restored Parliament. This document asked for action to be taken against papists, the sanctification of the sabbath and the protection of the ministry in the pulpit. In addition, they asked for the now defunct Cromwellian 'triers' to be replaced by a committee of clergy to act as a committee for the 'approbation' of ministers admitted to livings. Finally, the ministers requested that a national assembly of divines be chosen by 'the ministers of the respective counties, with due qualifications' to attend to 'the healing of our sinful and woful divisions'. However, this request was made in the context of a requirement that Parliament 'still own' the Westminster assembly's confession of faith, its catechisms and its form of church government.[43] These demands therefore looked to the terms of ecclesiastical settlement suggested both in 1648 and at the close of Richard's Parliament. The provision of a clergy-selected assembly of divines was seen as a means both to counter the sectarian interest and frustrate the growing sentiment towards returning to the pre-civil war episcopalian Church of England. The ministers' *Desires* also closely followed Monck's speech to Parliament of 21 February, which talked of establishing 'a moderate presbyterian government, with a sufficient liberty for tender consciences'.[44] However, just as Monck expressed in private that he was not 'engaged against bishops', the ministers' *Desires* allowed the proposed assembly of divines a free hand in finding a solution to the issue of the national church.

A number of suggestions for the settling of church polity were being openly discussed. The case for the establishment of a reduced episcopacy as a means of settling the Church of England had been growing since the mid-1650s, particularly since the posthumous publication of James Ussher's *reduction* manuscript in 1656.[45] Henry Hammond had built on Ussher's scholarship to remount a case for the apostolic descent of diocesan episcopacy.[46] The growing confidence of advocates of episcopacy was demonstrated by John Gauden, soon to be appointed bishop of Exeter. Gauden used a sermon before the city on 28 February 1660 to preach against presbyterian polity, although he offered the olive branch of episcopacy 'joined with presbytery' in consolation.[47] In light of the chaos of the later 1650s many presbyterians were becoming tempted by reduced episcopacy as a means of retaining something of the presbyterian system in a stable national church. In autumn 1656 Gauden had been in discussion with presbyterians in London and Essex to find an accommodation with godly episcopalians. Although it is unclear who was present at these discussions, the meeting had led to tentative agreement that Ussher's reduced episcopacy could form the basis of future unity.[48] Nevertheless, Gauden's presbyterian counterparts had advised that the title 'bishop' should be eschewed in favour of 'president'.[49] Richard Baxter did much to clear the way for the acceptance of reduced episcopacy among presbyterians. In the first of his *Five disputations on church government*, published in March 1659, Baxter abandoned one of the distinctive features of the Westminster assembly's presbyterian position, the so-called 'third proposition' that 'many particular congregations may be under one presbyterial government'. Baxter argued that in the immediate post-apostolic church, each church, of a size equivalent to a larger seventeenth-century parish, was governed by a single 'bishop'. In cities, this 'bishop' was joined by 'presbyter' assistants, just as rectors in large country parishes in England had curates to take care of their chapelries. In making these arguments, Baxter was seeking not only to dismantle the Westminster assembly's presbyterianism, but also to counter the position advanced by episcopalian thinkers such as Hammond, who saw the ancient bishops described by Ignatius of Antioch as the foundation of future diocesan episcopacy.[50] Baxter's arguments were increasingly persuasive among many presbyterians, as can be seen from the later words of the minister John Howe, who said that his ordination in the early 1650s by Charles Herle and his curates at Winwick was an example of the 'scriptural bishop' acting with the 'presbytery of which the Apostle speaks'.[51]

The appeal of moderate episcopacy in 1659 and early 1660, however, can be overstressed. Other presbyterian works from the same period, for example Newcomen's *Irenicum* or Clarke's *Golden apples*, were still looking to accommodate presbyterianism with congregationalism. The Manchester classis's *Censures of the Church*, published in May 1659, opposed the institution of Ussher's moderate episcopacy and defended the Westminster assembly's presbyterianism.[52] In March 1660 James Sharp reported that many of the leading London ministers were still opposed to reduced episcopacy.[53] The London ministers' *Desires* can be seen, therefore, as a final push for a presbyterian settlement. The *Desires* formed the basis of the Long Parliament's spurt of religious legislation in the first two weeks of March 1660. Edward Harley's committee for religion proposed measures to establish a classical presbyterian church system with sufficient latitude for tender consciences. The Solemn League and Covenant was ordered to be reprinted, placed and read in churches.[54] The Westminster assembly's confession of faith, which, like the version approved by the Long Parliament in August 1648, was shorn of its clericalist chapters on church censures and synods, was finally voted as the national confession of faith in England and Wales.[55] Harley's committee appointed leading London presbyterian clergy to do much of the leg work for this legislation, such as bringing the Westminster confession to the press or acting on the new committee for the approbation of ministers.[56] However, given the absence of any measures to put pressure on the restored Long Parliament's successor (such as the clerical assembly proposed by the ministers' *Desires*), the Parliament's enactment of its religious legislation was at best indicative, and ultimately pure tokenism. As a result, the presbyterian ministers, led by Calamy, considered drafting a petition for the Long Parliament to continue sitting. The presbyterians feared that if Parliament dissolved, old parliamentarians would lose the ability to direct a negotiated settlement with the king on the terms of the 1648 Newport treaty, including the church settlement passed in 1660.[57] On 11 March, Monck took steps to neutralise the London ministers' petition, meeting Calamy, Ashe and Sharp privately in his coach. According to Sharp, the presbyterian ministers convinced Monck that the continuation of 'a Commonwealth', which he had publicly declared for before the Army only four days before, 'was impracticable'. However, the ministers urged on Monck that the presbyterian interest was reliant on 'keeping up this House, and settling the government' with Charles Stuart 'on terms'. Playing on the ministers' fears, Monck insisted on the dissolution of the Long Parliament, stating that his political credibility rested on it. In addition, Monck warned, the threat from another republican insurrection would remain until a free Parliament was elected. Consequently, Calamy and Ashe left the meeting after Monck had satisfied them 'of the necessity of dissolving this house, and calling a new parliament'.[58]

Calamy's and Ashe's advice to Monck that the continuation of a republic had become 'impracticable' raises the question when the London presbyterians began to actively consider a Stuart Restoration. As has been seen, the London presbyterians had always been monarchists, albeit holding to a constitutionally limited kingship circumscribed by Parliament and the Covenant. Nevertheless, the ministers' acquiescence in Oliver Cromwell's administration and their deeper support for Richard indicates that, all things being equal, the ministers had come to terms with the Protectorate. In addition, there remained a good deal of ambivalence among presbyterians about the restoration of Charles Stuart. Both lay and clerical presbyterians were eager to preserve the parliamentarian programme encapsulated in the Newport treaty. Simeon Ashe declared this view in his October 1658 funeral sermon for the Countess of Manchester. The 'true ends' of the civil war, Ashe stated, were set out in the Solemn League and Covenant. The war had been fought to 'restore peace, preserve religion, establish fundamental lawes, and secure the ancient privileges of Parliament' against a king 'misguided by evil councellors'.[59] James Bunce, the presbyterian-royalist alderman, declared very much the same sentiments in his homecoming speech of March 1660. His support for Parliament in the 1640s was, he said, 'for the maintaining, not the infringing' of the 'privileges of parliament' and for 'the moderation of a kingly government' according to the Solemn League and Covenant.[60] Many London presbyterians were far from enamoured with reports of Charles Stuart's loose morals and his leanings towards Roman Catholicism. This aversion to Charles was only confirmed further by his apparent disregard for the Covenant.[61] More serious than problems with Charles personally, however, was the presbyterian fear that the restoration of the Stuart monarchy would mean that they would have to accept the return of old royalist and episcopalian interests to positions of power.

Such a step was a difficult one to accept for many London presbyterians. Zachary Crofton complained in December 1659 that 'authority, like a tennis ball, hath been cast up and down for him to catch that catch can' so that 'revolution is the constant attendant on usurpation'. For Crofton, a restoration on the terms of the treaty of Newport and the Solemn League and Covenant was the best means to break the cycle of disorder that had consumed English politics.[62] Likewise, in February 1660 Edmund Calamy expressed the view that he was 'weary of the late charges, and willing to close with the royal party, or at least not averse to them'.[63] This willingness to find an understanding with outright royalists was commented on by John Milton in his February 1660 *Readie and easie way to establish a free commonwealth*. Milton warned the 'new royaliz'd presbyterians' that their support for Parliament in the civil war would not be forgotten by a restored monarchy.[64] Such fear helped drive the internal 'great contests' reported by John Robinson in March 1660 as taking place between London presbyterian ministers for and against a return of the Stuart monarchy.[65]

Presbyterian fears that their hope for an 'Isle of Wight' settlement was under threat were heightened by the new-found royalist exuberance of the spring of 1660 and the growing royalism of the country.[66] Alderman Robinson noted that the 'extravagant discourses' of pro-episcopalian preachers such as Matthew Griffith, George Masterson and Thomas Pierce were doing 'much harm' to the strategy of enticing presbyterians to accept a return of the Stuart monarchy.[67] Charles Stuart's declaration of Breda, made on 4 April, can therefore be seen partly as a response to calm the fears of former parliamentarians, especially those religious presbyterians near to Monck.[68] The issuing of the declaration was preceded by the Calvinist conformist clergyman George Morley's arrival in London as Edward Hyde's agent in church matters. Morley's aims were to silence those episcopalian preachers who were damaging the king's position in London, and to attempt to win over 'the more moderate presbyterian clergy' who were willing to submit to episcopacy.[69]

The presbyterian ministers' ability to bargain was complicated by the position of their political patrons, many of whom were looking to secure the political aims of the old parliamentarian cause ahead of its religious demands.[70] Since June 1659, the Earl of Manchester and other political presbyterians had been negotiating with Viscount Mordaunt for a Stuart restoration based on the terms of the 1648 treaty of Newport.[71] On the other hand Sir Edward Hyde and his circle were determined that any restoration would be on the king's terms alone.[72] As David Underdown noted, the political presbyterian group was not united to the extent necessary to drive a hard bargain against Hyde's resolve. The growing royalist tide in England after the dissolution of the Long Parliament, especially in the country, made such negotiations more difficult for the presbyterian politicians.[73] This inevitably meant abandoning whatever commitment to a presbyterian church settlement they formerly had in order to focus on preserving their constitutional demands. By the second week of April 1660,

Manchester had promised Morley that 'he will serve the king by disposing the presbyterians to admit of episcopacy'.[74]

In addition to the flagging resolve and diminishing political capital of the presbyterian politicians, many of the city's lay presbyterians were caught up with the presbyterian-royalist leadership who had long sought a restoration of the Stuart line based on trust rather than terms. On 27 March, a meeting of the city's common hall returned the presbyterian-royalists Richard Browne and William Vincent (a nephew of John Langham, who himself was returned for Southwark), together with the city's Recorder William Wilde and John Robinson as London MPs for the convention Parliament. The return from exile of James Bunce, Langham's brother-in-law, who had fled to the royal court in 1648, provided a further powerful voice to those lay presbyterians who sought an unconditional restoration of the Stuart monarchy. Bunce made it clear that he was for a presbyterian accommodation with episcopacy and a 'restauration' of Charles Stuart 'without infringing the royal prerogative'.[75]

In light of the absence of any viable political support for a presbyterian church settlement after the dissolution of the Long Parliament, the London religious presbyterian leadership were forced to seek an accommodation with Charles' episcopalian agents. An initial meeting took place with George Morley around 19 March. By 27 March Sharp reported that he was receiving overtures for further meetings. However, he was shy of such a meeting, as he perceived its purpose was for the episcopalians to cut a deal with the Scottish presbyterians in order to divide the Scots from their English brethren.[76] Such a threat led the London ministers to seek the counsels of Lauderdale and Sharp as to the position that both English and Scottish presbyterians should take. Lauderdale met the London ministers on 23 March and a further meeting occurred on 5 April. It was agreed that the Scottish and English presbyterians would push for the king 'to be restored on Covenant terms'. The main purpose of this meeting, however, appears to have been to convince those presbyterian ministers who were wavering over, or opposed to, the restoration of the monarchy that the time had come to unite behind it. Lauderdale's arguments were probably similar to those he raised with Baxter in correspondence on 31 March, when he argued that any sense of loyalty to the 1650s regimes, particularly to Richard Cromwell, was overridden by the prior obligations to Charles I and his heirs. Given the struggle ahead, Lauderdale and Sharp advised the London presbyterians to meet amongst themselves and resolve 'on the terms they would stick to' in their negotiations with the episcopalians.[77]

This advice reveals that the London ministers were divided on the issue of what form of church government to bargain for in a Stuart restoration. Although the London presbyterians were reported by Sharp and Morley as being 'resolved to stick to their principles' and 'very high in their demands' in the first week of April, by the following week divisions had become apparent in the search for accommodation.[78] The royalist churchman John Barwick's analysis of this shift in position was that the ministers recognised from the Parliamentary elections that their interest was 'so faint' that they needed to compromise.[79] How far the former ministers of the Province of London were willing to surrender the essentials of presbyterianism, however, is debatable. Although Edward Reynolds appeared to accept the restoration of diocesan episcopacy, albeit with legal safeguards against abuse, Edmund Calamy and others would only go so far as to accept the outlines of a reduced, presidential episcopacy.[80]

The opening of negotiations with Morley coincided with the arrival of Richard Baxter in London on 13 April at the invitation of Lauderdale, who hoped to talk Baxter into being 'the great instrument of union'.[81] Baxter's time in London was inauspicious from the start: he immediately fell out with Morley. A general meeting arranged on 25 April to discuss the nature of the restoration of episcopacy was poorly attended, with only Baxter, John Gauden, Nicholas Bernard and Thomas Manton showing up, so that 'little was done but only desires of concord expressed'.[82] By the first few days of the convention Parliament, the London presbyterian ministers found that their leading political allies had all but deserted them on the issue of the religious settlement. This made accommodation a necessity and caused the presbyterians to shift towards a policy of reconciliation with episcopacy.[83] With the loss of hope for the survival of the bulk of the presbyterian system after the dissolution of the Long Parliament, the city ministers began to look at strategies to preserve what they could of the 1640s reformation within an episcopal settlement.

The convention Parliament and the Worcester House Declaration

The London presbyterians' turn towards accommodation with the returning episcopalians was spurred on by the poor showing and tactical blunders that plagued presbyterians in the elections for the convention Parliament. The restored Long Parliament's legislative safeguards to return old parliamentarians to seats in the convention failed dismally.[84] Attempts by peers led by Manchester to control the House of Lords were equally foiled. Such was the reaction against former parliamentarian candidates that Lord Wharton, seeking to make common cause between presbyterians and Independents, could only make a generous list of 124 MPs in the convention who might be called upon to support presbyterian and Independent measures.[85] Further, those members of Parliament who can definitely be associated with old parliamentarian or Reformed protestant positions were still divided by the mutual sense of betrayal echoing from the interregnum.[86] A similar pattern can be discerned among the clergy. While ministers such as Thomas Case looked to make common cause with Lord Wharton and other Independents, many presbyterians stood aloof from any such alliance; a position reciprocated by many congregationalists.[87] The distance between presbyterians and Independents only grew greater following John Lambert's attempted insurrection after his escape from the Tower of London on 10 April.[88]

In any event, the mood of the country electorate had turned, to use Robert Beddard's phrase, 'violently Anglican'.[89] The campaign issuing from the presbyterian pulpits proved ineffective at preventing a majority of cavalier-Anglican candidates from being elected.[90] This opposition to presbyterian sermons was replicated in Parliament itself, with more than sixty members opposing the nomination of Calamy and Baxter to preach at the day of humiliation on 30 April. John Gauden, on the other hand, was nominated without question.[91] Gauden's sermon focused on Parliament satisfying the need for justice and he advised the members to single out the ringleaders of the revolutionary period for punishment, but to show mercy to lesser men who showed genuine repentance.[92] Baxter counselled MPs to look to their own individual iniquities over the previous twenty years and to humble themselves by personal repentance before seeking to punish the sins of others. He advocated that MPs should show charity to those of differing judgements and focus on the continuing need for reformation by establishing parish discipline.[93] Calamy, whose sermon was not published and exists only in manuscript, preached the doctrine that moderation 'is the very marrow and spirit of church and state'. He counselled Parliament to act in a spirit of forgiveness and not seek vengeance: 'let this day make an act of oblivion, and bury all odious expressions and names of reproach in the grave of forgetfulness'. In matters of religion, Calamy preached for Parliament to show a temperate attitude to those protestants holding to the same fundamentals. He advocated that English protestants should 'accommodate and beare with one another'. Calamy advised Parliament to first establish doctrinal agreement before turning to matters of church government, warning that 'if your settlement bring in persecution of the godly, God will never bless it'.[94]

As we have seen, the declaration of Breda of 4 April, read in the House of Commons and the London common council on 1 May, was designed to ease presbyterian concerns at the danger of a *revanchiste* restoration of the house of Stuart. It had the effect of disarming any residual parliamentarian militancy in the common council, which expressed the city's thanks to Charles by sending a delegation of presbyterian-royalist-leaning citizens to The Hague.⁹⁵ Charles's general offer of liberty of conscience, however, was more than the presbyterian ministry were willing to accept, potentially offering toleration to Roman Catholics. The king's failure to promise a synod of divines also proved less than what ministers had hoped for.⁹⁶

Taking advantage of the declaration, George Morley continued his ministerial conferences to reduce London's presbyterians into conforming to an episcopalian Church of England. By 4 May it was becoming clear that the presbyterians would struggle to preserve any aspects of the 1640s reformation. After meeting with 'the chief of the presbyterian ministers', Morley was confident that the presbyterians would 'be persuaded to admit of, and submit to episcopal government, and to the practice of the liturgy in public'. The real issue, Morley perceived, would be requiring those ordained by presbyterian classes to be reordained by a bishop.⁹⁷ His conference was discussed by the London ministers on 7 May 'in a general assembly' at Sion College.⁹⁸ It was agreed that a delegation of the most prominent presbyterian ministers would travel to the Netherlands to thank Charles and to seek a general synod of the three kingdoms to settle the church.⁹⁹

The presbyterian ministers, however, remained divided on issues of church government. The majority appear to have accepted that if parish discipline and a degree of conciliar church government was to survive, it would need to be integrated into a restored episcopacy. The model for this integration was James Ussher's reduction scheme, which had been recently touted by both Baxter and John Gauden.¹⁰⁰ Following the Sion College meeting, Morley met the presbyterian leadership again on 9 May, where he convinced Calamy and Reynolds to agree to comply with episcopacy and the liturgy.¹⁰¹ The presbyterian delegation at Breda declared that the London presbyterians were 'no enemies to moderate episcopacy', although they also stressed their obligation to the Solemn League and Covenant. Despite a cordial welcome from Charles, the delegation was 'much unsatisfied' when Charles vented 'some warmth' after they suggested he discontinue the use of Book of Common Prayer in his private chapel.¹⁰² Nevertheless, after Charles's return to England, he continued the show of cordiality that he had shown to the presbyterian ministers at Breda. On 20 May he met the ministers at St Paul's Cathedral and accepted a bible from Arthur Jackson. By late June ten presbyterians, including Calamy, Manton, Reynolds, Ashe, Bates and Case, were sworn in as royal chaplains by the Earl of Manchester.¹⁰³ Baxter would later complain that these were token appointments, with only Calamy, Reynolds and Baxter preaching before the king. Calamy, who preached once to Charles, is said to have ultimately refused to perform his services as a royal chaplain in order to avoid reading the Book of Common Prayer in surplice and tippet.¹⁰⁴

By mid-June the king offered the ministers a 'conference for agreement' through Lord Broghill and the Earl of Manchester. This led to an informal meeting at Manchester's lodgings. Charles declared that he hoped the presbyterians and episcopalians could find an accommodation by 'meeting in the mid-way' and asked for a written platform from the presbyterians to begin negotiations.[105] These moves towards accommodation, however, were deeply unpopular with some of the presbyterian clergy. According to Sharp 'the presbyterian cause [was] wholly given up and lost' in England and he considered the presbyterian concessions 'destructive to' Scottish interests.[106] He noted that the English presbyterian leadership had calculated that they could not secure presbyterian government in a synod of divines and thus had no option but to accept Morley's position.[107] This meant returning to an agenda similar to the ideas broached before the Williams committee in the spring of 1641. Sharp believed that the London presbyterian leaders feared that if they did not accept episcopacy either 'open profanity' or 'Erastianism' would be the rule in the Church of England.[108] Zachary Crofton also noted the difficult compromises reached, commenting that the presbyterian leadership 'professed in private debates with their brethren another judgment of the Covenant and episcopacy than what is now reported of them'.[109]

That the abandonment of presbyterianism was a realisation of the ministers' limited room for manoeuvre is confirmed in a letter from Calamy, Ashe and Manton to the Edinburgh ministers of 10 August. The London presbyterian leaders observed that 'the general stream and current is for the old prelacy in all its pomp and height, and therefore it cannot be hoped for that the presbyterial government should be owned as the public establishment of this nation'. Faced with the choice of a 'bare toleration' which, they feared, would allow 'papists and sectaries' to multiply undisturbed, the only course likely 'to secure religion' was 'by making presbytery a part of the public establishment'. This could 'not be effected but by moderating and reducing episcopacy to the form of synodical government, and a mutual condescendency of both parties in some lesser things'. The ministers advised the Scots that such a strategy had been adopted because it 'is all we can for the present hope for; and if we could obtain it, we should account it a mercy'. In conclusion, they pleaded with the Edinburgh ministers not to consider their decision a betrayal 'from our principles, or apostacy from the Covenant' but to realise that expediency required compromise in order to preserve what aspects of presbyterian church government were possible within a restored episcopal Church of England.[110]

Sharp felt that the London presbyterian leadership had given too much away to Morley and predicted that 'matters ecclesiastick in England will be reduced to their former state'. This feeling was evidently shared by some of the presbyterian ministers meeting at Sion College. In early June the majority of them voted to send a petition to the common council and Parliament 'to put the king in mind of the Covenant' on the point of religion. This petition was apparently timed to coincide with a similar petition from presbyterian ministers in the northern counties. Both petitions faltered when Edward Reynolds refused to sign and the London petition was blocked in the common council after the rumour was spread that it was influenced by Scottish covenanters seeking to disrupt the Restoration.[111] Crofton put the failure of the petition down to the 'overprudent cowardice of some' as well as the 'state strategems and court complement' of others.[112] The Sion College dissidents also perceived that, by agreeing to put their position in writing, the presbyterian leadership had fallen into the trap of giving their bottom line away too soon.[113]

The growing discontent within Sion College over the presbyterian leadership's concessions was heightened by the perception that the cause of the Solemn League and Covenant was under attack.[114] In June, John Gauden provoked a presbyterian reaction by publishing a letter of advice to Lawrence Bromfield, a 1640s presbyterian activist, attacking the Covenant and arguing for the full restoration of episcopacy.[115] This elicited popular and vitriolic responses from some presbyterians, arguing that the Covenant still remained a national obligation.[116]

Despite the misgivings of some presbyterians about putting together a written platform, the presbyterian position statement was drawn up by Calamy and Reynolds, with assistance from Baxter and Edward Worth, later bishop of Killaloe.[117] It was proposed that the Book of Common Prayer should be revised by a cross-party committee and that certain ceremonies, such as kneeling during the sacrament of the Lord's supper, should be left to the individual conscience as things indifferent.[118] The parish minister was to be 'learned, orthodox and godly', was to preach, catechise and to have power to exclude 'such as are insufficient, negligent or scandalous' from the Lord's supper. Only those who showed a competent knowledge of the Christian faith were to be confirmed by the bishop, and such confirmation was only to be administered with the approval of the parish minister.[119] In matters of ecclesiastical polity, the presbyterian paper stressed that the bishop was merely a president lacking any sole right of ordination and jurisdiction and was required to act with the advice of presbyters. The *Proposals* required that there should be a bishop joined with a presbytery in every town or city 'as a fit means to avoid corruptions, partiality, tyranny and other evils'. These president-bishops would be elected by the clergy themselves. In essence, the *Proposals* were suggesting that ecclesiastical jurisdiction would be vested in presbyteries, which would act in very much the same way as the presbyterian classis and provincial assemblies had done in the late 1640s and 1650s, albeit with a fixed moderator-bishop. It should be stressed that the *Proposals* were ambivalent in their advocacy of such a 'reduced episcopacy', considering it to be 'the lowest degree of corruption of church-order' from the original New Testament presbyterian pattern.[120]

An example of how these arguments could be made to fit into a more grass-roots presbyterian frame can be seen in the November 1660 pamphlet *Complaints concerning corruptions and grievances in church government*. This pamphlet argued that although the church government of the New Testament had been presbyterian, by 'the latter end of the apostolick age' churches had allowed a presidential bishop who was not 'authoritative', 'being only for order and unity'. This was a permissible practice but it was not 'an apostolick constitution, or divine right'. The pamphlet argued that, even after the emergence of such presidential bishops in the immediately post-apostolic church, the bishop oversaw the congregations of an area no larger than one city.[121]

Unsurprisingly, the bishops rejected the presbyterian ministers' proposals. The bishops criticised the presbyterians' insistence on the election of city bishops by the local presbytery and the demand for a mixed government of bishop and presbyters acting together. Pointing out that, since the reign of Henry VIII, the choice of suffragan bishops had been a prerogative of the king, the bishops attacked the presbyterian view of city presbyteries as 'the government of many', an allusion to the classical language of democracy in mixed government. The bishops declared that 'we cannot but wonder that the [...] government by one single person' should be said to be so 'so liable to corruptions'. Such arguments, alluding to the recent restoration of monarchy, was 'a most dangerous insinuation' that smacked of chaotic republicanism.[122]

Despite the cold rejection of the bishops' reply, on 4 September Charles issued his own draft of a *Declaration* that accorded with his promise to meet the presbyterians half-way. Charles promised that preaching bishops were to be chosen for each diocese and if the size of a diocese proved to be impracticable, he would appoint sufficient suffragan bishops to make episcopacy effective on the ground. Although the bishops would retain the powers of jurisdiction, ordination and confirmation, such acts would be done on the advice of the dean and chapter and on the information of the local minister. In addition, the king would appoint a commission to review the Book of Common Prayer and the ceremonies it contained. In the meantime, ministers who scrupled at using the cross in baptism could refuse to do so, on the condition that any parents who wished for the sign of the cross to be used would be permitted to seek another minister to perform the baptism. Charles's draft *Declaration* therefore rejected the main presbyterian features of Calamy's and Reynold's *Proposals*, while at the same time making concessions to puritan criticism of the Church of England. Upon reading it Calamy, Reynolds and Baxter declared to Hyde that 'it would not serve to heal our differences'.[123]

The king's draft *Declaration* was also accompanied by offers of preferment to the leading presbyterian clergy. Reynolds, Baxter and Calamy were offered bishoprics and deaneries were offered to Thomas Manton, William Bates and the Yorkshire minister Edward Bowles.[124] The offer of preferment clearly proved tempting. Reynolds accepted the offer of the see of Norwich before 9 September.[125] Calamy's grandson, born five years after his grandfather's death, was still repeating in the eighteenth century what must have been an often told family lament that if Calamy had accepted the bishopric of Coventry and Lichfield he could have left his family an endowment worth £20,000.[126] Anthony à Wood thought that the difference between Calamy and Reynolds was the differing ambitions of their respective wives.[127] The clergyman Simon Patrick offered a more political explanation, arguing that the presbyterian leaders were sounding out their brethren as to the terms by which they could accept episcopal preferment and still keep face.[128] Within the presbyterian camp, Matthew Newcomen was horrified at the prospect that his brother-in-law Calamy might accept a bishopric and wrote to Baxter to put pressure on Calamy to refuse the king's offer of Lichfield and Coventry.[129]

With the exception of Reynolds, the presbyterian leadership appear to have resolved to only accept the offers of episcopal preferment if the 4 September *Declaration* was enshrined in law.[130] It should be remembered that the presbyterian leadership had already conceded that episcopacy and the liturgy would form the basis of the Church of England. It is possible that the presbyterians had calculated that they could establish a power base in the Lords by working alongside moderate episcopalian bishops, such as Gauden, and godly lords such as Manchester and Wharton. They would also have the representation of a number of presbyterian and Calvinistic deans in Convocation.[131] They realised, however, that the offer of preferment was part of a divide and rule strategy and, without the *Declaration* having legal force, they would be called upon to enforce conformity against their brethren. On the other hand, if the king's *Declaration* was to become law, the presbyterians could accept the positions offered as a means of enforcing it and protecting the presbyterian compromise.[132] As will be seen below, the *Declaration* failed to pass through Parliament and, coupled with the presbyterian leadership's disunity over the offer of bishoprics and deaneries, the presbyterians' political calculus failed, weakening their bargaining position with the royal administration thereafter.[133]

The presbyterian rejection of the king's offers of preferment would lie in the future, however. The next significant meeting between the presbyterians, the king and the episcopalian clergy took place on 22 October at Hyde's London residence Worcester House. This conference pitted the leading presbyterians against the principal episcopalian divines.[134] The clergy were joined by Charles, Hyde and a group of largely presbyterian politicians.[135] The critical debates at Worcester House were over reordination and the proper status and authority of the bishop. In addition, the issue of the power of the parochial ministry to have some control over local discipline, a basic demand of the presbyterian clergy since 1641, was a pressing concern on the presbyterian side.[136] Accounts of the meeting issuing from presbyterians suggest that Baxter and Calamy entered intemperate debates with Morley and Gunning, although, as Bosher pointed out, the episcopalian account is that the parties 'agreed in all matters, and very suddenly'.[137] It is possible that the negative presbyterian perception of the Worcester House conference was coloured by their internal disagreements about what the nebulous concept of 'primitive episcopacy' meant in practice. The Worcester House conference floundered when Hyde read out a request from Independents desiring the right to worship peacefully. This raised the spectre of toleration for Roman Catholics by royal prerogative. Such a measure was too much for the impolitic Baxter who, despite John Wallis's prudent advice to remain silent and let the bishops lay out their case first, spoke out against the measure. The conference continued to show further division among the presbyterians, with the lay politicians and Simeon Ashe arguing for greater compromise, but Calamy vetoing Baxter's suggestion that a paper should be presented to show the delegates' distance from more 'rigid' presbyterians.[138] Charles, perceiving these internal conflicts, realised that compromise was more likely to be achieved by the senior clergy on both sides. He therefore nominated Calamy, Reynolds, Morley and Henchman to draft an agreed version of the *Declaration*. This committee was to operate under the moderation of the old parliamentarian political presbyterians Arthur Annesley and Denzell Holles.[139]

The final version of the Worcester House Declaration was completed and published on 25 October. It is clear that Calamy and Reynolds, supported by Annesley and Holles, had managed to prevail in inserting basic 'presbyterial' concepts, if not exactly presbyterian demands, into the revision. The final Declaration moved from a vague commitment to considering the appointment of suffragan bishops in 'any diocess [that] shall be thought of too large an extent' to a more direct statement that 'the dioceses, especially some of them, are thought to be of too large an extent'. The king therefore would appoint as many suffragan bishops as would be 'sufficient' to join with local presbyters in the administration of the church. The exercise of episcopal jurisdiction over church censures was envisaged to require the advice and assistance of the presbyters of the diocese, including the minister of the parish to which any particular case related. The local minister's consent was also required before a bishop could confirm a candidate's admission to the Lord's supper. The basis of the local minister's consent was to be the candidate's 'credible profession of their faith' and knowledge of the rudiments of the Christian faith. In order to facilitate the bishop and suffragan bishops being advised by the presbyters of a diocese, Calamy and Reynolds convinced their opposites that the local representatives of the deans and chapters should be joined by an equal number of ministers annually elected by the presbyters of the diocese. These changes to polity therefore represented the minimum aspirations of the presbyterian ministers for the reformation of the Church of England. Although there was no room for ruling elders, if it had been brought into effect the Declaration would have allowed presbyterians to practise their parochial ministry on terms not too dissimilar from the practices of the 1640s and 1650s. This goal was assisted by a degree of latitude in ceremonial conformity, with provisions being added that would allow the Lord's supper to be received while sitting. In addition, the wearing of the surplice would be optional and no minister would be required to take the oath of canonical obedience.[140] The issue of those ordained by presbyterian classes in the 1640s and 1650s was solved by the adoption of the formula of the 1571 Subscription Act allowing clergy ordained within communions other than the episcopalian Church of England to hold ecclesiastical livings upon giving assent and subscription to the Church of England's thirty-nine Articles. Although this statute had originally been aimed at the Elizabethan Roman Catholic clergy, its wording would have allowed presbyterians ordained by a classis to take livings within the Restoration Church of England without the need for episcopal reordination.[141]

Richard Baxter was surprised and 'exceeding glad' when he read the final draft of the Declaration and believed that it was 'such as any sober honest ministers might submit to'.[142] The completed Declaration did not, however, meet with such acclaim from all of the London presbyterian ministers. The presbyterian leadership took the published Worcester House Declaration to their brethren with a view to obtaining a vote of thanks. This garnered immediate protest from Arthur Jackson and Zachary Crofton, who refused to sign the Declaration because its support for prelacy was contrary to the Covenant. In March 1661, in a tract directed against Gauden but also implicitly critical of the direction of presbyterian negotiations for comprehension, Crofton cited the Smectymnuus tracts to argue that episcopacy 'was of humane invention on diabolical occasion, by which the man of sin was made manifest'.[143] Nevertheless, the majority of presbyterians did agree to sign the address, published on 16 November.[144] The address declared that although the Declaration was 'not exactly suited to our judgement', it contained sufficient godly elements to be a basis of compromise. Robert Baillie, from the distant vantage point of Glasgow, believed that the English presbyterian ministers had been 'befooled and bewitched' and now acted like 'fools and knaves'.[145]

With the convention Parliament reconvening on 6 November, Calamy and the London ministers attempted to use their contacts in Parliament to have the revised Declaration made law.[146] As noted above, the aim behind this was to establish the Declaration in law before the king dissolved the convention on 24 December. This would provide the necessary security for the presbyterian clergy to carry on negotiations in the next, undoubtedly more 'Anglican', parliament. Led by William Prynne in the House of Commons, a bill to put the Worcester House Declaration on a statutory footing came to its first reading on 28 November. A successful counter-attack on the bill was mounted by cavalier MPs, who finally defeated it by twenty-six votes, after the Independent MPs joined them on the basis that it did not afford the gathered churches any prospect of toleration.[147] The defeat of the Worcester House bill thus saw the unravelling of the presbyterians' political hand, with Manton and Bates refusing the offer of their deaneries shortly after the bill's failure.[148] As the congregationalist minister William Hooke would tell John Davenport in March 1663, the presbyterians found themselves 'very much hated and reproached by the episcopal party' for their challenge to the national church.[149] With the defeat of the Worcester House bill, the presbyterians faced a restoration of episcopacy without any legal protection for their position and the hard choice between unconscionable conformity or leaving the national church they had struggled to reform.

Conclusion

The last years of England's republican period marked the internal collapse of classical and synodical government in the city. Ironically, the same period led to an up-turn in the fortunes of the London presbyterians, with a Parliamentary presbyterian settlement, complete with the Westminster confession, being a serious contender for the form of church government to be established under Protector Richard and the restored Long Parliament.

Until it became painfully clear that the restored Long Parliament had failed to make adequate provision for a lasting religious settlement, few London presbyterians concerned themselves with the establishment of a compromise with the growing episcopalian mood. This position would change with the realisation that Charles Stuart would be crowned king without any of the conditions agreed with his father at Newport in 1648.

It is possible that Charles Stuart's episcopalian negotiators such as Morley, Mordaunt or Gauden did not think that the re-establishment of episcopacy would be as total and one-sided as it would soon turn out to be. This probably led Calamy and other presbyterians, who yearned for the Church of England to be whole again, to expect that they would be able to retain substantial features of the presbyterian system within the Restoration Church of England. The *Proposals* drafted by Calamy and Reynolds for the Worcester House conference, with their blend of pre-civil war puritanism, 1640s presbyterianism and the Baxterian take on reduced episcopacy, suggest that it was believed that the Restoration Church of England would blend presbytery with episcopacy. Indeed, Charles II certainly encouraged the presbyterians to believe that this was possible.

Yet even these concessions, however much they pandered to the art of the possible, were too much for the presbyterian leadership's episcopalian counterparts. With the failure of the Worcester House Declaration to become enshrined in law, a reaction set in against the presbyterian 'reconcilers' within their own camp, reinvigorating dissident voices against further compromise with episcopacy. The final tribulations of the London presbyterian movement would be ejection and nonconformity, which will be the subject of chapter 12.

Notes

1 T. Harris, 'The bawdy house riots of 1668', *HJ*, 29:3 (1986) 544; G. Southcombe, 'Presbyterians in the Restoration' in *The Oxford history of protestant dissenting traditions*, vol. 1, ed. J. Coffey (Oxford, 2020), p. 74.
2 For these concerns, see [George Thomason], *Six new queries* (1659).
3 De Krey, *London*, pp. 4–5, 9.
4 *Ibid.*, pp. 21–2; G. S. de Krey, 'Ireton, John (created Sir John Ireton under the Protectorate), 1615–1690)', *ODNB*.
5 Edmund Calamy, *An historical account of my own life*, ed. J. T. Rutt, 2 vols (2nd edn, 1830), I, pp. 379–80.
6 Mordaunt, *Letter book*, pp. 21–2.
7 On Booth's uprising see Underdown, *Royalist conspiracy*, ch. 12 and J. S. Morrill, *Cheshire 1630–1660: county government and society during the 'English revolution'* (Oxford, 1974), ch. 8.
8 *Cal. Clarendon SP*, IV, pp. 340, 348; *CSPV, 1659–60*, p. 57; F. Guizot, *History of Richard Cromwell and the restoration of Charles II*, trans. A. R. Scoble, 2 vols (1856), I, p. 450; Abernathy, 'The English presbyterians', p. 31; De Krey, *London*, p. 26.

9 *CSPV, 1659–60*, p. 57; Underdown, *Royalist conspiracy*, pp. 279–80; De Krey, *London*, p. 23.
10 Guizot, *Richard Cromwell*, I, p. 450.
11 *CCRB*, I, pp. 408–9; De Krey, *London*, pp. 24–6; Worden, 'Campaign for a free Parliament', p. 163.
12 *CCRB*, I, p. 413.
13 *Cal Clarendon SP*, IV, p. 340.
14 Baxter, *RB*, II, p. 229.
15 LMA, JCC41, fo. 208; *CJ*, VII, pp. 787–8; Sharpe, *London*, II, pp. 354–5; De Krey, *London*, p. 27.
16 Abernathy, 'The English presbyterians', p. 33; De Krey, *London*, pp. 28–9.
17 Abernathy, 'The English presbyterians', p. 34; De Krey, *London*, pp. 29–34.
18 Sharpe, *London*, II, p. 358.
19 Abernathy, 'The English presbyterians', p. 35; De Krey, *London*, pp. 34–6.
20 D. C. Elliot, 'Elections to the common council of the city of London, 21 December 1659', *Guildhall Studies in London History*, 4:4 (1981), 152–201. For the centrality of the politics of the city in this period, see Worden, 'Campaign for a free Parliament', pp. 164–8.
21 Elliot, 'Elections to the common council', pp. 175–9.
22 Sharpe, *London*, II, pp. 360–61; De Krey, *London*, pp. 38–40.
23 F. Guizot, *Monk: or the fall of the Republic* (1851), pp. 142–5; Worden, 'Campaign for a free Parliament', p. 163.
24 LMA, JCC41, fo. 218r; Sharpe, *London*, II, p. 364.
25 Pepys, *Diary, 1660*, p. 9.
26 B. Worden, 'The demand for a free Parliament, 1659–60', in Southcombe and Tapsell, *Revolutionary England*, pp. 182–3.
27 Pepys, *Diary, 1660*, p. 16; De Krey, *London*; pp. 41–2; Sharpe, *London*, II, pp. 364–5.
28 De Krey, *London*, pp. 43–4; Worden, 'Campaign for a free Parliament', p. 163.
29 [Anon.], *Things just and necessary which the Parliament must do* (1660).
30 Mordaunt, *Letter book*, p. 150n, 163n, 165; Davies, *The restoration of Charles II*, pp. 256–8; Underdown, *Royalist conspiracy*, p. 299.
31 Pepys, *Diary, 1660*, p. 19.
32 [Anon.], *To the reverend, learned and grave divines* (1660).
33 London presbyterian ministers, *A seasonable exhortation of sundry ministers in London* (1660).
34 *Ibid.*, p. 3.
35 *Ibid.*, pp. 5–7.
36 *Ibid.*, pp. 14–20; De Krey, *London*, p. 56.
37 Abernathy, 'The English presbyterians', pp. 38–40; Sharpe, *London*, II, pp. 366–7; Pepys, *Diary, 1660*, p. 47.
38 De Krey, *London*, p. 49.
39 Sharpe, *London*, II, p. 369; De Krey, *London*, p. 57; Pepys, *Diary, 1660*, p. 55.
40 Wodrow, *Sufferings*, I, p. vi.

41 *Ibid.*, pp. vii–viii; De Krey, *London*, p. 52.
42 Wodrow, *Sufferings*, p. vii; Sharp, *London*, II, p. 371; Abernathy, 'The English presbyterians', p. 40.
43 Wodrow, *Sufferings*, p. li.
44 Cited in Bosher, *Restoration*, pp. 101–2.
45 James Ussher, *The reduction of episcopacie unto the form of synodical government* (1656).
46 Henry Hammond, *Dissertationes quatuor quibus episcopatus jura* (1651); J. W. Packer, *The transformation of Anglicanism 1643–1660 with special reference to Henry Hammond* (Manchester, 1969), pp. 108–27.
47 J. Gauden, *Kakourgoi, sive mediacastri: slight healers of publick hurts* (1660) pp. 59–60, 78–9, 105–6; Davies, *The restoration of Charles II*, p. 297; Bosher, *Restoration*, p. 121; Abernathy, 'The English presbyterians', p. 46.
48 *Thurloe SP*, V, pp. 597–601; *Cal Clarendon SP*, III, p. 192.
49 *Thurloe SP*, V, pp. 597–601.
50 R. Baxter, *Five disputations of church-government and worship* (1659), 'The preface', p. 5, 'Disputation 1', pp. 16–17, 80–3, 101.
51 *The whole works of the Rev. John Howe MA with a memoir of the author*, ed. J. Hunt, 8 vols (1822), I, p. vii.
52 The First Classis of the Province of Lancashire, *The censures of the church revived* (1659), pp. 85–101.
53 Wodrow, *Sufferings*, pp. ix–x, Abernathy, 'The English presbyterians', pp. 40–1, 44; Buckroyd, *The life of James Sharp*, pp. 50–2.
54 *CJ*, VII, p. 862; Guizot, *Richard Cromwell*, II, pp. 376–7; Davies, *The restoration of Charles II*, pp. 297–8; Bosher, *Restoration*, pp. 102–3; De Krey, *London*, pp. 57–8.
55 *CJ*, VII, pp. 858, 862; Guizot, *Monk*, p. 188.
56 *CJ*, VII, pp. 862, 867, 897–8; Wodrow, *Sufferings*, p. xii; De Krey, *London*, p. 57.
57 *Cal Clarendon SP*, IV, p. 606; *Nicholas papers*, IV, p. 202; Abernathy, 'The English presbyterians', p. 43 n. 101; De Krey, *London*, p. 59.
58 Wodrow, *Sufferings*, pp. xii–xiii; Baxter, *RB*, I, p. 214; R. Hutton, *The Restoration: a political and religious history of England and Wales, 1658–1667* (Oxford, 1993), p. 102.
59 Simeon Ashe, *The faithfull Christians gain by death* (1659), 'To the Right Honourable Edward, Earl of Manchester', sig. A3.
60 James Bunce, *Alderman Bunce, his speech to the Lord Maior, aldermen and common council of London* (1660), p. 5. For other presbyterian attempts to appropriate the language of the 'good old cause' to the parliamentarianism of 1648, see Worden, 'Campaign for a free parliament', p. 177.
61 'A letter written by a minister in London' in Zachary Crofton, *Berith anti-Baal* (1661), p. 14.
62 Crofton, *Berith anti-Baal*, pp. 5, 9–12.
63 HMC, *Report on the Manuscripts of F. W. Leyborne-Popham, Esq* (1899), p. 221; De Krey, *London*, p. 54.

64 *The complete works of John Milton*, vol. VI *Vernacular regicide and republican writings*, eds N. H. Keeble and N. McDowell (Oxford, 2013), p. 509.
65 HMC, *Calendar MSS Ormonde*, I, pp. 335–6.
66 R. Beddard, 'The Restoration church' in *The restored monarchy 1660–1688*, ed. J. R. Jones (Basingstoke, 1979), pp. 155–75.
67 *State papers, Clarendon*, III, p. 716; Bosher, *Restoration*, p. 108; De Krey, *London*, pp. 62–3.
68 De Krey, *London*, pp. 62–3.
69 *State papers, Clarendon*, III, p. 630; Bosher, *Restoration*, pp. 106–14; Abernathy, 'The English presbyterians', pp. 46–7.
70 Baxter, *RB*, II, p. 229.
71 Mordaunt, *Letter Book*, pp. 81–3, 95–6, 110–11; *State papers, Clarendon*, III, pp. 628–9; Davies, *The restoration of Charles II*, pp. 304–5; Abernathy, 'The English presbyterians', pp. 29, 42; D. R. Lacey, *Dissent and parliamentary politics in England, 1661–1689: a study in the perpetuation and tempering of parliamentarianism* (New Brunswick, NJ, 1969), pp. 7, 308, 321.
72 Bosher, *Restoration*, p. 98.
73 Underdown, *Royalist conspiracy*, pp. 307, 330; De Krey, *London*, pp. 60–1.
74 *State papers, Clarendon*, III, p. 728.
75 Bunce, *Speech*, pp. 2–6. For the excitement generated by Bunce's return see *The Diurnal of Thomas Rugg, 1659–1661*, ed. W. L. Sachse (1961), p. 65.
76 *Cal Clarendon SP*, IV, p. 599; Wodrow, *Sufferings*, p. xv; Abernathy, 'The English presbyterians', p. 44.
77 *Thurloe SP*, VIII, pp. 865–7; Wodrow, *Sufferings*, p. xvii; CCRB, I, pp. 429–30.
78 Wodrow, *Sufferings*, p. xvii; *State papers, Clarendon*, III, p. 722.
79 *State papers, Clarendon*, III, p. 723.
80 Ibid., p. 727; Bosher, *Restoration*, p. 114.
81 CCRB, I, pp. 429–31; Baxter, *RB*, II, p. 215.
82 Baxter, *RB*, II, p. 218.
83 Abernathy, 'The English presbyterians', p. 46.
84 *A&O*, II, p. 1472.
85 Abernathy, 'The English presbyterians', pp. 55–7; Crawford, *Denzil Holles*, pp. 189–90.
86 Abernathy, 'The English presbyterians', p. 60.
87 *Cal Clarendon SP*, IV, p. 639; Bosher, *Restoration*, p. 117.
88 De Krey, *London*, pp. 62–3.
89 Beddard, 'The Restoration church', pp. 156–8, 161–4. See also Abernathy, 'The English presbyterians', p. 52.
90 *State papers, Clarendon*, III, pp. 731–2; Wodrow, *Sufferings*, p. xv.
91 *The diaries and papers of Sir Edward Dering Second Baronet, 1644–1684*, ed. M. F. Bond (1976), p. 35; J. Spurr, *The Restoration Church of England 1646–1689* (New Haven, CT, 1991), p. 32.
92 John Gauden, *Megaleia theou, God's great demonstrations and demands* (1660), pp. 34–5, 39.

93 Richard Baxter, *A sermon of repentance* (1660), pp. 17–19, 42–3.
94 Congregational Library, London, MS II.a.5, fos 164–83 (cited here: fos 170, 177, 179–80, 181, 183). Calamy's sermon ties in with the various discourses of early modern moderation examined by Ethan Shagan in *The rule of moderation: violence, religion and the politics of restraint in early modern England* (Cambridge, 2011).
95 LMA, JCC41, fos 231–2. The delegation included the former Lord Mayors Thomas Adams and Abraham Reynardson, the presbyterian-royalists John Langham, James Bunce and William Vincent, and the presbyterians Thomas Chamberlain and Lawrence Bromfield.
96 Abernathy, 'The English presbyterians', pp. 60–1.
97 *State papers, Clarendon*, III, p. 738; Bosher, *Restoration*, pp. 126–7.
98 LMA, CLC/198/SICA/008/MS33445/00 (Sion College court of governors' minutes, 1631–1716), fo. 204; Wodrow, *Sufferings*, p. xxi. The London ministers' address to Charles Stuart is not recorded, but was possibly the published *A declaration of the presbiterians concerning his majesties royal person* (1660).
99 *CJ*, VIII, p. 20; *LJ*, XI, p. 18. The ministers were Edward Reynolds, William Spurstowe, Edmund Calamy, Thomas Manton, Thomas Case and a 'Mr Hall', possibly George Hall.
100 Gauden, *Slight healers of publick hurts*, pp. 78–9.
101 *State papers, Clarendon*, III pp. 743–4; Bosher, *Restoration*, p. 127; Abernathy, 'The English presbyterians', pp. 57, 64–5; Spurr, *Restoration Church of England*, p. 31.
102 Clarendon, *History of the rebellion*, VI, pp. 231–2.
103 B. Till, 'The Worcester House Declaration and the restoration of the Church of England', *Historical Research*, 70:172 (1997), 204; Rugg, *Diurnal*, p. 92; Baxter, *RB*, II, p. 218.
104 Baxter, *RB*, II, p. 229; HMC, *The manuscripts of S. H. Le Fleming, Esq, of Rydal Hall* (1890), p. 26; Wodrow, *Sufferings*, p. xxxiv.
105 Baxter, *RB*, II, p. 230; Wodrow, *Sufferings*, pp. xxxvii, xli; Till, 'The Worcester House Declaration', pp. 205–6.
106 Wodrow, *Sufferings*, pp. xxviii, xlii.
107 Ibid., p. xxviii.
108 Ibid., p. xxxiv.
109 Crofton, *Berith anti-Baal*, 'To the Reader', sig. B2.
110 Wodrow, *Sufferings*, pp. lxii–lxiii.
111 Ibid., pp. xxxiii–xxxiv; HMC, *le Fleming MSS*, p. 26.
112 Crofton, *Berith anti-Baal*, 'To the Reader', sig. B3.
113 Wodrow, *Sufferings*, p. xlii.
114 Bosher, *Restoration*, pp. 154–5.
115 John Gauden, *Analysis: the loosing of St Peter's bands* (1660).
116 Zachary Crofton, *Analepsis, or St Peter's bond's abide* (1660); Zachary Crofton, *The anatomy of Dr Gauden's idolised non-sense and blasphemy* (1660); William Wickins, *The kingdom's remembrancer* (1660). For this debate see Abernathy, 'The English presbyterians', p. 69; Vallance, *Revolutionary*

England, pp. 180–6; C. Haigh, 'Conscience and conformity: some moral dilemmas in seventeenth-century England', *Journal of Anglican Studies*, 11:1 (2013), 69–70.
117 Baxter, *RB*, II, pp. 232–59.
118 *Ibid.*, pp. 234–6. For the debate on liturgical reform in general see C. Haigh, 'Liturgy and liberty: the controversy over the Book of Common Prayer, 1660–1663', *Journal of Anglican Studies*, 11:1 (2013), 32–64.
119 Baxter, *RB*, II, p. 233.
120 *Ibid.*, pp. 233–4.
121 [Anon.], *Complaints concerning corruptions and grievances in church government* (1660), especially pp. 4–8.
122 Baxter, *RB*, II, p. 243.
123 *Ibid.*, pp. 259–65.
124 Abernathy, 'The English presbyterians', p. 77.
125 NA, SP 29/14, fo. 106.
126 Calamy, *An historical account*, I, p. 55.
127 Anthony à Wood, *Athenae Oxonienses: an exact history of all the writers and bishops who have had their education in the University of Oxford*, ed. P. Bliss, 3 vols. (Oxford, 1691), III, p. 1085.
128 Simon Patrick, *A friendly debate* (1668), p. 111.
129 *CCRB*, II, p. 7; Baxter, *RB*, II, p. 281.
130 Baxter, *RB*, II, pp. 281–2; Calamy, *An historical account*, I, pp. 55–6.
131 Abernathy, 'The English presbyterians', p. 77. Calamy had been on friendly terms with Lord Wharton during the interregnum, and in 1658 requested that Wharton be the sponsor at the baptism of his son. See Bodleian Library, University of Oxford, Ms. Rawl. letters 50, fo. 1.
132 Baxter, *RB*, II, pp. 281–2; Bosher, *Restoration*, p. 194.
133 Reynolds's early acceptance of the see of Norwich and Baxter's rejection of the bishopric of Hereford on 1 November 1660 meant that Calamy's attempt to accept episcopal preferment as a bargaining position was frustrated; see Baxter, *RB*, II, p. 283.
134 The presbyterians present were Reynolds, Calamy, Ashe, Manton, Wallis, Spurstowe and Baxter. The episcopalians were represented by Morley, Gauden, Sheldon, Henchman, Cosin, Barwick, Hacket and Gunning.
135 Monck (now Duke of Albermarle), Manchester, Ormonde, Arthur Annesley and Denzell Holles.
136 Till, 'The Worcester House Declaration', pp. 209–10; Baxter, *RB*, II, p. 278; Haigh, 'Conscience and conformity', p. 71.
137 Bosher, *Restoration*, pp. 186–7.
138 Baxter, *RB*, II, p. 278; Abernathy, 'The English presbyterians', p. 75. Annesley and Holles both appear to have been 'reduced episcopalians' by religious preference.
139 Baxter, *RB*, II, p. 278.
140 *LJ*, XI, pp. 179–82; Baxter, *RB*, II, pp. 259–65.
141 A. H. Wood, *Church unity without uniformity: a study of seventeenth-century*

English church movements and of Richard Baxter's proposals for a comprehensive church (1963), pp. 158–61. Wood provides a table of the differences between the original Worcester House declaration and the final version at pp. 153–7.

142 Baxter, *RB*, II, p. 279.
143 Crofton is often seen as a die-hard 'rigid' presbyterian. However, he was willing accept 'presbyterial episcopacy' on Ussher's model: see Crofton, *Berith anti-Baal*, pp. 12, 14, 18, 21, 26–9; Crofton, *Analepsis*, pp. 2, 6.
144 Baxter, *RB*, II, pp. 284–5; London ministers, *To the Kings most excellent maiesty. The humble and grateful acknowledgement of many ministers of the gospel in and about the City of London* (1660). For a similar declaration from the Lancashire presbyterian ministers see Oliver Heywood, *Oliver Heywood's life of John Angier of Denton*, ed. E. Axon (Manchester, 1937) pp. 24–7.
145 Baillie, *L&J*, III, pp. 414–15.
146 Baxter, *RB*, II, p. 384; Bosher, *Restoration*, p. 195; Till, 'The Worcester House Declaration', pp. 225–6.
147 *CJ*, VIII, pp. 176, 188, 194; Bosher, *Restoration*, p. 196; Abernathy, 'The English presbyterians', p. 78.
148 Matthews, *CR*, pp. xii–xiii; *Memoirs of the Verney Family*, ed. M. M. Verney, 4 vols (1899), IV, p. 7.
149 A. G. Matthews, 'A censored letter. William Hooke in England to John Davenport in New England, 1663', *Congregational History Society Transactions*, 9 (1924–6), 274. This letter is a transcription of NA, SP 29/69, fos 6–9.

12

Epilogue: the Cavalier Parliament, the Great Ejection of 1662 and the first years of dissent

This chapter, which serves as an epilogue to this work, explores the London presbyterians' preparation for a time of persecution after the failure to obtain statutory confirmation of the revised Worcester House Declaration. This proved essential for the presbyterian transition to nonconformity. As one informer in March 1661 put it, the city's presbyterians continued 'to walke in the very same way as they did in the first war', seeking to maintain the puritan style of worship and aiming to reform the doctrine and discipline of the church.[1] Most London presbyterians did not give up hope that reforming the Church of England was still a possibility. Yet, as this prospect became less likely after the election of the Cavalier Parliament, the London presbyterians were forced to confront the choice between submission to the restored church and forming conventicles that met separately if not in separation from the Church of England. These options caused considerable debate but, as will be argued, the majority of ministers and many lay presbyterians maintained their mid-century bonds of fellowship and religion as they organised the foundations of Restoration nonconformity.

'Bang the bishops': the London elections to the Cavalier Parliament

The failure of the Worcester House Declaration to become law indicated to many London presbyterians that the decision to preserve elements of 'Christ's discipline' through a reconciliation with the returning episcopalians had been an improvident course of action. In October, the Convention Parliament made an example of William Drake, the 1640s presbyterian activist and protagonist in Love's plot, for publishing a 'distempered' book arguing that the Long Parliament had not been lawfully dissolved and that it should be revived to complete its work.[2] As well as questioning the legitimacy of the Convention Parliament and thus the legality of the Restoration, Drake's work was seen as particularly scandalous because it deployed the political theory of the co-ordinate power of the three estates.[3] Although

Drake's prosecutors thought that other minds, most probably London presbyterian clerics such as his brother Roger, were behind the publication, this investigation proved inconclusive and Drake's prosecution seems to have been quietly dropped.

The elections for what would become known as the Cavalier Parliament led other London presbyterians to catch the attention of the authorities. Jeremiah Baines, the Southwark brewer, former ruling elder and MP in the first Protectorate Parliament, was reported to have been bound over on 21 March for speaking 'seditious words' in relation to the upcoming elections. Baines's treatment only spurred on Southwark parliamentarians, as the next day he was selected by a meeting of 'three and four score persons of schismatical opinion' to stand in the Southwark election with the former Rump MP Colonel George Thompson. Baines's troubles with the authorities probably explain why he was not ultimately selected as a candidate in the Southwark election, but, in any event, he was replaced by the old London presbyterian grandee Sir John Langham. The attempts to elect Langham (who had sat in the Convention) and Thompson, however, were unsuccessful, allegedly owing to government-orchestrated foul play on the day of the election.[4] Across the Thames, the campaign to elect Reformed protestants for the city, led by the ministers Lazarus Seaman and Zachary Crofton, was a total success.[5] The campaigning of Seaman and Crofton was largely aimed at a public rejection of the Restoration bishops. One correspondent thanked God 'that Mr Crofton is still at liberty; he preaches that bishops are a human institution, and led to the papacy', a theme taken directly out of the 1641 Smectymnuus tracts. Another observer said that Crofton's lectures at St Antholin, Budge Row drew so many listeners that a 2,000-strong crowd gathered in the streets outside the church building to hear Crofton 'bang the bishops, which theme he doth most exquisitely handle'.[6] Crofton's preaching was accompanied by the publication of pamphlets taking aim at the restoration of episcopacy and the liturgy, attacking the compulsory use of the Prayer Book, bowing to the altar and the demand for the reordination of those ministers ordained by presbyterian classes.[7]

During the hustings for the London elections it was reported that large crowds of people gathered crying 'no bishops, no bishops'.[8] When attempts were made to prevent Captain John Jones, the 1640s presbyterian activist and ruling elder, from standing for Parliament, the crowd menacingly cried out 'A Jones! A Jones! till it was otherwise resolved'.[9] Consequently the city elections returned the presbyterians John Fowke, Sir William Thompson and John Jones and the Independent William Love as its representatives. The evidence suggests that the motivation of the electorate rested on dissatisfaction with the course of the Restoration religious settlement. John Jurin, a colonial merchant and presbyterian common councillor in the 1640s, declared that the city's Parliament men had been elected 'to take down the pride of the bishops, who daily entrench on honest, godly ministers'.[10] Another commentator noted that 'all the members are against lawn sleeves and formal worship'.[11] The city election therefore served to increase the sense of partisan politics in the city.

The presbyterian ministers behind the election campaign looked further afield than London, however. The election results led to a letter-writing campaign with correspondence sent to many of the cities and boroughs in the country in order to influence the national general election. Many of the letters were sent to the York minister Edward Bowles, presumably for onward transmission to the northern network of Reformed protestants.[12] Although the campaign was foiled by the government's interception of the letters through the postal service, many of them were from known London presbyterians including the ministers Thomas Vincent of St Mary Magdalen, Milk Street and John Meriton of St Nicholas Acons, as well as from the former ruling elder William Ashhurst.[13] The election campaign demonstrated that the London presbyterians, while accepting the return of monarchy, were still willing to mobilise for many of the same religious issues that had caused them to support Parliament in the early 1640s.

Gilbert Sheldon, the Clarendon Code and the attack on the last vestiges of presbyterian London

The intercepted letters from the March election showed that dissident presbyterian feeling was anti-episcopal rather than anti-monarchical.[14] One cause of this surge of anti-episcopalian sentiment was the campaign of Bishop Gilbert Sheldon to gain control of the diocese of London. In early 1661 Sheldon had begun a series of test cases against popular presbyterian incumbents in the city. Among his primary concerns was to reinstitute the use of the Book of Common Prayer. One of the March letter writers noted that 'there are more churches that have not the reading of the Common Prayer than that have it; but the bishops have sent readers to some, and will do so to all. It is feared they will be too forward in imposing in that way, if the Parliament back them.'[15] In February 1661 a faction of parishioners at St Paul, Covent Garden successfully appealed directly to Sheldon to force Thomas Manton to use the Book of Common Prayer.[16] A similar campaign was conducted against William Bates of St Dunstan-in-the-West and Thomas Jacombe of St Martin, Ludgate in March, although they proved to be less pliant than Manton, pleading 'conscience' and 'the King's Declaration' against Sheldon. Bates sought a partial compromise by ordering 'the psalms, two lessons, ten commandments, and creed to be read', but

Jacombe and his leading parishioners threatened legal action to 'hinder any one from officiating in his church without his leave'.[17] At St Benet, Paul's Wharf, the godly churchwarden Stephen Trigg refused to obey the chancellor's order to prevent the parish's presbyterian minister John Jackson from preaching without the Book of Common Prayer.[18]

One of Sheldon's strategies to quash presbyterian resistance was to constitute select vestries on parishes to control the minister, such as that settled in April 1662 at Bates's parish of St Dunstan-in-the-West.[19] Nevertheless, the imposition may have backfired somewhat, as the select vestry included Alexander Normington and Edward East, both of whom had served as the parish's ruling elders in the late 1650s.[20] In other cases, such as that of William Taylor at St Stephen, Coleman Street, or at St Mildred, Poultry where the presbyterian Thomas Wills had been elected, Sheldon refused to allow the parish its choice of minister, imposing his own candidate.[21] The importance of parishioners in resisting Sheldon, particularly former presbyterian ruling elders, is noteworthy and suggests some of the roots of presbyterian partial conformity during the Restoration.[22] Nevertheless, parishioner resistance was ultimately limited. The vestry was more than just a religious entity and vestry service was an essential part of the demands of active citizenship and social mobility in London. Furthermore, many of the substantial parishioners who had been excluded from or avoided vestry office under the parliamentarian regimes were again able and willing to take office.

In addition to seizing control of the city's parishes, Sheldon also ensured that the diocese was sterilised of presbyterian influence in Convocation. Baxter and Calamy had been chosen to represent the diocese, but Sheldon used a technicality to prevent them from sitting.[23] Of perhaps greater psychological effect was his victory in wrestling control of Sion College from London's presbyterians, who on 7 May conceded defeat to Robert Pory, Sheldon's candidate for president.[24] By the close of 1661 Sheldon had thus managed to capture much of the diocese of London from presbyterian influence.

As a further attempt to undermine the resolve of the presbyterian interest in London and its area, Sheldon advertised swift episcopal reordinations in 1662 for ministers who had been ordained by presbyterian classes.[25] The evidence of reordination from the Clergy of the Church of England database (CCEd) suggests that only about four ministers who had served in the London presbyterian system at the end of the interregnum chose to be reordained between 1660 and 1662, although this figure is perhaps too low, as more of the eleven ministers from this cohort who conformed must have been reordained by August 1662.[26] Those who did accept episcopal reordination had all obtained it by 1661 and had largely chosen to be ordained by Robert Sanderson, the accommodating Calvinist Bishop of Lincoln, or the free-handed Thomas Sydserff, Bishop of Orkney.[27] As Ken Fincham and Stephen Taylor have argued, the offer of episcopal reordination was a national policy designed to reintegrate many would-be presbyterian nonconformists into the restored episcopal church, with a working figure of 25 per cent of presbyterian ordinands taking up the bishops' offer.[28] This policy played on the fact that almost all presbyterians were committed to the idea of a national church and that ejection threatened their livelihood, especially those with families and little personal wealth. That so few within the London presbyterian movement chose to be reordained between 1660 and 1662, compared to ministers outside London, may suggest that pressure from within the presbyterian clerical community acted to cause individuals to resist the episcopalian pressure for reordination.

The *coup de grâce* to London's presbyterianism in the parishes, however, would be given by the Cavalier Parliament. From the first sitting of the Parliament on 8 May, the city's presbyterians were forced into a posture of defence.[29] The London presbyterians had built their political influence on the institutions of Parliament, the city and the parishes. With less than fifty Reformed protestant members in the House of Commons, the godly Lords largely satisfied with offices, the return of the bishops to their seats and Sheldon's campaign to restore episcopal rule in London, the political foundations of religious presbyterian influence had all but eroded away.[30]

The March elections showed that, in their attempt to preserve the Church of England intact, the presbyterian clerical leadership had essentially conceded everything of the presbyterian discipline to the episcopal party. The new Parliament continued the trend set a year before by re-establishing legal uniformity and conformity to the restored Church of England. In the changed environment of 1661, government policy was to offer minor concessions to presbyterians through the use of the royal prerogative.[31] Despite resistance from William Prynne in the Commons on 17 May, the Covenant was ordered to be publicly burned at various sites in the city. This provocative act signalled to London's presbyterians just how far they were required to bend the knee to be comprehended within the restored Church of England.[32] Their sense of defeat was further compounded by the debacle of the Savoy conference on the Book of Common Prayer, which ran from April into the summer.[33] In accord with government policy, the episcopal party, led by Sheldon, were willing to offer concessions on the Prayer Book if the presbyterians could sufficiently prove their objections.[34] The presbyterians' starting point was to set out a catalogue of the historical objections that English puritans had long mounted against the Prayer Book.[35] Perhaps an indication that the presbyterian leadership had already conceded defeat, Richard Baxter was entrusted with most of the debate with the episcopal party.³⁶ This gave Baxter free rein to advance his proposal for a complete and radical revision of the liturgy. By the late spring of 1661 the episcopalians had no desire or political need to accede to such demands and Baxter's insistence on his wholesale revision of the liturgy, coupled with his intemperate debating style, proved to be the undoing of the Savoy conference.³⁷ The work of revising the liturgy was therefore completed in the purely episcopalian environment of Convocation.³⁸ However, the failure of the Savoy was just as much the result of the tactical failure of the London presbyterians to secure their position in 1660 and the bishops' seizure of the strategic advantage after the return of Charles II as on Baxter's considerable ineptitude as a negotiator.³⁹

Not without justification, Hyde, and probably Charles, were irritated with Baxter and the presbyterians for the failure of the Savoy conference. With the collapse of the *détente* between the London presbyterian leadership and the episcopalians, the loyalty of presbyterians was called into question. Between September and December, Edward Potter, a government spy, named the dissident presbyterian ministers William Jenkyn, Samuel Annesley, Thomas Gouge and Thomas Woodcock as among those preaching against the government.⁴⁰ The renewed question of presbyterian loyalty assisted the passage of the Corporation Act in December. This test act required those holding civic office to abjure the Solemn League and Covenant and to take communion in the Church of England.⁴¹ Few presbyterian councillors (around seven) survived the imposition of the Corporation Act in the 1662 elections, with many citizens who had formerly supported presbyterianism losing other positions of public trust, such as the governorships of hospitals.⁴² The Act anticipated the May 1662 Act of Uniformity, which required all ministers to have received episcopal ordination, to abjure the Solemn League and Covenant and to give 'unfeigned assent and consent' to the entirety of the Book of Common Prayer.⁴³

In March, it was reported by a government informer that the London presbyterian ministry were setting 'up meetings' and appointing 'daies of fasting' in order to prepare 'the people that now persecution is approaching and prophaneness and idolatry is coming in like a flood'.⁴⁴ The 1661–2 preparations for the approach of dark times are encapsulated in a carefully prepared manuscript volume of sermons made by Walter Boothby, the former ruling elder of St Mary, Aldermanbury. Boothby collected sermons preached by Edmund Calamy, Thomas Watson, Simeon Ashe and other London presbyterian ministers in the period 1661–2, recording many of the themes explored by David Appleby in his comprehensive study of the Bartholomew's day sermons of 1662.⁴⁵ A common theme, preached by both Calamy and Watson, was to warn the faithful against trimming their sails to the Restoration church order for an easier life. In a sermon on Job, preached on 24 April 1661, Calamy counselled the godly that they should expect hard times to come. While 'yesterday, and the day before were joyful dayes and glorious days', the 'good things of the gospel' were now receding from England. The 'catholike remedy' for such times, Calamy explained, was to imitate Job and 'retain thine integrity' to the ways of God.[46] On 9 April 1661 Thomas Watson taught that, 'notwithstanding the wicked do flourish and [be] raised up on high, and the godly they are laid low and bruised', yet it was 'a golden maxime, without dispute, that however things go in the world, yet God is good unto his people'. In a similar vein, on 28 June 1662, Calamy acknowledged that 'the prosperity and the flourishing condition of the wicked and ungodly is and always shall be a sore temptation, and stumbling block unto the godly'. Yet the faithful should not envy such people, as the ultimate reward for those who profited from sin was to be 'sent from Christ's presence and burned in the everlasting fire'.[47]

The London presbyterians, therefore, were forced to rest their future aspirations for their ministry on the prerogative schemes for comprehension that had been proposed by the king, Hyde and Bishop John Gauden. These plans would give the king a power to exempt ministers from some of the requirements of the Act of Uniformity. The belief that nonconformity would be a temporary state of affairs, which could be alleviated by the king's use of prerogative powers, continued to inform presbyterians after the ejection of August 1662. Edmund Calamy, in an apparently impromptu December 1662 sermon at St Mary, Aldermanbury, prayed that the presbyterians would be returned to the Church of England by royal prerogative.[48] This was encouraged in Charles's ill-fated declaration of indulgence of 26 December 1662 and was promised again in February 1663 when Calamy, Bates and Manton were told they would soon be returned to their places under the king's dispensing power.[49] Yet even these schemes were defeated by Sheldon and other bishops, who saw in them an unconstitutional power that could be used by the king to support toleration for Roman Catholics. The king's use of his prerogative to favour presbyterians was thus decisively scuttled by Parliament in early 1663.[50]

London presbyterians and the beginning of dissent

For the London presbyterians, Black Bartholomew's day would therefore prove to be the decisive break with the Church of England. The main reasons for refusing conformity were the requirements of reordination, 'unfeigned' consent to the Book of Common Prayer and prelatical episcopacy, and for renunciation of the Solemn League and Covenant.[51] Of seventy London ministers who can be identified as holding a parochial position at the Restoration and who had been delegated to either a London classis or the Provincial assembly during the 1640s and 1650s, eleven can be described as conforming. Of these eleven perhaps five were episcopalians who had conformed under the parliamentarian church administrations. The clearest example of this is Nathaniel Hardy, of St Dionis, Backchurch, who had attended meetings of the fourth London classis in the 1640s, but in 1660 was made Dean of Rochester.[52] Six from this cohort, however, had shown commitment to the cause of presbyterianism in the 1640s and 1650s.[53] Of this group, the most surprising conformists were John Meriton of St Nicholas Acons, who is reported to have 'warmly spoken' against the Act of Uniformity, but nevertheless conformed after Bishop Sheldon permitted him to drop the oath of canonical obedience, and George Smallwood, who had been elected moderator of the twenty-fifth meeting of the London Provincial assembly.[54] Meriton's conformity was so surprising that the cavalier satirist Sir John Birkenhead could not decide whether he was a trimmer or a presbyterian Trojan horse.[55] Around fifty-eight ministers, or just under 83 per cent of those presbyterians still in parish positions who had taken part in the London presbyterian system, were ejected in either 1660 or 1662. Of these, two or three were after-conformists who returned to the national church after 1662.[56]

It is apparent that there were divisions among the London presbyterians over their future stance facing the Church of England after the ejections. Having been imprisoned in the Tower since March 1661 for his attack on the bishops, the usually militant Zachary Crofton alienated many of his presbyterian friends, including Edmund Calamy and Roger Drake, by his insistence that presbyterians hold full communion with the Church of England's parish worship and eschew conventicles.[57] The London presbyterians' stance in the face of the restored national church was therefore one of deep disappointment and ambivalence.[58] David Appleby's study of the Bartholomew's day sermons has shown that the ministers' general position was to warn the godly against the dangers of outright separatism, while at the same time encouraging the continuation of the godly style of worship, in private gatherings if necessary.[59] In his 1662 farewell sermon William Jenkyn had counselled that 'the chamber, the field or the riverside is holy'. 'If there be a heaven on earth', Jenkyn preached, 'it is to enjoy the company of saints', a construction that could be read to encourage the godly to meet in conventicles.[60] The call for ejected ministers to resume preaching was made by Matthew Poole in 1664, who is reported to have said that 'every one of the ejected ministers should take to his own pulpitt againe and see if the people will not stand by them'. Poole's advice to his brethren was repeated the same year in print by the Somerset minister Joseph Alleine.[61]

Poole and Alleine were only putting into words what had already become practice in London and elsewhere. One London nonconformist in 1663 described presbyterians holding weekly meetings for 'private devotions' where 'nothing but Christ crucified is preached among us'.[62] Between 1662 and 1665 at least twenty-seven of the ejected London presbyterians were reported as holding regular conventicles or preaching to assemblies meeting in taverns, coffee shops and private houses.[63] The homes of Arthur Jackson in Whitefriars and Thomas Doolittle in Bunhill were singled out by government agents as regular conventicles, as was the house of Frances, Countess of Exeter in Little Britain.[64] These conventicles appear to have largely hosted preaching and fasting, although there is some evidence that ejected ministers were also celebrating the sacraments with their lay followers.[65] It was reported that Bartholomew Beale, the auditor of the imprest of the Exchequer, had Arthur Jackson baptise one of his children, even though the child 'was not weake'. Beale had earlier that year been informed on for paying for the supper of Jackson's conventicle after a fast.[66] In addition, in February 1663 Ralph Smith, a presbyterian stationer and the publisher of Thomas Edwards's *Gangraena*, who had become concerned that presbyterian conventicles were drifting towards separatism, observed that 'some presbyters not only absent from publique assemblies, but also celebrate the Lord's day by preaching and ministration of the Lord's supper, to a select company in private'.[67] The general picture from this evidence is of regular presbyterian preaching and the occasional ministration of sacraments outside the regular parish worship of the Church of England from as early as late 1662.[68]

One of these government reports, made in 1664 by the spy Edward Potter, described London presbyterians as holding fasts 'every week' along with 'friquent conferences and collections of money whereby to hold theire party together'. According to Potter's intelligence, the centre of the presbyterians' 'intelligence and corrispondencies' was the house of one 'Mr Benbow' in Ironmonger Lane. This was almost certainly John Benbow (or Benbo), one of the presbyterian common councillors elected in 1659 and a former ruling elder of St Martin, Ironmonger Lane.[69] The 'intelligencers' who met at Benbow's house included William Yorke, formerly a ruling elder of St Botolph, Aldgate and the ministers Thomas Lye and Thomas Woodcock. Through weekly dinners at Benbow's house, these presbyterians were said to have managed contacts throughout the three kingdoms. Potter and other informers also reported that Edmund Calamy managed a fund for the relief of ejected ministers and had been given £500 from Lady Mary Armine (who was noted as a frequent attender at presbyterian conventicles) to distribute to impoverished ministers.[70]

In his study of the 1662 sermon literature, David Appleby has sought to downplay the notion that there was such a level of presbyterian organisation in London.[71] As this study has shown, the London presbyterians had formed very close bonds of friendship and organisation over the previous twenty-year period. It seems very unlikely that the August 1662 ejections substantially interrupted those connections. While the image of conspiratorial meetings of London presbyterians described by Sir John Birkenhead in his scurrilous tract *Cabala*, or in Potter's intelligence, were no doubt exaggerated for polemical or mercenary reasons, they were not too far removed from the mobilisations and meetings of the London presbyterians that had occurred over the previous twenty years. In addition, references to the presence of known godly patrons in the early Restoration period such as Lord Wharton, Sir William Waller, Richard Hampden, Lady Armine and the Countess of Exeter adds coherence to government intelligence accounts.[72] More importantly, the inclusion of former, and often obscure, ruling elders such as Benbow, Yorke and the dissenter Alderman William Webb, suggests that there was continuity between the presbyterian movement of the 1640s and 1650s and the emergence of Restoration dissent.[73]

Conclusion

Although intelligence reports of the continuation of the former 'Sion College conclave' into Restoration nonconformity must serve as the epilogue to this study, it suggests that the narrative of Restoration presbyterianism needs reassessment. Historians have often worked on the basis of a division between 'dons and ducklings', with the older presbyterian clergy seeking comprehension but a younger generation edging towards an emancipation from the idea of a national church.[74] That view is increasingly coming under attack.[75] In particular, the notion of a generational divide among presbyterians is untenable given the role in the emergence of presbyterian nonconformity of older presbyterian ministers such as Arthur Jackson, William Jenkyn and Edmund Calamy. Of the fifty-eight ministers who had served the Province of London prior to 1660 and who were ejected from their livings, twenty-eight were reported as holding conventicles between 1662 and 1665. After the plague year of 1665, more former London presbyterian ministers would preach to conventicles, with at least twenty-eight survivors from the 1650s Province of London taking out licences as presbyterians during the royal indulgence of 1672.[76] These presbyterian conventiclers were careful to deny that their meetings were gathered churches and the meetings were seen as supplemental to the worship of the parish church. Nevertheless, even with this qualification of their activities, some former London presbyterians were not prepared to be tainted with the appearance of schism. These included Samuel Clarke, one of the authors of the 1646 'high presbyterian' treatise *Jus divinum regiminis ecclesiastici*, or the impetuous Zachary Crofton, who took up work as a cheesemonger and farmer, before becoming a school master.[77] If government intelligence is even half-believed, the London presbyterian ministers were capable of envisaging both the possibility of a future comprehension within the Church of England and the necessity of providing religious instruction to voluntary gatherings without considering the latter to be truly schism. George Southcombe and Ann Hughes have drawn attention to how Restoration presbyterian print kept alive the memory of the mid-seventeenth-century presbyterian experiment and propelled the presbyterian community forward.[78] The collective meetings in taverns, homes and coffee houses also continued the practice of the 'Sion College conclave' long after that establishment closed its doors to the presbyterians. Even into the 1680s Edmund Calamy's grandson remembered travelling with his mother from Tooting to Dyers' Hall in the city to learn the Westminster assembly's *shorter catechism* from Thomas Lye, a veteran minister of 1650s London presbyterianism.[79] It was this organisation that bridged the civil war and interregnum period into the Restoration. This continuity would provide the basis for the presbyterian politics of religion to resurface in the king's indulgence of 1672, the exclusion crisis and the glorious revolution.

Notes

1 BL Egerton Ms. 2543, fo. 331.
2 Thomas Phillips [i.e. William Drake], *The Long Parliament revived* (1660). Drake (not to be confused with the MP Sir William Drake) is described as 'a merchant of London'. His identity can be discerned from the fact that Drake had been involved in Chancery litigation in 1658 with a Philip Thomas, whose name was inverted by Drake to form his *nom de plume* (see NA C 7/345/138, papers in the case of *Thomas v. Drake*). Drake was defended by Silius Titus and Edward Massie, his fellow presbyterian-royalist conspirators in the 1650s, along with the political presbyterians Denzell Holles, Arthur Annesley and Thomas Bampfield, all of whom acknowledged him to be a 'great sufferer already for the royal cause'. For Drake's prosecution see *State Trials*, V, pp. 1363–9; *CJ*, VIII, pp. 186, 187, 192–3, 198; *LJ*, XI, pp. 200–1, 206–8, 211–12.
3 Phillips [i.e. Drake], *Long Parliament revived*, p. 12; *The Long Parliament twice defunct* (1660), pp. 19–20, 27–8; J. T. Neilson, 'National confusion over the issues of the English Restoration' (Ph.D thesis, Florida State University, 2005), p. 28.
4 BL Egerton Ms. 2543, fo. 35; *History of Parliament: the house of Commons 1660–1690*, ed. B. D. Henning, 3 vols (1983), I, p. 415. Baines, along with his former tenth classis ruling elder Robert Terry, was still being monitored by

government agents in August 1663, when he was described as 'a prime promoter of the late warres': see SP 29/79, fo. 131.

5 NA SP 29/32, fos 175–6; R. L. Greaves, *Deliver us from evil: the radical underground in Britain, 1660–1663* (Oxford, 1986), pp. 62–3; De Krey, *London*, pp. 75–6.

6 NA SP 29/32, fos 203, 174–6. *Smectymnuus redivivus*, the 1654 reprint of Smectymnuus's 1641 *An answer to an humble remonstrance*, was reprinted five times by the presbyterian publisher John Rothwell between 1660 and 1661.

7 Zachary Crofton, 'An epistle to the Reader' in Giles Firmin, *The liturgical considerator considered* (1661), sigs A2r–b4v; Zachary Crofton, *Altar-worship, or bowing to the communion-table considered* (1661); Zachary Crofton, *A serious review of presbyters re-ordination by bishops* (1661). For Crofton's pamphlet polemics, see J. Warren, 'Polity, piety and polemic: Giles Firmin and the transatlantic puritan tradition' (Ph.D thesis, Vanderbilt University, 2014), pp. 99–100, 109–10, 115; Haigh, 'Liturgy and liberty', pp. 44–6, 49.

8 NA SP 29/32, fos 184, 187.

9 *Ibid.*, fo. 209.

10 *Ibid.*, fo. 221. For Jurin see Lindley, *Popular politics*, pp. 72 n. 189, 206 n. 36, 207.

11 NA SP 29/32, fo. 219. 'Lawn sleeves' was a colloquial term of abuse for bishops.

12 P. Withington, *The politics of commonwealth: citizens and freemen in early modern England* (Cambridge, 2005), pp. 260–1.

13 NA SP 29/32, fos 180, 183, 188, 193.

14 De Krey, *London*, pp. 76–7 n. 77; Bosher, *Restoration*, pp. 208–10.

15 SP 29/32, fo. 224. John Murphy's and Ronald Hutton's research indicates that the Prayer Book had largely fallen into disuse in many London parishes during the 1640s and 1650s. See Hutton, *The Restoration*, pp. 171–2; J. M. Murphy, 'Oliver Cromwell's church: state and clergy during the Protectorate' (Ph.D thesis, University of Wisconsin, Madison, 1997), pp. 246–9.

16 *The kingdomes intelligencer*, No. 9 (25 February–4 March 1661), p. 134; *Mercurius publicus* (21–28 February 1661), pp. 127–8; *The Diurnal of Thomas Rugg, 1659–1661*, pp. 153–4; A. Richardson, 'Thomas Manton and the presbyterians in interregnum and Restoration England' (Ph.D thesis, University of Leicester, 2014), pp. 125, 132.

17 NA SP 29/32, fos 183, 109, 167.

18 Matthews, *CR*, pp. 290–1.

19 See P. Seaward, 'Gilbert Sheldon, the London vestries and the defence of the Church' in *The politics of religion in Restoration England*, eds T. Harris, P. Seaward and M. Goldie (Oxford, 1990), pp. 49–74.

20 RLPA 247r (DWL transcript, p. 182).

21 NA SP 29/32, fos 167, 191; Bosher, *Restoration*, pp. 207–8; Seaward, 'Gilbert Sheldon, the London vestries', pp. 60–4; Matthews, *CR*, p. 535.

22 See J. D. Ramsbottom, 'Presbyterians and "partial conformity" in the Restoration Church of England' *JEH*, 43:2 (1992), 249–71.

23 Baxter, *RB*, II, p. 333; Bosher, *Restoration*, pp. 213–15. As John Spurr notes, moderate rather than high episcopalian candidates dominated the 1661 Convocation: see Spurr, *Restoration Church of England*, p. 40.
24 LMA, CLC-198-SICA-008-MS33445–00 (MS Sion College court of governors' minutes, 1631–1716), fo. 206; Baxter, *RB*, II, p. 334; Bosher, *Restoration*, p. 216.
25 D. J. Appleby, *Black Bartholomew's day: preaching, polemic and Restoration nonconformity* (Manchester, 2007), p. 176; K. Fincham and S. Taylor, 'The restoration of the Church of England, 1660–1662: ordination, re-ordination and conformity' in *The nature of the English revolution revisited: essays in honour of John Morrill*, eds S. Taylor and G. Tapsell (Woodbridge, 2013), pp. 211–12.
26 https://theclergydatabase.org.uk/jsp/search/index.jsp. With the exception of Nathaniel Hardy, the majority of the eleven conformists appear to have been too young to have been ordained prior to the civil wars.
27 For reordination see Fincham and Taylor, 'The restoration of the Church of England', pp. 197–232. According to the CCEd, those reordained by Bishop Sanderson of Lincoln included Henry Hurst of St Matthew, Friday Street (5 March 1661), John Meriton of St Nicholas Acons (28 May 1661) and Francis Raworth (28 October 1661). Bishop Sydserff of Orkney reordained the conforming John Rumney of St Thomas the Apostle (4 December 1661) and possibly Samuel Smith of St Benet, Gracechurch (1 January 1662) (CCEd ID 166543). Of these five, Hurst and Smith were ejected in August 1662, although Smith conformed later.
28 Fincham and Taylor, 'The restoration of the Church of England', pp. 213–14, 218–19, 225–6. See Zachary Crofton, *A serious review of presbyters re-ordination by bishops* for a presbyterian condemnation of reordination. For summaries of the debate on episcopal reordination see G. F. Nuttall, 'The first nonconformists' in *From uniformity to unity 1662–1692*, eds G. F. Nuttall and O. Chadwick (1962), pp. 174–82 and Warren, 'Polity, piety and polemic', pp. 75, 79–80, 87–91, 99–100, 236.
29 De Krey, *London*, p. 78; HMC, *le Fleming MSS*, pp. 27–8; Abernathy, 'The English presbyterians', p. 81.
30 Lacey, *Dissent*, p. 30; P. Seaward, *The Cavalier Parliament and the reconstruction of the old regime, 1661–1667* (Cambridge, 1989), p. 163; P. Seaward, 'Circumstantial temporary concessions: Clarendon, comprehension, and uniformity' in *Settling the peace of the Church: 1662 revisited*, ed. N. H. Keeble (Oxford, 2014), p. 79.
31 Seaward, *Cavalier Parliament*, pp. 163–4, 172.
32 Bosher, *Restoration*, p. 221; Abernathy, 'The English presbyterians', p. 81; Lacey, *Dissent*, pp. 31–3; De Krey, *London*, p. 78; Seaward, *Cavalier Parliament*, p. 164.
33 For the Savoy conference see Baxter, *RB*, II, pp. 303–68; E. C. Ratcliffe, 'The Savoy conference and the revision of the Book of Common Prayer' in Nuttall and Chadwick (eds), *From uniformity to unity*, pp. 91–148; H. Davies, *Worship and theology in England: from Cranmer to Baxter and Fox, 1534–1690*, 2 vols

(Grand Rapids, MI, 1996), II, pp. 365–73; G. J. Segger, *Richard Baxter's Reformed liturgy: a puritan alternative to the Book of Common Prayer* (Farnham, 2015), pp. 46–50.
34 Ratcliffe, 'The Savoy conference', pp. 124–5, 127–8.
35 Davies, *Worship and theology*, II, p. 369.
36 Baxter's prominence at the Savoy conference was ascribed by one observer to the fact that Edmund Calamy had fallen ill in 1662, having suffered 'one fall after another'; see *The Mather papers*, Collections of the Massachusetts Historical Society, 4th ser., vol. 8 (Boston, MA, 1868), p. 195.
37 Gilbert Burnet, *Bishop Burnet's history of his own time* (1838), p. 123.
38 N. H. Keeble, *The Restoration: England in the 1660s* (Oxford, 2002), pp. 116–17.
39 T. Cooper, 'Richard Baxter and the Savoy conference (1661)', *JEH*, 68:2 (2017), 326–39.
40 NA SP 29/41, fo. 135; SP 29/43, fo. 189; Greaves, *Deliver us from evil*, pp. 70–2.
41 De Krey, *London*, p. 79; Vallance, *Revolutionary England*, p. 180.
42 Elliot, 'Elections to the Common Council', pp. 167, 198 n. 118; De Krey, *London*, pp. 73, 80–1.
43 Lacey, *Dissent*, p. 21.
44 BL Egerton Ms. 2537, fo. 331. As Geoffrey Nuttall pointed out, Baxter (and no doubt his London presbyterian colleagues) perceived the likely direction of their fate from the late spring and early summer of 1660; see Nuttall, 'The first nonconformists', p. 157.
45 Congregational Library, London Ms. I.f.18.
46 *Ibid.*, fos 156–7, 121.
47 *Ibid.*, fos 3–6, 695–704.
48 Edmund Calamy, *Eli trembling for fear of the ark* (1663), p. 22; Seaward, *Cavalier Parliament*, p. 184. It seems likely, however, that Calamy preached this sermon with the knowledge of presbyterian courtiers such as Manchester in order to test the waters for the King's projected indulgence; see NA, SP 44/9, fo. 224 (I am grateful to George Southcombe for this reference).
49 Baxter, *RB*, II, pp. 429–30; *The Mather Papers*, pp. 207–8; Abernathy, 'The English presbyterians', pp. 86–8.
50 Bosher, *Restoration*, pp. 258–64; Abernathy, 'The English presbyterians', pp. 82–5; Lacey, *Dissent*, p. 52; Seaward, *Cavalier parliament*, pp. 179–80; J. Rose, *Godly kingship in Restoration England: the politics of the royal supremacy, 1660–1688* (Cambridge, 2011), pp. 94–6.
51 Nuttall, 'The first nonconformists', p. 158; J. Spurr, *English puritanism 1603–1689* (Basingstoke, 1998), p. 130.
52 For Hardy see Tai Liu, 'Hardy, Nathaniel', *ODNB*. Other ministers in this category probably include Ralph Harrison (CCEd 163736), who had been ordained by Bishop Robert Maxwell of Kilmore in 1648, and who only attended one session of the Provincial assembly, Thomas White of St Mary Hill (Tai Liu, *Puritan London*, p. 143), George Gifford (CCEd ID 142828) and Thomas Marriot (CCEd 164808), both ministers from the unformed ninth classis who

agreed to attend meetings of the London Provincial assembly after 1657, when the Province invited ministers willing to assist with the assembly.

53 John Seabrooke of St Andrew Wardrobe (CCEd ID 120577), John Meriton of St Nicholas Acons (CCEd ID 72349), George Smallwood, from 1661 of St Margaret, New Fish Street (CCEd ID 143696), Francis Raworth of St Leonard, Shoreditch (CCEd ID 101397) and John Rumney of St Thomas the Apostle (CCEd ID 166182/166140). These ministers had all signed declarations or dedications to presbyterian tracts in the 1640s and 1650s. The sixth minister was John Dalton of St Mary Bothaw (CCEd ID 162355), who had attended the London Provincial assembly three times as a delegate and been elected scribe for the assembly's twenty-first session.

54 S. Dunn, *Memoirs of the seventy-five eminent divines whose discourses form the morning exercises* (1844), p. 210; Fincham and Taylor, 'The restoration of the Church of England', p. 219 n. 60.

55 [John Birkenhead], *Cabala, or an impartial account of the non-conformists private designs* (1663), pp. 9, 10, 13, 15, 16.

56 I have based these calculations on entries in Matthews, *CR*; RLPA and the CCEd. The after-conformists were Samuel Smith of St Benet, Gracechurch and Thomas Wills of St Botolph, Billingsgate. A third may have been Thomas Hutchinson of St Michael Royal, although this identification is uncertain. For biographical details of the after-conformists, see Matthews, *CR* and CCEd.

57 Zachary Crofton, *Reformation not separation* (1662); R[alph]. S[mith]. *Jerubbaal justified* (1663); Zachary Crofton, *The saints care for church communion* (1671), 'To the Courteous Reader', n. p., first page.

58 Crofton's opponent in support of presbyterian non-communion with the offending parts of the Restoration Church of England was the London presbyterian minister Thomas Douglas; see T. P. [i.e. Douglas], *Jerub-baal, or the pleader interpleaded* (1663) and T. P. [i.e. Douglas], *Jerubbaal redivivus* (1663). For studies outside of London that point in this direction see D. Beaver, *Parish communities and religious conflict in the Vale of Gloucester, 1590–1690* (Cambridge, MA, 1998), pp. 245–321 and S. S. Thomas, *Creating communities in Restoration England: parish and congregation in Oliver Heywood's Halifax* (Leiden, 2013).

59 Appleby, *Black Bartholomew's Day*, pp. 219–20; A. Hughes, 'Print and pastoral identity: presbyterian pastors negotiate the Restoration' in Davies, Dunan-Page and Halcomb, *Church life*, p. 170.

60 William Jenkyn, *The burning yet un-consumed bush* (1662), pp. 32, 34; [Birkenhead], *Cabala*, p. 6.

61 SP 29/109, fo. 72; [Joseph Alleine], *A call to Archippus* (1664), p. 21; M. Winship, 'Defining puritanism in Restoration England: Richard Baxter and others respond to *a friendly debate*', *HJ*, 54:3 (2011), pp. 707, 709–10, 713.

62 [Anon.], *A mystery of godliness and no cabala, or a sincere account of the non-conformists conversation from the 24 August* (1663), pp. 3–7.

63 In particular the Half Moon and Seven Stars on Ludgate Hill was singled out as a location for presbyterian conventicles, as was the Helmet in Basinghall Street, owned by John Hardy (or Harding), possibly the same person who signed the

November 1645 city petition in support of presbyterian government (NA SP 29/94, fo. 5; SP 29/100, fo. 13). William Bates was said to hold a conventicle at Mrs Monday's coffee house at Temple Bar (NA SP 29/93, fo. 5) and presbyterian ministers were said to meet regularly at a coffee shop in Soper Lane (SP 29/109, fo. 72v).

64 NA SP 29/71, fo. 143; SP 29/92, fo. 5; SP 29/99, fo. 15; SP 29/100, fo. 13; SP 29/105, fo. 54; SP 29/121, fo. 46.
65 George Lyon Turner noted that conventicles recorded by government agents were generally held on weekdays, not Sundays. See DWL Turner MSS 3a, fo. 23.
66 SP 29/100, fo. 13v; SP 29/99, fo. 15.
67 S[mith], *Jerubbaal justified*, p. 4.
68 For further discussion, see my '"I cannot go on, yea, but I must never go back": Zachary Crofton, the Restoration Church of England and the dilemmas of partial conformity, 1662–1665' in *Aspects of conformity in English protestantism, 1560–1714*, eds E. Counsell and J Griesel (forthcoming).
69 RLPA fo. 123 (DWL transcript, p. 114); Elliot, 'Elections to the Common Council', p. 175.
70 NA SP 29/109, fos 72r-v; SP 29/121, fo. 46; SP 29/67, fo. 105; SP 29/67, fo. 112; SP 29/93, fo. 5; J. Eales, 'Armine (*née* Talbot, other married name Holcroft), Mary, Lady Armine (1594–1676)', *ODNB*.
71 Appleby, *Black Bartholomew's day*, pp. 19, 172.
72 NA SP 29/93, fo. 5.
73 For Webb, see De Krey, *London*, p. 131 n. 31.
74 See e.g. R. Thomas, 'Comprehension and indulgence' in Nuttall and Chadwick, *From uniformity to unity*, pp. 191–253; R. Beddard, 'Vincent Alsop and the emancipation of Restoration dissent', *JEH*, 24:2 (1973), pp. 161–84.
75 Hughes, 'Print and pastoral identity', pp. 169–71.
76 The twenty-eight ministers who had been ministers of the Province of London and held conventicles up to the plague in 1665 were Samuel Annesley, Arthur Barham, William Bates, Daniel Bull, Edmund Calamy, Thomas Case, John Crodacott, Thomas Doolittle, Thomas Douglas, Samuel Fisher, Matthew Haviland, Henry Hurst, Arthur Jackson, John Jackson, Thomas Jacombe, William Jenkyn, Thomas Manton, Benjamin Needler, Matthew Poole, John Sheffield, Robert Tatnall, William Taylor, Thomas Vincent, Thomas Watson, Stephen Watkins, John Wells, William Whitaker and Thomas Woodcocke. The congregationalist Joseph Caryl, who had been moderator of the fourth London classis was also reported as preaching at conventicles. Elias Pledger of St Antholin, Budge Row, who signed numerous presbyterian petition and pamphlets, also held conventicles from 1663. Those who are reported as having conventicles between 1666 and 1670 include Thomas Gouge, Thomas Lye, Abraham Pinchbecke, Gabriel Sangar and Lazarus Seaman. Those taking out licences in 1672 were Richard Adams, Samuel Annesley, Arthur Barham, William Bates, William Blackmore, Haselfoot Bridges, Daniel Bull, Thomas Case, Zachary Crofton, Thomas Doolittle, George Fawler, Henry Hurst, John Jackson, Thomas Jacombe, William Jenkyn, Thomas Lye, Thomas Manton,

Matthew Poole, Lazarus Seaman, John Sheffield, Robert Tatnall, Thomas Vincent, Peter Vinke, Gabriel Sangar, Thomas Watson, John Wells, William Whitaker and William Wickins. Some ejected ministers continued their ministry as chaplains. For example, Thomas Jacombe was chaplain to Frances, Countess of Exeter and William Wickins was chaplain to Alderman John Forth. See Matthews, *CR*; George Lyon Turner's notes preserved in DWL Lyon Turner MSS 3a; NA SP 29/71, fo. 143; SP 29/93, fo. 5; SP 29/99, fo. 15; SP 29/100, fo. 13; SP 29/105, fo. 54; SP 29/109, fo. 72; SP 29/111, fo. 105; SP 29/121, fo. 46.

77 P. Lake, 'Reading Clarke's *Lives* in political and polemical context' in *Writing lives: biography and textuality, identity and representation in early modern England*, eds K. Sharpe and S. N. Zwicker (Oxford, 2008), p. 313; NA SP 29/82, fo. 74; Crofton, *Reformation not separation*, pp. 3–7. Crofton was, however, licensed as a presbyterian in 1672, the year of his death: E. C. Vernon, 'Crofton, Zachary (1626–1672)', *ODNB*.

78 G. Southcombe, 'Dissent and the Restoration Church of England' in *The later Stuart Church, 1660–1714*, ed. G. Tapsell (Manchester, 2012), pp. 195–216; Hughes, 'Print and pastoral identity', pp. 162, 168–9.

79 D. L. Wykes, 'Calamy, Edmund (1671–1732)', *ODNB*.

Conclusion

In September 1666, Edmund Calamy travelled to London in a coach from his residence in Enfield, a location near enough for a day's visit to the city, but far enough away to comply with the Five Mile Act that had expelled many presbyterian ministers from their homes a year before. From his coach, Calamy saw London, whose inhabitants were still recovering from the decimation of the plague of the previous year, destroyed 'in ashes' after the Great Fire. His grandson recorded that Calamy 'seeing the desolate condition of so flourishing a city, for which he had so great an affection, his tender spirit receiv'd such impressions as he could never wear off. He went home, and never came out of his chamber more; but dy'd within a month.'[1] Calamy, who Richard Baxter considered 'the guide' of the London presbyterians, was buried on 6 November in the remains of St Mary, Aldermanbury, near where his pulpit once stood.[2] The plague and subsequent fire were seen by many of Calamy's mourners as divine judgement for the treatment of the ejected of 1662.[3] In many respects Calamy's death marked a transition to a new phase of puritanism, one that, despite continuing hopes of comprehension, would forever remain outside of the Church of England.

This study has sought to provide a narrative and analysis of the London presbyterian movement from the inside, principally as a movement for the further reformation of the Church of England and for the political conditions that would permit such reformation. In so doing it has sought to complicate the common characterisation of London's religious presbyterians as the arch-conservative or even 'counter-revolutionary' force who held back the parliamentarian revolution. Seventeenth-century historians have long warned against the anachronistic use of the term 'radical', arguing that it often puts an unwelcomely modern, often romanticised, gloss on discussions of seventeenth-century politics.[4] By the same token, similar caution must also be applied to the use of the nineteenth-century designation 'conservative', or reliance on allusions (such as 'counter-revolution') to the revolutions of the modern era. These analogies often have the effect of making ideological comparisons that are neither appropriate nor effective to describe the nature of the mid-seventeenth-century crisis in Britain and Ireland.[5] Like many of the political and religious positions that informed parliamentarian politics, the London presbyterian movement grew out of a long-standing 'godly' vision that had been part and parcel of much of the oppositional politics in the Elizabethan and early Stuart periods. As Phil Withington has noted, visions of a godly commonwealth were particularly prevalent in the urban political culture of England. It is therefore unsurprising that English presbyterianism found its constituency largely in cities and towns, for example York, Exeter, Manchester and, above all, London.[6]

The political tenets of a mixed constitution based on 'co-ordinate' powers in Parliament and an ecclesiastical settlement that encouraged godliness, but at the same time shielded religion from being used as a tool of the monarch's personal power, became the touchstones of what 'the parliamentarian cause' meant for a substantial number of its supporters. The London presbyterians stood in this tradition and remained committed to it as the revolutionary turn of events in December 1648 set in course a series of alternative constitutional and religious experiments in the English state. For the London presbyterians, the best way to protect the aims of the parliamentarian cause was the British confessional and military alliance enshrined in the Solemn League and Covenant and the proposals for a limited monarchy contained in the Newcastle Propositions or the treaty of Newport. In this vision, Reformed protestant doctrine would be protected by the dismantling of the king's royal supremacy and the adoption of a localist but conciliar form of church polity in the national church. These projected reforms were part of the early parliamentarian 'war party' vision of the aims of the civil war and the view, sometimes expressed in surveys of period, that the political presbyterian alliance of the mid-1640s was a mere rebranding of the early-1640s 'peace party' is unsustainable in light of this study. The London presbyterians' leverage with the city's government and with the Scots meant that they had a substantial voice within the composite alliance that made up the political presbyterian 'party'. Their demands for a settlement according to the Newcastle Propositions, the Covenant and a presbyterian reformation of the Church of England envisioned a very different constitutional future to those among their allies who wished for a negotiated peace on terms that went not much further than what had been confirmed by Charles I in 1641. As the Erastian debate shows, unlike the majority of MPs in Parliament the London presbyterians favoured community-based church structures which settled ecclesiastical power in the parish and locality, rather than the state. The political vision of the London presbyterians, therefore, looked to a 'further reformation' settlement, a vision that while never 'radical', cannot be classed as entirely 'conservative'.

The presbyterians' political thought looked to the classical mixed 'co-ordinate' constitution of government by the one, the few and many. This view applied both to church polity and the political state, the structures of which naturally mirrored each other in accordance with the Calvinist two-kingdoms theory that was increasingly adopted by presbyterians over the 1640s. This necessarily entailed a rejection of that strand of parliamentarian thought, closely associated with the revolution of 1649, which held that governors were merely the officers, trustees or agents of the people whom they served. This political view had a religious mirror image in those gathered congregations that saw ecclesiastical officers as the representatives of the body of the faithful. Nevertheless, as can be seen from the presbyterian tracts justifying Parliament's defensive war, presbyterian political theory did put a stress on elected political representatives as the people's compelling voice in the constitution. In discussions of church polity a similar emphasis was put on the ruling elder as the elected voice of the congregation, even if such power was to be shared in presbyteries and synods with the 'aristocratic' element of the ordained ministry, who received the power of the keys of the kingdom of heaven directly from Christ as king.

For London's presbyterians, as for many of the parliamentarians, the politics of the civil war and the republican period were politics of religion. This is not to argue, however, that the civil wars were religious wars. As with the early modern European 'wars of religion' in general, the British conflicts of the mid-seventeenth century blended confessional politics (albeit between protestants) with political ambitions and constitutional struggles, rather than being driven solely by religious zeal.[7]

The struggles of the London presbyterian movement also demonstrate the importance of theology for the politics of the mid-seventeenth-century crisis. It is sometimes argued that the soteriological debates that form the focus of historians of the early Stuart period were not as important by the time of the civil war, which saw a focus on ecclesiology. Nevertheless, presbyterianism in the 1640s resulted from the grievances of moderate puritan clergy who, generally, had previously conformed and those non-conformists who were not prepared to give up the Church of England. This radicalisation was caused by the increasing perception that the doctrinal 'foundations' of the protestant religion were under threat in the Caroline Church of England, from both Laudians and sectaries, particularly the antinomian fringe that had emerged in London during the early Stuart period. Opposition to the Laudian canons of 1640, together with the outbreak of the covenanter revolution in Scotland, were the banners under which clerical and lay resistance to Charles I's monarchy could gather, but this was fuelled by a decade of growing unease with the direction of the Church of England. For a sizeable proportion of the clergy and laity, the means to protect the ecclesial marks of true doctrine and pure sacraments in the Church of England were through a thorough reformation of polity. The ends of this vision of 'reforming the Reformation itself', however, provided a further spur to political conflict. The working out of sometimes fuzzy notions of church polity, discussion of which had often been self-censored by the godly during the early Stuart period, proved to be increasingly divisive among former friends and allies within the emerging parliamentarian camp. The Westminster assembly managed to create a synthesis from originally disparate theories of the underlying ecclesiology behind presbyterian polity, a synthesis most clearly expressed in the collective works on church polity by the London Provincial assembly. Nevertheless, attaining this synthesis among those committed to a national church settlement came at the price of a substantial falling-out with congregationalists and those politicians, scholars and lawyers who insisted that any further reformation of the church must retain the state's 'Erastian' supervision. While the quest to preserve the doctrinal foundations of Reformed Christianity looked to mark the path to reconciliation among Calvinists in the 1650s, the fracturing of protestantism and the political uncertainties of the Protectorate meant that attempts to settle the 'foundation' of religion proved repeatedly futile.

These theological conflicts were made all the more bitter, however, because they were reflected in the internal political conflicts that gnawed away at the parliamentarian alliance from within. This work has attempted to show that a cautious move towards presbyterianism existed among many of the English godly clergy prior to the Solemn League and Covenant, even if this was underplayed publicly to preserve godly unity. However, the British alliance of 1643, necessary to put the covenanter armies in the field against the king's nearly victorious forces, sought to make a presbyterian settlement the price of that alliance. The reaction and discontent caused by the narrowing of political options resulting from the Anglo-Scottish alliance allowed previously disparate collectives of 'radicals' to find that their minority political voice and constituency was increasingly backed by those in power opposed to the political settlement that the Covenant entailed. The force of the divisions within parliamentarianism was fully revealed in the internecine crises of 1647 and 1648. Yet, as the debates in the Parliaments of the 1650s show, a substantial constituency of the political nation remained in favour of what were essentially 'presbyterian' positions, of an alliance of magistracy and ministry, as a means of settling the nation.[8]

Recent historical writing has focused on the political effects of the information revolution that accompanied the civil wars and interregnum.[9] The explosion of print has been linked with a focus on mobilisation, organisation and politics defined not as allegiance, but as organising towards, and giving voice to, common objectives or freeing up 'radical' expression. This study has attempted to show that London's presbyterians were among the pioneers in the uses of the information revolution. In order to further their objectives, London presbyterians campaigned to gain control of the licensing of civil war print, the enforcement operations of the Stationers' Company, and seized key positions on the city's common council, particularly its religious committees. In the mid-to-late-1640s the presbyterians were thereby able to engage their opponents asymmetrically, contesting for popular support in a world that still saw print as an extension of oral and private manuscript culture. The strategies used by presbyterians included the weaponising of local gossip and rumour and the printing of once private letters, debates and recollections. This study has provided a number of case studies of how the information wars of the civil war acted to give the semi-private world of face-to-face discussion and manuscript transmission greater reach in the conflicts that served to fracture the parliamentarian cause. This use of printed information was added by London's presbyterians to more common public centres of information dissemination such as the pulpit, bookshops, the Exchange and election hustings to develop a formidable campaigning machine for the 'Covenant-engaged' interest.

The London presbyterians quickly perceived that such institutional control was of critical importance to the new arena of public politics. Although there were exceptions, the presbyterians' access to and appreciation of such 'institutional power' emerges as a fundamental difference between the presbyterian citizens explored here and the 'radicals' so richly explored recently by David Como.[10] Indeed, as Philip Baker has noted, the London presbyterians often forced 'radicals' to react to their political initiatives.[11] However, as the recent works of Baker, Phil Withington and Christian Liddy have shown, mid-seventeenth-century parliamentarians were not as innovatory in their political methods as has sometimes been thought and all sides drew on common political techniques and strategies that were part and parcel of citizen political action in the pre-modern period.[12]

Nevertheless, the change in the London presbyterians' political fortune and the loss of their institutional power bases during the last years of the 1640s and early 1650s brought about the New Model Army's revolution, and led the presbyterians to deploy many of the subaltern tactics formerly used by their sectary opponents. Opposing the new republic, the 'Sion College conclave' adopted the rhetoric and mantle of the 'oppressed godly' as a strategy to criticise what the presbyterians saw as a military-backed minority regime's seizure of legitimate government. As Christopher Love's trial shows, this could include the use of explicitly Lilburnian strategies and rhetoric, as well as the deployment of the Christian tradition of martyrdom.

Having been purged from almost all of the institutional bases that they had captured in the 1640s, the deployment by the presbyterians of these 'weapons of the weak' was, on one level, a reflection of the desperate state of affairs in which they found themselves. Yet their involvement with the tragically misconceived covenanter-royalist alliance also shows that the London presbyterians remained strategically placed in politics. This faithfulness to principles would see the London presbyterians increasingly restored to former positions of trust and influence in the Protectorate as the 'radical' parliamentarians, who had pioneered the short-lived revolution of 1649, tore themselves apart in the shifting Cromwellian experiments of the rule of the saints.

Ultimately, however, the return to the chaos of military and sectary interference in 1659 proved too much for the London presbyterians. Although it is not clear that they considered the restoration of Stuart monarchy as their first step, they were quickly brought round to the idea by the promises of the Stuart court and their own political allies within the old parliamentarian camp. The presbyterians' response to the bedlam of 1659, being fatigued by years of turmoil, meant that they sought to salvage what they could of their vision of a Reformed church settlement in the Restoration settlement. The return to episcopacy, something Charles Stuart and his negotiators made clear was non-negotiable, was quickly conceded. However, the presbyterians' hope rested in the new king's commitment to a broad settlement of the Church of England and the redrafted Worcester House Declaration becoming law before the *revanchiste* cavalier-Anglican reaction fully set in. In many respects the failure of the Worcester House Declaration to reach the statute book showed the writing on the wall to most London presbyterians, who took to preparing the faithful for the evils to come. This, together with Charles II's somewhat remiss promises to use the royal prerogative to protect loyal presbyterians, in part explains the disengagement of the presbyterian leaders at the Savoy conference and the relatively peaceful acceptance of Black Bartholomew's day.

I began this study by suggesting that the London presbyterian movement was a historical failure, but one that revealed much of the nature of the British revolutions. The failure of the London presbyterian movement, however, does not mean that it did not leave any legacy. In the political sphere, as Mark Goldie's research into the intellectual world of Roger Morrice has shown, the civil-war-parliamentarian political theory of mixed monarchy, limited by its co-ordination with the houses of Parliament developed by London presbyterians, would remain the political theory informing Whig political thought into the eighteenth century.[13] In religion, the most obvious legacy of mid-seventeenth-century presbyterianism is the worldwide use of the Westminster assembly's confession of faith and its other confessional standards, especially in Scotland, the USA, Canada, Australia and South Korea. Although this can largely be traced to a Scottish or Ulster Scots inheritance, many of the London presbyterian ministers noticed in this study contributed to the drafting of these doctrinal standards or contributed to their explication. The works of London presbyterian ministers such as Thomas Watson, Thomas Vincent and Thomas Manton have remained in print long after the local presbyterian movement that sustained them was forgotten. Indeed, as stated in the introduction, mid-seventeenth-century London presbyterians are currently experiencing something of a renaissance in the field of historical theology, being the subject of doctoral-level scholarship and academic monographs.

In addition to theology, the English culture of protestant dissent can be seen as a further enduring contribution by the London presbyterian movement. While London presbyterians were clearly not the only dissenters, their early organisation of conventicles was predicated on their interregnum practices. That such presbyterian conventicles were often attended, and protected, by the well-to-do and powerful, provided an environment where the culture of religious nonconformity could emerge; as John Coffey has noted, it has 'enjoyed a disproportionate cultural influence across the Anglophone world'.[14] The London presbyterian movement of the mid-seventeenth century may have been a failure on its own terms, but understanding it reveals important aspects of the nature of the British revolutions in particular and the religious culture of the early modern (and indeed modern) Anglophone world in general.

Notes

1 Edmund Calamy, *An account of the ministers [...] ejected or silenced after the Restoration in 1660*, 2 vols (1713), II, p. 7.
2 Sharon Achinstein, 'Calamy, Edmund (1600–1666)', *ODNB*.
3 See for example T[homas] V[incent], *Gods terrible voice in the City* (1667), pp. 25, 27.
4 The classic discussion is C. Condren, *The language of politics in seventeenth-century England* (Basingstoke, 1994), ch. 5. I am in agreement with Philip Baker that the word 'radical' can be used in historical discussions of the seventeenth century to refer to the extremes of a spectrum, or those ideas or individuals that sought an axiomatic change in society and the constitution. See P. Baker, 'Rhetoric, reality and the varieties of civil-war radicalism' in *The English civil war: conflict and contexts, 1640–49*, ed. J. Adamson (Basingstoke, 2009), pp. 202–5.
5 For example, Valerie Pearl's anachronistic and distorting comparisons to the French and Russian revolutions: 'London's counter-revolution', pp. 29–56.

6 Mendle, *Dangerous positions*; Withington, *The politics of commonwealth*, ch. 8.
7 Morrill, *The nature of the English revolution*, p. 68; G. Burgess, 'Was the English civil war a war of religion? The evidence of political propaganda', *Huntington Library Quarterly* 61:2 (1998), 173–201. For further meditations on the war of religion idea see *England's wars of religion, revisited*, eds C. W. A. Prior and G. Burgess (Farnham, 2011).
8 Little and Smith, *Parliament and politics during the Protectorate*, pp. 114–20; ch. 9.
9 A topic most fully explored in Peacey, *Print and public politics*.
10 Como, *Radical parliamentarians*.
11 Baker, 'London's liberty in chains discovered', p. 566.
12 *Ibid*.; Withington, *The politics of commonwealth*; Liddy, *Contesting the city*.
13 M. Goldie, *Roger Morrice and the puritan whigs* (Woodbridge, 2016), pp. 164–85. As Professor Goldie notes (p. 167), Morrice was particularly influenced by the Yorkshire presbyterian Philip Hunton, whose work had been brought to print by the London ruling elder John Bellamie between 1643 and 1644.
14 J. Coffey, *The Oxford history of protestant dissenting traditions*, vol. 1: *The post-reformation era, c.1559–c.1689* (Oxford, 2020), p. 37.

Index

Abbot, Robert 184
Adams, Richard 309–10 n.76
Adams, Thomas 149, 152, 157, 164 n.88, 166 n.145, 206
Alford, John 227–9
Alle, Thomas 127
Allein, Francis 130, 131, 136 n.82, 136 n.84, 231
Alleine, Joseph 301–2
Allhallows, London Wall 82
Allhallows the Great 21, 247
Ames, William 39
Anderson, Mr 83
Andrews, Thomas 136 n.82, 161 n.24, 218 n.90, 243
Annesley, Samuel 261 n.8, 299, 309–10 n.76
antinomians 78–9
Apologeticall narration (1644) 94, 95–9, 106, 110
Armine, Lady Mary 302–3
Asham, Anthony 223
Ashe, Simeon 21, 26, 71, 81, 126, 141, 158, 184, 186, 212, 222, 223, 231, 250, 256, 257, 263 n.55, 270, 273–4, 279, 280, 299–300
Ashhurst, William 201, 296
Atkins, Thomas 222
Austin, John 245
Axtell, Daniel 70

Bacon, Nathaniel 203

Baillie, Robert 24, 25, 28, 85, 96, 107, 126, 136 n.79, 139–40, 141, 143, 171, 186, 250, 256, 286
Baines, Jeremiah 75, 139, 166 n.145, 227, 251, 295, 304 n.4
Bakewell, Thomas 82, 247–8
Ball, John 21, 40, 41
Ball, Thomas 21
Balmford, Samuel 253, 257
Bampfield, Joseph 154
Bampford, Patrick 145
Barbour, Edward 4, 83
Bard, Maximillian 164 n.93, 185
Barham, Arthur 309–10 n.76
Barton, William 162 n.45, 227, 230
Bastwick, John 18, 139
Bates, William 253, 255, 279, 283, 286, 296, 297, 309–10 n.76
Baxter, Richard 2, 22, 28, 37, 186, 230, 246, 250, 252, 254, 259, 268, 272–3, 276, 277, 278, 279, 281, 283, 284, 297, 298–9
Bayley, Thomas 98
Baynes, Paul 22, 37, 39, 50
Beale, Bartholomew 184, 302
Bellamie, Edward 152, 164 n.88
Bellamie, John 97, 120, 127, 128, 136 n.79, 136 n.84, 141, 152, 153, 154, 159, 161 n.22, 164 n.88, 172, 178, 207, 218 n.90
Ben Israel, Manassah 255
Benbow, John 302
Best, William 40

Beza (de Bèze), Théodore 37, 44, 45, 46, 47, 48, 49
Bickerstaffe, Anthony 164 n.93
Biddle, John 245, 254
Birkenhead, Sir John 301, 303
Bishops' Wars 19, 24
Blackmore, William 177, 309–10 n.76
Blackwell, Elidad 181
blasphemy ordinance (1648) 198, 204
Bodin, Jean 100
Book of Common Prayer 17, 24, 57, 179, 184, 188, 196, 282, 295, 296, 298, 300, 305 n.15
Booth, George, 1st Baron Delamer 268
Boothby, Walter 127, 136 n.79, 164 n.88, 299
Bourne, Immanuel 135 n.51
Bourne, William 28
Bostock, Robert 97, 151
Bowles, Edward 74, 283, 296
Boyle, Roger, Lord Broghill 252, 255, 280
Bradshaw, William 39
Bridge, William 71, 72
Bridges, Haselfoot 309–10 n.76
Bridges, John 49
Brinley, Lawrence 127, 162 n.45
Bromfield, Lawrence 164 n.88, 164 n.93, 166 n.145, 167 n.146, 281
Browne, Joseph 179
Browne, Richard 226, 270, 276
Browne, Samuel 131
Brownrigg, Ralph 52
Bucerus, Gerson 22
Bull, Daniel 309–10 n.76
Bullinger, Heinrich 120
Bunce, James 155, 161 n.22, 164 n.88, 164 n.93, 166 n.145, 206, 207, 226–9, 268, 274
Burges, Cornelius 21, 23, 26, 27, 52, 77, 102, 140, 156, 201, 211, 212
Burges, John 37
Burgess, Anthony 152
Burroughes, Jeremiah 4, 15, 42–4, 71, 72, 74, 177

Burton, Henry 18, 28, 54, 56, 80, 177
Bury St Edmunds, Suffolk 15, 17
Busher, Leonard 85
Butler, James, 1st Duke of Ormonde 208, 220

Calamy, Edmund (1600–6) 15, 21, 25, 26, 27, 29 n.3, 35, 42, 52, 53, 58, 67–8, 76, 77, 79, 80, 82, 103, 107, 108, 109, 123, 131, 141, 157, 158, 169, 172, 177, 182, 184, 201, 210, 211, 212, 222, 223, 231, 234–5, 246, 253, 255, 256, 257, 258, 260, 263 n.55, 268, 270, 271, 273–4, 277, 278, 279, 280, 281, 283, 284, 286, 297, 299–300, 301, 302, 303, 307 n.48, 309–10 n.76
Calderwood, David 105
Calvert, Giles 245
Calvin, Jean 37, 44, 49
Campbell, Archibald, 1st Marquess of Argyll, 8th Earl of Argyll 201, 202, 226, 229
Canne, John 41, 56, 81
Canons of 1640 16, 19–22
Carter, William 263 n.55
Cartwright, Thomas 36, 44, 103
Caryl, Joseph 178, 230, 255, 263 n.55, 264 n.69, 309–10 n.76
Case, Thomas 74, 76, 127, 158, 184, 185, 223, 226, 278, 279, 309–10 n.76
catechising 83, 103, 172, 255, 265 n.91, 270, 304
Cawdrey, Daniel 21
Cawton, Thomas 173, 200, 221, 235, 268
Cecil, Frances, Countess of Exeter 302–3, 310–11 n.76
Chamberlain, Thomas 155, 269
Chamberlen, Peter 247–8
Charles I 8, 11, 18, 20, 71, 72, 85, 119, 141, 146, 148, 151, 153, 195, 208–9, 213

Index

Charles II 10, 221, 226, 227, 228, 242, 269, 270, 274, 279, 282, 300
Chandieu, Antoine de 105
Chetwynd, Philip 206
Cheynell, Francis 246, 252, 254
Chidley, Katherine 81
City Remonstrance (1646) 143–4, 146
Clarke, Samuel 21, 22, 71, 76, 259, 273, 303–4
Classis (presbyterian)
  Amsterdam classis 40
  First Lancashire (Manchester) classis 181, 273
  First London classis 114 n.75, 172
  Second London classis 174–5, 182, 185
  Third London classis 185
  Fourth London classis 4, 171, 175, 177–80, 186, 301
  Fifth London classis 170
  Seventh London classis 178
  Ninth London classis 174, 307–8 n.52
  Tenth London classis 174, 186, 191 n.50
  Eleventh London classis 174, 185
  Twelfth London classis 185
Clement of Rome 19
Coleman, Thomas 6, 77, 103, 121
Coke, Sir Edward 51
Coke, Thomas 225–6
committee for accommodation 106–7, 122–4, 134 n.29
conformity
  'after-conformity' 301, 308n. 56
  definitions of 16, 18, 21, 30n. 9, 37
  restoration 297–8, 301
congregationalism 8, 9, 28, 41, 56, 66 n.143, 81, 82, 97, 98, 99, 258, 273
Conventicles (post-August 1662) 301–3, 308–9 n.63, 309 n.76, 317
Convocation 20, 22
Cooper, William 182, 253, 256, 257, 258, 271

Copley, Lionel 142
Corbet, Miles 222
Cotton, John 79
Covenanters, Scottish 4–5, 8, 18, 19, 22, 24, 68, 76, 94, 107, 121, 139, 197, 202
  'Protestors' and 'resolutioners' 255–7
Cranford, James 21, 81–2, 97, 98, 127, 139–40, 141, 151, 196, 202–3, 221, 228, 247, 248
Crewe, John 21, 27
Crodacott, John 184
Crofton, Zachary 190 n.41, 255, 268, 274, 280, 295, 301, 304, 309–10 n.76
Cromwell, Oliver 107, 109, 184, 196, 201, 213, 236, 250, 251, 252, 253, 257, 285
Cromwell, Richard 11, 186, 257, 258, 260, 267, 271–2
Cromwellian Protectorate 10–11, 186, 250, 254–5, 256, 257, 258, 259, 260
  First Protectorate Parliament 251–2, 295
  Second Protectorate Parliament 254–5
  Third Protectorate Parliament 259
  'triers' and 'ejectors' 252–3, 271
Crisp, Tobias 78
Cullum, Thomas 152, 164 n.88, 166 n.145
Cyprian of Carthage 27

Dalton, John 308 n.53
Davenport, John 40, 80, 286
Declaration of Breda (1660) 275, 278
Dell, William 254
Denne, Henry 78
Dering, Sir Edward 54, 55
Dethicke, John 218, 243
Devereux, Robert, 3rd Earl of Essex 4, 106, 108, 109, 110, 119, 130, 138–9, 141, 143

D'Ewes, Sir Simonds 55
Dickson, David 171, 256
disputations, religious 246–9
Dod, John 21, 41
Doolittle, Thomas 302, 309–10 n.76
Douglas, Thomas 308 n.58
Downame, George, Bishop of Derry 37, 39
Downame, John 21
Downing, Calybute 24, 26, 42
Drake, Roger 185, 228, 229, 231, 246, 247, 295, 301
Drake, William 162 n.45, 166 n.145, 226–30, 294–5, 304 n.2
Duke of Ormonde *see* Butler, James, 1st Duke of Ormonde
Dury, John 221, 250, 252
Dyke, Daniel 264 n.69

Earl of Essex *see* Devereux, Robert, 3rd Earl of Essex
Earl of Manchester *see* Montagu, Edward, 2nd Earl of Manchester
Earl of Northumberland *see* Percy, Algernon, 10th Earl of Northumberland
Earl of Warwick *see* Rich, Robert, 2nd Earl of Warwick
East, Edward 297
Eaton, John 78
Edwards, Thomas 6–7, 56, 58, 79, 96, 97, 124, 141, 145, 156, 157, 158, 178, 179, 251
elders, ruling 2, 36, 39, 41, 42, 43, 44, 46, 51, 56, 57, 63 n.72, 69, 79, 102–5, 114 n.72, 169–73
Engagement, the (1649–50) 222–5, 232
episcopacy 22, 27, 28, 47, 51, 59, 282, 284
  'primitive' or 'reduced' episcopacy 3, 27, 28, 37, 38, 49, 209, 272, 282
'Erastianism' 6, 9, 54, 59, 99, 119, 129, 280, 312, 314

Erastus, Thomas 6, 120
Erbury, William 244
Erle, Sir Walter 196, 214 n.9
Evelyn, Sir John, of Wiltshire 146, 196
excommunication 119–22

Fairclough, Samuel 264 n.69
Fairfax, Sir Thomas 158, 206, 210, 211, 212, 233, 234
Farnworth, Richard 254
Fawler, George 309–10 n.76
Fawne, Luke 261 n.18
Felton, Nicholas, Bishop of Ely 15
Fenn, Humphrey 21
Feake, Christopher 184, 254
Featley, Daniel 52
'feoffees for impropriations' 17
Ferne, Henry 69, 71
Fiennes, William, 1st Viscount Saye and Sele 19, 21, 70, 106, 107, 127, 139–40, 143
Fisher, Samuel 172
Foote, Thomas 255
Fowke, John 136 n.82, 161 n.24, 218 n.90, 243, 295
Fulke, William 36
Fuller, John 182
Fuller, Thomas 52, 53
Fyge, Valentine 145, 185, 269, 270

Gace, John 136 n.79, 161 n.22, 164 n.88
Gataker, Thomas 2, 28, 177
Gauden, John, Bishop of Exeter 272, 277, 278, 279, 281, 283, 300
Gayer, Sir John 145, 164 n.88, 166 n.145
Gellibrand, Thomas 167 n.146
Geree, John 53
Gething, Maurice 136 n.79, 164 n.88, 253, 261 n.9
Gibbons, John 230
Gibbs, William 136 n.84, 218 n.90
Gifford, George 307 n.52
Gillespie, George 42, 104

Gillespie, Patrick 256
Glyde, Richard 136 n.79, 161 n.22, 164 n.88, 164 n.93
Glynne, John 149, 155
Glover, John 201
Godfrey, Lambarde 256
Goffe, William 231
Goodwin, John 21, 75, 80, 82, 83, 98, 149, 169, 179, 200, 209, 212, 243, 247, 254
Goodwin, Thomas 42, 82, 85, 98, 99, 122, 179, 193 n.113, 252
Goring, George, 1st Earl of Norwich 205
Gouge, Thomas 299, 309–10 n.76
Gouge, William 17, 83–4, 222, 247, 248
Gower, Stanley 202
Gower, Thomas 127, 136 n.79, 152, 160 n.10, 164 n.88, 164 n.93, 261 n.9
Green, John 85
Greenhill, William (Congregationalist minister) 42, 193 n.112
Greenhill, William (Presbyterian ruling elder) 87 n.10, 164 n.93
Greville, Robert, 2nd Baron Brooke 26, 69
Gurdon, John 222

Hacket, John 52
Hall, George 173, 184
Hall, Joseph, Bishop of Exeter 4, 9, 44, 49, 51, 52, 208
Hall, Nathaniel 136 n.79
Hamilton, James, 1st Duke of Hamilton 199, 202, 204, 205, 206, 207, 225
Hamiltonian engagement (1647–8) 199–204, 207, 225
Hammond, Henry 258, 272
Hampden, Richard 303
Hardy, Nathaniel 301, 306 n.26, 307 n.52
Harford, Anthony 172

Harley, Edward 273
Harley, Sir Robert 26, 28
Harris, John 195
Harrison, Ralph 307 n.52
Harvey, Edmund 142
Haviland, Matthew 309–10 n.76
Henderson, Alexander 24, 42, 49, 57, 76
Herle, Charles 71, 72–4, 80, 96, 100, 103, 109, 201, 206, 273
Herring, John 186
Herring, Julines 21
Herring, Michael 87 n.10, 136 n.79, 136 n.84, 161 n.22, 224, 261 n.2
Hesilrig, Sir Arthur 270
Heyrick, Richard 75
Hildersham, Arthur 21
Hill, Thomas 52, 246
Hills, Henry 245, 255
Hobbes, Thomas 223, 245, 246
Hobson, William 136 n.84
Holles, Denzell 75, 145, 148, 152, 153, 154, 155, 284, 304 n.2
Holmes, Nathaniel 56, 80, 83, 98
Holy Trinity, Queenhithe 174
Hooker, Edward 87 n.10, 136 n.79, 152, 159, 161 n.22, 164 n.88, 166 n.145, 167 n.146, 178, 207
Hooker, Thomas 139
Hudson, Samuel 100
Hurst, Henry 307 n.27, 309–10 n.76
Hutchinson, Thomas 308 n.56
Hyde, Sir Edward 275, 284, 300

Ireton, John 267, 268, 269

Jackson, Alexander 136 n.79
Jackson, Arthur 20, 185, 270, 279, 285, 302, 303, 309–10 n.76
Jackson, John 297, 309–10 n.76
Jacob, Henry 38
Jacombe, Thomas 184, 264 n.69, 268, 296, 309–10 n.76
Jaggard, Thomas 222
James VI and I 38, 49

Janeway, Andrew 82
Jekyll, John 226, 229
Jenkyn, William 156, 184, 200, 202, 211, 221, 226, 228, 235, 253, 255, 268, 299, 301, 303, 309–10 n.76
Jerome of Stridon 27, 46
Jessey, Henry 264 n.69
Jesson, William 136 n.79, 207
Jessop, Constant 19, 20, 22, 37
Johnston, Archibald, Lord Wariston 256
Jones, John 123, 127, 136 n.79, 143, 152, 159, 160 n.10, 161 n.22, 164 n.88, 166 n.145, 295
Jurin, John 295
Juxon, Thomas 126, 127, 128–9, 131, 142, 143, 146, 148, 153, 158

Kendall, William 87 n.10, 136 n.79, 161 n.22, 164 n.88
Kettering, Northamptonshire 21–2
Kiffin, William 244, 267
Kirton, Joshua 261 n.18
Knightley, Richard 21

La Peyrère, Isaac 254
Lambert, John 231, 269, 278
Langham, John 145, 152, 161 n.22, 164 n.88, 166 n.145, 206, 207, 270, 276, 295
Larner, William 245
Laud, William, Archbishop of Canterbury 8, 16, 17, 184
Lawrence, George 72
Lawrence, Henry 196
Lee, Walter 159, 167 n.146
Leech, Francis 254
Levellers 209, 213
Ley, John 22, 28, 178
Lilburne, John 151, 230
Lilburne, Robert 226, 255
Lilly, William 246
Lockyer, Nicholas 80
Loder, John 173
London, government and institutions
   common council 128, 129, 140, 141, 142, 143, 145, 146–7, 148, 206, 207, 209, 210, 269, 278
   common hall 145, 206, 276
   elections 128, 140, 145, 146–7
   militia committee 152, 153, 154, 157, 158, 164n. 88, 201, 205, 207, 267
London Provincial assembly 4, 102, 103, 104, 171, 173, 174–6, 180, 181, 182, 184–8, 212, 229, 243, 247, 249, 250–1
Lord Brooke see Greville, Robert, 2nd Baron Brooke
Lord Saye and Sele see Fiennes, William, 1st Viscount Saye and Sele
Lord's supper 38, 83, 120, 126, 169, 172, 173, 175, 246, 284, 302
Love, Christopher 10, 71, 72, 109, 156, 158, 182, 195, 212, 220, 221, 222, 223, 224, 226–35, 242
Love, Mary 212, 220, 230, 231
Ludlow, Edmund 70
Lye, Thomas 302, 304, 309–10 n.76

Mabbot, Gilbert 155
Mainwaring, Randall 74
Mainwaring, Robert 136 n.79, 164 n.88, 207
Maitland, John 2nd Earl of Lauderdale 276
Manton, Thomas 173, 182, 231, 234–5, 253, 255, 256, 257, 258, 260, 263 n.55, 264 n.69, 271, 277, 279, 280, 283, 286, 296, 309–10 n.76
Marriot, Thomas 307–8 n.52
Marshall, Stephen 22, 23, 26, 35, 53, 54, 70, 71, 84, 107, 108, 208, 250, 252, 263 n.55
Marten, Henry 154
Martindale, Adam 181, 221
Maslyn, James 178

Massie, Edward 143, 152, 158, 202, 226–9, 304 n.2
Maxwell, Robert, Bishop of Kilmore 307 n.52
Meredith, Christopher 97, 98, 127, 136 n.79, 159
Meriton, John 296, 301, 307 n.27, 308 n.53
Mills, Peter 136 n.79
Milton, John 51, 244, 254
Mohun, Lord 108
Monck, George 258, 269, 270, 271, 272, 273–4
Montagu, Edward, 2nd Earl of Manchester 106, 109, 118, 130, 139, 149, 201, 229, 268, 275, 277, 279, 280, 283, 307 n.48
Montereul, Jean de 130
Morély, Jean 105
Morley, George, Bishop of Worcester 275, 276, 277, 279, 284
Morton, Thomas, Bishop of Durham 52
Mosse, Francis 178

Nalton, James 30 n.20, 135 n.51, 235, 268
Nayler, James 255
Nedham, Marchamont 220, 226
Needler, Benjamin 309–10 n.76
Newcastle Propositions (1646) 145, 149, 153
Newcomen, Matthew 35, 141, 259, 273, 283
Newport, Treaty of (1648) 11, 195, 208–9, 274, 275
Normington, Alexander 297
Nutt, Thomas 83
Nye, Philip 84, 85, 252, 255, 263 n.55

Offspring, Charles 17, 21, 125 n.51
Okey, John 231
ordination, 181–2
    episcopal reordination 284, 285, 295, 297, 298, 300, 307 nn. 27, 28

Oudart, Nicholas 126, 148
Overton, Richard (Leveller) 26, 28
Owen, John 244, 250, 252, 256, 257, 258, 267

Packe, Christopher 127, 136 n.79, 164 n.88, 218 n.90, 243, 253, 255
Paget, John 40–1
Painter, Henry 84
Papillon, Thomas 155
Parker, Henry 70
Parker, Robert 37, 39, 50, 79
Parker, Thomas 98
Pembroke Hall, Cambridge 15
Pennington, Isaac 25, 75, 152, 222
Pepys, Samuel 269, 270
Percy, Algernon, 10th Earl of Northumberland 75, 96, 144, 149
Perne, Andrew 21
Peters, Hugh 79, 80, 211
Petition and Remonstrance of the clergy (1641) 23, 25, 26, 27
Pinchbecke, Abraham 309–10 n.76
Player, Thomas 171
Pledger, Elias 309–10 n.76
Poole, Matthew 104, 258, 301–2, 309–10 n.76
Potter, Edward 299, 302, 303
Potter, Henry 167 n.146, 226, 230
Powell, Vavasour 178, 247
Poynts, Sednham 158
Presbyterian church polity 2, 39–51, 99–106
Price, John 157, 200–1
Price, William 77
Pride, Thomas 209, 210, 213, 231, 246
Protestation (1641) 53–4, 212
Prynne, William 6, 18, 48, 74, 127, 286, 298
psalters 251
Puritans 16, 36–7
    use of term 16

Rainolds, John 38, 48
Randall, Giles 4, 78

Rathband, William 21, 81, 96
Rawlinson, John 184
Raworth, Francis 307 n.27, 308 n.53
Reynardson, Abraham 210, 221
Reyner, William 264 n.69
Reynolds, Edward 224, 255, 258, 261 n.8, 268, 270, 277, 279, 281, 283, 285
Rich, Henry, 1st Earl of Holland 149
Rich, Robert, 2nd Earl of Warwick 15, 26, 42, 69, 106, 139, 149, 211, 229
Ricraft, Josiah 139, 162 n.45
Roberts, Francis 111 n.113, 126, 127, 135 n.51, 140
Robinson, Henry 98
Robinson, John 184, 269, 270, 276
Roborough, Henry 80, 82, 178
Rochford, Essex 15
Root and Branch petition (London) (1640) 23, 24, 25, 27
Root and Branch bill (1641) 35, 53–5
Rothwell, John 261 n.18
Rous, Francis 78, 107, 171, 223, 235
Royal Exchange, London 5, 127, 128, 140, 315
Rumney, John 306 n.27, 308 n.53
Rushworth, John 156
Russell, James 136 n.79
Rutherford, Samuel 79–80, 256, 257

St Alphage, London Wall 82
St Andrew, Undershaft 181
St Anne, Blackfriars 17, 83, 180
St Antholin, Budge Row 17, 24, 174
St Augustine, Watling Street 126, 127
St Bartholomew by the Exchange 173, 221
St Benet Fink 21, 76
St Benet, Gracechurch 175
St Benet, Paul's Wharf 183
St Botolph, Billingsgate 175, 183
St Bride, Fleet Street 170, 172, 186, 209–10
St Dunstan in the West 82
St Gabriel, Fenchurch 101
St Giles in the Fields 185
St John, Oliver 106, 107
St Lawrence, Old Jewry 173, 222, 230
St Leonard, Eastcheap 171, 172
St Magnus the Martyr, London Bridge 230
St Martins in the Fields 192 n.89
St Martin, Ironmonger Lane 177
St Mary, Abchurch 179
St Mary, Aldermanbury 15, 25, 169, 177, 180, 235
St Mary Magdalen, Bermondsey 249
St Mary Magdalen, Milk Street 76, 127
St Mary, Newington Butts 186
St Mary, Stoke Newington 183
St Michael, Bassishaw 141
St Michael, Cornhill 170, 172, 177
St Michael, Crooked Lane 179
St Michael, Wood Street 20, 139
St Olave, Old Jewry 170
St Olave, Southwark 75
St Paul, Covent Garden 173
St Peter, Cornhill 170, 177
St Peter, Paul's Wharf 183
St Peter, Westcheap 170, 185
St Saviour, Southwark 221
St Stephen, Coleman Street 75, 169, 247
St Stephen, Walbrook 210
Salter's Hall sub-committee 75
Sancroft, William 131
Sanderson, Robert, Bishop of Lincoln 298
Sanger, Gabriel 253, 309–10 n.76
Savoy declaration of faith and order (1658) 258–9
Savoy conference (1661) 298–9,
Seabrooke, John 308 n.53
Seaman, Lazarus 100, 102, 103, 104, 105, 108, 224, 235, 243, 268, 295, 309–10 n.76
Sedgwick, Obadiah 109, 210, 253
Selden, John 6, 78, 79, 120
separatism 41, 58, 82, 85

Sharp, James 256, 257, 258, 259, 260, 271, 273–4, 276, 280
Sheffield, John 309–10 n.76
Sheldon, Gilbert, Bishop of London 296, 297, 298, 301
Shute, Richard 177
Simpson, John 78, 247
Simpson, Sydrach 173, 252, 263 n.55
Sion College, London 5, 67, 82, 119, 126, 129, 140–1, 148, 180, 107, 212, 279
Skippon, Philip 164 n.88, 204, 205, 206, 207, 211
Skinner, Thomas 149, 157
Slater, Samuel 263 n.55
Smallwood, George 301, 308 n.53
Smectymnuus 35, 43, 44–51, 54, 99–100, 208, 305 n.6
Smith, Ralph 97, 98, 197, 302
Smith, Samuel 306 n.27, 308 n.56
solemn engagement, London (1647) 150, 153–4
Solemn League and Covenant (1643) 76, 77, 85, 86, 94, 98, 118, 128, 140, 141, 143, 146, 152, 197, 201, 205, 212, 222, 223, 225, 228, 229, 233, 270, 273, 274–5, 279, 281, 299, 300, 314
Sowton, Daniel 18
Sparke, Michael 245
Spencer, John 85
Sprigge, Joshua 245
Sprint, John 37
Spurstowe, William 35, 42, 253
Stapilton, Sir Philip 142, 145
Stationers' Company of London 5
Steuart, Adam 96, 97
Story, James 136 n.79, 164 n.93
Stoughton, John 15
Suckling, Sir John 53
Swynfen, John 201
Sydserf, Thomas, Bishop of Orkney 298, 306 n.27
Symonds, Joseph 177–9
Synod of Dort 15

Tate, Zouch 107, 108, 203
Tatnall, Robert 309–10 n.76
Taylor, William 75, 169–70, 221, 297, 309–10 n.76
Terry, Robert 304 n.4
thirty-nine Articles of religion 78, 196, 285
Thomason, George 42, 127, 159, 226, 246
Thompson, Sir William 295
Tichbourne, Robert 136 n.82, 161 n.24, 211, 243, 269
Titus, Silius 226–8, 304 n.2
toleration 7, 123, 196, 251
Travers, Walter 36, 38–9
Trigg, Stephen 297
Turner, Richard 87 n.10, 136 n.79, 164 n.88
Turner, Sir Robert 44
Twisse, William 52, 84
two-kingdoms theory, Calvinist 6, 36, 67, 119, 121–2, 130, 132
Tyndale, William 50

Underhill, Thomas 75, 157, 183, 251, 254, 261 n.18
Underwood, William 75, 139
Ussher, James, Archbishop of Armagh 9, 28, 49, 51, 52, 208, 252, 272, 273
Uxbridge treaty (1645) 109–10

Vane, Sir Henry, Jr 55, 105, 107, 122, 230, 231, 244
Vaughn, Joseph 166 n.145, 167 n.146
Venn, Anne 19
Venn, John 19, 54, 109
Venner, Richard 127, 136 n.79, 152, 160 n.10, 161 n.22, 164 n.88
Venning, Ralph 261 n.8
Vicars, John 57, 58, 75, 109
Vincent, Thomas 296, 309–10 n.76
Vincent, William 261 n.9, 276
Vines, Richard 2, 99, 131, 173, 208, 209, 263 n.55, 264 n.69

Vinke, Peter 309–10 n.76
Vow and Covenant (1643) 76
Vyner, Thomas 136 n.79, 176, 243, 253

Wadsworth, Thomas 186
Walker, Clement 156, 201
Walker, George 79, 98, 103, 104, 129
Wall, John 200
Waller, Sir William 75, 118, 139, 303
Wallington, John 18, 218 n.90
Wallington, Nehemiah 3, 4, 13 n.18, 18, 80, 151, 152, 157, 158, 171, 172, 202, 205–6, 224, 235
Wallis, John 101, 284
Walwyn, William 95, 121, 141, 149
Ward, Nathaniel 223
Waring, Richard 136 n.82
Warkman, Lawrence 261 n.2
Warner, John 75, 136 n.79, 176
Watkins, Sir David 75
Watkins, Stephen 221, 309–10 n.76
Watson, Thomas 75, 210, 261 n.8, 299, 309–10 n.76
Webb, Nathaniel 251, 254, 261 n.18
Webb, William 207, 248, 303
Welde, Thomas 68, 79
Wells, John 309–10 n.76
Wentworth, Thomas, 1st Earl of Strafford 53
West, Francis 205
Westminster assembly of divines 2, 67, 77–9, 83–4, 94, 99–105, 106, 120, 121, 131, 196
Westminster confession of faith (1647) 196, 203–4, 252, 273, 316
Wharton, Philip, 4th Baron Wharton 278, 283, 303

Whitaker, Jeremiah 21, 22, 210, 212, 249–50
Whitaker, William 182, 309–10 n.76
White, John (MP for Southwark) 54, 69
White, John (minister of Dorchester) 52, 53
White, Thomas 82, 307 n.52
Whitelocke, Bulstrode 121
Wickens, William 309–10 n.76
Widmerpole, Nicholas 145, 167 n.146
Wildman, John 149
Williams, John, Bishop of Lincoln 9, 44, 52
    Williams's committee on innovations in religion 52–3
Williams, Roger 244
Wills, Thomas 308 n.56
Wilson, Roland 136 n.82
Winthrop, John 70, 84
Witham, George 136 n.79
Witham, Peter 200, 222
Woodcock, Thomas 299, 302
Woodcocke, Francis 71, 74
Woodcocke, Thomas 309–10 n.76
Woodwood, Hezekiah 97
Worcester House Declaration (1660) 277–86, 294
Worcestershire association 250–1
Worth, Edward, Bishop of Killaloe 281

Yorke, William 302
Young, Thomas 35, 38, 47, 51

Zepper, Wilhelm 50
Zwingli, Huldrych 120

EU authorised representative for GPSR:
Easy Access System Europe, Mustamäe tee 50,
10621 Tallinn, Estonia
gpsr.requests@easproject.com